STEVIE RAY VAUGHAN

DAY BY DAY,
NIGHT AFTER NIGHT

STEVIE RAY VAUGHAN

DAY BY DAY,
NIGHT AFTER NIGHT

His Early Years, 1954–1982

Craig Hopkins

Backbeat
Books

An Imprint of Hal Leonard Corporation
New York

Copyright © 2010 by Craig Hopkins

Author website: www.StevieRay.com

Published in 2010 by Backbeat Books
An Imprint of Hal Leonard Corporation
7777 West Bluemound Road
Milwaukee, WI 53213

Trade Book Division Editorial Offices
19 West 21st Street, New York, NY 10010

Stevie Ray Vaughan: Day by Day, Night After Night is a two-volume work:
His Early Years, 1954–1982 and *His Final Years, 1983–1990*.

Front cover photo courtesy of James Elwell and Cutter Brandenburg.
Back cover photo of Vaughan by Byron Barr.
Back cover guitar crafted by Tim Davis. Photo copyright Craig Hopkins.

Printed in China through Colorcraft Ltd., Hong Kong
First Printing

Book design by Kristina Rolander
Cover design by Damien Castaneda

Library of Congress Cataloging-in-Publication Data

Hopkins, Craig L. (Craig Lee)
  Stevie Ray Vaughan : day by day, night after night / Craig Hopkins.
    v. cm.
  Includes bibliographical references and index.
  Contents: v. 1. From Thunderbird to Blackbird : 1954-1971 ; Early years in Austin : 1972-1977 ; Triple threat to double trouble : 1978-1980 ; Power trio : 1981-1982
  ISBN 978-1-4234-8598-8
  1. Vaughan, Stevie Ray–Chronology. 2. Double Trouble (Musical group)–History–Chronology. I. Title.
  ML419.V25H68 2010
  787.87'166092–dc22
  [B]
                                      2010019778

www.backbeatbooks.com

In memory of
Bo, Bud, Palin and Belle

COURTESY JANNA LEBLANC

COURTESY JOE COOK

Contents

A Texas Ray of Sunshine

by Stevie's uncle, Joe Cook

I hear a blues riff in the still of the night.
Is that you "Little Boy Blues?"
Your cross was found on some faraway hill
They say where wild flowers grow.
Are you up there somewhere playing your blues?
Oh Lord, I think I know.

Guitar slingers, the best of blues singers
Came to Alpine Valley to play.
Some brought their new songs
Some played the old songs
All jammed at the end of the day.

Now Queen Anne's Lace, bittersweets grace
That faraway field where they lay.
Going back to Chicago, the 'copter flew too low
And some didn't make it all the way.
Gone is another guitar hero
And I'm missing you "Little Boy Blues."

PHOTO BY WILLIAM SNYDER © SONY MUSIC ENTERTAINMENT

I'm laying in my bed
These things going through my head
Trying to make some sense of it all.
For when you're down, you're trying to rebound
Searching for something you can use.
Call down a Texas Ray of sunshine
And play some of the little boy's blues.

Though a friend is gone, his music is living on
For we've all been touched by him in some way.
Like waves on the ocean, his music brings emotion
As he carries us along on his cruise.
Now God is the power we need in our darkest hour
Just call on Him and leave it in His hands.
He gave us music to enjoy, and a special Oak Cliff boy
To help bring the world His good news.

I pray this ache in my heart will some day part
When we understand what it's all about.

Remember the dreams we've had
And the things his songs have said.
To keep on keeping on just might be our cues.

Thanks for caring, thank you for sharing
Your gift of music and your warm smile.
Peace and comfort remain
Your blues sweep away the pain
For your songs were from your heart and soul.
Thank you so very much, you had that magic touch
Your blues guitar was the very best.
An old Strat Fender, a serious string bender
You brought new life to the blues.

Call down a Texas Ray of sunshine
And play some of this little boy's blues.

Acknowledgments

Special thanks to Martha Vaughan, Janna Leblanc, Byron Barr, Randy Jennings, Donnie Opperman, Alex Hodges and the many who granted interviews (listed in Footnote 1) and contributed photos (credited throughout the book); forgive me for not listing y'all here. Extra special thanks to Donna Johnston for her many hours of proofreading the original edition of this book.

Sincere thanks to Kathleen Aisling, Don Anderson, Rollie Anderson, Paul Barlow, Shon Beall, Marc Benno, Stan Blackburn, Wayne Blagdon, Bruce Bowland, Cutter Brandenburg, Jeremy Brown, Michael Byrns, Rene Carillo, Renee Carter, Dana Causey, Gary Cockrell, Brent Combs, Joe and Margaret Cook, Bill Crawford, Tony Czech, Paul de La Haye, Jeanne Deis, Bob DiRenzo, Dobbs/Jackson ("Mr. Valco," www.valcoamp.com), Jim Edwards, Erik-Jan Engelen, Rosemary Englishbee, Herman Fillingane, John-Christophe Fluckiger, David Jo Frame, Manny Gammage, Joella Gammage, Deb Gaspard, Paolo Gonnelli, Warren Goodwyn, Scott Haasl, Darrin Harvey, Charlie Hatchett, Dan High, Eric Hendershot, Benita Hennessy, William Hermes, Ray Hill, Jani Hiltunen, Alex and Karen Hodges, Michelle Holland, Harry, Virginia and Steve Hopkins, Rick and Mary Horgan, George Hostilo, Lynda Howard, Beverly Howell, John Hutchinson, Tohru Itoh, John Jackson, Alan Jamnik, Drew Jiritano, Steve Kalinsky, John Kalnin, Zoltan Katona, Craig Keyzer, Jay Kreper, Snorri Kristjansson, Greg Krikorian, Larry Lee, James Leising, Barbara Logan, Lonesome Dave, Carla Lowe, Marta Lozano, Lynn and Bob Madewell, Mike Marchione, Mike Mettler, Russ Morgan, Adam Muhlig, Andrew Mullin, Daniel Negrini, Marie Neile, Deborah Nigro, Don O., Allison O'Cain, Ron Parry, Bruce Pates, Joe Nick Patoski, Paul F. Price, William Pritchett, Bob Randall, Joe Renaud, Margaret Richter, Xavi Robertson, Randall Rodriguez, Michel Ronchi, Laurent Roussel, Luciana Rzegocki, David Schulze, Andy Schwartz, Philippe Sergent, Kumi Smedley, Jane Smith, Derrick Sorensen, Mike Stanton, Lew Stokes, Scott Thistlethwaite, Tom Tierney, Steve Toney, Jan Tonnesen, Rick "Chainsaw" Turnpaw, Todd Turpitt, J.J. Vicars, Ron Wages, Paula Washburn, Michael Weaver, Russell Whitaker, Mark Wilkerson, Bill Willmot, Marion and Rien Wisse, Bubba Wood, Riccardo Zacchi, Texas State University's Southwestern Writers Collection and all I have unintentionally omitted.

Introduction

"And now for something completely different"

Fans of British television comedies will recognize that catchphrase from *Monty Python's Flying Circus*. This book is completely different from what I envisioned in late 2006. I won't bore you with the original plan, but over 100 interviews and almost 1000 illustrations later, you have this ... *thing*. Is it a biography? A chronicle? A 10,000-piece puzzle? A door stop? It certainly felt like a puzzle to me, the assembler. The result, I hope, is as complete a picture of Stevie Ray Vaughan as you are likely to find. An essential missing piece is, of course, a soundtrack – which I assume you already have in your CD or MP3 player.

You have in your hands all the facts I could find in a reasonable amount of time, presented in the words of the witnesses rather than in my own. Just like in a trial. Imagine that – a former trial lawyer presenting witness testimony to flesh out a lengthy list of facts.

The framework was created by merging extensive, segregated compilations of information from over seventeen years of research. Added to that framework are quotations from people who were there and any other interesting information I could find about the events, performances and persons involved in Stevie's daily life.

The layout of the book combines the advantages of two formats – a biographical story and a chronicle. The strength of this approach is threefold. First, there is a tremendous amount of information. Second, all the information is presented chronologically, so that the reader gets all the facts within a single timeline. Third, the visual cues used in the layout make it easy for those wishing to skip over the minutia to read the story.

Biographer Donald Spoto observed, "We are part of a culture of gossip and innuendo." Some might argue that because Stevie was a celebrity, all information is fair game. No less a musical legend than Johannes Brahms said, "What would become of all historical biography if it was written only with consideration for other peoples' feelings?" Maybe that is partly the reason this book might not be considered a biography. Certain information, while interesting, would only serve to unnecessarily embarrass or hurt persons whom Stevie would not want to hurt or embarrass.

I have intentionally excluded those facts that would be considered sensational in the negative sense, with the exception of those critical to an understanding of Stevie or significant events in his life. For example, the awesome inspirational power of Stevie's recovery from substance abuse cannot be understood without Stevie's own statements about the causes and extent of his substance abuse and about his recovery. My overriding ethic was to publish something the Vaughan family and Stevie's fans would appreciate and enjoy, while at the same time providing an honest historical record.

Another aspect of my approach that may be completely different from other SRV biographers is that there are quotes from more than one person about the same event. Rather than merely paraphrase everyone and put things in my own words, I prefer to quote each person, giving the reader the words and recollections of those who were there. I was not there, so in most cases I have chosen not to summarize or pick one recollection over another. Admittedly, it makes the story a little less smooth, but it is more complete.

It is a remarkable story, and I hope you can accept the somewhat unconventional format. If nothing else, it is easy to find a place to stop without waiting for the end of a chapter!

Explanations of the layout

ABBREVIATIONS

The name of the band, beginning in 1978, was *Stevie Ray Vaughan and Double Trouble*, and much of the data in this book pertain to the band and not just Stevie. For brevity's sake, the full name of the band is not typed repeatedly. This is not meant as a slight to Stevie's bandmates. The reader should assume all performance references are to Stevie Ray Vaughan and Double Trouble unless specifically noted to the contrary. Similarly, Paul Ray and the Cobras is often listed simply as The Cobras. Marc Benno and The Nightcrawlers may be listed as The Nightcrawlers, but keep in mind that The Nightcrawlers existed after Marc left the band, and the full name of the band was The Nightcrawlers. Particularly in the discographical listings, the band name is abbreviated "SRV & DT." There are some references to Stevie as "SRV" and to Jimmie Vaughan as "JLV."

ACCURACY

Every reasonable effort has been made to determine the date of each event. In some cases, the information is placed according to a reasonable estimate of the time it occurred.

Most gig information comes from published itineraries or the band's records. If there is reason to doubt a particular piece of information, it is noted. In some cases, the reader will find a gig listed as "unconfirmed," yet with an indication there is a recording of the show in existence. How can it be unconfirmed if there is a recording, you ask? In those cases, the bootlegger's information is all the author has, and bootleggers' information is notoriously suspect.

WHAT ARE ALL THOSE SYMBOLS?

The visual cues described below are provided for your ease in finding various types of information. The default is, of course, plain text without special symbols. This is used for two types of information: the "story" and performance dates. I did not feel the need to symbolize the concert listings because, in a very real sense, the gigs *are* the story. All these years of research have revealed one essential truth – music and the performance thereof were the essence of Stevie's life. While no amount of research is likely to provide a complete list of every performance Stevie gave, the information herein definitely shows that there wasn't time for much else. Days for which there are no entries, between 1983 and 1986 in particular, were probably travel days or days filled with interviews, record store appearances and other promotional activities. Stevie made hundreds, if not thousands, of appearances at radio stations and record stores around the world while on tour. There being no reasonably accessible source for discovering those appearances, only syndicated radio shows are included.

⊙ **Discography.** Authorized audio releases, followed by the date (if known), ARTIST, title, label, catalog number, type (CD, LP, cassette, 45 rpm 7-inch, CD single (CDS), 12-inch single, etc.), and any comments. For lack of more accurate information, release dates for singles are listed with the album, though they may have actually been released before or after that date. SRV & DT songs and SRV guest appearances appear on many compilation albums and CDs. These compilations and rereleases are not listed unless noteworthy. However, I have included most of the American releases through 1990. Releases in other countries are not listed unless noteworthy or interesting (e.g., picture sleeve, different artwork, additional tracks).

🎥 **Commercial and promotional video** on VHS, laserdisc and DVD formats.

📺 **Television broadcast video.** The length of the video is expressed in hours (x), minutes (y) and seconds (z) (i.e., x:yy:zz) and is based on the video in the author's archive, which may or may not be complete.

📡 **Radio shows.** Syndicated radio shows that were sent to subscriber radio stations. Dates given are broadcast dates, not recording dates, except in the case of live shows such as *Rockline*. Radio shows broadcast after November 1997 are not listed unless noteworthy. However, many radio shows continue to be repackaged and rebroadcast.

🥾 **Bootleg.** Bootleg video (🥾) and audio (📼) are recordings made either (a) with authorization but not for broadcast, commercial or promotional release or (b) made without authorization. Stevie on bootlegs: "It's funny, I don't like it when people have bootlegs of my stuff, but I'm glad I got to hear these other people [Jimi Hendrix is one example he gave], so you know how that goes."[1] An interviewer once commented, "Stevie's record rack is filled with every Hendrix album available, including several European imports and bootlegs that we had never seen, or heard, before."[2]

— **Song Titles:** I have included representative set lists for those who find it interesting to see how Stevie's shows changed over the years. Some songs were rarely performed, others almost every night for months or years at a time. The set list information comes largely from bootleg audio and video recordings and may or may not be complete for each show. In the case of bootleg video, the list is typically only the songs on the video in the author's archive. When available, information is given about songs performed with special guests.

Album titles are in italics; song titles within the body of a paragraph are in quotation marks. Thus, *Texas Flood* refers to the album, and "Texas Flood" or 'Texas Flood' refers to the song. As noted above, song titles within a set list of several songs are merely indicated with a dash prior to the title.

📖 **Bibliography.** I was tempted to leave the bibliography out of the mix, but it provides a picture of when Stevie started getting publicity and what was being said. Some publication names and/or dates are incomplete or unknown because fans have sent me clippings without complete information. In some cases, content is unknown because the article was listed somewhere as having SRV content, but I have not located a copy of the article.

🏆 **Awards.** Sales certifications by the Recording Industry Association of America (RIAA) and other achievements and recognitions.

💲 **Sales.** Significant sales of collectibles. I did not include a price guide to memorabilia because that information becomes obsolete too quickly.

[1] **Endnotes** are unconventional in that there is only one endnote number per source. This is purely a space-saving device. Because of this efficient format, the endnotes in this volume also apply to the companion volume, *His Final Years, 1983–1990*. All quotes are from interviews by the author unless noted otherwise. The endnotes are at the end of the book.

[x] Within some quotes, there are words inside brackets which are the author's words rather than those of the person being quoted.

There are a few intentional misspellings to emphasize Texas pronunciation (e.g., thang, sanger).

Illustrations. Placement of illustrations is chronological except where noted otherwise. All photographs are copyrighted and are credited on the page on which they appear. See also the list of photographers' websites near the end of this book. All uncredited photos are © Craig Hopkins. In a few instances the photographer's identity could not be determined after a reasonable search and are credited courtesy of the person providing the photo. Should the photographer be identified after the publication of this book, appropriate credit can be provided in a corrigenda and in any future printings of the book. Unless otherwise noted, all posters and other artifacts pictured in the book are from the author's collection. Poster artists are credited when the artist's identity appears on the poster.

Band personnel. Stevie was a member of over twenty bands and many of the band members have been interviewed for this book. A handy reference to the bands, personnel and dates begins on page 218.

COURTESY JOE COOK

COURTESY JOE COOK

STEVIE RAY VAUGHAN

DAY BY DAY,
NIGHT AFTER NIGHT

Blackbird. © JEANNE DEIS

From Thunderbird to Blackbird 1954–1971

"I just play."

Some of Stevie Ray Vaughan's friends interviewed for this book have commented that he was elevated to the level of guitar deity after he passed away. Based on the evidence herein, one might argue that the anointing of Stevie as a guitar hero began long before he died. He is rightfully recognized as one of the greatest electric guitar players, often placed on the top tier of polls with only Jimi Hendrix, Eric Clapton and Jimmy Page.

As for those friends, their point was not that such recognition of his musical talent was undeserved, but that they knew him as a gentle man, quick with a smile and, yes, bursting at the seams with talent. But "guitar hero"? Stevie would – and did – say no: "I just play."

Did he ever play! Lawd-a-mercy! That boy rarely put the guitar down. Many have recalled that the guitar seemed to be an appendage to his body, especially that "old junker" of a Fender Stratocaster he called Number One. Not only was it Stevie's tool to produce the blues, it *looked* like the blues and is perhaps the most individually recognizable guitar of all time – not just because of its appearance, but because of what Stevie coaxed and, at times, forced it to do.

Stephen Ray Vaughan, October 1954. COURTESY MARTHA VAUGHAN

This written celebration of Stevie Ray Vaughan only serves to document as completely as possible the life of the man who made the music. The music itself and Stevie's place among the legends of rock and blues can only be assessed aurally.

Magazine writers and documentarians often quote Stevie's celebrity peers, but the goal here is to create a portrait of the man painted by those who knew him best, on stage and off.

1954-1960

October 3, 1954: Stephen Ray Vaughan is born at Methodist Hospital in the Oak Cliff area of Dallas, Texas, southwest of the central business district.

MARTHA VAUGHAN: "I went for my checkup that day, and he just decided it was time. Dr. Henderson's office was close to Methodist Hospital, so we went on over to the hospital."[1]

The weather on Stevie's birthday was partly cloudy and warm with a low around 75 degrees and a high of 90 – a typical North Texas early fall day. Stevie weighed just 3 pounds, 9.25 ounces and was 17.5" long with light red hair. Martha: "I had to leave him there until he weighed five pounds. I think it took about three weeks or so." Stevie was three-and-a-half years junior to his big brother, Jimmie Lawrence Vaughan, born March 20, 1951.

Martha Jean Cook had encountered Jimmie Lee Vaughan in the early 1950's when she would go to the 7-11 convenience store to get ice cream after work as a secretary. In those days, the convenience store really was convenient – they had curb service. Jim would bring Martha her ice cream, and one day he got the gumption to ask her out. She thought he was very handsome and had wonderful, big arms. JIMMIE VAUGHAN: "She said he had pretty arms. I mean, he had everything else pretty too, but that's what she always told us."[2]

JIMMIE: "My dad and mom could really dance good. They had a dance in Dallas called The Push, and one of the things they did was they'd get dressed up and go dancing all the time. So, my dad loved music, my mother liked music. My mother was always listening to black gospel singers on the radio. My dad liked western swing and big band."[3]

Jim was known as "Big Jim" after the birth of his first son. Vaughan, of course, is spelled with two a's, something few

people seem to pay attention to. Even the record company has used the wrong spelling, as have countless nightclubs and newspapers. STEVIE: "Well, it's an English spelling, but somewhere along the line, someone with the "a" in their name, the last "a," had some kind of criminal deal going on, so they

Stevie and mother, Martha. COURTESY MARTHA VAUGHAN

changed the spelling of it to try to hide that. And most of the family behind him agreed [*laughs*]. A few of us went 'What the heck?' you know? At least, that's how the story goes."[4]

Stevie's birth certificate. COURTESY ALEX HODGES

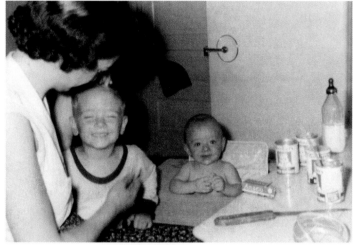

"What do you mean, 'No shirt, no service'?" COURTESY MARTHA VAUGHAN

At the time of Stevie's birth, the Vaughans lived at 4114 Rockford Drive in the Cockrell Hill area of Dallas. The site is now a parking lot. The family moved several times during Stevie's childhood – a month here, two months there. Little Rock, Baton Rouge, Shreveport. Jimmie attended part of the first grade in Jackson, Mississippi.

"Back then we lived in quite a few places," MARTHA recalls, "because it was before we bought our first house in '61 or '62.

Methodist Hospital, Dallas, as it looked when Stevie was born. It has since been expanded and remodeled. COURTESY DALLAS PUBLIC LIBRARY

"C'mon Dad, I gotta get to the gig!" COURTESY MARTHA VAUGHAN

[When Stevie was born,] we were probably in a duplex in Cockrell Hill. We lived mostly in the Dallas area, but we did live in Mississippi for a while, and Oklahoma, but just for a short time. My husband was an asbestos worker, you know, and we travelled around when there wasn't any work here in Dallas. After we bought the house, sometimes he would go and I would stay here. By that time the kids were in school, so I had to stay here."

JIMMIE VAUGHAN: "It wasn't really a comfortable 'Leave It To Beaver' kind of a deal, you know. There was a lot of tension, and there was moving all the time, and never really getting to know people. They were great parents, and my mother's the sweetest mother in the world. And I love my dad. There was a lot of happy times and it wasn't all weird and crazy, but there was a lot of that too. We didn't ever know what our old man was gonna do, you know. He'd go off like a rocket. [But] we had the absolute best parents in the world for being the guitar players that we are, when I look back on it now."[3]

"Nice hat, but do you have one in black?"
COURTESY MARTHA VAUGHAN

Stevie thinks Jimmie's pose is hilarious in this still from an early home movie. COURTESY DELBERT WILEY

🎞 Dallas, TX. Family home movies 1955-1959. 17:23. Filmed by Stevie's uncle, Delbert Wiley. It features Stevie and Jimmie playing in the house and yard, with most of the footage from holiday gatherings. No audio.

In 1960, Stevie started school at New Friends School in the Cockrell Hill area of Dallas. MARTHA: "It was kind of like a kindergarten. I was working, and that's where I left him, so that's where he started school. They had first grade there [too]."

Stevie suffered from sinus problems and had surgery (year unknown) that removed some of the cartilage in his nose. This left Stevie with a flatter nose. JIMMIE: "He had some kind of sinus thing; Stevie had it real bad. It's like, Stevie got all the stuff – like he broke his leg two or three times. It would break, take the cast off, and it'd break again in a week. He was sort of a frail little kid. It seemed to go away after he grew up a little bit."[3]

1961

The exact year isn't known when Jimmie first started playing guitar, but it was probably in the summer of 1961 just before Stevie turned seven. JIMMIE: "This guy named Robert Louis Stevenson was a friend of my dad's. They had a son who was a singer in a band who was away at the Navy. My parents would go over there on weekends and play dominoes, and I'd play with the guy's drums and his guitars and stuff. I broke my collarbone playing football [in the yard], and they gave me this crummy guitar with three strings on it. I started playing it and Stevie watched me learn how to play."[3]

MARTHA: "Somebody brought a guitar over and left it, and he picked it up and started messing with it. Big Jim picked out a song and said, 'Well, if you can do that, I'll just go buy you a guitar. So he went to Sears

Possibly Stevie's first portraits. COURTESY MARTHA VAUGHAN

and got him a guitar. He took it from there, and Stevie right behind him. It was amazing."

Big Jim encouraged Jimmie's pursuit of music. JIMMIE: "He'd always tell me that he didn't want me doing what he does. Anything would be better than that."[2]

"My father decided one day that, 'Son, you need to learn your majors and minors.' So he made me go down to this place on Jefferson Street called Boyd's Guitar School. I went to two lessons. The first lesson, the guy said, 'Okay, what can you do?' and I started playing something. He said, 'No, that's not right; you can't do that' and gave me a book and said, 'You got to do this, and you got to learn this.' I found out by following the notes the song was 'Mary Had a Little Lamb' or something like that, so I just played it. I went back the next week and tried to do that, and he wouldn't have it, so he said, 'You're too far gone. If you're not going to pay attention to what I'm saying, I don't think you should come back.' And that was it. I didn't want to go there anyway.

"[I learned] by ear, by listening to the radio and watching people. My father also had some guys that worked at his local who were guitar players. There was one guy

COURTESY MARTHA VAUGHAN

named Leonard, and he had played rhythm with Chuck Berry. He showed me how to play John Lee Hooker and Chuck Berry, and they would also play country."[3]

STEVIE: "My first instrument was shoe boxes and pie pans, with clothes hangers for sticks!"[5]

In 1961, the Vaughan family bought a home at 2557 Glenfield in the Oak Cliff section of Dallas. This was Stevie's home until he moved to Austin at the end of 1971. The house was built in 1955 and had approximately 1100 square feet of living space. Stevie returned to this home for several months after rehab in 1986, and Martha lived there until 1993.

COURTESY CONNIE BRIGGS

COURTESY MARTHA VAUGHAN

2557 Glenfield. © CRAIG HOPKINS

NEW FRIENDS SCHOOL

Kindergarten class, probably spring 1960. Stevie in striped shirt near center. COURTESY MARTHA VAUGHAN

After attending kindergarten and first grade at New Friends School, Stevie completed his elementary education at Lenore Kirk Hall Elementary School in Dallas.

October 3, 1961: Stevie receives his first guitar on his seventh birthday, a Sears toy guitar with western motif.

STEVIE: "Far as I can remember, I got my first guitar on my birthday in '61, so I was seven, I guess. It had cat gut strings and it was one of them – not a Gene Autry or a Roy Rogers – but it was made out of Masonite, with the little stencils on it, you know? I had to take three of the strings off, 'cause it wouldn't tune, and I started out trying to play kinda bass riffs. Didn't make any sense, but I tried it.[6] I took three of the strings off and played bass for Jimmie when he'd play guitar. Tore 'em off and spread 'em all over the neck, and then you can thump right."[7]

JIMMIE: "Daddy bought us out of the Montgomery Ward's catalog this Airline record player, where the speakers'd come out with wires on either side, and we used to both stand in front of 'em with our guitars [strikes a cool pose] so it looked like we had amps. We were hooked."[2]

COURTESY CONNIE BRIGGS

STEVIE: "I wanted to play drums, but I didn't have any drums. Then I wanted to play saxophone, but all I could get out of it was a few squeaks. My big brother played guitar, so I figured I'd try it too. He would leave his guitars around the house and tell me not to touch 'em. That's basically how I got started – sneaking into his room and playing his guitars. It didn't take me any time to figure out that was what I wanted to do."[8]

JIMMIE: "When I left [the house] I would say, 'Don't touch my guitar because I'm going to get you. Leave my guitar alone.' And of course when I would leave, he would go straight in there and play with my guitar and try to learn what I had been playing."[9]

MARTHA: "Stevie was pretty much a loner. The guitar was his life, just about. Jimmie would go with friends to a game or something. He'd leave the house and tell Stevie, 'Now don't you touch my guitar!' And the minute he got out of sight, Stevie would go in there and pick up that guitar and play it the whole time he was gone [*laughs*]! I remember that very well."

STEVIE: "I started out trying to learn that song about Thunderbird wine by The Nightcaps. I'd get a clothes hanger and I'd use something for a fake mic, and I'd put the stereo speakers behind the flower boxes on the porch. My girlfriend would walk by and I'd act like I was doin' the song. She came up the driveway and told me to take the Nightcaps off the record player and stop acting like a fool! So I figured I ought to try to learn something."[2]

"I would sit down and listen to something [on a record], and if I couldn't find it on the neck yet, I would learn to find it *singin'* it the best I could. Trying to find the sound with my lips and mouth, doing some bastardized version of scat singing. Then I would learn how to make the sound with my fingers that I was making with my mouth."[6]

Among the first songs Stevie learned to play were "Wine, Wine, Wine" and "Thunderbird" by The Nightcaps. Stevie often said that Jimmy Reed songs were also among the first songs he tried to play.

1962

March 3: First photo taken of young Stevie and Jimmie with their guitars. It appears on the *Family Style* album jacket.

Big Jim and Martha were music fans and loved to dance. They would go see performances by Jimmy Reed, Fats Domino and Bob Wills. Members of Bob Wills' band, The Texas Playboys, would sometimes come to their house to play dominoes. Big Jim would call the boys out to show folks what they could do on their guitars. Not a bad gig – playing for members of one of the most important Texas swing bands of all time – and in your own living room!

Stevie with his first guitar. COURTESY MARTHA VAUGHAN

The boys with their father, "Big Jim" Vaughan
COURTESY MARTHA VAUGHAN

JIMMIE: "[Stevie] was a little shy, I guess. It was more like just sort of polite. I mean, he wasn't obnoxious. He was very nice, you know; he wasn't mean or anything. I mainly remember that he wanted to go everywhere; wherever I went, he wanted to go. And he always wanted to know what was going on, what we were doing, why we were doing it, and just real curious. We were just normal brothers. I would go first and then he would. I think it was normal; seemed normal to me."[3]

1963

Stevie goes to the record store to buy his first record and asks for the wildest guitar record they have. The clerk sells him Lonnie Mack's "Wham!" Lonnie, the master of the Gibson Flying V, had used the time left over at a session for the Charmaines to cut the two sides, including an instrumental version of Chuck Berry's "Memphis, Tennessee," shortened to just "Memphis." The song peaked at number five in the Top 40 in 1963. "Wham!" was the follow-up single and reached number 24 in September 1963. Nine-year-old Stevie had been playing guitar for two years.

COURTESY MARTHA VAUGHAN

STEVIE: "I remember [Jimmie] bringing home Hendrix records, Buddy Guy, Muddy Waters, B.B. King. The first record I ever bought was Lonnie Mack's 'Wham!' in '63. I'm glad it wasn't the Monkees or something. It's a great record. I played it so many times, my dad broke it. I played 'Wham!' over and over and over and over and over, and when I didn't think it was loud enough anymore, I borrowed somebody's Shure P.A. Vocalmaster and put mikes in front of the speakers and turned it up. It was loud in my room. After my dad broke it, I just got another one."[11]

Paul Ray, who grew up near the Vaughan brothers in Oak Cliff, recalls the "Wham!" story differently. It was *his* record that he had loaned to Jimmie.

STEVIE: "As soon as I saved up enough money, I went out and bought a Lonnie Mack album. It was just incredible. He did all that wild-ass, fast-picking, whammy bar stuff, then he'd do a ballad, and it would sound like a cross between gospel and the blues – incredibly soulful and eerie. Lonnie Mack really taught me to play guitar from the heart, to really tap your insides."[10]

Stevie's first electric guitar is Jimmie's hand-me-down Gibson Messenger ES-125-T (3/4 scale).

The author has set up several SRV memorabilia exhibitions in Texas and has heard many people claim they "grew up down the street" from the Vaughans. It must have been a mighty long street. At the Dallas Guitar Show in 2004, a man was viewing the exhibition and told his story. "I grew up down the street from Stevie Vaughan," he said, just like all the others, but then his story diverged from the pack. "He used to come over and kiss on my sister." Well, that was one the author doesn't hear all the time, but it gets better. "Yeah, if you look real close at photos

of Stevie, you'll see he had a scar just above one eye. That's where I hit him with a rock I threw from the roof of my house." Of the countless people who claim to have grown up with the Vaughans, he is the only one who has admitted to assault and battery!

1964

STEVIE: "Jimmie and I found out that the only way to meet girls was to either play football or play in a band."[12]

Jimmie's first band is the Swinging Pendulums, with Ronnie Sterling (bass) and Phil Campbell (drums). JIMMIE: "Me and a few buddies of mine started trying to play parties and the morning pre-school dime dances. We'd play anywhere we could – talent shows, battles of the bands. And we were good right from the start, I think. We played through the summer, six nights a week. We used to sing through the old Seeburg jukebox, and we had Silvertone amps. We made fifty dollars apiece [at] the Hob Nob Lounge in Dallas.

"Daddy was our manager. He'd put our shit in the back of the pickup and take us to the gig. I was on top of the world, [but] Stevie was too young.

The Pendulums. (l-r) Ronnie Sterling, Jimmie Vaughan, Phil Campbell. COURTESY MARTHA VAUGHAN

They wouldn't let him out of the house. I didn't hang out with him because he was only my kid brother. I was off with old guys,

COURTESY MARTHA VAUGHAN

guys a year older than me. So he was having trouble getting away with it. What can you do when you're nine years old? I remember once, our parents took us to that ... what was the name of that club, the fancy one with the Playboy bunny girls? The In Crowd. We was gonna do the Sunday talent show, and when these beautiful women showed up mother covered his eyes."[2]

MARTHA: "Big Jim really supported them. Wherever Jimmie needed to go, [he would drive him]. He backed him 100%. I was concerned about it, because I'd heard so many stories about the problems other people got into. But Big Jim didn't seem to be concerned, and of course it gave him a chance to go out too [laughs]."

With the older Jimmie advancing so quickly, it was only natural that he received most of the early attention, as Martha recalls. "I don't remember going to see Stevie like we did Jim. That might have been why he got into such trouble early on, because we weren't there to supervise."

As is common among many, if not all, families, the first born gets a bit more attention. The oldest does everything first – first steps, first words, sports, and perhaps first to play an instrument and perform in public. In a household where elder brother Jimmie was successfully blazing a trail in music, little Stevie was naturally a few steps behind and out of the spotlight. He was certainly encouraged, but as Jimmie arrived at a more rebellious age, there was obviously some concern that perhaps the younger son should pursue a more conventional lifestyle.

February: Doyle Bramhall gets his first drum set and soon joins The Chessmen from Denton, Texas.

1965

June 26: Cockrell Hill Jubilee, Hill Theater, Dallas, TX. This may be Stevie's first public performance. Stevie wrote "first band, first performance" on the back of the photo shown here. One of the band members has identified it as the Cockrell Hill Jubilee, and Martha kept a handbill from the show in the family photo album. The date is from the correct time period. Given that The Chantones were using some of The Pendulums' equipment (and possibly personnel), both bands probably played that night.

The Chantones is Stevie's first band. Their first performance was at the Cockrell Hill Jubilee Talent Contest, using The Pendulums' equipment. The other band members were Jimmy Bowman, vocals and sax, and Gerald Mason on drums. For a short time the band featured Billy Gable on rhythm guitar, soon to be replaced by Glenn Anderson. They didn't have a bass player, but the bass player in the photo may be Ronnie Sterling of the Pendulums.

STEVIE recalls that first band: "We played at the Cockrell Hill Jamboree [actually, Jubilee] Skate Rink. We finally figured out we couldn't play – any of us![13] In the Chantones, we thought we had a band, and we played a talent show and realized in the middle of our song [Jimmy Reed's "Baby What You Want Me to Do"[10]] that we didn't know the whole thing!"[5]

The Hill Theater was the first of a chain of theaters opened by movie and recording star Gene Autry in 1946. For a brief time, it was the Cockrell Hill Jubilee, and shortly after Stevie's performance there, it closed and was later converted to an auto parts store. It was destroyed by fire in 1999.

Stevie's uncle, JOE COOK, recalls the venue: "This was in an old Cockrell Hill movie house. They had matinees and a Battle of the Bands contest. Stevie was playing in places like that, and Jim was playing in a Battle of the Bands at Yellowbelly Drag Strip.

"We were following [Jim's career], because we hadn't realized what Stevie was capable of doing. He was just the little brother, and we had never seen him play, other than in the back seat of my car one time on the way to a family reunion. He took his guitar,

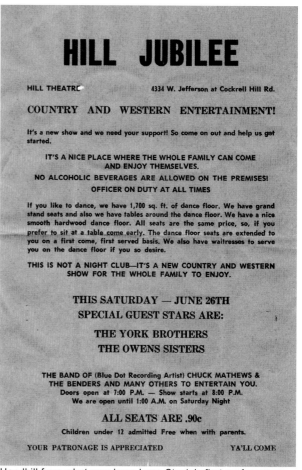

Handbill from what may have been Stevie's first performance.
COURTESY MARTHA VAUGHAN

On the back of this photo Stevie wrote, "First band. First performance." (l-r) Vaughan, Mason, Bowman, unidentified. COURTESY JANNA LEBLANC

seems like he was about nine years old, and said, 'Hey, Uncle Joe, listen to this,' and he played a little run and picked out a little piece. I said, 'Stevie, that's pretty good. You keep that up and you'll be as good as Jim one of these days!'"[14]

Drummer GERALD MASON: "It would have been '65-'66. We never had a bass player. Mostly it was me and Stevie and Jimmy singing and playing a little saxophone. He was playing that little Gibson guitar with a single pickup. I think it was one of those little Alamo amps, but we hoped we'd get to borrow Jimmie's big Silvertone amp sometimes. We were doing things like 'Gloria,' 'Don't Let the Sun Catch You Cryin','' 'House of the Rising Sun,' and that kind of stuff. It always tickles me when I see online that Stevie played in early Dallas blues bands like The Chantones. I thought, '*blues* band?!' We had my mother in her '61 Ford Country Squire wagon hauling us around [*laughs*]!

"The way I met Stevie, his cousins Mark and Gary [Wiley] were younger, but we played together some when I was maybe ten, and they were seven or eight. They would tell me about their cousin Jimmie, and then Stevie's parents started going to our church.

"[The Cockrell Hill Jubilee] was a theater, then a roller rink, and sat dormant for a few years. Then a policeman in Cockrell Hill named Bellamy opened it up for a short time as a western nightclub on Saturday nights and a teen dance club on Friday nights.

"One of the first places we ever played in public. If you walked out of that theater to the intersection of Cockrell Hill Road and Jefferson, there was a street lamp in the [median]. There was a little square, elevated box, big enough for a band to be on. There was a merchant with a cafe or something, and he had a local newspaper trying to promote all the businesses in Cockrell Hill. He started sponsoring a talent show there. We

The Hill Theatre where Stevie made his public debut. The marquee has been comically altered by the author. COURTESY DALLAS PUBLIC LIBRARY

Stevie and unidentified man.
COURTESY MARTHA VAUGHAN

that was kind of fun. It was something like a national teen congress at the Adolphus Hotel, and I don't know how we got tied into it, but they were having a big dance. Kenny and the Kasuals were the main band, and we were the break band. There was another band called Sweet Pea and the Lovers! Stevie played his guitar behind his head, and the guys in Kenny and the Kasuals wanted to talk to him, and we got all pumped up about that. [Kenny Daniels' band was among the most popular and successful bands in the Dallas area.] That was probably the only big thing we ever did, if you want to call it that. We were just a break band, but it was a lot of fun!

entered that talent show in the open air at that intersection. Scared to death!

"The Chantones didn't get to play many places, but Jimmie and The Pendulums were really talented. Jimmie and The Pendulums played there, and we played during their break. Then, at the end of the night, we all played together for a little bit. Phil Campbell played piano, and I played drums. I really don't know if the bass player [in the photo] is Glenn Anderson or not. Might be, or it might be Ronnie Sterling just helping out.

"I do not remember the name of the place, but Bellamy probably did name it The Cockrell Hill Jubilee or something like that. We jokingly had said he should call it the Bellamy-A-Go-Go. The photo was taken from a lower position than the stage, and that would have been about how it was in that theater, and the decor would have fit with what the place looked like. The stage was pretty small and was where the screen had been. The floor was flat with small round tables out a way from the stage to have room for the dancing, and at the very back, I think there was an elevated balcony-type area. When it was a roller rink, that area was where people sat. Probably would have been in 1965, and probably summer. It did not stay open very long at all.

"We played in the little circular auditorium at the Hampton/Illinois library, a few parties. We did one deal

"Jimmy Bowman was a year older than me, and Stevie was two years younger than me and was still in elementary school

The Chantones circa 1965. COURTESY JOE COOK

when this first started. A guy named Billy Gable said, 'Hey, we need a drummer. We've got a band and Jimmie Vaughan's brother plays guitar for us.' Billy Gable left and Glenn Anderson was in for a short time, and even a guy named Phil Coaster for a very, very short time. [The band] was together for a couple of years, seems like.

PARTIES	BANQUETS

The Chantones
The Best in All Fields of Teenage Music

GERALD MASON	JIMMY BOWMAN
FE 9-9064	FE 1-0856
GLENN ANDERSON	STEVE VAUGHAN
FE 1-4419	FE 1-5809
DANCES	SOCK HOPS

Facsimile created by the author from an original provided by Martha Vaughan.

"We were kids, but we were gung ho and wanted to be like a real band, so this guy at the print shop next door to where I worked said, 'If you'll help me, I'll help you make some business cards.' I was scared to death to stick my hand down in that machine, but he said, 'You've got to pull this one out and put that one in before it clamps down again.' He laughed and started doing it for me. We only printed about 150 of them, but, boy, were we proud of them. We were *official* [*laughs*]. [The card pictured is a recreation of the card from a very low resolution copy of the only known surviving Chantones card.]

"We used to go up to the Rocket Skating Rink on either Friday or Saturday and watch the Penthouse Five play for the sock hop after the skating session and talk about how we would take over that gig some day [*laughs*]. [The reader should note that all references to skating rinks are to *roller* skating, not ice skating.]

"I can't swear to this, but seems like Stevie and Jimmy [Bowman] did a demo record, a 45. 'Bring It On Home to Me' was on one side. Jimmy brought it by to me and was real proud of that. I think they were calling themselves The Apolcorps, before all that came up with The Beatles and Apple Records. They thought that was a neat spelling. I thought it was something he did with Stevie."

PAUL KESSLER knew Jimmy Bowman somewhat later and recalls that "he really

was a good singer. He was older than us, and he made us kids a lot better. And I think he played the sax." Despite an extensive search, Jimmy Bowman could not be located.

The Rocket Skating Palace in Cockrell Hill sounds a lot more palatial than it probably was. The *Dallas Morning News* noted one adult's reaction to a visit years after Stevie played there. "She went to the Rocket Skating Palace one Saturday night a few weeks ago and found, to her horror, people were actually skating to rock music."[15] Horror of horrors! Roller skating to rock music! What will these depraved kids do next?

📖**July 10, 1965:** *The Dallas Morning News*, "Dallas After Dark: Young Players Driven to Job," Francis Rafetto: "The Pendulums, a trio of rock-and-roll musicians 14 and 15 years of age, are probably the only combo in town playing in a beer-dispensing tavern but too young to go to work without their parents. 'We parents take turns driving them to work and staying with them,' said Douglas Campbell, Oak Cliff businessman and father of Phil Campbell, 15, expert drummer since Christmas. 'They're too young to drive.' The good-natured parent said about rock-and-roll: 'If people danced like that in my wife's and my day, we'd have never met.

Stevie sits in with The Pendulums circa 1965. COURTESY JOE COOK

It's like they are throwing rocks at each other.' "Other members are Jimmie Vaughn [sic], 14, lead guitar, and Ronny Sterling, 15, bass [sic]. The combo, paid $75 a week each by the Beachcomber, 5015 West Lovers Lane, wears red-and-white candy striped T-shirts. The young boys on the stage put on a bouncing version of 'Long Tall Texan,' ad-libbing some of the lyrics. The trio started their first professional engagement last Tuesday and have a week to go. As the young musicians expertly and enthusiastically dealt with another tune, the stage jumped, the bar vibrated, and the customers clapped and stomped in appreciation. Mr. Campbell remarked, 'At least this job got those drums out of the house for a while.'"

1966

By 1966, the primary impact on Stevie's life is the fact that his big brother, at age 15, has already gained a reputation as an accomplished and popular guitar slinger. Jimmie was playing in a band made up mostly of college-age young men, an indication of just how good he was, considering how vast the age gap typically is between a fifteen-year-old and guys in their early twenties. Twelve-year-old Stevie often commented that what came so easily for Jimmie was more difficult for him, but what else was he going to do? The excitement created by his brother's music was consuming young Stevie.

Late summer: Doyle Bramhall recruits Jimmie into The Chessmen.

The local music rag stated in a retrospective: "Jimmy [sic] advanced rapidly to a berth in The Chessmen, a veteran touring rock band on the way to becoming one of the state's most outrageous acts. Sixteen year-old Jimmy [sic] approached Clapton in taste and finesse, while horrifying unsuspecting onlookers by taking an axe to TV's, drums, guitars, and once, almost, a fan. It was the kind of on stage demolition derby with which The Who were at that point still experimenting."[16]

JIMMIE: "[The blues] was very unpopular. I was the only guy I knew that played that, you know. I had to learn other stuff so I could play in the band, like what was on the radio. The Chessmen was a band that did, like, Yardbirds and The Beatles or whatever was on the radio. Chessmen was a copy band – we played fraternities."[3]

CUTTER BRANDENBURG recalls those early days and the band's singer: "Doyle had more than a voice. Doyle could write

Stevie and unidentified band circa 1966. COURTESY JOE COOK

songs, which was a rarity. A lot of guys could play, but a lot of them couldn't write. But Doyle could write a tune and he could play drums. *Asleep* he could play' better than a lot of people."[17]

Doyle was among the first to pay attention to Stevie as a guitarist. Not too surprisingly, Stevie's own family was just as focused on Jimmie as those in the Dallas music scene. Comments such as "Keep it up, Stevie, and you might be as good as Jimmie some day" were not uncommon in the family.[14]

Five years older than Stevie, Doyle would remain a friend, occasional band mate and song writing partner for the rest of Stevie's life. DOYLE's vivid recollection of meeting Stevie: "Jimmie and I were in a band called The Chessmen together when we were teenagers in Dallas. He was 15 and I was 17, so I could drive and he couldn't, and I would go by and pick him up. One time – this was sometime in 1966 – he wasn't ready, so he waved me in. I was sitting in the living room, waiting, and Jimmie walked from the back bedroom to the kitchen, and I heard this guitar playing going on from the other direction.

"I walked down the hall, and a bedroom door was a little ajar. I looked and there was this little skinny twelve-year-old kid sitting on the bed, playing Jeff Beck's 'Jeff's Boogie.' As soon as he saw me, he stopped playing, and I said, 'Don't stop.' He gave me this shy little smile and said, 'Hi, I'm Stevie,' and I said, 'Hi, I'm Doyle. Keep playing. You're very good.' Thirty seconds later, Jimmie ran up and said, 'Let's go.' I didn't even know Jimmie had a brother, and I [thought], 'There's *another one*?' Because Jimmie was so good, and it was clear that Stevie had it from the get-go too.

"Stevie always made it look easy. Even at the age of twelve he definitely had a feel for the guitar. There was a period of time in the mid-sixties that I would only see Stevie every other month or so. From the time you saw him this month and then the time you saw him two months later, you could tell that he had been playing a lot. He had so much passion for his music.

"He was very quiet, but also very curious. He was always kind of looking around the corner for what's around there and wanted to know how he could be better. If he was fixing an amplifier, if he was buying a pair of boots, or if he was playing his music or talking with you, he wanted to know how everything worked and had a real passion for it. If you knew Stevie, when he got comfortable with you he would talk. You could talk with him about anything."

BILLY ETHERIDGE: "I had been a member of The Chessmen with Jimmie; I played guitar as well as keyboards. Jimmie and I would be back in the bedroom at his parents' house playing guitars, and Stevie would sit on the end of the bed trying to play along. He would be swinging his feet, and they didn't touch the floor [*laughs*]. He would have been about 12 – a little bitty punkin."

Guitarist MARK POLLOCK, who took over Charley's Guitar Shop in 1985 after Charley died: "Me and Jimmie's ex-wife's brother were best friends. We went over to Jimmie's and little Stevie's house. I think Doyle might have been there and Billy Etheridge. Stevie came bounding out of the house, this fourteen-year-old kid with incredibly big hands, bounding out the house with I think an Epiphone Casino – some kind of Epiphone. He never took it off, and he's talking to you while he's playing the guitar. He never once quit playing the hour or two hours we were there.

"He was always nice and polite. Basically, he was a lot nicer than Jimmie. I've known Jimmie years longer, and we're worlds apart. When Stevie was in Dallas, he was at Charley's. If Stevie were still alive, he'd still call me every once in a while. I got postcards from him from all around the world. The irony is, I have never gone out and bought an SRV album, yet I have the first four Fabulous Thunderbirds albums – more my style. But Stevie's my friend and Jimmie isn't. But you have to remember, without Jimmie, there would have been no Stevie. You can't discount that."

October: Stevie sees Christian-Charles dePlicque, known then [and therefore in this book] as Christian Plicque, singing "Treat Her Right" in The Misters at the Texas State Fair. Five years later, Stevie would remember Christian and recruit him to sing in Blackbird.

Stevie's parents were beginning to take notice, but with increasing apprehension. STEVIE: "Yeah, most of the time they were very supportive. Jimmie left home when he was 15 to go play on the road, and here I was, 12, and doing gigs and they're going, 'Uh-oh, here he goes too.' It got kind of rough there for a little bit. They didn't really want me to be taking off at 13, so it was a little bit tenuous there for a while. For the most part they've been very supportive."[129]

After The Chessmen, Jimmie joins Sammy Loria and the Penetrations. No doubt what was on their minds when they named that band! Around this time, fifteen-year-old Jimmie left home and school, and for several years he didn't see much of his little brother. Jimmie moved to an apartment with the other guys in the band.

"I started making a little money in The Chessmen – $300 a week and I was fifteen. I mean, that was a million dollars. I remember going down on Jefferson and buying every B.B. King record they had. You could buy Telecasters for $75 – they couldn't give them away. I was doing really bad at school. I quit going to school and didn't want to do what anybody told me. Being gone and coming home late and everybody was starting to get high and everything, you know. I finally collided with my dad big time, and we had a fight and I ran off.

"The next time I saw [Stevie], we had been apart for a couple of years, and he could really play then. When I left, he really started playing all the time because he didn't have anything else to do, I guess. I left him a Telecaster [actually a Broadcaster], but I always felt bad about leaving him. My dad was still there, and one of the things I didn't like about him was he drank a lot. I felt bad about leaving my mom and Stevie."[3]

Though unconfirmed, it has been reported that Stevie auditioned for the band Freestone but was rejected because he didn't know any Beatles songs.

1967-68

L.V. Stockard Junior High School in Dallas is the next stop in Stevie's education.

The summer of 1967 is a new dawn in young Stevie's life. Jimmie found a Jimi Hendrix 45 in the trash at the mall behind the studio for the Dallas teen dance TV show, *Sump'n Else*, hosted by Ron Chapman. He took the record home, and it was the first time Stevie heard Hendrix. Amazingly, Jimmie's band would open for Hendrix the next year. He recalled in a 1991 interview that the record was "Purple Haze," which was released in the United States in August 1967.

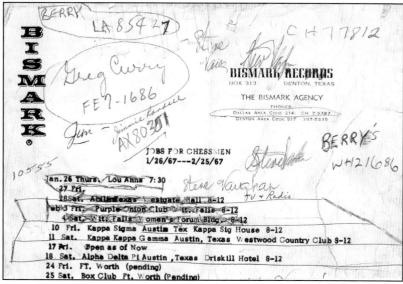

On the Chessmen booking notes pictured herein Stevie appears to be practicing his autograph – not unusual for a twelve-year-old. COURTESY MARTHA VAUGHAN

Sump'n Else was filmed at NorthPark, which was itself a big deal – the largest climate-controlled retail center (mall) in the nation when it opened in 1965. You know, everything is big in Texas! There were several large windows where shoppers could look into the studio from the mall concourse. There were several attractive teenage girls who were hired as regular dancers, but at age six or seven, the author was more interested in hoping the TV cameras would pan across the audience and he would end up on TV!

Stevie's last non-music job was working for $0.70/hour at the Dairy Mart near the northwest corner of Glenfield and Hampton. Martha recalls it was one lot north of the corner. After falling into a barrel of grease, Stevie quit and devoted his life to music. "When I was about twelve, I had been a dishwasher for a while, and part of my job was to clean out the trash bin. That involved standing on these big 55-gallon barrels with wooden lids on them, where they'd put all the hot grease.

"One day I was out there cleaning out the bin, having a blast, and the top broke and I fell in. Just as I finally got out – I'd been up to my chest in grease – they came with two fresh hot vats of

boiling grease and I got out just in time. If I'd taken a break later, I would have been a fried guy! The woman fired me because I broke the lids on the barrel, and right then and there I decided, 'Wait a minute. This is not what I want to do. I want to play guitar like Albert King!' And that's the last job I've had other than playing guitar. So, thank you, Albert, for helping me there.[5]

"I went home with smoke coming out of my ears. I put on the meanest record I had, *King of the Blues Guitar* by Albert King, and right then I made up my mind that I was going to be a guitar player like Albert King."[10]

By 1967, Stevie had experimented with some public performances with The Chantones and, possibly, Epileptic Marshmallow, though the latter seems to have disappeared almost completely from history. The Chantones sounds like it should be a '50's doo-wop group, and Epileptic Marshmallow certainly had a name befitting the '60's hippie music era. STEVIE: "It was just the worst name we could think of.[2] We played National Guard Armory gigs – sloe gin and apricot brandy and daddy's bourbon if you could sneak it into your flask – opening for bands like The Mystics."[18] Nothing is known of the personnel, where they played or how long the band existed.

Then along comes The Brooklyn Underground, the first of Stevie's bands to have any success or longevity. The members were Paul Kessler and Steve Vaughan (guitars), Randy Martin (bass), Billy Metcalf (vocals) and Bobby Ragan (drums). By their accounts, Brooklyn Underground probably started in late 1967 and lasted about eighteen months, which would take Stevie through most, if not all, of 1968.

Guitarist PAUL KESSLER: "I think it's pretty safe to say that Brooklyn Underground was the first organized band that

One of the photos of Jimi Hendrix that Stevie carried. The man at right is unidentified. COURTESY CRAIG HOPKINS

Paul Kessler
Randy Martin

Billy Metcalf
Steve Vaughn

The Brooklyn Underground
"ENTERTAINMENT FOR PARTIES · DANCES · CLUBS"

Bobby Ragan
FE 1-4208

Richard Wilson, Mgr.
CA 4-1698

Note the misspelling of Vaughan on this early business card. In later years his contracts imposed a fine if his name was misspelled on the marquee.
COURTESY RANDY MARTIN

Steve was in. I know we did it over a year, and I want to say it was almost two years. We were actually playing some pretty big deals – I think we would make five hundred dollars and split that – and we were a bunch of fourteen-year-old kids! These days you get some good older musicians and they don't split that much money [*laughs*].

"The main reason we got Stevie in the band was because we considered Jimmie to be the best guitar player in Dallas, and we thought maybe some of that might rub off on us. We never saw him; we'd have to go pick Stevie up and Jimmie was never there. He never came to see us play or nothing."

The band didn't change permanent members, but occasionally the need for a substitute would arise, as Paul remembers. "There were times when someone couldn't show up to play, and generally it might be Steve, just because he was a year younger and not driving. Danny Sanchez was one of the other guitar players we could get. At that time he was really way better, and we didn't have to put

The Brooklyn Underground. COURTESY RANDY MARTIN

up with Stevie playing too loud at practices. I'm in a band now, and at practices you need times to talk and be organized, and I preach that to the other guys. But maybe I'm wrong, because the only other guy I knew that was aggravating at practice was Stevie, and he got famous [*laughs*]!

"He wasn't *Stevie Ray Vaughan* then, he was just another kid playing the guitar. We knew he had some talent but really had to put a leash on it back when he was fourteen years old. At that time, how good your band was was how current the stuff was you were playing. If you were playing a Top 40 hit that had just hit the radio, you were pretty good; if you were sitting there playing old Buddy Holly tunes, you weren't that cool. I remember *Are You Experienced?* came out with 'Purple Haze' and we were pretty

impressed with the bands that were doing those songs, and next thing you know we're doing them. Stevie jumped on that stuff pretty quick.

"I think his big influences at that time would have been his brother, Jimi Hendrix, Eric Clapton, Jeff Beck. ... We were playing The Beatles, Kinks and Yardbirds, that kind of stuff.

"We played Candy's Flare, which was an old National Guard armory. We called them sock hops, where we all danced and chased women. We were kids; they didn't sell booze or anything like that, but it was a big gathering for kids. Our parents would drop us off and pick us up at midnight. Pretty harmless stuff – maybe the occasional fight, but we didn't know anything about people doing drugs. We did several gigs at the Oak Cliff Country Club and some churches that had once-a-month gigs.

"A lot of good guitarists came out of Oak Cliff during that time. I don't know if they were influencing each other, but there were a lot of venues for young bands to play. I knew lots and lots of kids who were playing guitar, and we'd get together and learn from each other. Nowadays, I guess most kids are in their house playing video games. We had to go down the street and find something in common with somebody, and that's how a lot of guys got good – playing with each other. We would feed off of each other; one guy'd know a little ol' lick and first thing you know we'd be playing a song.

"Steve mainly liked to improvise leads, and I never was too good at that, so I knew the chords and played rhythm. Most of the showy stuff he liked to do, but every now and then I would learn to do some leads exactly like they were on the record.

"He was a pretty introverted, quiet kid, focused on that guitar. But we were all pretty introverted, you know – it took a lot of guts to go ask some girl to dance with you at that age. We'd laugh and cut up, but I don't think he cared about sports or girls or anything else too much. Looking back, I guess it was about the only thing he was good at; he wasn't particularly handsome or well-built. I was poor, but I thought he was poorer than me; I don't remember him having any really good guitars. It kind of teaches you a lesson that if you focus and stick with something, there is some opportunity out there."

RANDY MARTIN: "Steve was about fourteen and joined our band. We'd go over to Desoto and play a sock hop on Friday nights, then on Saturday nights, periodically, we'd play out at Candy's Flare in Oak Cliff. Steve would come over and sometimes stay the night at my parents' house in Oak Cliff. My neighbor was Bobby Ragan, the drummer in the band.

"When we would go somewhere that served alcohol, if Steve's dad knew about it, he wouldn't let him play with us. We would have to get a stand-in guitar player, and many times it was Danny Sanchez.

"The biggest thing I remember about Steve is that he was funny, he was a joker. Back then he had a little hollow-body Gibson SG guitar, and he couldn't keep it tuned. It would go out of tune in the middle of a song [*laughs*], and he'd try to tune it while we were playing.

"He loved Hendrix, and when he'd start playing a lead in a song, people would turn around and gravitate toward the stage to see this little kid play guitar. He wasn't refined back then. He had nervous energy and didn't know how to put it all together, but it was incredible to see a little kid play guitar like that. He had a gift, but his equipment wasn't very good. We thought we were big time though. We had business cards and the name written on Bobby's drum."

The relative age gap between Stevie and Jimmie may have been at its widest point. Not only was Jimmie approaching his late teens and Stevie barely in his teens, but Stevie was playing guitar – one of the only things Jimmie had going for him besides his looks. The brothers both recounted numerous times in interviews that Jimmie's parting words anytime he left the house had been, "Don't touch my guitar," often followed by, "or I'll beat your ass." According to some, that's exactly what happened. But getting the back of his head slapped didn't deter Stevie from playing or taking Jimmie's guitars to jams and gigs.

February 16, 1968: The Chessmen open for Jimi Hendrix at the State Fair Music Hall, Dallas.

DOYLE BRAMHALL: "We hung out during the day a little bit and after the [Hendrix] show a little bit. They invited us, Jimmie, myself and the band, the next morning to have breakfast before they took off for Houston. It was his first American tour, and we had heard about him and heard one of his recordings just shortly before we actually played with him. We were just so excited. It was like, 'What is this? We've got to hear this guy.' Not only did we get to hear him, but we got to open for him. It was definitely one of the highlights of my life.

COURTESY MARTHA VAUGHAN

Christmas 1968.
COURTESY MARTHA VAUGHAN

"Hendrix walked up to Jimmie; his wah-wah pedal had broken. Jimmie had a pedal at the time, and [he was] asked if he would like to trade his pedal for Hendrix's, and Jimmie said sure! So they traded pedals." Jimmie Vaughan's recollection: "We opened the show for him, and I saw him play, but I never talked to him again. He bought my wah-wah pedal. I had a brand new one, and he broke his. The roadie said, 'I'll give you fifty bucks and the old one.' I said, 'Okay.' That was about it. We weren't friends or anything."[19]

1969

STEVIE: "I spent a lot of time at the Dairy Mart when I was a kid. I used to work there. I had two paper routes too — one for each paper. Lost them both. I was never trying to be deliberately crazy or wild. I was running with some kids doing the usual stuff, you know, staying up late at night and drinking beer once in a while."[20]

RODDY COLONNA: "Stevie would call me up at night and go, [imitates Stevie] 'Hey Roddy, what're you doin'?' I said, 'Oh, nothin' much.' He says, 'You wanna go out tonight?' I had a '67 Dodge van, and I'd go by Burns' Dairy Mart and pick him up. He just wanted to get out of the house – things weren't that great around there, so he wanted out. We'd go out and shoot some pool, you know, down on Davis Street at some broken down old pool hall, or go out and eat barbecue on our way to Dallas – The States Barbecue. Go hang out at the Pizza Hut or something.

"Stevie had a little 'sit-in' circuit; he'd go and sit in with different bands. We'd go over to the Aragon Ballroom over in South Dallas – it was an all-black club – and I'm just a regular, skinny white kid and Stevie's getting me in the door, 'Hey, can he come in with me? I'm gonna sit in.' He'd have his guitar with him. He got to sit in with this soul band. 'Hey!' you know, they'd wave at us. Then we'd leave and go over to The Fog and he'd sit in with somebody – play 'Crossroads' verbatim, you know, every note that Eric Clapton played.

"He could emulate people, I mean, he would copy and learn every note of Hendrix and just about anything he liked. He could sit and play air guitar and know every nuance. He could do it with his mouth [*laughs*]."

After Jimmie's stints in The Chessmen and The Penetrations, Janis Joplin allegedly tried to convince him to move to California with her.[16] Instead, Jimmie formed a new band called Texas. PAUL RAY recalls: "Jack Caldwell said, 'If you've got any balls, you'll call yourselves 'Texas." It was Jimmie and Doyle, turning into a bluesy band – Billy Etheridge, Tommy Carter. They replaced Tommy Carter with Jimmy Chilton. They were a really good band; they played The Cellar in Dallas and Fort Worth, and that's where the speed started. After Chilton died, Jimmie and Jamie Bassett and Phil Campbell showed up in my apartment in Dallas – they knew I'd been a singer – and said we want to play blues and nothing but blues.

"We started playing a place called The Closing Gap on Lovers Lane. One Sunday in '69, Stevie's mom and dad came by with Stevie to see our jam just to see where Jimmie was working. I had this big ol' Gretsch Country Club guitar – it looked like a coffee table – big ol' blond, single cutaway, bad ass guitar. Stevie picked it up and started messing with it at the break. I sat down next to him on the stage and I said, 'Do you want to play one?' And he thought we were just going to sit there and goof around during the break. He didn't know I hadn't turned the P.A. off – it was still on. So I said, 'Okay. Just play,' and he started playing 'Stormy Monday' and I sang. Everybody was kind of going [stares with mouth open]. He wasn't Stevie like we know Stevie now, but he was definitely heading that way. I was just sitting there going, '*Another* one! Here comes another [Vaughan]!' I'm guessing this was the spring of '69."

STEVIE: "When I was about fourteen, I used to ride a cab down to Hall Street in Dallas, sneaking in to see T-Bone Walker and Freddie King. At the same time, Eric Clapton was coming out, and it was like, 'Oh, it's okay for me to do this.' Somebody else is doing it who's not black. Guitar was the way for me to get out and do it, do my own thing."[21]

For twelve weeks in 1969, he attends Graham High School in Graham, Texas, then returns to finish the year in Dallas at Kimball High.

March: Reese Wynans is part of a jam session that ultimately leads to the formation of the Allman Brothers Band. Some actually refer to him as an original member. In 1985, Reese would become a member of Double Trouble.

May 30: Corsicana High School, Corsicana, TX. Stevie joins The Southern Distributor, replacing Jim Cullum on guitar. For this first gig with the band, Stevie receives $18 after what he owes for guitar strings and Finger Ease.

COURTESY PATRICK MCGUIRE

JIM CULLUM: "Southern Distributor probably hit its stride about 1968 and started getting better gigs. Pat's father, Hal McGuire, was the manager. He got us some good exposure, took all the photographs, built a light show around it. So we were a little better than the average band."

After playing with The Southern Distributor for a couple of years, Jim was ready to move on to something else but offered to help the guys find his replacement on guitar. "We put the word out that we were looking for someone and listened to two or three other guitar players. I remember this kid that had a guitar case kind of bigger than he was, pulled out a [guitar] that had seen better days, and just absolutely blew everybody away. I'm thinking, 'Holy cow! Where'd you learn how to do that stuff?' And the kid says, 'Oh, my brother kind of taught me some stuff.' 'Well, who's your brother?' 'Jimmie Vaughan.' And that floored everybody too. Jimmie was kind of a guitar hero in our circle. I think everybody looked at each other and went, 'Yeah. We'd be stupid to turn this away.'

"Stevie and I spent a lot of time together. I can't show him how to do anything, but I can show him the structure of the songs and where we take breaks. We were a cover band, but we had our own slant on things. I continued to hang around a little bit, and there were probably some times we alternated lead breaks.

Ledger showing Stevie's first gig with The Southern Distributor and expenses for his strings and Finger Ease. COURTESY PATRICK MCGUIRE

COURTESY PATRICK MCGUIRE

"His playing was phenomenal for a fifteen-year-old kid. He was light years ahead of almost anybody else I'd been around, and I'd been fortunate to be around some really good players.

"I guess the thing I remember about him most was he was not consumed with ego. I think he knew he was good, but if you were asking him how he did something, he would stop and show in detail how he did it. That was a refreshing change from the other guitar players I'd been around. They were very secretive and ego driven and protected what they do. Stevie was very giving of his knowledge and techniques. He was a fun guy to hang around."

Summer: Stevie's girlfriend in 1969 and into 1970 is Vicki Virnelson.

VICKI: "Both of us had a mutual friend, Tom Russell, and his dad was a builder, and he had a development going in. Tom was supposed to work this concession stand his dad set up for the people coming to see the houses. Of course he didn't want to do it, so he enlisted Stevie and me. Making hot dogs and pouring Cokes for everyone.

"We were both fourteen, between ninth and tenth grade. As fourteen-year-olds will do, one thing led to another and we ended up seeing each other for most of our sophomore year [1969-1970]. He was playing in a band in Irving [The Southern Distributor] and I would go watch them practice.

"We dated through that year – going to the State Fair, football games. We went to Red Bird airport to see the blimp at Texas-OU weekend [college football rivalry]. Stevie was really shy and quiet. We would talk on the phone for hours. He'd be in his room and he'd play his guitar and say, 'Listen to this song.' I remember one was 'Baby, Don't Cut Your Hair.' I'd listen to old blues songs with him over the phone. I didn't even know he had an older brother [*laughs*]. He had already moved out and married Donna.

"I remember [Southern Distributor] played at the Lamplighter Club. It was like a teen club, whereas [Candy's] Flare wasn't a club. Candy's dad just rented the place out. There was a fellow that came up one night after Steve played 'Jeff's Boogie.' Every band

did 'Jeff's Boogie' as a break song. He said, 'I bet you can't do that double-time.' He didn't think this fourteen-year-old kid could do it. Stevie played it, like, triple-time. He was just awestruck and he just walked off. The other song he played a lot was 'Sittin' On Top of the World,' which was Cream. They had to play rock and roll because the kids didn't know blues."

Asked about particular memories of Stevie, Vicki laughed and said, "Yes. I was talking with a lady recently when I was getting new glasses. ... I told her I had lost my glasses once at the State Fair, and she said she lost hers once at the beach. We just kind of rolled our eyes because we both knew why our glasses weren't on our faces! Steve and I were sitting and 'resting' under this big oak tree at the Fair, and of course I took my glasses off... .

"I still make my E's like backward 3's, and I got that from Steve."

Southern Distributor

The Southern Distributor (l-r) Mike, Pat, Stevie and Darryl. Stevie has graduated to a 1951 Fender Broadcaster. © HAL MCGUIRE, COURTESY PATRICK MCGUIRE

June 7: Lee Park Recreation Center, Dallas, TX (The Southern Distributor)

June 13: YMCA, Grand Prairie, TX (The Southern Distributor)

June 14: YMCA, Grand Prairie, TX (The Southern Distributor)

June 27: Carrawood Apartments, Dallas, TX (The Southern Distributor)

June 28: Camp Crusis, Granbury, TX (The Southern Distributor) The band played for a junior-high-age church camp dance.

"We Deliver" — The Southern Distributor truck with Pat driving. © HAL MCGUIRE, COURTESY PATRICK MCGUIRE

July 5: United Service Organization (USO), Dallas, TX (The Southern Distributor)

📖**August 20:** *Irving Daily News*, "The Southern Distributor and their light show will furnish entertainment Friday at Northwest Recreation Center, 2800 Cheyenne. Admission costs $1 for the barbecue, $1 for the dance scheduled from 7 p.m. until midnight. Members of the group include Mike Steinbach, drums; Pat McGuire, rhythm guitar, organ and vocals; Steve Vaughan, lead guitar; Darryl Haynes, bass guitar; and Jim Cullum guest performer."

Hmm ... concert, light show, barbecue and dance for two dollars. It appears people got a lot more for $2 going to see Stevie play in 1969 than folks get these days paying $300 for the Rolling Stones or Paul McCartney.

August 22: Northwest Recreation Center, Irving, TX (The Southern Distributor) 7 p.m. to midnight, admission $1.

The band's tag was "Pseudopsychosonicoptic," which at first glance looks like something Mary Poppins would say, but which stands for simulated (pseudo) psychedelic (psycho) sound (sonic) and sight (optic). What a brilliant part of the sixties rock lexicon! The band's name logo was drawn by the manager, Hal McGuire, father of guitarist Pat.

PATRICK McGUIRE: "Back then, the parents were very involved. Steve's parents would bring him over, or my parents would go pick him up – whatever it took to make it all work. My dad knew where bands played and wasn't afraid to go knocking on doors, so he got gigs lined up for us.

"I played rhythm guitar and some keyboard. Jim and I did the bulk of the singing, and Darryl did some. Jim Cullum was the guitarist Steve replaced. He quit and we put an ad in the *Dallas Times Herald* in the Musical Instruments section that we were looking for a guitarist. Stevie actually came and auditioned for us [*laughs*], and we said, 'Wow! This guy can do it.'

"We were all astounded at how well he played for his age. He played things like 'Jeff's Boogie' – all kinds of things which were intricate and difficult even for guys quite a bit older. He was into the old blues artists. What I remember more than any other thing is how much he practiced – at least five hours a day. He didn't have much social life; I don't know how well he did in school, but I don't suspect he did too well because all he did was play guitar. I mean he lived, ate, breathed guitar – that was it. He definitely idolized his brother. Steve was very shy and he let his guitar speak for him. He didn't sing.

"The band would practice at my house, but I used to take my guitar and practice with him in his bedroom in Oak Cliff. I was just astounded at his knowledge of music – the blues especially – and how much he worked at it and how dedicated he was.

"My mom, Zoe McGuire, called him 'Little Stevie Wonder' and everybody else called him Steve. She wasn't talking about [the famous] Stevie Wonder, but talking about the fact that he was little and a wonder. She called him Stev*ie*, and I didn't know anyone else who did.

"We were a pop rock band. We did the songs they played on KLIF – Beatles, Doors, Yardbirds, Byrds, Kinks – all those kinds of things. Of course, Steve wanted to play blues, so we tried to pacify him, but the funny thing was, we said, 'Man, you're never going to make any money playing blues!' [*Laughs*] It was definitely what he wanted to do, and we pacified him to a certain degree, but we were doing our thing. He sure showed us, didn't he? Even after the band broke up, we all stayed friends, and we all pulled for him and were really happy for him when we heard about Carnegie Hall and those things he did.

"We played mostly school dances, YMCA's, National Guard armories (Candy's Flare), things like that, because back then there were teen dances. There aren't anymore, but there were tons of them back then. The photo in the paper was for a recreation center dance, which were very common. We played in the gymnasium of the recreation center in Irving."

The Southern Distributor had been playing those teen dances since about 1966 or 1967 with Jim Cullum before Steve came into the band on May 30, 1969. But by this time, the original members were seventeen years old and being pulled in separate directions as they approached the end of high school.

Drummer MIKE STEINBACH: "Pat's father was a jazz musician and professional photographer and was our manager. We were together about two years and were a fairly established band – high school gigs, YMCA on Irving Boulevard, rec centers, proms; played the National Guard armories, which was a popular thing to rent out and have dances with a live band. We played East Texas, North Texas and into Oklahoma even.

"We were making, like, $15 apiece per night, getting to travel. At age fifteen, sixteen – it was like being rock stars. In the late sixties it was better than any other part-time job for a teenager. We were studs [*laughs*]! We didn't think we were then, but I can't believe it, looking back. We were really lucky to have it come together with the right people and adult supervision. With Pat's dad Hal there, it opened the door to the other parents' approval.

"We had a light show, which was one of our big selling points, and it was a really good one. Pat's dad built it; he was an all-around guy and built a lot of the electronics. Pat and Jim both originally had built their amplifiers out of mail-order kits! Toward the end they got the Kustom amps with the tufted vinyl. The light show, at one time we had two guys running it. We had two or three overhead projectors which would project the mixed-up oil and colored water on the walls; we had a strobe light and an 8mm projector for showing old commercials from the fifties. It was really a big deal and got us a lot of shows.

"We played the Texan Club, a private club in Oak Cliff when I was sixteen, and I remember some drunk yelling, 'Turn off that damn flicker light!' [Laughs] The strobe was a little too much for him."

PATRICK: "Psychedelic light shows were a pretty big deal. You'd have a strobe light and a movie projector projecting old movies, slide projectors projecting anything – just random things – then oil, water and food coloring in a pie plate on an overhead projector. We had a couple of those. So a bunch of images covering all of the walls wherever you were playing. My brother Michael ran the light show."

The Southern Distributor in 1969 was probably the only time any of Stevie's bands had a semblance of an elaborate light show or decoration. Even into the arena shows twenty years later, Stevie was content with just playing music. (See Trey Hensley's remarks in late 1989.) The one exception seems to be the Carnegie Hall show in 1984, for which Stevie had custom stage risers made and painted blue and gold.

MIKE: "We did a lot of Doors because they were brand new, current hot stuff. We also did Hendrix ('Fire' and 'Foxey Lady'), some Cream, English blues-rock, Stones, fair amount of Beatles – we were very eclectic and had harmony on most songs. We were definitely rock and not bubble-gum. The Hendrix and Clapton tunes fit Stevie real well, plus a couple of Jeff Beck songs.

"Jim Cullum was our first lead guitar player and sang most of the lead vocals. He quit, so we auditioned guitar players. Most

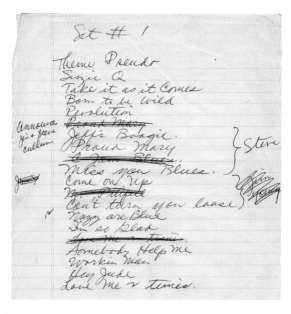

Set lists noting the songs on which Stevie was featured.
COURTESY PATRICK MCGUIRE

of our business was at Arnold & Morgan Music in Garland (the place to buy equipment in those days), and a guy named Dan recommended Jimmie Vaughan's little brother. I still remember he described him as 'adequate' [laughs]! He came over to Pat's house where we rehearsed, and our mouths dropped! The kid was fourteen. We auditioned him on 'Jeff's Boogie,' really fast instrumental guitar, and he played it note for note.

"He could play Hendrix and Clapton note for note at fourteen, which was pretty amazing. He sang, but not [on stage]. He was a sweet little kid, and I do mean little – he looked fourteen. I was seventeen, but at that age, that's a big difference. Pat, Jim and Darryl were sixteen. I was the only one with a driver's license, and I would borrow Pat's mom's car to go pick Stevie up.

"He lived and breathed music – that was all he cared about. He used to call me up and play licks over the phone. Nice as he could be, extremely talented. Unfortunately, he was already into diet pills [amphetamines].

"Stevie was in the band maybe six to nine months at the most and was the last guitar player. I don't remember exactly why the band broke up. I think Hal McGuire, Pat's dad, was losing interest in it, and everyone was wanting to go in different directions. The picture in the Irving paper was toward the end of Southern Distributor."

DARRYL HAYNES, bass player for The Southern Distributor, responded succinctly when asked why the band broke up: "Girls [laughs]. They sort of messed things up, because our attention got placed other places. That's probably the real reason.

"I remember spending the night over at Steve's house. He slept with his guitar. He didn't put it down. About four o'clock in the morning I said, 'Can't we go to sleep?' We were practicing the Cream album – he wanted to get it down perfectly, and I had to get my part down too. We played a lot of Beatles and Doors.

"We always practiced at Pat's house – two or three times a week late at night until the neighbors started calling the police. The light show was so good Pat even rented it out to other bands. I remember a couple of these places we played had a light board behind the stage. [The lights flashed in response to sound.] The goal was to never let the light board go black. So you had to go from one song to another and could never stop. That was a challenge."

Patrick's brother, CHRISTOPHER McGUIRE (now an accomplished classical guitarist): "Steve was a little younger than the others, and he kind of empathized with me because I was kind of the punky little brother that hung around. He was really such a nice person. He would pay attention to me, and we played together during the rehearsal breaks. He taught me all the parts to the tunes they were playing and how to pick solos off the records by picking up the needle and playing a little part, imitating it. He was very patient and sat there for hours after rehearsals and would help me with things like that.

"He was around the house for at least one rehearsal a week and then would have one or two gigs every Friday and Saturday night. They would play out of town frequently, but mostly locally. The Jaycees would put on dances, until they caught on that that's where all the kids were exchanging drugs and beer. The civic leaders thought they were doing a good thing for the youngsters, and then they found out that's where everyone was getting their pot [laughs]!

"I have no idea whether Stevie had started using drugs, because he wouldn't have let me know – I was the kid. He was the youngest guy in the band, but he was the older guy that I looked up to.

"He was also playing in two other bands at the same time, but they didn't have many gigs. What little money he made was with The Southern Distributor. It was mostly a cover band, but they did some of Stevie's things that would show him off. He did 'Jeff's Boogie,' but he had a couple of his own licks that he did. Even as a fifteen-year-old he was taking tunes like that and doing his own thing with them.

"I was thirteen or fourteen, and one night I snuck out with Stevie and went to The Cellar. We ended up getting on stage with Johnny Winter!"

In 1969, Stevie met Robert "Cutter" Brandenburg, who started out giving Stevie rides and eventually became the band's roadie. Cutter served two long stints with Stevie and has published his own memoir of life on the road, *You Can't Stop a Comet.*

Also in 1969, Stevie acquired his first Fender Stratocaster, a 1963 maple neck. GARY COCKRELL recalls Stevie using his brother's hand-me-down guitars: "He just had his brother's old Telecaster at the time, so when I brought a friend's vintage Strat into the club, he totally lit up and went around showing it to everyone. He really wanted that guitar, but it wasn't mine to sell."

After playing the 1969 Woodstock Festival as a member of Johnny Winter's band, Tommy Shannon met Stevie for the first time at The Fog club in Dallas. By remarkable coincidence, it was the same club in which he had met Winter. TOMMY: "I'd been playing with Johnny Winter and we'd just broken up and I flew

back to Dallas where I lived before I moved up to New York with Johnny. I went back to this club that I used to play at called The Fog. I remember walking in and all my old friends were there. All of a sudden I heard this guitar playing in the background and I looked up there on stage, and there was this skinny little awkward kid. He was just incredible even then. I remember he was very humble – he really respected all these big guys around him. He didn't realize he was already better than them.[3]

"[Stevie] wasn't really with a band then, he was sitting in, and I'll never forget it. He blew me away. A couple of notes and you knew there's something really special there. I got up and played some with him."

In '68 or '69, Stevie tried out for the band Dallas City Blues. The band was gigging regularly at Candy's Flare, with Fredde Walden on drums and Bobby Rogers on bass. Fredde says Stevie wasn't hired because he was too young, despite blowing them away at the audition with a rendition of "Sunshine of Your Love" by Cream. Ten years later, as Stevie was putting together Triple Threat Revue and looking for a drummer, he got Fredde back, saying, "I'm worrying about playing with you because you're so *old!*"[17]

ROLLIE ANDERSON: "I used to play in a band called Dust at Candy's Flare in the Oak Cliff National Guard Armory near Red Bird. The deal there was that two bands played, trading one-hour sets. On our breaks, Stevie (then known only as Jimmie's little brother) would come hang out and ask if he could play my Telecaster while the other group played. Stevie would sit behind the equipment (not plugged in) just playing his heart out to no one but himself with a grin on his face."

👀 **date unknown:** The End of Cole Avenue, Dallas, TX (sitting in with Marc Benno's band, Jomo) These instrumental blues tunes, totaling approximately fifteen minutes, are the earliest known surviving recordings of Stevie.
  – slow blues 11:22
  – uptempo blues 3:20 (incomplete)

In 1969, musician Marc Benno sees Stevie play for the first time. Marc had just been half of the Asylum Choir with Leon Russell and would later record "L.A. Woman" with The Doors. MARC: "That was an incredible thing. At the time, Jimmie used to beat Stevie up for playing his licks. He would tell him, 'Do *not* play the same lick that I play. If you do, I'm gonna hit you in the mouth.' Stevie would play the lick just like Jimmie, so Jimmie took him out in the back and beat him up.

"Jomo was kind of [a play on] mojo. Blair Smith on guitar, I'm on guitar, Wally Wilson is on bass, and David Davis on drums. The End of Cole Avenue was around the corner from Knox Street. It was BYOB – bring your own blanket. It was freezing – they didn't have any heat, so we made a new deal about BYOB. It was the new version of The Outcasts, which played at the Studio Club from like '64 and '65. In '66 that band disbanded and we put another thing together that was similar. I think we added Blair Smith and became Jomo. We'd gone down to the Vulcan Gas Company, came back when they opened up this club in Dallas called The End of Cole Avenue. Stevie walked in, wearing a white T-shirt and weighing about a hundred pounds, and asked if he could sit in."

"I hadn't seen him for a while, and I didn't recognize him. He wanted to sit in, and I said, 'I don't think so.' Then he said he was Jimmie's brother, and I said, 'Yeah, okay. You can use my guitar.' He had his own guitar and ran out and came back in with a [1951 Fender] Broadcaster. No case – he just brought it in over his shoulder and poured it out – 'Here's the licks I know.' Stevie's tone is the biting, Fender tone. The other, muted guitar tone is Blair Smith playing a Les Paul. He did his thing, but he had an Albert King influence. It was pretty, clean, smooth, hot – it was wonderful. [The recording] is so pure of him at his very beginnings – it really paints a picture of where it started. At the same time, it was that effortless flow where the guy never ran out of stuff to play or made errors. He charmed the whole place pretty quick."

MARK POLLOCK recalls the club: "It was called the End of Cole Avenue. There were no table and chairs, you sat on the floor on pillows, if you could get a pillow. Me and Jimmie and Donna, his future wife, went there to see Freddie King one night. That was probably '69."

The End of Cole Avenue was short-lived: the owner, Claude Albritton, thinks it opened in 1968 and closed in less than two years. The only references the author could find that were reasonably trustworthy were also from 1969. Benno most often referred to this recording as having been made in 1969, though it's remotely possible it could have been earlier, when Stevie was fourteen.

October 3: Stevie's fifteenth birthday.

Girlfriend VICKI VIRNELSON: "I remember saving my money to get Steve a birthday present. I got him some dress shoes, because he didn't have any, and a pocket watch which he had for a long time. We bought this pocket watch at the strangest little jewelry store downtown. It had gorgeous carving on the front and a silver chain."

November 13: Stevie, Vicki Virnelson and Jan Jones attend The Rolling Stones concert in Dallas.

VICKI: "We went to Moody Coliseum, and our friend Jan Jones' dad drove us and picked us up. We sat next to the top row, almost looking through the girders to see them. Chuck Berry was the

beginning act. And it was neat that the first time Stevie was on the Grammies [in 1984], he was part of a tribute to Chuck Berry and played on stage with him. In the first or second year of the Texas lottery, Jan's dad won fifty-six million dollars!"

Stevie moved on to Justin F. Kimball High School. Had he finished, he would have been in the class of 1972. "When I was in school, it was berserk, especially high school. I had to get a note from the principal every day saying I looked all right to go to his school [probably a reference to his long hair]. Jimmie got chased by the girls and beat up by the football players. I was playing 'til 6:00 in the morning and going to school at 7:15, and it didn't work."[22]

STEVIE: "I took music theory for one year in high school and flunked all but one six-week period. That's because I couldn't read music, and the rest of the class was already eight or nine years into it. The teacher would sit down and hit a ten-fingered chord on the piano and you had to write all the notes down in about ten seconds. I just couldn't do it. It was more like math to me."[8]

JIM RIGBY, who recorded with Stevie in 1970, recalls, "He was, I think, a loner, basically, and in school he was just trying to get by. People said he was a 'druggie.' I can't imagine playing in clubs and coming to school the next day – how exhausted he must have been. In some ways he was not plugged in to anything at Kimball, but in other ways there was this real sensitivity that you could see. And when you watched him play music, he went to a different place. That was the thing that I remember most. He was in the room with you, but he was in a different place.

"It was like something was coming through him and moving his body and his hands. It was a real eerie feeling. Some of it was talent, but some of it was love. It's like the eyes roll back in the head almost, and there's some bliss that certain performers get, and they go to this place. It's like they say that when you watch great racers, their head doesn't move – you can tell who the great racers are because they're in a zone."

Despite his lack of success in the classroom, Stevie perfected his craft through constant practice. "I played it on the curb, on the porch, in my room or walking down the street. And if I didn't have my guitar with me, I'd either want it or was taking a break. I remember I had to put it down if I had to fight somebody. We lived in a tough neighborhood in Dallas, and some of the kids couldn't understand why I wanted to play guitar and not go rip somebody off. But I'm glad I kept playing. Some of those guys are now dead."[23]

DENNIS DULLEA: "A guy I worked with came up to me when I was playing one time, and said, 'Hey, can this guy sit in with you? He's really good.' I said, 'Well, I guess so.' I think Stevie was fifteen. He came up, took my guitar and played, and he was incredibly good for fifteen. Broke one of my strings, blew one of the speakers out on my Twin Reverb, then he handed my guitar back and said, 'Thanks,' and walked off."

1970

Stevie's artistic talent qualifies him for an experimental art class at Southern Methodist University called Imagination's Growing Place. STEVIE: "It was a night class and it was a few kids from all over the city. It was completely wide open. We brought records and talked and worked. If you were working on a piece of sculpture and you decided to come in and smash it, you did it. If you wanted to look at it, you did that. The class was great, I learned a lot in it, but it was on the nights when I was supposed to be rehearsing."[20]

MARTHA VAUGHAN: "He won a little scholarship to a program out there. Stevie was a good artist. In fact Jimmie draws too, or he did. Mostly it was cars that they drew [laughs]. One of the first things Jimmie drew was a car wreck that he saw when we were coming home one day. When we got home, he immediately sat down and drew a picture of that wreck."

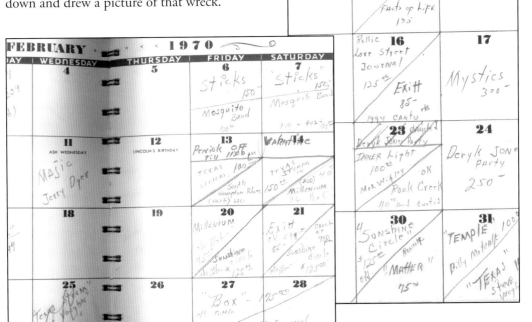

Candy's Flare booking calendar showing Stevie in Texas Storm in early 1970.
COURTESY CHRISTIAN BROOKS

January 31: Candy's Flare, Dallas, TX (Texas)

February 13: Candy's Flare, Dallas, TX (Texas Storm)

February 14: Candy's Flare, Dallas, TX (Texas Storm)

The above three gigs come from M.L. King's personal calendar for Candy's Flare, shown below. Candy is his daughter's name. Note the January listing for Texas and mid-February listings for Texas Storm. Either the January listing abbreviated the band name (most likely) or this identifies when the band changed. For both months, the band contact is listed as Steve Vaughan, perhaps because he was still living at home and easier to reach. Steve would have been playing bass on a Barney Kessell guitar or a borrowed Fender.

MIKE KINDRED, who would later be keyboard player in Triple Threat Revue, recalls seeing Stevie play bass: "I met Stevie at the National Guard Armory in Oak Cliff; it used to be called The Flare, and then it was Candy's Flare. It was run by a guy, I forget what his straight business was, who thought a lot of his daughter Candy and wanted to provide a place for the kids to get together and hear live bands on the weekend. I went up there one night to hear Jimmie. Stevie was playing bass, and I couldn't get Stevie to say anything. Later I found out Jimmie had told him to keep his mouth shut [laughs]."

Whereas his earlier bands were cover bands, Jimmie recalls Texas Storm as being "when [we] went trying to do something different, you know. Trying to do what we wanted. It was just like art – you want to draw what you want to draw. You don't want to draw what somebody tells you to draw."[3]

DOYLE BRAMHALL: "Jimmie and I were in a band called Texas in Dallas back in early '69, and we were playing at The Cellar. Anyway, we had been going, since '66, down to Austin to play. We went back down to Austin in '69 to play a few dates, messed around playing more of the blues stuff down there. Texas broke up and we immediately formed Texas Storm, and I guess for about four or five months we played a few dates around Dallas. It was Jimmie on guitar, Phil Campbell on drums, Stevie played bass and I sang.

"You don't know back then where it's going to head. We just wanted to play the music we wanted to play, and Stevie said, 'I'll play bass.' We got to go down to Austin and play the Vulcan Gas Company a couple of times and a couple of other gigs on the east side of Austin. Then we broke up and Jimmie and I moved our families to Austin at the same time and started Storm in '70. So it went Texas, Texas Storm, Storm."

Regarding Stevie's bass playing, Doyle recalled, "Oh, he was great! He and Jimmie both are. I've found that most good guitar players are great bass players. Jimmie and Stevie and my son are great bass players. They tend to think more in the Hammond B-3 [organ] bass, left handed or foot rather than they do regular bass. You can talk to any of the guitar players, and if you hear them play bass, it's more of the organ bass than guitar bass. We listened to a lot of Jimmy Smith records, and if you listen to Jimmy Smith, he does that real solid in-the-pocket stuff."

Texas Storm was the only time Stevie and Jimmie were truly members of the same band. The age difference was still significant, but it wasn't quite as noticeable with Stevie now fifteen and Jimmie eighteen. Asked about the dynamic between them at that time, Doyle responded, "Oh, it was brother stuff. We just wanted to play. Jimmie was the guy, and Stevie knew his place [laughs]. There weren't any fights as far as I knew, but there was definitely an older brother-younger brother 'You know who the man is' kind of a deal."

A less than stellar review of Stevie's bass playing came from drummer John Hoff, who would later be a member of Stevie's band Blackbird. "Adequate" was his assessment.

Stevie, Doyle and Phil at Lee Park, Dallas. COURTESY JAN HARRIS

Jimmie and Stevie at Lee Park, Dallas. COURTESY JAN HARRIS

Doyle Bramhall, Stevie. COURTESY JAN HARRIS

Another who witnessed Stevie holding down the bottom end was GARY COCKRELL: "I was playing in a band called Millennium. We had a gig at Candy's Flare in Oak Cliff, a skating rink. We shared the gig with Jimmie Vaughan's band and alternated sets for four hours. Jimmie had just left The Chessmen and was now strictly playing only blues and Stevie was playing bass — an old Fender Precision bass that was bigger than him! Stevie was easier to talk to than Jimmie, so we talked guitars for a while. He said he really liked playing bass and how he liked doing those slow bass lines going down the neck. He was so into music, as we all were!"

DENNY FREEMAN: "I remember hearing Stevie play bass one night in Austin. One of the places we played in the early days was the I.L. Club, a black club on the east side. I heard Jimmie and Doyle were playing there, and Stevie was playing bass. Stevie must have been fifteen or sixteen. I didn't hear him play guitar until he moved to Austin in '71 with Blackbird. Jimmie was sixteen, I think, when I first heard him play. Both of them were already good guitar players at sixteen or seventeen, better than most people.

"Stevie had a ways to go yet, but he had jumped on the Albert King thing and was already a pretty fiery lead guitar player. I mean, we all have to go somewhere for something, and Stevie went to the Albert well, and I think Jimmie pretty much went to the B.B. well."

February 28: According to a fan, Liberation formed on this date. It is a nine- to ten-piece horn-driven, jazz-rock band with Scott Phares (bass), Mike Day (drums), Steve Lowrey (organ), Steve Vaughan (guitar), Wes Johnson (sax), Scott Leftwich (trumpet), Jim Trimmier (sax+), Larry Chapman (trombone), and Christian Plicque (vocals). The short-term original singer was Mike Reames. Scott Phares was replaced on bass by Robert Penhall shortly before the band broke up at the end of the summer.

Singer CHRISTIAN PLICQUE: "I was working as a Toy Buyer Junior Executive Trainee at Neiman-Marcus. He came in looking for me. How he found me is still a mystery! But he said he was looking for a black singer to form a band and he had heard me sing at the Fair the year before [probably a couple of years]. I thought, 'This guy must be joking! I have this fine job at this great store and my future, financially, is secure. And he wants me to leave and work with him?!' But he was so on fire and excited about the possibilities that I thought, 'Oh well, I'll at least go and see what he is into.' Never thinking I would begin a band with him.

"Stevie and I had several bands before Blackbird, but one of our biggest bands was Liberation. It was made up of Oak Cliff musicians and was a horn band. I think we had five horns, keys, bass, drums, Stevie and me. We mostly did Chicago-type songs. We didn't make money but we sounded good. We got our name because we were a racially mixed band and wanted people to know that all of us could work together no matter what color. Also our music was very liberated.

"There was no other band in Texas to our knowledge playing that kind of music, certainly not in Dallas. As in most bands, from time to time there was arguing about what songs we would do and so on. I think that is why we got tired of horns and wanted a smaller group. Jim Trimmier was our arranger and sax player. Very talented. Again, this was just another short-lived band on our way to Blackbird. Stevie and I tried all kinds of combinations searching for the right thing. Blackbird was it."

Sax player JIM TRIMMIER: "In the fall of '69 I was in Liberation, and then in the spring of '70 I had tonsillitis with complications and was laid up for six weeks out of school. When I came back, they were saying, 'Man, you gotta get back with us. We learned 'Vehicle' by The Ides of March, and we got a new guitar player.' He was great. I remember he could play 'Jeff's Boogie,' some Hendrix and all kinds of things."

Drummer MIKE DAY: "It was in my last year of high school [1969-1970] and Scott's too. Jim Trimmier was in the school band and he was a really good sax player. That was at a time when [the band] Chicago was really popular, Blood, Sweat & Tears, The Ides of March. I really liked that sound, so I approached him about playing in the band. He had some contacts with other horn players who were really good. The thing about Jim Trimmier was his ability to write music – hear something and sit down and write out the parts for everybody."

Original guitarist SCOTT PHARES: "Jim Trimmier was such a musical genius, he could sit and listen to a Chicago song, and within thirty minutes he could write out all the horn parts and go, 'Okay, we're ready!' He was the director over the horns, and they just kicked ass."

MIKE: "We had auditions for a bass player, and that's when Stevie showed up. [He was coming from playing bass with Texas Storm, which may explain why he auditioned for bass in Liberation.] He was just Steve Vaughan then – no Stevie Ray.

I'd seen him play in some band, Brooklyn Underground or something, and he had a guitar and a Silvertone amp and was just real good. He did a wonderful job of playing bass during our first session. During our first break he went over, picked up [Scott's] guitar and started playing. That's when Scott Phares said, 'This is ridiculous. You're playing lead, I'll play bass.' That was pretty big of him to acknowledge the talent there, but it was obvious. He was willing to change instruments just to be part of that band."

SCOTT: "I knew who Jimmie was, and I had heard Jimmie had a younger brother that was a really hot guitar player. Liberation was rehearsing at Mike Day's house, and I was still the guitar player. We were putting together some Chicago songs and I was having a hard time doing some of the Chicago guitar riffs at the time. We didn't have a bass player, and somebody knew a kid that would come over and play bass with us during rehearsal, and if he can do it, we'll ask him to join the band. Steve came over and played bass on one or two or three songs, and we said, 'Hey kid, as long as your mom will let you make the gigs you can play with us.' We went to take a break and Steve asked me, 'Can I play your guitar?' And I said, 'Sure.' He picked it up and just played circles around me! I said, 'Look. I will be the bass player, you're obviously the better guitar player.' We pretty much swapped equipment. Steve had an old '52 or '53 Telecaster that had absolutely no finish on it whatsoever. I guess it was one of Jimmie's guitars, because if you turned it over on the back it had 'Jimbo' carved in it." [It was a 1951 Fender Broadcaster.]

MIKE: "[Liberation] was pretty special. I don't think Stevie had done anything on the scale we were doing. We were playing the big clubs in Dallas at that time – The Fog, Soul City, The Rickshaw. The band was pretty large. At one time we had two singers, five horns. I think it was The Fog, our first gig on that little circuit, and there was some band playing, then they finished and people were filing out the door until we got up and hit the opening of 'Vehicle' by The Ides of March, and they just stopped in their tracks and the place started filling up more so than it was before. It was a big sound with all the horns, but in spite of all that instrumentality, a fifteen-year-old guitar player steals the show!

"It was amazing to watch him jump off the stage and start going into his riffs, and seeing how it affected the crowd. It was such an interesting mix of music, because he always wanted to play the blues. He came across it honestly – he lived it too. We'd go over to pick him up and his dad would say, 'Oh no you're not,' and punch him in the face. It was kind of tough on him, so he didn't spend a lot of time at home. In fact, he kind of lived at my house for a good part of the time, and he hung out with Cutter a lot. When Stevie'd stay at my house, we'd sit out in the front yard drinking cheap wine, have a couple of acoustic guitars and a singer. We'd be making up nasty blues songs and rolling down the hill [laughs]. He was a funny guy, a fun guy. He had this kind of hawk sound that he could make. Girls were always real interested in him, being the front man.

"Cutter was good at keeping Stevie's ego up, keeping him positive. He was true, he wasn't lying to him – [Stevie] didn't have bad days. He was always striving to try to be as good as his brother Jimmie. And we always said, 'Stevie, you've already passed him!' It was kind of meteoric how things went. We played a gig at the Adolphus Hotel and ZZ Top came in. To watch Stevie and Billy [Gibbons] get up and trade licks was pretty cool.

"The guy who was running the little circuit in Dallas had connections with the group that ran Ceasar's Palace, the hotel in Lake Tahoe, and the Newport in Miami, and they had a circuit of their own that they wanted us to play. It was very interesting – these were guys you would consider were more like [hesitates] the group who ran the Las Vegas circuit for a long time – organized type ... Very nice, but people you wouldn't want to cross. They loved us and were ready to book us, which would have been pretty good, [but] Stevie was fifteen, so they said, 'You'll have to replace the young lead player.' We said, 'We don't think so.' They also wanted us to back up The Coasters, which is not what we were interested in doing musically.

"I think we all had a little different aspirations, and Stevie was committed to playing the blues. Stevie and I and some other members of the band would go off and play other clubs under made-up names, and we'd just jam, just play blues. I enjoyed that, but it wasn't where my interests really lie. I was starting to get into more orchestral-type rock, music like Yes, Genesis, Gentle Giant – a lot of meter changes, more complex music.

"In Liberation we did a pretty wide variety of music – Chicago, Blood, Sweat & Tears, and then we did Cream or something with Clapton or a lot of Hendrix. And we played blues – watching the black people come up and talk to Stevie and say, 'You're black!' [Laughs] I think that meant more to him than any of the accolades that anybody else showered on him."

STEVIE: "There's nights when I feel like I play better, and there's nights that – for a lack of a better way to say it – I feel like the whitest guy that walks."[4]

April 12: Jimmie's band plays at Lee Park in Dallas, TX.

Liberation keyboardist STEVE LOWREY recalls going with Stevie to Lee Park to see Jimmie Vaughan play. "The day we went out there to watch them play, they had what I believe they referred to as 'the Lee Park massacre.' A couple of kids jumped in Turtle Creek, the cops pulled them out, a riot ensued, tear gas, the whole nine yards."

Lee Park was established in 1903 near a very expensive area called Highland Park, but the park is actually in the Oak Lawn area of Dallas. There is a large equestrian statue of General Robert E. Lee and an ante-bellum-style events hall erected in 1939. Its large front porch and the sloping lawn near Turtle Creek was a popular place for spring and summer outdoor concerts. MIKE KINDRED: "I wasn't playing the fateful day that everybody jumped into Turtle Creek nude that caused such a scandal, but I was playing the next weekend with Stevie when they had the SWAT team to make sure nobody got naked again!"

There was a lot of media coverage of the melee, but the newspaper accounts do not refer to any nudity on the part of the teens. Many recall such an incident occurring during a Lee Park event, but it may not have been this weekend. Apparently, two kids went for a swim to cool off in the creek, the police ordered them to get out, and in the highly charged atmosphere of the times, the crowd turned on the police. Of the 3,000 or so on hand, it was said that 300 were "involved" in the disturbance that local police termed a riot. Some 150 police officers were dispatched to the scene, one was cut by a thrown bottle, and five police vehicles were damaged. Arlington House, the events hall in the park, was closed to future Sunday events by the Park Board, and the city council, police department and ad-hoc citizens groups debated the situation for several weeks.

An event the following weekend drew an increased police presence. This time the swimmers were left alone and although the kids and police postured toe-to-toe when police tried to clear the streets around the park, no violence was reported. The bands that played those two weekends were not identified in the several articles in the *Dallas Morning News*. Whether Jimmie's band played the day of the melee or Stevie's played the following weekend is not confirmed.

Jimmie had established his reputation as a guitar player around Dallas, but it was difficult to find places to play blues. California was known to have a great music scene, so the band took off to see first hand if all the stories they had heard were true.

PAUL RAY: "[Storm] went to California; we were supposed to make a demo. We played at the Experience and the Whisky A-Go-Go on Sunset, and it was horrible – it was just a nightmare because Jimmie and Phil showed up all fucked up on speed. They were going so fast that they were playing in slow motion, just like a movie camera would go in slow motion. We were opening for Junior Walker and the All Stars at the Whisky A-Go-Go. I counted off the first number and they started playing half that speed.

"After the first set the guy said, 'Come tomorrow and I'll pay you, but you're fired – you're not going to play tomorrow, you're not even going to play your next set.' So we busted up on Sunset Boulevard – I went to San Francisco and they went to Oakland."

📖**May:** *Sundial* (Sunset High School yearbook) Stevie appears in a photo from sometime during the school year. The keyboard player is Steve Lowrey, and the bass player (behind Stevie) may be Mike Hargrove. Jimmie Vaughan's Les Paul appears to be in the background, which Stevie almost certainly did not have permission to borrow!

STEVE LOWREY: "Sunset High School had a thing called Musicians Club, and I got invited to go over one night and played with Steve Vaughan. In the picture, I'm playing the keyboard, and that would have been taken around the time of Liberation, but this was just a group of miscellaneous musicians. It was just an excuse to have a dance and have some kids come in and play. It wasn't very organized, and I don't think it was well received by school officials [laughs]."

Guitarist ROCKY ATHAS remembers: "We used to go to jam sessions together, and one time when Sunset High School was having one, Stevie called me, saying 'We should go.' [But] we went to Kimball High, and they wouldn't let us in at Sunset High. He goes, 'Well, we'll just sneak in,' and that's exactly what we did! When we went in, they said, 'This is only for the Sunset guys. You can watch, but you can't play.' All of a sudden, one of the amplifiers blew. Stevie had his Silvertone in my car, and we rolled it in. He said, 'You can use my amp, but let me play.'

JAM SESSION MEMORIES

1969-1970 Members

TOM HIETT	JAMES LOVELL
STEVE WHITE	ANGI WALTERS
DON McMINN	CHARLES WIRZ
MIKE HARGROVE	JAMES WILLIAMS
DAVID BROWN	ROY ORBISON
ROBERT WARE	ERIC CLAPTON
TAMMY TODD	WARD McCAIN
VICKI GARDNER	DANNY KNOX
CINDY MITCHELL	TERRY KNOX
DOUG PITT	KIETH MOON
DONNIE SPURRIER	KIETH RICHARDS
RICKY CHILDS	RICHARD TIDWELL
JEFF BECK	LOUIS JONES
RANDY KOUNAS	KENT MOFFIET
SKIP RUBY	ROBERT PLANT
JIMMY PAGE	DANNY BURRIS
JOHN CURIEL	JOE CASTILLO
DAVID FONTENOT	ROCKY STONE
ROBERT BOX	JOHNNY CRENSHAW
CHRIS LAWERENCE	MIKE MALONE
BRUCE MATLOCK	FRANK ZAPPA
RICKY McCURLEY	RICK FARINA
DALE TROOT	MICK TAYLOR
TEX RITTER	ERIC BURDON
JOHN MAYALL	JOHNNY WINTERS

Sunset High School yearbook. Note the fictitious members!
© SUNSET HIGH SCHOOL, DALLAS TX

When a photo of the jam appeared in Sunset's yearbook, there was Stevie! That was so funny because all the guys who put it on didn't get a picture in their own annual."[25]

May: Jimmie Vaughan and Doyle Bramhall follow Denny Freeman's lead and move to Austin. Singer Paul Ray would follow in August.

By the summer of 1970, the migration of musicians from Dallas to Austin was in full swing, and DENNY FREEMAN was on the leading edge. He recalls, "It wasn't because it was a music town. They had music before we got there, but we all moved there because if you had long hair, Austin was the type place that was long-hair friendly. It was a freak-friendly place. Because of the university, there were a lot of freaks there – enough that there was a 'presence' for a small town. It wasn't a real rough, industrial or conservative town.

"This was only a few years after the whole '60's explosion happened. *Sgt Pepper* had just come out in '67, Hendrix and Cream in '67-'68. Woodstock. Something had changed, and all that stuff was still new.

In '65-'66, very few people had long hair. If you grew your hair long, you were making a somewhat risky statement, and it was a real polarizing thing. There was hostility and suspicion, but there was also a camaraderie, because if you had long hair you had something in common with each other. Now long hair doesn't mean anything.

"So there was music in Austin before us, and some cool places to play, but Austin was a nice town with cheap rent and beautiful hippie girls, and it attracted musicians, and they're still moving there. Now they're moving there because it's a music town, but we moved there because it was a cool town."

PAUL RAY: "Jamie Bassett and Denny Freeman moved [to Austin] first, and it wasn't much later Jimmie and Doyle, who were trash men in Irving at the time, gave it up and moved down, then me and Diana came in August. Phil didn't move; I wish he had – it would have saved his life.

"The Armadillo [World Headquarters, a classic Austin venue] was just opening up. .... Storm played the first night of the Armadillo ... no, it wasn't, it was the weekend, they opened for Freddie King. That was before I was in the band [for the second time] – Jamie Bassett was still playing with them. [Then] Jamie found Jesus and went back to Dallas. They got Danny Galindo from the 13th Floor Elevators to play bass, but he wouldn't play pass-the-hat jobs. He wanted a ten-dollar guarantee, which back then was like a thousand-dollar guarantee now.

"They were playing in East Austin – the I.L. Club [owned by Ira Littlefield]. They were going to play The One Knite, which is now Stubb's. Jimmie called and said, 'Hey, we're going to play some Jimmy Reed and John Lee Hooker stuff at this place called The One Knite; come on down 'cause Galindo won't play – it's pass-the-hat. Lewis [Cowdrey] has his bass, and I know you can play bass.' I ended up being the bass player for three years and drummer for part of that time. It was fun. It was Lewis, Doyle, me and Jimmie. I quit The Storm in '73."

On the difficulty of making it in music in Dallas, Paul says, "You didn't get your name in the paper unless you killed somebody back then. They didn't have ads for anything except strip joints – [Jack] Ruby's Carousel, Athens Strip, where Lulu Roman used to strip – 350 pounds if she's an ounce, *bending* the pole [*laughs*]! It was wonderful; we were throwing money at her!"

DOYLE: "There wasn't much of a music scene [in Austin]. People were just starting to move in from Houston, Lubbock, Dallas, all over Texas. There was just a few clubs you could play [blues] – the I.L. Club on the east side, and Vulcan Gas Company was on the west side of the freeway. [But] Austin was a place you could come play your music and dress the way you wanted to. It was pretty much a little San Francisco. In Dallas or Houston, if you didn't play rock and roll and you didn't look a certain way, you didn't play. The cops in Dallas and Houston didn't care too much for you."[3]

JIMMIE VAUGHAN: "There was no blues *scene* unless you went and saw T.D. Bell or W.C. Clark. You could go to the I.L. Club or Ernie's Chicken Shack and see somebody play the blues, but there was no blues *scene*."[3]

May 2: Conquistador Room, Marriott Hotel, Dallas, TX (Liberation); fraternity party
- And When I Die
- Uncle Jack
- To Love Somebody
- Star Spangled Banner
- Spoonful
- Crossroads
- I Should Have Quit You
- Texas
- Vehicle
- I've Been Abused
- 25 Or 6 To 4
- Fever
- Only the Beginning
- I'm a Man
- blues
- Jeff's Boogie
- Soul Man
- Out of Sight
- Whole Lotta Love
- Rock Me
- Poem 58
- Sweet Lorraine
- Thunderbird
- You Shook Me
- Sunshine of Your Love
- Hideaway
- Light My Fire
- Cold Sweat
- Communication Breakdown
- Hoochie Coochie Man

SCOTT PHARES: "That was the night Steve went around to all the tables after the gig was over and started drinking all the drinks left on the tables – a cheap and easy buzz for a kid who was too young to buy liquor."

May 19: (venue unknown) Dallas, TX (Liberation); appears to be a rehearsal session
- Evil Woman
- Fever
- Vehicle
- Mississippi Queen (practice)
- You Shook Me (slide practice)

◉ **June 6:** (venue unknown) Dallas, TX (Liberation)
- I'm A Man
- Vehicle
- Poem 58
- Spoonful
- South California Purples
- I Should Have Quit You
- Texas
- Evil Woman
- Fever
- Cold Sweat
- Hoochie Coochie Man
- Hideaway
- Thunderbird
- Soul Man
- Mississippi Queen

◉ **June 10:** (venue unknown) Dallas, TX (Liberation)
- Rock Me
- Red House (recording incomplete)
  tracks below are from May 2 and June 6:
- Uncle Jack
- Star Spangled Banner
- Spoonful
- I Should Have Quit You (with impersonation of President Richard Nixon as an intro)
- I've Been Abused
- 25 Or 6 To 4
- Fever
- I'm A Man
- Jeff's Boogie
- Whole Lotta Love
- Poem 58
- To Love Somebody

The above gig information comes from recordings made by John Hutchinson. He was a high school student who had a hobby of recording music with a portable reel-to-reel deck. The audio quality was not superior, which is understandable given that it was not patched into a soundboard.

SCOTT: "We were strictly a cover band. We did a lot of Chicago, Blood, Sweat & Tears; we did some Crosby, Stills and Nash, 'Almost Cut My Hair'; we did a song off the Jeff Beck *Truth* album called 'Let Me Love You,' and Stevie wailed on that one; and 'Rock Me Baby.' We did some Led Zeppelin; Steve played 'Whole Lotta Love' for an S.M.U. frat party. He would eat everything up – any song he had a solo on, he would kick ass [*laughs*]. We played a dance in the Kimball [High School] gym one time, right after we got together and rehearsed ourselves well enough that we could handle a dance where we had two sets

worth of music. I remember when Steve would cut loose on a solo, everybody would stop dancing and watch him play guitar.

"We played downtown at a club called Arthur's, next to the Adolphus Hotel. That was the night ZZ Top walked in off the street and played for free and took two of our sets. Steve and Billy Gibbons played about two or three songs together. I think one of them was 'Wine, Wine, Wine.' [Jim Trimmier says it was at The Cellar, and Stevie sang 'Thunderbird.'] They played some blues songs, and he and Billy got up and traded riffs, and they tore the house down [*laughs*]. It was awesome. It was one of those magical evenings. Stevie fit in like a glove on a hand. When they walked in off the street that night, we were just finishing our first set or were between songs. I think it was Billy that came up and talked to our singer and said something to the effect, 'We're fixing to release our first album; we want some exposure in the Dallas area; we don't want any money, we just want to take two of your sets tonight.'

"I remember one of [our] guys saying, 'Are you guys any good?' And he said, 'Well, if you don't like us, you can ask us to leave and we'll leave.' Of course, they got up and played and it was like, 'Holy ...!' And that was the summer of '70, either right before or right after graduation."

SCOTT continues, "Steve had a real long guitar cord, and whenever he took off into a solo he'd jump off the stage and go walk around. All the dancers would watch him play his ass off [*laughs*]. He was quite a showman. But he loved to get high, he loved amphetamines, and he loved malt liquor. He liked to do speed and he liked to get drunk. And he liked to play. He didn't have a car, so I'd bring him home from school in the afternoons over on Glenfield, and we'd go back into his bedroom, where he had an old hi-fi stereo. He'd put on an Albert King or B.B. King record and sit there and play along with a blues song. He always had some new lick he'd learned and wanted to show me. He taught me a lot on guitar. He taught me one song, 'Fever,' but it was a jazz version.

"Steve, of course, was a very gaudy dresser. I always told him he was born the wrong color. He liked the hats with the big plumes. He came to Arthur's one night, and I just cracked up. Back then, everybody was dressing up like hippies – long hair, bell-bottoms – and Steve showed up one night in a sequined jacket that had these big ostrich feathers pluming up out of the collar. It was a knee-length jacket with these ostrich feathers that fanned out all the way around his head in the back. He had on a ragged cowboy hat and these yellow sunglasses that were about two-feet wide [*laughs*]! He could really dude it up! He had on his bell-bottom jeans and some sort of boots.

"He was a good kid; he was fun to be around and was very inspirational. He had the strongest hands of anyone I've ever known in my life. He was a skinny little kid. I remember wrestling with him out in the front yard over at Mike Day's house one day. I probably outweighed him by twice his weight, but he was very strong. I couldn't believe how strong his hands were."

Scott's time in Liberation was short. "In the summer of '70 they got another bass player, named Robert Penhall, who had been with the band Rose Colored Glass. They had a single out called 'I Can't Find the Time to Tell You,' and they were on American Bandstand once and were a one-hit wonder. Shortly after that, Liberation fell apart. There were ten guys and so many personality conflicts. Three guys would want to do something, and two guys wouldn't, or the horn players wouldn't. It didn't last long at all."

JIM TRIMMIER: "Over the summer we got a guy named Bob Penhall, a guy that I hung out with in high school. He was a real good bass player – played upright and also electric, read music – good musician. I remember Scott Phares' mom calling me and denouncing me for firing him. I can't remember the reason why; I think Bob was just the better bass player."

DON TANNER: "Bob Penhall was a student at North Texas, and when we had the audition at the Loser's Club, [the prospect of going on the road] scared him to death, and he went back to finish his education. He brought us bass player after bass player to try out, and even brought a bass player from the Dallas Symphony. He showed up in a tux, and I said, 'No, no. This isn't going to work.'"

JIM: "I believe Steve was a sophomore and I was a senior, and we would meet after school and ride in my '65 Dodge Dart for hours and hours, just doing what teenage guys do. He had a Telecaster [actually, Broadcaster] that had 'Jimbo' carved into the back of it, with two volume controls and no tone control – no case. I think it was a guitar Jimmie had given him to get him off his back.

"He would sit in the passenger seat and play and play and play, all the time. And it wasn't like he was practicing, he was just serious playing all the time. He played with a good tone back then, didn't make mistakes, played the blues wonderfully. I remember a John Lee Hooker album with a song called 'Boogie Woogie All Night Long,' and it had kind of a false ending – Hooker didn't hit the lick quite right, and Stevie loved that lick and would play that lick over and over and over again. He would play it on the record, play the lick, and go back and back and back.

"We played through the summer. We had a gig at The Fog club for two weeks. I think it was fifty dollars a man per *week*. The club had been closed for some kind of liquor violation, and we had the club for two weeks, rehearsing in the club. I believe that's the gig that Tommy Shannon came in and heard Stevie play.

"Later on we played Arthur's in the Adolphus Hotel. Our band was real loud with all the horns and two lead singers, and that was the night ZZ Top came in. I had never heard of them, but Stevie was real excited about them. Their first album might have been released, but they were an unknown band. I believe Billy Gibbons and Dusty Hill didn't have beards at the time.

"My recollection of ZZ Top that night was that it was the first time I heard a band play a room – neither too loud nor too soft. They brought in their equipment but balanced themselves to the room, and it was proper and right and not overbearing.

I'm pretty sure Stevie sat in with them that night, but I don't remember for sure."

Billy Etheridge, former member of The Chessmen with Jimmie and later a member of The Nightcrawlers with Stevie, was the original bass player for ZZ Top. He had already left the band, and Dusty Hill took over on bass. Billy says he quit because "playing bass in ZZ Top was boring." He was "a keyboard player primarily, and a guitar player secondarily" and wanted something more personally challenging. Plus, "I'm a jazzer and a blueser, and it was this straight ahead, blow the hair off your head … . We'd played a gig with B.B. King and we had 19 Sunn amps, and B.B. had one little Vibroverb or something with a mic on it. So I moved back to Austin."

Liberation was at least a nine-piece band, the largest of Stevie's career. Jim and Mike recall that there were some smaller versions of the band that played when the whole group wasn't available.

DON TANNER: "A friend of mine was a trombone player [Larry Chapman], and I played trumpet. [Don just sang in the bands with Stevie.] I really didn't want to go back to college. He called me one day and said, 'Man, I'm in a horn band. We're doing a lot of Chicago, Blood, Sweat & Tears. We need a singer bad. There's this kid that plays guitar. Man, you won't believe it.' I told him I would audition, so he brought me over a Chicago album to learn '25 or 6 to 4.' I saw them play before I auditioned at some dirt race track. Stevie had worked up a rendition of 'Spoonful.'

"I auditioned at Mike Day's house and knocked their socks off. I took Mike Reames' place in Liberation. We played The Fog and a little gig at Arthur's at the Adolphus Hotel. Cutter was hauling Steve around and helping us hustling equipment. The Fog was the worst gig I ever played in my life. You played all night – 45-minute set, 15-minute break, 45-minute set, 15-minute break … then, at the end of your *four* 45-minute sets, you had an hour break or hour and a half. We'd go next door and have something to eat, rest, then go back and start the whole thing over again 'til five o'clock in the morning. After midnight, the place would empty out, except for some drunks. It was a hard gig to play. Rough on the voice trying to do that all night long.

"Liberation was doing Chicago, Blood, Sweat & Tears, early Spirit, some John Mayall, Buddy Miles and Electric Flag. A lot of horn music, and then we'd give those guys a break for the lip and we'd do Spencer Davis, Clapton's 'Crossroads,' maybe some Steve Miller, and probably some Three Dog Night, I hate to say.

"We auditioned one time at the Losers Club on Mockingbird. We didn't have a clue, but we were actually auditioning for Cornell Gunther and the Coasters. Cornell and them were sitting at the bar, but we didn't know who they were until after the audition. They wanted to put us on tour with them to Florida, but we couldn't do it because Big Jim wasn't going to let Stevie go because of his age.

"Stevie was a little upset, but Big Jim ruled with a stern hand, and he knew he was under age. Stevie just said, 'I'll wait until he can't do anything about it, and then I'll do what I want to do.' And he did [*laughs*]. Neither of us was too upset. I wasn't too thrilled about everybody dressing in the same show clothes – the show band stuff. That wasn't me." Can you imagine Stevie in a lounge show band suit?

LARRY CHAPMAN: "We started the band ... probably early 1970. The first night we ever practiced, I think at Mike Reames' house, the first song we learned was 'Get Ready,' Ides of March. Kimball High School wanted to hire us to do a junior-senior prom, and we didn't know but ten songs, so we just replayed 'em a couple of times. The principal didn't want us to play there because he didn't like Scott and he didn't like Vaughan because they had long hair. He didn't like 'em worth a durn.

"When we auditioned for the people that were going to hire us, he come runnin' down that aisle: 'You're not going to play here! You're not going to play at this school! Leftwich, I was on you all last year to cut your hair!' Leftwich was in *college* now. [*Author laughs*] He didn't like Stevie Ray either and now ... I was at Kimball [in recent years] on business, and you walk into Kimball High School and there's Vaughan's picture up there! Walk in the front door and there's a big picture of him.

"That was our first job – Kimball. We played at the Shamrock Roller Rink couple of times, played at the one in Pleasant Grove – we were too loud out there and the guy turned the electricity off on us. We played the Rocket in Chalk Hill; we played one time in Devil's Bowl up on a big stage. They had some kind of a Woodstock-type deal with bands all day. We reopened The Fog – it had been shut down. They were auditioning three bands, and the band right in front of us tried to play 'Vehicle' with no horns. We decided right then our first song was going to be 'Vehicle.' We got that slot.

"We played two or three clubs right there around Oak Lawn – The Orange Crate, Purple Orchid or something like that. Last time I played with them was at the Shamrock, end of July or early August 1970." Asked what they could earn on a typical one-night gig, Larry replied, "Probably $200 – split ten ways. For a week at a club we might get $900. So $90 each for a week.

"Jim Trimmier was great at writing out the parts for all of us. I thought Stevie was just about as good a guitar player at sixteen as when he died. He was fantastic. We were playing '25 Or 6 To 4,' and Stevie Ray got in the middle of the dance floor and did that lead break for about twenty minutes. Wes Johnson was up on stage doing the [wah] pedal for him, and he got tired, so I walked over there and did the pedal for a while. It was a nice little break for the horns. Somebody finally had to go out and tell him to come back [on stage]. It was great. He could just hear a song and he could start playing it.

"One time, ZZ Top came into Arthur's and said, 'We heard y'all have a good guitar player, and we'd like to hear him play.' We were going on break, and they said, 'Do y'all mind if he jams

with us for a little while?' He wanted to do it and we wanted the break so, 'Sure, go ahead!' We took about a twenty-minute break while he played with ZZ Top.

"That old blond guitar that he had ... Stevie told us that Jimmie tore it up, and he got it out of a cardboard box in pieces and put it back together himself. He glued it all back together.

"We were at Scott Leftwich's house trying to learn '25 Or 6 To 4,' and Christian couldn't sing it. I got Don Tanner and said, 'Don, learn this song. We're going to go up there tomorrow, and you're going to sing this song and try out for the band.' He was a pretty good singer, and so now we had two singers. Plus Don could double on trumpet, which came in handy on a few songs."

---

date unknown: Shamrock Roller Rink, Lancaster, TX (Liberation)

Liberation. (l-r) Leftwich, Vaughan, Phares, Chapman
COURTESY CONNIE FOERSTER

Larry Chapman provided the photos of Liberation, taken by his cousin, Connie Lusk Foerster, at Shamrock. Having a nine- or ten-piece band, you'd think there would be more photos of the band, but these are the only ones the author could find.

WES JOHNSON (sax): "Early in Liberation's life, The Coasters were in town looking for a drummer, sax player and a guitar

Liberation. (l-r) Leftwich, Trimmier, Chapman, Vaughan, Phares, Reames, Lowrey. COURTESY CONNIE FOERSTER

Liberation. (l-r) Vaughan, Reames, Lowrey. COURTESY CONNIE FOERSTER

player to back them in Florida during the upcoming summer. We auditioned at the Losers Club in North Dallas during the early morning hours (4 a.m.). The Coasters were there and asked Stevie and me to join their group. Stevie had to decline because of his age, and I didn't want to leave my day job in Dallas."

STEVE LOWREY, keyboards for Liberation: "I met Steve for the first time at the home of Scott Phares about 1969 through Cutter. A band was being formed and Scott was the guitar player. I had been invited to play keyboards. I was introduced to Steve, who was actually brought in to play bass for the band. I don't believe he actually owned an electric guitar at the time. Practice droned on for a couple of hours and a break was finally taken. It was during this break that Steve picked up what I believe was Scott's Telecaster and proceeded to blow everybody's minds. The decision was then made unanimously that Steve would play guitar. He was almost as good at the tender age of 15 as he was when he left us.

"We were playing covers of Chicago, Blood, Sweat & Tears, Steve Miller, just about anything we could. Pretty much horn-oriented stuff. But he would come over to my house and we would play blues for two or three hours – my folks would actually sit and watch this. Who knew [*laughs*]?

"The band got a few gigs around the Dallas area, which was amazing in that the band as a whole wasn't much to get excited over. We weren't a full-time, hard-working band. We probably did it every other weekend, or if we got lucky, something that would carry us through the week. Seems like we did a lot more rehearsing than gigging, because we were so young. We never played The Cellar. One noteworthy gig, however, was one we did at The Fog club on [3508] Oak Lawn.

"It was at this gig that, to my knowledge, was the first time Steve ever sang in public. It was pretty wild. The singer called 'Crossroads' as next song to play. Before it was counted off, Steve leaned over to the singer and told him he'd like to try to sing the song. He took a microphone and put it out on the dance floor. It was one of those underlit dance floors – kind of pre-disco.

"We started the song and Steve started to sing. He had a soft quality to his voice that would later become part of his

distinctive sound. He held his own and brought down the house with a ferocious playing style that was probably equalled only by someone like Eric Clapton, Jimmy Page or Jimi Hendrix at the time. It was an amazing scene.

"A few weeks later we got a gig at a downtown Dallas club called Arthur's. It was a strange gig because we worked our asses off for a week for next to no money, but we were all underage and playing in a very adult scene. Very cool. One night, out of the blue, in walked Billy Gibbons, Dusty Hill, Frank Beard, manager Bill Ham, members of a new band called ZZ Top. We struck up a conversation with them, and they asked to sit in during one of our breaks. Steve sat in with them as well as myself. My friends, that was a moment! Needless to say, young Steve rose to the occasion and was quite a match for the older, more seasoned Gibbons.

"What happened with the singer, Mike Reames, is that he had trouble with his throat that week at Arthur's, and Christian Plicque came in because he knew Steve. I think at a point we used Christian more, but he didn't do many gigs. Steve was in the band maybe six to eight months, and once he was gone, the band kind of fell apart.

"Steve was fun, but just a kid. He knew he had this ability, but he didn't let it go to his head or wear it on his sleeve. We just laughed and cut up like fourteen-, fifteen-year-old kids would do.

"I remember we went over one time [to the Vaughans' house] and Jimmie wasn't around. He got out the amp and guitar and said, 'Let me show you what I figured out!' And he started doing this crazy figure eight strum that he had come up with. He said, 'I figured this out last night!' And he'd sit and play 'Little Wing' or something.

"Those are the memories I have most – sitting in my parents' living room. What he taught me was that it's okay to unlock what's inside of you and let it come out into the music. I'd never been around anyone that did that. It made a difference in the way I approached what I was doing, and it makes a difference to this day. That's the memory that I've got, right there.

"I took lessons and studied theory for five or six years and threw all of that away and started playing rock and roll – and didn't get it until I met him."

LARRY CHAPMAN: "Lowrey needed a Leslie amplifier for his organ, and we found him one, or he found one and we let him have some of our pay to buy it. I thought it was the greatest thing in the world. That thing would start spinning, and boy, it sounded great! He was a good organ player."

Original singer for Liberation, MIKE REAMES: "We started kicking around the idea of having a band that would do a lot of Chicago Transit Authority, Blood, Sweat & Tears, Al Bloomfield, that sort of thing. We had a multitude of players in Oak Cliff, and certain ones were just better than others, and they were the most sought after. When Scott brought Steve to us, we were wondering, 'Well, why hasn't someone else picked this guy up a long time ago?'

FROM THUNDERBIRD TO BLACKBIRD 1970

"But you have to realize we were eighteen and in college, and he's *sixteen* years old.' [When you're eighteen,] you almost weren't going to associate with someone that was sixteen years old, you know. Of course we realized that he was a big talent, although his main interest was always the blues. If we asked if he wanted to contribute a song, he'd say, 'Yeah, let's do an Elmore James tune,' or this or that.

"We were about a ten-piece wall of sound. We did 'Vehicle,' by The Ides of March, because that had just come out. In the after-hours places that stayed open until four or five in the morning, about 4:30 we'd be coming out with 35-year-old blues things that people had never heard – 'Yeah, let's play that one. What the heck.'

"It was kind of funny because none of us had ever worked with horn players before, and we thought horn players were always ready to go. Scott informed me that every three or four songs you need to give the horn players a chance to rest! That's where we'd slide in Zeppelin and different things, like 'I'm a Man.'

"[*Laughs*] We were on the Arthur's stage doing the usual beginning of 'I'm a Man' by Chicago with a lot of percussion instruments. Normally Steve would just go right into the feedback and off we go. Well, all of a sudden he turns around and keeps trying to turn the volume pot up and nothing's happening. One of the guys launched into the rain chant from Woodstock while Stevie was trying to get his amp to work. That went on for two or three minutes, but it seemed like two or three hours! The amp started working and we went on with the song. So instead of taking its customary seven or eight minutes, it took fifteen.

"The owner came up to us later and said, 'Man, that was great! Y'all need to do that every night!' There was no way it was going to happen like that every night. We tried it a couple of times deliberately after that, but it was never pulled off quite like it was the night it was accidental."

With four horns, the band definitely had a big sound. Mike continues: "At some point everybody said, 'With this act, you ought to go to Vegas, go do the lounges and so on. The only problem was that Steve was so much younger than everyone else that we were going to have all kinds of problems getting him into any casinos to play, especially if there was any liquor being served. We had to promise absolutely that he wouldn't drink, but he was such a good guitar player that everybody wanted to buy him a drink [*laughs*]. We had to take care of this, and Steve was just having a good time."

The band's engagements were not just one night here and there, as Mike explains. "Whenever we played places like Arthur's, The Fog, Soul City, Gertie's, normally it was two or three days in a row. It would pay you to have set your equipment up as opposed to one-night stands. Especially community centers where you set up the equipment, tear it all down, and in between perform – and then wonder when you got home why you're so tired."

Liberation wasn't the last of Stevie's forays into bands with horns. Paul Ray and the Cobras featured sax players, as did the original Double Trouble. Despite the focus on sounds similar to Chicago Transit Authority and Blood, Sweat & Tears, Stevie was able to fit into the mix and put the blues on the back burner. As Mike Reames said, "Talent fits in anywhere," and Stevie had it in spades. "Even if you have to fake it, talent will see you through."

---

date unknown: Devil's Bowl Pop Festival, Devil's Bowl Speedway, Dallas, TX (Liberation)

Vocalist MIKE REAMES: "[The Devil's Bowl Pop Festival] was shortly after our engagement at Arthur's downtown. I just remember thinking, 'This is the hottest I've ever been in my entire life.' It was 113 degrees when we hit the stage! And the other thing I remember about that gig – it was the first time I'd ever been at a place where there were so many people all watching one thing. You get up on stage and look out there at this sea of faces, and you think they're all looking right at you. You know how it's weird when people stand and look over your shoulder? It's like having 20,000 people looking over your shoulder at the same time [*laughs*]."

Stevie said his first club gig was at Arthur's in Dallas, next to the Adolphus Hotel.[24] He said this in the context of Liberation, but it seems he would have played in clubs with Texas Storm before that. Perhaps he meant as a guitarist, and did not consider playing bass with Texas Storm as "his" gig. There is no conclusive evidence that Brooklyn Underground or The Southern Distributor played clubs. (Candy's Flare was only an armory rented out for teen dances.)

STEVIE: "My first club gig was at a place called Arthur's on Commerce Street, downtown [Dallas]. We worked several nights there, and then after hours at a place called The Fog. We had an 11-piece band, worked eight days in a row and made $650 for the week. Then we started playing the Funky Monkey. Played that gig from 10:00 to 6:00 with 10-minute breaks, one 20-minute break to eat on."[24]

Late summer: Stevie and Christian form the band Lincoln, named after the American luxury car. The band consists of Stevie, Christian, Don Tanner (vocals), and Brad Smith (drums); the bass and keyboard players' names are not known.

CHRISTIAN: "[Lincoln cars represented] class, and we wanted or thought of ourselves as a class act. Pretentious, eh? Lincoln as I recall didn't play together very long. I seem to remember we argued more than we played. We were all from such different backgrounds, and that really made it hard. Don [Tanner, the other singer] and I got along great though. We did a lot of duo stuff, Sam and Dave, The Righteous Brothers and so on. The keyboard player didn't like rehearsing. Stevie and I were just the opposite and were rehearse freaks."

Lincoln. (top right) Christian-Charles dePlique; (bottom middle) Stevie Vaughan; (bottom right) Don Tanner; others unidentified. COURTESY CHRISTIAN-CHARLES DEPLIQUE

DON TANNER: "I remember sitting out in the front yard drinking wine. Stevie got sick. I told him, 'Don't you drink that Spinyata.' He drank a half gallon and got sick, and that's the last time he ever touched it. He was deathly ill.

"I don't remember why Liberation ended. It just kind of faded away as people left to do other things. And then Stevie and Christian and I found a drummer named Gabriel Saucedo. I know Gabriel played with us a few times, but [seeing the photo] I guess Brad Smith is the guy standing next to the bass player. We found a bass player, but it was one of these deals where, 'Yeah, I'll play bass with you guys, but you have to let my friend play keyboards.' Both these guys were music majors at North Texas [a Denton university with a strong music program]. We did a lot of Lee Michaels, and the keyboard guy ate that up and could sing just like Lee Michaels.

"Lincoln did Joe Walsh, James Gang, Eric Clapton, Lee Michaels – it was more rock and roll than Liberation. At least my side was; I don't remember much of what Christian sang. Christian would get up and do his deal, and then I'd get up and sing, because we clashed a little bit, voice-wise. He had this stage presence that he didn't really have to do anything and people paid attention.

"We all got together and got a repertoire up and started playing The Lamplighter. Christian was in with these rich kids in the Preston Road area, and that's where the Lamplighter was. At that particular time, I was Stevie's taxi! I think Cutter broke loose and went to work for Ian Hunter. I'd go pick Stevie up for practice, take him home. There'd be times we weren't playing, and I'd pick him up and head for Lemmon Avenue. It was so ironic that everyone knew who he was. We'd just walk into a club – 'Well hi, Stevie. How're you doin'?' We'd hit all these clubs, and it wouldn't be thirty minutes and we'd be sitting in with a band.

"Stevie was more mature than a fifteen-year-old. He had good sense about him for a fifteen-year-old back then. I was six years older. He never bitched in the band. If we wanted to do it this way or that way, he'd speak his peace, but if more than one of us wanted to do it the other way, he went along with it. It didn't bother him any.

"Of course, I kept him in strings. I asked him what he wanted. He says, 'Black Diamond.' Well, Black Diamond strings are steel strings, not round-wound and not flat-wound. His fingers were so strong he could pull 'em like they were Super Slinkys. They weren't but like three dollars a set and lasted about a week. And I've seen him break 'em! You ask any guitar player who knows anything about Black Diamond, and they'll tell you they're steel strings, will rust in about a week and they're very, very difficult to [bend]. It just blew my mind. He liked the sound.

"I remember he asked me one night, 'Man, can you teach me how to sing?' I said, 'Steve, I wish I could, but what I have is God-gifted, just like your guitar playing. I know you can carry a tune; all you need to do is work on your vibrato and put the two together, and eventually it'll work out.' And it did."

September: Tempo 2 Studios, Dallas, TX. Stevie's first recording session.

The early fall of 1970 was an historic time for Stevie because he entered a recording studio for the first time. John Bothwell began what was planned as an ongoing project to give Dallas teenage bands an opportunity to record and have albums to sell for their own fund raising. The studio, at 7275 Envoy Court in the Trinity Industrial District, northwest of downtown Dallas, was called Tempo 2, operated by Bill Jones and Don Zimmers. The first project was to select several bands consisting of kids in South Dallas high schools and let them each record two songs for the album, titled *A New Hi*. Bothwell organized financial support from Howard Carr and Frank Bozeman and enlisted recording engineer Bill Jones and assistant engineer Mike Sibley.

Recollections of whether a competition or audition was held differ, and five bands were selected to record, including a band called Cast of Thousands. The group was Bobby Forman, Jim Rigby, Steve Vaughan, Stephen Tobolowsky, Mike McCullough, and Chris Lingwall.

The group had started around 1968 with Rigby and Forman writing songs and Tobolowsky singing. When they started to entertain, they would do musical satire, sketches and skits. RIGBY: "The problem was, we weren't very good." Fortunately for Tobolowsky, he got better – better enough to become a successful actor in Hollywood. Look him up on the internet and you are almost sure to exclaim, "Oh, *that* guy!"

Tempo 2 Studios, Dallas, TX. © CRAIG HOPKINS

Forman stayed in the music business and performs with his daughters in a group called Shanti Shanti.

Stevie hadn't been a member of the band before, but they were smart to enlist him for the new Cast of Thousands. JIM RIGBY: "[Bobby] and I were writing songs at the time and then Tobolowsky started singing with us. I had left for college when Bobby heard about an opportunity to cut a record like Bloodrock had done in Ft. Worth. There had been a battle of the bands; Bloodrock won and got an album.

"So Bobby was going to put together the best band he could find; I mean, this was a ringer band. The one person he had to have was Stevie Vaughan. He was just in a whole different league than us. It was obvious from the very start. It was like we were T-ball and he was Barry Bonds! I mean, we were okay –

Cast of Thousands: Forman, McCullough, Vaughan, Lingwall, Rigby, Tobolowski. COLLECTION OF CRAIG HOPKINS

we could get by. But when we were in the studio, the people in the booth were absolutely mesmerized. They were literally leaning forward to watch his hands when he played."

ROBERT FORMAN: "Someone had approached me and said, 'We need a representative from this school [Kimball High].' As I recall, each high school was supposed to send a representative, and there was nobody coming from our school. I took my two buddies who had graduated [Rigby and Tobolowsky] and found two other guys who could do something [Lingwall and McCullough], and I wanted to use Stevie because he was such a monster guitar player. At the time, I knew him as Steve Vaughan, and at fifteen years old he was a monster. I forget what the gig was, but I saw Stevie play and I went, 'Jesus Christ, this guy is an amazing guitar player, and he's a kid!' He was way, way more advanced than anyone I had worked with. So I tried to amalgamate the whole thing together into something that we represented as a band from Kimball High School."

Forman's recollection is that there really wasn't a competition or audition because there was no other band from Kimball trying to get the slot on the record for that high school.

RIGBY: "Always, from the very beginning, he was just possessed by the music. You watch him play and it was like a wolf fixated by something – like something grasped him. He wouldn't follow the drummer or the bass – everyone had to recalibrate. He was so good."

Rigby and Tobolowsky were already in college, making this a bit less than a true high school band. RIGBY: "Mike and Chris were added just for this one project. Stevie, of course, was in a whole different league than the rest of us. He was influenced by Hendrix at the time and his hand was like a hummingbird flying up and down the guitar neck. I can still picture his fingers blurring together. It was quite an experience to play with him. He was real quiet. He showed up for the rehearsal driving a station wagon, and in the back was every kind of musical gadget that existed at that time – wah-wah pedals and fuzz boxes and all different things just piled in there.

"He was talking about a new style. At that time, he was kind of a Hendrix clone – he was all speed; he didn't have any of the nuance that he later developed. But he was just beginning to work on that style of taking a C chord and sliding it up the neck and turning it into E, and that freed up some of his other fingers to do lead things. None of us had ever seen that before. He was really excited about this new thing he was working on."

The band recorded two songs, "Red, White and Blue" with Jim Rigby singing lead vocal, and "I Heard a Voice Last Night" with Bobby Forman singing lead. RIGBY: "We didn't trust [John Bothwell], so we used two of our songs we didn't like that much, and if we got to cut an album, we would use the [better] songs. 'Red, White and Blue' was a take-off on 'Okie From Muskogee,'

Original master tape for *A New Hi.* COLLECTION OF BILL JONES

which was real popular then. What we wanted to do was have a redneck version of the same thing, and then Stevie would break into this real wild lead thing, and then we'd go back to the song."

FORMAN: "We were being sarcastic. We thought we were playing social commentary, kind of funny in our behavior. I was juxtaposing Stevie's cool guitar playing against our silly songs. It was fun, but it wasn't like it was any big deal for him – he could rip out licks on anything. I told him to first play something really crappy and then go nuts, you know? So he played this real limited, very marginal guitar thing, and then the second half he goes [mimics rapid guitar riff] and did this Stevie Ray Vaughan stuff."

RIGBY, now a minister, recalls, "The other one ['I Heard It Last Night'] had more of a spiritual bent – the sense of being called." Rigby wrote the lyrics and Forman the music on both tunes.

FORMAN: "I remember Steve sat on his amp while he played, which I thought was kind of weird. But it was great because he was really good. I remember he had to do a second take because his first take, he didn't like it. I thought his first take was great, but it was a little out of time. Actually, the [second take] is a little out of time. If you listen to it, he ripped into his guitar, and then he kind of picks up the tempo and pulls back.

"[Stevie] was very intense. He knew he was really good, kind of a predestined guy. He didn't care about school at all, he only cared about that guitar. He was so good he could play anything, any time, any place, in any key. He was very clear about what he was here for." Oddly, Forman didn't realize he was Stevie Ray Vaughan until after Stevie died. "One day it occurred to me that *Steve Vaughan was Stevie Ray Vaughan* [*laughs*]. I hadn't put the whole thing together because I had left it all behind in high school."

Regarding his clear recollection of Stevie, engineer BILL JONES said, "It was really kind of wild. I thought maybe he was a ringer! Stevie Ray was kind of quiet. I mean, he was there and he just got down and played." Asked if Stevie's guitar playing stood out even at age sixteen, Jones exclaimed, "Oh yes. Oh my god, yes!" But he said, 'I always thought that Stevie Ray was playing the wrong lines to the changes in the blues, but he really was … you know how two wrongs can make a right? He would do a suspension of the particular thing going to the next chord. Where me being a fundamentalist in jazz, I would say you shouldn't go there so quick. But he did that consistently, and he did it on that record too. It's kind of a wild thing. He's playing around on a particular chord basis, which was a chord that – I being an old jazz guy – I would say is wrong. But it wasn't wrong because he did it consistently, and that's the way he wanted it to be done. Which was part of his genius more than anything else."

There were probably two takes of each song, as Jones recalled. "They would just rehearse for a little bit, and then we'd say, 'Okay, let's go.'" Unfortunately, the 8-, 16- and 24-track tapes have long since disappeared, but Jones kept the original two-track master.

The exact date of Stevie's first studio recording is unknown. BILL JONES: "The studio was actually a warehouse and had a little bit of treatment but not very much. We had a big fan that would go on in the summer time, so we had to cut it off and do a couple, three takes as quickly as we could. It wasn't the dead of summer. I want to say maybe October. It had to be 1970 [because the tape numbers are 70-101 and 70-102]." JIM DAWSON, who played in one of the bands on *A New Hi*: "The recording took place

at Tempo 2 Studios, whose primary business was commercial jingles. They were located in the Mockingbird Lane/Carpenter Freeway area. My best recollection is that we did the recording at Tempo Studios in late September 1970. It took them about 6-8 weeks to complete and press the records."

In addition to the air conditioning fan that had to be turned off during recording, there was a train track right behind the building that prevented recording any time a train went by. Bothwell was concerned about the expense of any time delays. RIGBY: "I was clowning around, and he was going crazy."

JONES: "[The project] was to go on and on, to have more things happen with that particular venue with other high schools. However, with the death of Marilyn, which was by the hand of John Bothwell [her husband], that just blew the whole thing. He was the promoter, and Howard Carr said, 'I don't want to have anything more to do with that.' The concept was a good one and could have gone on a long time and had a lot more people experience recording. To see how people did that [make recordings], that's what the value of that thing was – to go into a studio, you get to see things and say, 'Oh, is that how they do that?' It was really a wonderful learning experience. I'm sorry it didn't go on."

JIM RIGBY: "We were supposed to be selling [the records], and the radio stations were playing them, and supposedly, whoever won the contest by getting the most airtime, would have meant we would have cut this other album. Stevie was really serious about his own band, and though he was really excited about the chance to record, he didn't have any intention of dropping the rest of his group." [Foreshadowing the Bowie tour debacle in 1983.]

📖 **December 23:** *Dallas Morning News,* "South Dallas Boys Might Become Stars," by Maryln Schwartz, re: *A New Hi*

Though the project was derailed when Bothwell was arrested for murder, he had started the promotion of the record, resulting in this Dallas newspaper article: "What started as an experiment might just make recording stars out of a group of South Dallas boys. John Bothwell, who is with Tempo-2 Sound Studios, said about six weeks ago he and his associates, Howard Carr, Bill Jones and Don Zimmers, decided it might be interesting to go into the city's high schools and see what kind of original music the students might be turning out. .... The album, *A New Hi,* is being sold by various organizations in the boys' schools and by the boys themselves. 'Although this has no connection with the schools,' said Bothwell, 'we're offering the album to any interested organization so that they might use it as a fund raiser. They get 75¢ for every album sold. The boys make $1 off every album they sell.' Bothwell said his studio was amazed at the outcome of the recording. 'The boys have not only great sounds, but very individual ones. We plan to promote it big and hope it catches on with everyone else the way it did with us.'"

Poster, album cover and credits - Stevie's first record. COLLECTION OF CRAIG HOPKINS

One of those individual sounds was created by Jim Rigby. BILL JONES recalls: "He's the one that blew into this strange trombone; it was not a complete trombone! It was like he played through a mouthpiece, and it was almost like playing a kazoo. He was the character of the group; he was really funny. He was so loose and nice, and they had good material." RIGBY: "Stevie's lead was so hot we couldn't think of anything to bridge it back into the song, so I took a trombone, pulled out the slide and did a hideous solo to bring the song back to earth. None of us were in his league. It was just the only way we could think of to try to get it back to where people could listen to the song again."

The exact number of copies produced remains a bit of a mystery. BILL JONES: "There had to be a thousand or thereabouts ... it might have been even less than that ... boxes of twenty-five [albums] and we had five bands – that's 250, plus there were a number of extras; maybe each school got a hundred. So that's it – 500 or a thousand." Musician JIM DAWSON: "As I recall, there were around 1,200 copies of that record pressed. Each band member was given one case of 25 records. We sold them during gigs or gave them to family members." Jim Rigby also recalls that each band member got a box. With twenty-five total band members, and twenty-five records in a box, that would be 625. Given that 1000 was not an unusual pressing quantity, that is the best estimate of the number of Stevie's first record.

The record was released with a poster showing each of the five bands. Jim Rigby recalls that they were lured back to the studio sometime after the recording session under some pretense, and the photo was taken at the studio of the band. "None of us knew they were going to take a picture, and that's why we didn't have our real instruments [the guitar Stevie is holding in the photo was just one that was in the studio], and nobody was dressed right – half of us were nerds with the button-down collars. The other [bands] had spandex and CO2 cloud in the background."

The best estimate from all the interviews is that the recording session was very near Stevie's sixteenth birthday. He may have been fifteen years old, technically, but it would be more accurate to say sixteen. Every previous reference has been that Stevie was seventeen because the album was published in 1971, the year Stevie turned seventeen, but that is clearly inaccurate.

There was no effort to try to keep Cast of Thousands together after the recording session. Rigby and Tobolowsky were in different colleges 200 miles apart, Stevie was already a professional musician, Lingwall and McCullough had only been called in for the session. Cast of Thousands was just a blip on the time line but provided Stevie's first opportunity to record.

Stevie becomes an uncle for the first time with the birth of Jimmie's daughter Tina.

Late 1970: Stevie joins a band called Pecos: Don Tanner, vocals; John Nixon, guitar; Stevie, guitar; Lynn Fisher, bass; and Joe Wilmore, drums.

Once again, the music stopped in the musical chairs of bands. Stevie and Don ended up with seats in a band called Pecos. DON: "That band [Lincoln] with Christian faded out; the two guys from North Texas got tired of not really making any money, and it was a long drive back and forth to Denton. I got with John Nixon and there was a guy there in town that opened up a small studio [Bob Cady]. He wanted John and I to be his publishing company for a quarter of the royalties. They had some country people come in that couldn't read or write, and we had a real hard time publishing their music, because you had to have the melody line, the lyrics, chords, the whole nine yards. You don't have to do that now. I spent many, many hours with a tape recorder and piano, and John with a guitar, trying to figure out what these people were trying to play. A lot of them were out of tune [*laughs*].

"During this time I thought I'd give Stevie a call, so I got a hold of him and asked if he knew of a bass player and a drummer; we could rehearse in the studio. That's when Pecos formed. Lynn Fisher was the bass player and Joe Wilmore played drums – he was crazy. That was short-lived; I think we worked for about three weeks. Stevie was always talking about playing at The Cellar. 'Man, I got us an audition at The Cellar.'

"So we went to The Cellar, and for whatever reason, John said he couldn't play. He sat down on the stage in the corner, and of course Stevie could play everything backwards and forwards. They wanted to hire us, but Big Jim wouldn't let Stevie do it, again because he was so young, and it was an all-night deal.

"After that, Stevie said, 'Well, it's not working out. I think we're going to go talk to some other guys closer to home. I think that is when Christian was talking to him, and David Frame, and I believe he got together with them." That band would become Blackbird.

Stevie practiced with the band but did not appear on the record because he couldn't get to enough of the practices. Guitarist for Pecos, JOHN NIXON: "DelMar was in Lancaster on the square. Bob Cady opened up the studio and was there to sell time – 'For X amount of dollars you get X amount of time, we'll make X number of records, and I'll try to promote you.' He needed some acts to sign, and Don Tanner's dad knew about this new studio and bought us time to make a record.

"I said to Don, 'Okay, we're going to make a record. Who're we going to put it together with?' And he brought Stevie in. We didn't even know [Joe Wilmore and Lynn Fisher]; we had met them through a newspaper ad in the Dallas paper. We wanted to get good musicians, but we were in a small town where there weren't very many musicians at all. We interviewed a lot of people and picked them out.

"Stevie, we called him Little Stevie, was just too young to be able get himself anywhere. Lancaster, even from South Dallas [where Stevie was], when you don't have a car and you're a kid, it's a pretty long haul.

"He was so into Eric Clapton – that's all he would play. It was ironic that when he passed away, he had been on stage with Eric that night. We used to get into some pretty spirited discussions about guitar licks and things. He said, 'I'm going to play like Eric Clapton,' and my favorite at the time was Jimmy Page, so I said I'd play like him. So we thought we had a real good mix of styles. I'll do the fast stuff, he does the slow stuff.

"We had a lot of fun practicing [at DelMar] at night. I ended up writing both songs. We did a number of rehearsals that were recorded, and then we'd stop and take a break and listen to it. [The author located Bob Cady, but no tapes were found.]

"Stevie was a typical, fun-loving kid; he didn't have a care in the world. We would play and have fun with it, but we were serious – we'd play four or five hours and realize we were so hungry we'd have to quit for a while. Then we'd come back and go at it.

"He used to tell me he didn't like studying, didn't like school, and couldn't get into it. 'Man, I just want to play guitar.' He didn't want to ride his brother's coattails, but you could tell he wanted to go that route and was in it for the long haul."

Studio owner BOB CADY remembers Stevie as shy and very quiet. "He didn't care anything about being a front man. We knew he was going to be great, but we couldn't get him to [step up front] at that age.

"I let them take over the studio at night, and they used that for rehearsal. We just had a place to practice, and then we'd go downtown to make the records.

"About 11:30 one night I got a phone call from the police: 'We're going to shut your office down – they're in there smoking marijuana and playing too loud, and you told us they would quit by such-and-such hour.' I said, 'Before you turn anything upside down, let me come down there and we'll stop this.' Sure enough, they were so loud probably half a mile away you could hear them! They were just playing rock and roll; they weren't smoking pot or anything. They weren't doing anything wrong, but after that they lived up to my expectations, rules and regulations."

DON TANNER: "Pecos did Jeff Beck, Free, Eric Clapton (*Disraeli Gears*), I'm thinking we did a Zeppelin tune, and some early Johnny Winter. Basically we were rock and roll. We did a couple of tunes off Jeff Beck's *Truth* album. Of course, playing Jeff Beck was a piece of cake for Stevie. But his style and John's style kind of clashed. There never was any hard feelings between them."

1971

⊙VARIOUS – CAST OF THOUSANDS, *A New Hi*, Tempo 2, LP, poster 24 x 36 has black and white photos of the five bands

📖**January 14:** *Lancaster Journal*, "Del Mar Signs Contracts," article regarding Bob Cady signing the band Pecos to his new studio

Page 2 Journal Thursday, January 14, 1971

...Lancaster acid rock vocalist Don Tanner and lead guitarist John Nixon, to the foreground of the photo are now under recording contract to Del Mar Studios. Other members of their group are Lynn Fisher, bass; Joe Wilmore, drums, and Stevie Vaughn, second lead guitar. The group calls themselves the "Pecos" and use the facilities at Del Mar for rehersal for a show, soon to be given in Dallas.

Del Mar Signs Contracts

From the *Lancaster Journal:* "Del Mar has all of the facilities of an uptown recording studio. Master tapes are cut, dubs are made and the recorded sounds, ranging from country-western to acid rock, are ready to be made into the finished record.

"Two of the first artists to sign a contract at Del Mar are Don Tanner and John Nixon, two well-known Lancaster musicians. Both of these boys broke into the entertainment field with the Kollum. Don, a vocalist, was first trumpet in the Tiger Band, and has played with Liberation and Lincoln groups. John, a lead guitarist, has been associated with Hole in the Wall Gang. Currently, the boys are with the Pecos, an acid rock group. The thing that makes this band unique is the fact they have two lead guitars. Currently the group is using Del Mar facilities to get a show together for a Dallas engagement."

📖**January 21:** *Knight Life* (Kimball High School newspaper), "Study Halls." See Stevie's letter to the editor pictured.

Late January: Blackbird "I" forms. Originally, the bass player was Bill, but no one recalls his last name, and there was a young drummer from Fort Worth whose name is also unknown. The young drummer may have been the son of the owner of the Zodiac club in Fort Worth.

Blackbird "I" definitely existed in early 1971, because there is a photograph of them with the caption "Blackbird" in the Kimball High School yearbook, published in the spring of that year. It is also firmly established that Stevie's next band, Deryk Jones Party (described below), existed with Stevie in the band in mid-August 1971 as evidenced by a published photograph from that time. Christian Plicque does not recall Blackbird "I" at all, despite the caption clearly indicating it was in fact Blackbird.

There were two distinct lineups for Blackbird, the first of which even traveled to Austin to play at the New Orleans Club on a bill with Krackerjack.

Study Halls

Dear Editor:

I have something to say about study hall teachers stepping in and causing trouble where it is uncalled for. There is in this school an organization of people connected with the Student Council called the Sounding Board. Any time that the student wishes to speak to a Sounding Board member the student signs his name on a slip in the Sounding Board room and a Sounding Board representative comes and gets this student out of study hall. If the student has several gripes or problems to be discussed he may sign up as many days in a row as he has problems. The study hall teacher has nothing to do with how many times the student may get. During the first week of December a student in my study hall was denied the right to go to Sounding Board because the teacher felt he needn't go after going the day before.

Thank you for your time,
Steve Vaughan

Stevie's letter to the editor of his high school newspaper. COURTESY MARTHA VAUGHAN

Table top advertising card drawn by Stevie Vaughan. © STEVIE RAY VAUGHAN, COURTESY MARTHA VAUGHAN

Based on all the interviews, the best estimate is that there was a complete break between Blackbird "I" and "II," with Deryk Jones Party between, and Blackbird "II" starting in the fall of 1971.

MIKE KINDRED: "I saw Stevie at The Fog club where Krackerjack went to get together and jam for the very first time. Uncle John Turner and Tommy Shannon had been cut loose from Johnny Winter, and they had driven from New York to Dallas and were at Lee Park when The Mystics — my band with Bruce Bowland and led by guitarist Robert Farris — were playing. They liked Bruce, and I just kind of yakked my way [into the band]. I was pretty nervous, but we jammed and they all dug it and we went out to California.

"When we came back at the end of 1970, Krackerjack took over the Austin scene. We were playing the New Orleans Club, the king of all clubs, at 12th and Red River. It was so refreshing after the tight-ass Dallas clubs. It was quite notorious, and Krackerjack certainly had its contribution to making it that way. I think there were a lot of parents that didn't want their kids hanging out down there. Krackerjack started off giving away one keg of free beer, and when we got up to eight kegs of free beer, we decided we didn't need to do that anymore [*laughs*].

The boys' gym is a more likable place, thanks to Blackbird.
Blackbird "I" (l-r) dePlique; Jimmy Bowman?; Bill (bass); unidentified drummer; Vaughan. © KIMBALL HIGH SCHOOL

"All of our buddies in Dallas were getting a hold of us and wanting to debut on our show, and a number of them did. Stevie's band was one of those. Stevie's band debuted in Austin on the Krackerjack show at the New Orleans Club in probably February or March of '71.

"It was a four-piece band. I'll never forget the drummer was so young he had to come down with his dad. His dad stood stock still, sternly watching the band play. As soon as the band stopped playing, he got his son by the scruff of the neck and drove right back to Dallas. This kid was, like, twelve or something – even younger than Stevie."

Roddy Colonna recalls that Blackbird had an incarnation with this young drummer and that they played the New Orleans Club in early 1971.

Classmate Leslie Crowder knew even then that Stevie was going to be famous some day. "We knew. I told him I was going to save all his school artwork, and when he became famous, I was going to sell it and become rich! He would just laugh. We knew there was something special there. He would play at the Flare a lot – that's where we got our first taste of Stevie."

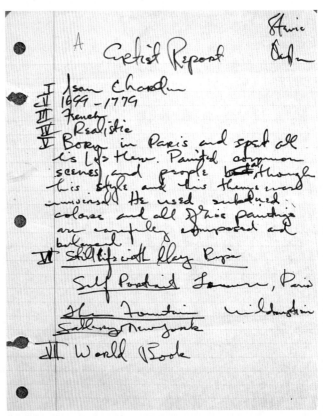

Stevie's school homework. © STEVIE RAY VAUGHAN, COURTESY LESLIE CROWDER

Watercolor by Stevie Vaughan © STEVIE RAY VAUGHAN, COURTESY LESLIE CROWDER

February 13: Spanish Fiesta, Kimball High School, Dallas, TX (Blackbird)

May 14: Zodiac Club, Fort Worth, TX (Blackbird) opening for the British rock/funk band Trapeze; Nitzinger also on the bill. Admission $3 or $5 per couple.

📖**May:** *Excaliber* (Kimball High School yearbook) The only appearance in any of Stevie's high school yearbooks seems to be the photo of his band Blackbird playing a dance in the gymnasium.

Summer: Stevie joins Roddy Colonna in the band Deryk Jones Party.

Deryk Jones Party had some regional success with singles recorded on the Bang label before Stevie joined. The members were Ron Hellner, vocals;

© LEW STOKES, COURTESY MARTHA VAUGHAN

Adam Palma, guitar; Steve Vaughan, guitar; Eric Tagg, bass; Ken Brooks, organ; and Roddy Colonna on drums.

The first reference to Stevie's participation in the band that the author found was in the *Studio Texas Newsbrochure,* which may have been produced by noted Austin artist Jim Franklin. There was no one named Deryk Jones, much like there was no person named Pink Floyd.

📖 *Studio Texas Newsbrochure,* date unknown. "Nowhere in the Texas area has there been a more dynamic professional act than the Deryk Jones Party. This season promises to be no exception as Texas' most popular group puts together a driving, funky sound that is sure to keep the D.J.P. at the top. In addition to the dynamic musical performance, the group gives a dazzling show that will long be remembered."

August 16: Bowie Elementary School, Corsicana, TX (Deryk Jones Party). This was a teen dance sponsored by the Corsicana High School cheerleaders as a fund raiser.

📖 **August 20:** *Corsicana Daily Sun,* photo of Stevie from the August 16 gig.

The only known photo of Stevie in this band was taken by a student journalist and appeared on the "Youth News" page of the local newspaper. Band member Ron Hellner's aunt sent him the clipping, which he saved. Given that Stevie's name doesn't appear in the paper and that the band was relatively obscure, it's a miracle this image survives. The author located the photographer in San Francisco, but he no longer has the photo, negatives, or any recollection of the event or of Stevie being in the picture.

RODDY COLONNA, drummer: "I first met Stevie in the school lunchroom at Kimball High School. He was kind of weird looking to me, a little bit, because he wore these big sunglasses and bell bottoms with this little sash thing, paisley shirt, and he wore a dickey too – ascot-type thing. One day he came up and sat by me in the lunchroom and started talking to me like he knew me. He was talking about his band. I had a car, and that made it good for him because he didn't have any wheels.

"He was just a kid; real friendly. At that school, the whole music and hippie thing wasn't going over too big with most of the students. Scrawny guys like Stevie weren't really picked on, but not really liked particularly. He was sort of a loner.

"I took a lot of music classes and was down in the band room a lot. They had rehearsal rooms and Stevie would come down there sometimes from study hall. He'd get them to sign a note so he could get out of study hall and come down there. I probably heard him play in a practice room. I thought he was pretty good.

"I got Stevie the guitar gig with [Deryk Jones Party], which had been The Cornerstones. Mike Rhyner was the drummer,

'I'm Gonna Take You Higher. . . .'
Local students dance to the music of Dallas' Derek Jones Monday night at Bowie Elementary School. The dance was sponsored by the CHS cheerleaders as a money-raising project. (Photo by Jolly Brown)

© JOLLY BROWN/CORSICANA DAILY SUN, COURTESY RON HELLNER

and he quit or something. Adam Palma was their guitarist, and they called me. We had played in garage bands together, but this was a gigging band that was playing frats and had an actual booking agent. Mike left and I auditioned and got the gig. It was a pretty good little band because it actually made money. They were a copy band, and we played all the frat houses in Texas and Oklahoma, junior colleges. We were one of the top bands [along with] Southwest F.O.B. Steve Sparks, the guitar player was getting married and I got Stevie the gig.

"We had this booking agent, and they wanted to change the name from The Cornerstones. It was the same band, but Stevie didn't play with The Cornerstones. They wanted us to change the name of the band and feature the singer more. His name was Ron Hellner, so his stage name became Deryk Jones."

Singer RON HELLNER: "The name came from Dan Lewis, who was our manager at Theze Few Productions. It was thought to have a British flair to it and was somewhat with the trend like Alan Price Set, Jimi Hendrix Experience, etc.

"My recollection is that the original Deryk Jones Party broke apart, and we absorbed the members in The Rogues, who included Skip Neilson, Eric Tagg. Skip and the drummer and the organist wanted to go back to school. Stevie came into the audition, and he wasn't nearly Top 40 enough, but we had Adam for that, and Adam was good at it. Stevie had that soulful feel to his playing that we really just didn't have. I was impressed that he could do what he did at that age. He would have been three years younger, and at that age it seems like an awful lot.

"I remember he didn't have a car, but he didn't seem to be interested in it because while the rest of us were out carousing and trying to score wine and liquor, he was sitting on the end of the bed playing his guitar. He was bashful, affable, easy to get along with, but he didn't have time for anything but playing guitar. He didn't chase the girls. When we'd get through playing, the rest of us would be ready to go out and get into something, [but] he'd want to go listen to someone else play. He was like a sponge for it.

"I can picture us on stage in the beach clubs in Galveston with Stevie and Adam in the band – The Bamboo Hut and the Grass Menagerie were the two hot beach clubs – and that would have been in the summer. I would say Stevie's tenure in the band was maybe six to ten months. The Studio Club and LuAnn's were the big deals in Dallas. I think we played at The Fog toward the end. At that point we had so much guitar talent that the tunes stopped being three minutes and fifty seconds – we'd do a set that contained four songs [laughs]. We had all this guitar talent and let it fly. They did some harmony guitar work. Adam, Eric and I sang, so we always had at least two-part vocals."

ERIC TAGG: "We were from North Dallas, and they [The Cornerstones] were from Oak Cliff, and we had a mutual respect for each other. Ron had adopted our band, The Rogues, as his backup band. This did not include Stevie yet – he was still a pup. Jimmie was already big, at least around Dallas. I remember seeing his band Texas open for Jimi Hendrix at McFarland Auditorium.

"In 1971, I graduated from high school. I didn't play with Stevie until I graduated. My band backed up Ron, and it was called Deryk Jones Party. The Rogues adopted the name of his band. Ron started replacing us with some of his original guys – Ken Brooks and Roddy joined the band in 1971, and that became the new version of the Deryk Jones Party. It was back to the old version plus me on bass.

"I was in with all these Oak Cliff guys, and I really relished that, because they were *funky*, you know? I was one of those snotty-nosed white guys from North Dallas. Then Stevie joined the band; I'm sure it was 1971. He and Adam had the double-stack Marshalls. We played a lot of Allman Brothers, Johnny Nitzinger, Eric Clapton-style. We had been more of a vocal band until Stevie joined, and then we were more of a kick-ass Derek

and the Dominos sound featuring the two guitarists. It was really loud.

"It didn't last long – six or eight months, and then Stevie left to go to Austin with Blackbird. It was at least late '71 because Stevie would call me from high school and say, 'Can you come pick me up after school?' He would call me after each period, 'Are you still coming?'

"Jimmie was more the straight blues; Stevie had the hot licks. He always had those real fast licks. It was more of a flashy style than Jimmie. He didn't know as much about playing through changes. You know how you play different scales with different chords? He would always just play the same blues licks through whatever chords were going by [laughs]. But it always had a lot of feel – a lot of funk.

"Roddy and Stevie were trying to teach me what funk was. I thought funk was just playing jerky. They said, 'No, it's not really playing jerky. You have to live it to play it.' It took me months to grasp the concept that these Oak Cliff guys were trying to teach me.

"I remember that it was on the trip to Galveston that I finally realized what it was. I drove the van to the gig on the beach, right to the edge of the sea. I got out and started walking into the ocean. I took my shoes off and started sinking down into the sand, you know? I stood there and felt myself sinking down into the earth, and I felt the grit and the salt and the *funk*. And that's when I finally grasped the concept they were trying to tell me. You've got to be grounded to the earth. Not jerky – *earthy*. You had to feel the grit and funk of the earth. Somehow it made sense to me.

"We played a lot of frat gigs, and they didn't know what they had there. We played The Cellar – $17 a night for eight hours. You alternated with another band, so you only played four hours, but you were there for eight. But in the summertime you had to do it to survive. There were no frat gigs then and not enough club dates to go around. A lot of bands broke up in the summer for that reason.

"I know he was getting together with [Blackbird], and he might have been rehearsing with them at the same time as Deryk Jones Party. Once we had our song list, we didn't rehearse much, so he could have been doing anything. [Blackbird] seemed to happen pretty fast. He lived with us a little bit that summer in The Trails apartments off Webb Chapel [Road, in Dallas]. He was there at least hanging out a lot in the summer of '71.

"I remember one time he was on top of the stairs, looked down and said, 'Same thang ever' day: get up and go to school, no need for me complainin,' my objection's overruled!' Some line he got out of a [Chuck Berry] song. He was already into blues, at *sixteen*. My dad was saying, 'What are you doing playing blues? You're eighteen years old. Don't you have to hang out in pool halls for, like, twenty years and lost a couple of lives before you can play blues?'

"We respected Stevie for having that blues idiom pretty well covered. He could play it, he could walk it, and, offstage, he could sing it. He could walk the walk. He was funny and easy going. We had a good time."

Guitarist ADAM PALMA: "My memory is that Stevie just tagged along on some of the gigs that we played that summer. We played in Austin and a bunch of frat gigs and a couple of beach clubs in Galveston. He wasn't officially a member of Deryk Jones. He wasn't with a band and just wanted to play whenever we would let him."

ERIC: "No, I remember him actually being a part of the band. Maybe we didn't gig too much. Like I said, we had to scrap to stay alive in the summer. That probably gave Stevie time to put the thing together with Christian and Noel and those guys [Blackbird]."

ADAM: "We were a pop band, playing Three Dog Night and stuff that was on the radio. The funny thing about Stevie was that he refused to play anything but rhythm and blues. Every once in a while we'd do something like Little Richard's 'Lucille,' and he'd get up there and do his thing, and he was great. He was definitely focused on being a blues guy."

RODDY: "We were a copy band, did all the Top 40 stuff – Three Dog Night, Otis Redding, Young Rascals. The singers were pretty good. Ron Hellner was the lead singer, and Ken Brooks was the piano player; Adam Palma on guitar and Stevie on guitar. Stevie got in there and was good – he could play a good lead and could learn the chords, but he didn't know the songs. It wasn't his thing, but he could play anything. (Liberation was doing Chicago.) He didn't stick to the arrangements as close as the guys in The Cornerstones did. We tried to play it just like the record, and he was more of an improvisation-type guy, you know.

"It was just for a few months, and then at some point I quit and Stevie and I parted ways for a while. And then Stevie got me an audition with Lincoln, and the bass player hated me. We went over to the Lamplighter Club – that's where they used to rehearse and play, and they wanted me to play 'My Back Pages' by Traffic, and I'd never even heard the song. So that didn't work out." [Contrary to Roddy's recollection, it is likely Lincoln preceded Deryk Jones Party.]

RON: "Adam and I were trying to stay in a commercial line because that's where we thought we needed to be to further our career. But Stevie wanted to play more rhythm and blues and abstract-type music. Eric was thinking about going to Europe. We played over on Jacksboro Highway [Sylvania] at Nitzinger's place, and we got a percentage of the door – I think we got six bucks. I walked out of there that night and said, 'I'm done with it.'"

Whether Stevie had already reformed Blackbird before Deryk Jones Party broke up is not clear. Roddy was in both bands and recalls a split before he rejoined Stevie in another band. In any event, the new lineup for Blackbird in the fall of 1971 became Stevie, Christian Plicque (vocals), Roddy Colonna (drums),

Kim Davis (guitar) and Noel Deis (organ). A little later, John Hoff joined on drums after David Frame came in on bass. Stevie usually sang two songs – "Thunderbird" and "Crossroads."

RODDY: "It seems like it was the fall of '71 when we cranked up Blackbird. We played gigs around Dallas and some showcase gigs where we'd rent the space. We did one at S.M.U. Then we started getting gigs in Austin at Alex Napier's club, Rolling Hills. I got married in the spring of '72 and moved to Austin. By the late fall or early winter of '72, Blackbird had broken up. David Frame had already left to join Too Smooth, and then we got Tommy [Shannon]. That's when the trouble began [laughs]."

STEVIE: "There was one place we played [The Cellar], you just didn't go there if you were black. If you were black and tried to get in, they'd ask for a reservation. If your name just happened to be on this fake list they had, they'd ask for $100 cover; you'd damn sure get rolled before you got very far into the club. If there was trouble, the owner and his goons [would] walk into the place with tommy guns, and they weren't kidding. If there were three bands playing, we'd have 2-hour breaks, so I'd go over to Hall Street to this club that you didn't go into if you were white [probably Funky Monkey]. But they fed me in the kitchen. I'd go over there and hang out, sit in whenever I could.[24]

"For a while, I was playing at The Cellar, in Dallas, and you would play a set for an hour. There was continuous music, as there was three bands or two bands, depending what was going on. Each band would play for exactly one hour and as the last band hit their last chord, the next band would come on the other side, plug into the same gear and hit it. That meant you would play for an hour then get two hours off. ... We would play a set for an hour, then go get into the car and go over to the other side of town and go sit in. We would have two hours, so we would be back in time to play our next set and then we would take off and go over again. [I was] fourteen. We were playing from ten at night until six in the morning. We were also trying to go to school, and that didn't work real well."[26]

By all accounts, Dallas in 1971 was not particularly supportive of the kind of music Stevie wanted to play. His band, Blackbird, was making trips to Austin to perform at the Waterloo Social Club at 7th and Red River, Alex Napier's Rolling Hills Club out in the hills south of town and other venues that were giving bands like Jimmie Vaughan's Texas Storm a place to play blues. It was still four years before Clifford Antone would open his club, but East Austin had the I.L. Club where blues was played.

RODDY COLONNA says the original lineup (without him) had played the New Orleans Club in Austin: "Me and Christian and Stevie got together to form a band, Blackbird. I kind of knew David Frame from playing with The Mystics, and I went steady with his sister. We had played together in a band called Natchul with David Deck that played guitar. We opened up for

Krackerjack at Candy's Flare one time, and that's where I met Uncle John and all them. It seems like right after Natchul broke up, we started Blackbird. Noel Deis was in on getting the band together too. We met Kim Davis too.

"The people liked Christian because it was so different. Hendrix was big, so having a black guy in the band wasn't a bad thing. He was real flamboyant by the time we moved to Austin – wearing these dress things, and big earrings – pretty wild [*laughs*]!

"Our first few gigs were at the Ali Baba Club. It was actually the old Ali Baba Club, and some guy had bought it and called it The Funky Monkey. They didn't have much of a crowd, but the guy did pay. When you played that club, you'd have to play like six sets a night. You know, you'd start at eight o'clock at night and go until two or three in the morning. We would probably make about $35 each a night. It was funky and dirty and dark. It was an old soul club for a long time – it wasn't a hot spot for young people. I had played there before with Freddie Empire. We would bring our own crowd when we would play there – twenty or thirty followers would come."

Blackbird was probably Stevie's first band that was not a Top 40 cover band. RODDY: "We were still a copy band, nonetheless. We played Allman Brothers, Lowell Fulson, we played 'Tramp,' and played some Janis Joplin stuff, a Rhinoceros funky rock tune, and 'Got Me Hummin'. We just played whatever we liked."

CHRISTIAN PLICQUE: "Who knew that Stevie would turn out to be such a great singer? I knew he would make it as a guitarist, but he was always so shy when it came to singing. The only songs I remember him singing over the five or so years we were together were 'Thunderbird' and 'Crossroads.' I could have gone home and slept and then come back and he still would have been playing the solo on 'Crossroads'! I remember when he would play it he would leap off the stage and jump on people's tables and play his solo right in their faces! He had this 30- or 40-foot guitar cord, and he would roam the clubs and the poor band just had to play on and on until he returned to the stage. His

minimum solos on 'Crossroads' were at least 30 minutes, no exaggeration!

"We had two guitarists in Blackbird. Stevie and Kim Davis. But when it came to who was going to play a solo, Stevie was always pushing for himself! Kim was a great guitarist too, no

Blackbird. (clockwise from top left) Deis, dePlique, Frame, Davis, Vaughan, Colonna. © JEANNE DEIS

doubt about that, but Stevie had a fire in him to play and nothing was going to get in his way. He was like a wolf after fresh meat compared to Kim. For example, Kim would not even consider getting out of bed for rehearsals until late afternoon, when all of us were up, knocking on his door in the mornings! He used to get so upset but would not rehearse until he was ready. We put up with him because he was a great guitar player and a fine person really. We all were spoiled in one way or another, me included. I was called 'Mr. Neiman-Marcus.'

"Stevie was the direct opposite of Kim: poor but happy and stuck to his guitar like glue. There were problems from time to time as in any band, but for the most part, Stevie and Kim worked really well together. We were doing that Allman Brothers thing and they sounded really good together.

"Frame sang one or two songs now and then, and Stevie sang his two songs, but the rest, four or five hours a night, was up to me. Kim and Stevie had 400-watt souped-up stacked Marshall amps, David with two monster acoustic bass amps, two drummers and Noel with more Marshall amps and two Leslies! I only had a small 200-watt Shure PA! And with no monitors! I think that is how I also developed into such a loud singer. I had no choice but to sing loud just to be heard. I always said that Vaughan played his amp on '12-and-a-half' volume!"

RODDY: "At first, the dynamic between Stevie and Kim was really good, but Kim really liked a lot of the new stuff that was coming out – Yes and bands like that really got his attention. Stevie was more into rhythm and blues. They did real well though. At rehearsals they would work out, 'You play this, I'll play that – you play lead, I'll play rhythm.'"

Kim Davis refused to be interviewed for this book, which did not surprise the people who knew him.

STEVIE: "[The Cellar] was the only place that would really let me do what I wanted to do, because nobody cared – they just had strippers and crabs. If you really wanted to come in there and play, they'd let you. A couple of times people would get pissed and start shooting at the stage. You ducked and kept playing. I played there from age 14 'til I was 18. There was a Cellar in Dallas and one in Fort Worth. We'd play two sets in one town, drive [30 miles] to the other club, and play two more sets. We got 90 bucks per night, per person. The only reason I could play there was because my parents didn't know about it.[27] We played The Cellar, the Funky Monkey and The Fox, where they had fake alcohol and strippers. We'd play from ten to six a.m., usually alternating with another band, which meant we could sometimes pick up another gig on the side. It was somewhere between what we do now and a sort of Allman Brothers/Cream thing."[18]

CHRISTIAN PLICQUE: "The days when we played at The Cellar in Dallas, I had to stand outside in the back during breaks because blacks weren't allowed in there."

Blackbird keyboard player NOEL DEIS: "Christian brought Stevie over and I thought, 'This kid sounds like Eric Clapton!' He was a little bit tentative, but he had a darn good sound. He had no equipment. I can't remember what he dragged over, but it wasn't much. Stevie went to Kimball and was the outcast kid that

was picked on by the local jock population. We had a couple of rehearsals, and then I met Kim Davis, who was also really good.

"We were heavily influenced by the Allman Brothers. When their first album came out [in 1969], it was a revelation. 'This is the direction we want to go.' Plus the blues stuff. Stevie was listening to Albert King and B.B. King. He played great slide guitar. Duane Allman isn't mentioned much as one of Stevie's formative influences, but he really did play Duane Allman a lot. I remember when he first started trying to play slide. Within about two or three months he was playing very aggressive, very confidant slide solos. He would play these blistering slide solos; Kim didn't play slide, so it really was kind of like Duane Allman and Dickie Betts.

"We had trouble getting gigs because we decided we were not going to be a commercial band. In Dallas, that was about the only places you could work was playing Top 40.

"We got some great players. Roddy was a good drummer. John Hoff was a great drummer too. We sort of said, 'Wow, he's really good. Let's snap him up too!' [Laughs] It was a seven-piece band. We had trouble making any money because it had to be split so many ways, but we played with a lot of soul and a lot of impact. We had a lot of raw, artistic energy.

"We got the Cellar gig, and I've never seen a more bizarre place in my life – a totally unique dump. I think someone described it as a Chinese dope den! The Cellar was almost like an X Files episode [sci-fi television show of the early 2000's]. Once you went into the doors of that place, it was like some other dimension! Kirkwood [the owner] actually looked a little like Mephistopheles. He had the thick eyebrows, sunken eyes, prominent cheekbones, and I believe he had a pointed goatee. He was a scary, Satanish looking guy.

"We had the gig for months, and then finally ... I didn't actually witness this event, but our relationship with The Cellar came to a grinding halt when Christian told me that Johnny Carroll, who was the manager of the Dallas Cellar, pulled his 45 out and pointed it at Stevie. The only thing I can say is they wanted to get out of there fast. Johnny was a frustrated guitar player and a guy you didn't want to stand close to. Everybody that worked there was chosen for their intimidation factor. They were always throwing someone out on the street."

Another band member says the incident with the gun never happened, but it does illustrate the nature of the times and the club.

RODDY: "When it would get dark, we'd head on over to The Cellar – get some Elf's Punch. This guy Elf that ran the place, he had a big trash can full of punch that he'd make with Everclear and Vodka and all this stuff [laughs]. It was free! They didn't have a liquor license, but they could give it away. So we'd go by and get him to spoon us out some of that. He was kind of a short guy with round glasses and wore a serape. [One time] a guy ran into [club manager] Johnny Carroll's office, shot him, and then Elf jumped out on the sidewalk and shot him in the back and killed him. So it was sort of a rough place [laughs]! A lot of girls running around in their underwear waiting on tables.

"The Cellar in Fort Worth had three bands a night, starting at about nine o'clock at night and go 'til about six. [The bands alternated sets], so you had two hours off between sets – plenty of time to go club hopping. Go sit in over here, go see someone play over there, and come back and do your set, then play pinball or there was always some girls. Johnny Carroll would say, 'Play a real long instrumental,' and these girls would get up there and strip. By the time she got her clothes off, the lights would go out, and a guy would shine a flashlight on her and she'd run off the stage. That meant either a cop's coming, or that's enough. You might see some tits, but that's about it. The girls wore the big bulls-eye bras and panties. It was real sleazy. The walls were painted black. Black lights were the new thing, and everything was painted in day-glo paint. 'Coffee and confusion' written on the wall."

The tandem of Stevie and Kim on guitars worked like a charm – Stevie, the improvisator, and Kim, who had the ability to more accurately recreate the sounds of the records. GARY COCKRELL: "I remember sitting with Stevie and listening to a band play 'Crossroads.' The guitarist played the solos note for note. After the tune I commented to Stevie that while I thought it was great the guitarist could do that, it lacked some punch or something. Stevie had nothing negative to say; he just replied that he couldn't copy solos note-for-note and was impressed that guitarist could."

Stevie's girlfriend for the next four years or so was Glenda Maples, a beautiful part-Native American girl with long dark hair. She left a difficult home life at age fifteen and moved into an apartment on Prescott near the nightclubs of Oak Lawn in Dallas. GLENDA: "Of course we couldn't stay away from it – The Cellar, The Fog, Soul City, all those places." Glenda's roommate and co-worker decided they should check out the music in Austin at the Waterloo Social Club, "and I thought, 'What the hell.' She had a little Mustang convertible, and we had about four gallons of sangria, so we proceeded to head down there, having a blast with the top down.

"I love to dance, and Stevie and the band were playing. I was kind of crazy and would dance by myself sometimes. If I liked the music I'd just get up and dance. All of a sudden I swung around this [post] and I looked up at the band and there was Stevie, and our eyes connected. Then ... he went home with me that night in the backseat of the Mustang.

"We kind of started it on and off – he was still in school and I was a bad influence. Martha [Stevie's mother] wanted him to graduate, but I was young and independent and he liked that. He started to stay with me more on Prescott.

"He was very shy and down to earth. [The attraction] wasn't so much the guitar as the physical eye contact. It was like, boom! Connect! He approached me after coming off stage, and I'll be damned if he didn't need a ride back to Dallas. Of course, I did take him straight home that night, although we did have a little fun in the backseat.

"We weren't real tight right then, but we did become very tight, and we didn't want to leave each other. If I was around, he was tight with me; if I wasn't, I don't want to think about what was going on. We were just, like, glued together. We even went to Sears and picked out sheets together, and we had this big future ... but he always told me his guitar would come first, and that was hard for me.

"I'll never forget the first time I was invited over to meet [Stevie's parents.] I'm so embarrassed when I think back on it. I'm a kind of natural person and I really never wear makeup that heavy, but I put blue eye shadow – all this stuff; I'm sure I looked like a freak. Martha cooked for us several times, and she let me know that if you made Stevie scrambled eggs, you had to remove the [white cords that connect to the yolk sack] or Stevie couldn't eat the eggs. For [Stevie's dad, whose health was starting to fail] she would put ice in the gravy and get all the grease off."

RODDY: "Stevie and his girlfriend Glenda lived over in East Dallas in this old house that was divided up into apartments. Stevie would always want a ride over to see Glenda, so I ended up stuck outside in the car, you know [laughs]. He'd do this to me all the time. 'Uh, can we go by my girlfriend's? I'll make it real quick ...' I was always trying to get money out of him for gas. I practically had to turn him upside down and shake the change out of his pockets. I remember gas was, like, twenty-two cents a gallon, and this '67 Dodge van just drank gas. Sometimes I'd give Stevie the ultimatum, 'We're not going any further until you give me some money!' [Laughs] And he always needed a ride out to Arnold & Morgan [Music] in Garland to get strings.

"He had this Epiphone that had sat in the sun in the window of the music store for years and was all bleached out. The bridge [he probably meant nut] was constantly wiggling loose because he was already starting to use heavier strings. He was always taking it back to get the bridge recemented into the guitar and getting the neck tuned. Constantly needing to go to the store, and Garland was a long way from Oak Cliff, and the van didn't have an air conditioner either! Cutter gave him a lot of rides too. Stevie was always needing a ride somewhere.

"I remember one night we ended up at this club on the Jacksboro Highway, and Bugs Henderson came and sat in. He set his drink up on Stevie's amp and started playing. It was a real small stage, and he backed up and hit the amp and spilled his drink in Stevie's amp and cooked it. Bugs just kind of ducked out [laughs]!

"He was younger than us, but he never had trouble getting in a club. When we started hanging out together, we'd go over to The Fog, and he'd say 'He's with me.' Heck, the drinking age was 21 then, and Stevie was about 16 and getting me into clubs."

GEOFF APPOLD recalls trading guitars with Stevie: "I had an Epiphone with the small humbuckers, and it looked exactly like a Gibson 335. I bought it in 1969 or 1970 for $200 in North Dallas, and the red finish had started to turn kind of yellow because it had been too close to the window in the store. This

49

friend of mine, Lynn Fisher, was a pretty good bass player and was the nephew of lounge piano player Pee Wee Lynn. Lynn came over and said, 'I've got this kid I'm playing with, and you just can't believe how good he is – it's Jimmie Vaughan's brother.'

"This was probably 1971, and I was teaching guitar in North Dallas and had about eight guitars. So Stevie comes over and he picks up this twelve-string guitar and starts bending the strings on it like they're Ernie Ball 9's [very light gauge strings]! I said, 'How can you do that?' and he said, 'Well, I got these hands ...' and he [held his hand out, showing the muscle between the thumb and first finger] that went like this [indicates a VERY large muscle]. 'My brother and I have arms like Popeye!' I'd never seen anything like it; he had phenomenal hand and arm strength. He was about sixteen. Even though he was dropping the tuning a half-step, he was still using these strings that were like pipes!

"Anyway, he picked up the red Epiphone and said, 'I'd really like to have this.' The next time he came over with this Telecaster [sic] that's been stripped – he had taken the finish off in high school shop, and you know how Fenders are, they have that seal on 'em, and you *really* have to go for it to get the finish off. The word 'Jimbo' had been scratched in the back of it.

"I said, 'Look. You have talent – take my guitar; I'm happy to take the Telecaster.' When I saw him years later, the first thing he said was, 'Hey, do you still have that guitar?' [It had been

Blackbird. (l-r) Frame, Davis, Deis, dePlique, Colonna, Vaughan. © CHAD SNEED

traded away.] He was obviously trying to reconnect with his early guitars, because every guitar he had had its own spirit and soul. I asked him why he wanted that Epiphone, and he said, 'Well, Freddie King was everything to me and I wanted to be like him with a hollow body Gibson/Epiphone. I saw Jimmie when the T-Birds did their 'Don't Mess With Texas' spot and told him the story. He got this weird look on his face and said, 'He had no right to give you that guitar – that was *my* guitar.' [*Laughs*] ... And this was sixteen years later!"

"Jimbo," the 1951 Broadcaster, is currently owned by a private collector in California. As of this writing, it is the only one of Stevie's early guitars to be located outside of Jimmie's possession. However, a number of guitars were stolen from Jimmie in 2007, and several had not been recovered when this book went to print.

Paul "Rocky" Miller, roadie for Blackbird, recalls that on the drives between Dallas and Austin, Stevie would be constantly playing guitar in the van. When he would find a new lick, he'd say, "Hear that? Did you hear that?" Sure enough, Stevie would find a way to work that new lick into the show that night. Rocky also recalls that "after a show there might be a big party somewhere, but if Stevie could find a guitar, he'd be off in a room by himself; not the life of the party. Stevie was pretty shy, but if you could get him out of his shell, he was funny and always very polite and nice."

Fall: David Frame joins Blackbird on bass.

NOEL DEIS: "Bill [had been] an excellent bass player and a very nice man, but David was part of the Oak Cliff crowd, and he hit it off with Roddy more than Roddy hit it off with Bill. Of course, that's sort of the basic underpinning: the drums and bass have to agree with each other. David was a great bass player. He laid down a very relaxed groove. Even though it was more of a rock band, he was more like the great R&B bass players at the time."

DAVID FRAME: "Stevie was in a band called Blackbird; I was in a show band and wanted to get back to 'real' music. The mafia was starting to close in on us, and it was really getting scary. Blackbird was the only band that was pure and not worried about doing the show circuit. Roddy Colonna on drums; Noel Deis on keyboards; Christian Plicque, lead singer; Kim Davis was equal guitarist to Stevie at the time. They were established and I auditioned at a club in Fort Worth. There was already a bass player, and I aggressively took his place. That's the last time I stole a gig – I never did that again because I felt bad. [Of course,] they didn't have to choose me [*laughs*].

"We played at The Cellar in both Fort Worth and Dallas, and that was really the only gig except the Funky Monkey, and it was an all-night thing too. Stevie was like a kid in a candy store. He loved everything, very naive; Glenda Maples was his girlfriend. He didn't have much of an ego; he was always nice and respectful."

Blackbird was obviously a big sound with two guitarists and two drummers. DAVID: "John Hoff and Roddy had different styles, but they learned how to play together. It was basically kind of like an Allman Brothers band. Stevie and Kim used to get up on the strippers' runway and do a dueling thing, and it was excellent. They would just take off and go on forever. And it wasn't just dueling solos; they would play harmonies together. They had licks where they would just [complement] each other and it was amazing. Stevie and Kim respected each other, and they dueled. It wasn't a competition, but it was constantly showing everything that they had.

"I was so impressed with Stevie. He would always have a guitar in his hands at home, unplugged, and be playing it – that's how he became who he was. My son ran into the music director at TBN, who told him that he ran into Stevie and asked him, 'What must I do to be good?' Stevie said, 'Go home, unplug your guitar, lay on your bed and play for forty years.' [*Laughs*].

"The only song he sang was 'Thunderbird'; him and I harmonized it. His voice was terrible – we couldn't get his tone right – but he later got voice lessons from Doyle and really belted it. I think the first time I heard him sing good was with the Cobras, and he sang 'Texas Flood.'"

RODDY: "We started doing gigs, and it was so loud I couldn't even hear my drums. Plus the Allman Brothers were coming along, and I wanted to add another drummer. John Hoff was a local drummer in Dallas and he was pretty good, so we got him."

JOHN HOFF: "They had Roddy and wanted another drummer to do an Allman Brothers kind of thing. I was pretty ecstatic about it. I saw James Brown play in my youth in Tulsa, and hell, I saw him play with three drummers one time.

"There was stuff that Roddy could do that I wasn't good at, and there was stuff I could do that Roddy wasn't good at. We'd trade off on stuff. He had a big Ludwig drum set, like John Bonham; I had a little Gretsch drum set that was a smaller jazz version. He had the deeper bottom end, and I had the higher end crack. Our nicknames for each other were Larry Ludwig and Gary Gretsch [*laughs*].

"We stayed on the twos and fours and worked around on the accents and fills. It worked out pretty good. We played Allman Brothers and stuff we wanted to hear, not so much what the audience wanted to hear. We had a gig at The Fog club on Lemmon – we played there and they fired us [*laughs*], but that didn't dampen anybody's spirit.

"At that point in time it wasn't about the money; it was about the fun. We had two guitar players, two drummers, bass player, Hammond B-3 player and a singer – that's a lot of guys in the band, so the money went pretty fast."

John concurs with virtually everyone else's sentiments regarding Stevie's spirit, even when Stevie was in his late teens. "He had a great sense of humor and was a practical joker. We always liked to twist off a bit, and he was an instigator in that, but when it came down to nut cuttin', we always tried to stomp on it pretty hard.

"He was a real giving kind of guy – he'd give you the shirt off his back if you needed it. All that we talked about was music, 24/7. I was into Stevie Wonder, and we used to talk about how to incorporate Stevie Wonder into other genres of music. We talked about that kind of stuff all the time."

NOEL: "Blackbird's biggest weakness was that we didn't have our own creative director; there was no songwriter writing songs that would have given the band a true identity. Some of our favorite songs were 'Engine Number 9' by Wilson Pickett, 'Statesboro Blues,' and we usually opened with 'Crossroads' and Stevie would sing it – usually just the three guys, Roddy, Stevie and David – then the rest of the band would come on stage.

"I remember Stevie and Kim trading solos on 'Statesboro Blues.' The jazzers would call it 'trading fours.' Stevie was playing slide, and you could practically see smoke coming off the strings – not something visual, but something you felt. Kim played riveting solos too.

"It's a shame there isn't a recording. The only tape I remember that we made was a demo tape with Charlie Hatchett in his little recording studio behind his law office. It wasn't very good. I think it was four songs, and it just didn't have a good sound quality. It didn't really capture the excitement that band managed to generate at that time either."

The author spoke with Charlie, who said the tape was stolen from his office many years ago.

BRUCE BOWLAND of Krackerjack: "When we got to Austin, we figured we needed representation, and Charlie Hatchett was the big guy down there. He had this little, like, Morgan building behind his office with egg crates in it [for acoustics]. All the bands went in there and made audition tapes, including us. It was gawd awful! Everybody overplayed the building, so it was muffled and it sucked."

Remember that at this time, Stevie and the others were typical teenagers, having a ball playing music and cutting up. DAVID FRAME: "Our big thing was pork skins – open the bag and smell the poot! It stinks real bad when you open a bag of pork skins, and the worse the smell, the better the pork skins. We had our own little silly language that we spoke – words we made up. Cutter used to sell Coke bottles to get Stevie a new set of strings. We had a Blackbird handshake: it was basically a soul handshake where you put your hands together and your thumbs are clasped like a brother handshake, then you release it and keep your thumbs clasped, your hands go out to the side, and then we flap our hands like a bird."

JOHN HOFF: "[The band and our girlfriends/wives] would hang out with each other all day, listen to Muddy Waters, 'Layla' and the Allman Brothers – I think those were the top three. And a lot of Freddie King too. I think we did the *Cannonball* album verbatim – we did every song on that record. Whatever Christian Plicque wanted to sing and that we could all agree on, we just played the shit out of it." Asked about Christian's stage persona, John replied, "Magnificent! Unbelievably great stageman. He always got the audience into it. On stage, great showman; backstage, things got a little weird, but everybody was a little crazy. He wore really cool silk scarves over his head and dressed to the truest of hipness back then. We all wore T-shirts and vests and tried to make the most of the shows – if we'd done laundry that week, or if your wife, girlfriend or mom had.

"Steve had a Guild guitar with huge strings like telephone wire. Steve and Kim played double leads, or one played rhythm and one played lead."

September 15: Allman Brothers Band, State Fair Music Hall, Dallas, TX (Stevie in audience)

RODDY COLONNA: "Dan Lewis was the booking agent for Theze Few Productions. His dad had a company that handled all the ushers for the State Fair Music Hall in Dallas. So through him, Stevie and I got free tickets to see the Allman Brothers. We had the two front seats in the balcony up on the right-hand side looking down on the stage. It left a big impact on us, the powerful sound that those guys had. Stevie was a big fan of Duane Allman. Two weeks later, Duane Allman died."

JOHN HOFF remembers going to the show, though he recalls Stevie sitting with him and Kim in a different part of the hall: "We went to see the Allman Brothers play, and me and Kim and Steve sat about eight rows back, dead center. I remember lookin' at them, and they were lookin' at me, and we all had tears in our eyes watching Duane Allman play guitar. What a great band that was. We tried to emulate that."

Earliest known handbill for Blackbird as headlining band.
© LEW STOKES, COLLECTION OF CRAIG HOPKINS

October: After about seven weeks of his final year of high school, Stevie quits.

STEVIE: "At the end of the year, the principal was announcing over the p.a. system that if I didn't pay my locker fees, I couldn't get my diploma, but I only went seven weeks. They were more interested in how much my hair had grown, if I looked clean enough to go to their school."[28] For a short time, Stevie moved in with his girlfriend Glenda.

Classmate Nick Nicholas recalls that Stevie wasn't the only one to quit school that day. Stevie and Nick were among several kids who were fed up with the school's focus on their hair length and walked out. Nick went back the next day after getting his long hair cut, but for Stevie it was the end of school and the next step toward life as a musician.

---

date unknown: Zodiac Club, Fort Worth, TX (Blackbird), opening for Krackerjack

---

Krackerjack was one of the most popular bands in Texas in the early 1970's. Singer BRUCE BOWLAND: "Blackbird opened for us at the Zodiac Club. Stevie was just a kid. I remember the Zodiac Club particularly because the police raided it that night, and they found some inebriates in the parking lot, came in and revoked the dance license. I jumped from the stage to a table and the police didn't like it and arrested me for dancing in an unlicensed hall. [*Author laughs hysterically.*]

"When we got downtown, I watched them pat down another guy they arrested, and they planted an ounce of marijuana on him. I thought, 'I am *soooo* screwed.' But they, you know, [apparently decided], 'He's just a sanger.'"

While Blackbird was doing well, Stevie was looking out for a better opportunity. He and Kim Davis auditioned for Dale Smith's band, Smith & Jones. Smith had asked Robert Farris of The Mystics to play, but he declined and suggested Little Stevie. When Smith learned Stevie was under 18, he initially passed. A couple of weeks later, however, having found no lead player, he auditioned Stevie and Kim. Both guitarists impressed him, but he only had enough money to hire Stevie. At the last minute, Stevie decided to stick with Blackbird and make the big move to Austin.[29]

Noel Deis recalls Alex Napier hearing Blackbird in Dallas and telling them, "You guys gotta come down to Austin." NOEL: "We got a gig at his place, the Rolling Hills Club out in the middle of the chaparral in South Austin. You could make as much noise as you wanted and nobody seemed to care. The first gig we did there was huge. I could tell it was going to be one of our home bases. We got into serious competition with Krackerjack, which was an established band."

October 22: Rolling Hills Club, Austin, TX (Blackbird)

October 23: Rolling Hills Club, Austin, TX (Blackbird)

The flyer artwork for the above two gigs was done by LEW STOKES: "Most of my posters brought me ten dollars, get-in-free/'I'm with the band,' and, for a short period of time, a free bar tab, but that quickly went south. I probably did 30-35 posters over the years, but I never could get focused enough to make it a business."

October 31: (venue unknown), Austin, TX.

The two photos on this page were taken at a Halloween gig with Stevie dressed in a green plaid jacket, clip-on tie, sash, leotard and his girlfriend's panties, with a scarf or tie around his leg and his hair in a ponytail. Playing a Gibson Firebird guitar too.

Stevie and David Frame. COURTESY BRUCE BOWLAND

Stevie in Halloween garb. COURTESY BRUCE BOWLAND

STEVIE: "I used to dress like Jimi on Halloween, and took to wearing scarves around my legs and hats like he wore. I figured that if Jimi was high as a kite when he played, I had to be high. The higher I got, the more obsessed I got. My worship got to the point where what killed Hendrix almost killed me."[10]

Late 1971: Stevie plays briefly in a band called Orchrist with Steve Lowrey and Mike Harrison (keyboards), Jas Stephens (drums) and Mike Howell (bass).

JAS STEPHENS: "We were into *The Hobbitt*. Orchrist is the goblin cleaver in the book. That's where we got the name. We needed something to kill the monster [*laughs*]. We thought we were going to break new ground. Everybody else was doing a lot of guitar stuff, so we were going to try to do an organ trio."

MIKE HARRISON: "We couldn't find a guitar player we really liked, so we decided we would just have a keyboard band. A buddy

told me, 'Stevie used to sit in with us all the time.' We were doing a lot of Moody Blues, Procol Harum – things of that nature – playing The Cellar circuit [Dallas, Houston, Fort Worth].

"The Cellar was insane [*laughs*]. This place stayed open all night until about seven in the morning. You'd have three to four bands a night, and the biggest draw would get the sets in prime times, and the other bands would fill in the hours in between, because you had twelve hours to fill!

"They sold highballs, but they weren't real highballs. In those days in Texas, you didn't have liquor by the drink. You could bring a bottle in and buy setups or fake drinks. One was rum flavored, one was whiskey flavored, and one was gin flavored."

DENNIS DULLEA: "The fake drinks were a few drops of bourbon extract or rum extract, put it in a Coke and sell it for three dollars! They had two Super Reverbs in each club, and you weren't allowed to bring in other amps. We got paid $15 each at between five and six o'clock in the morning – in one dollar bills. The big acts like Bugs Henderson got $20."

MIKE HARRISON: "The waitresses all walked around in bras and panties. Every once in a while there'd be one who was shy and wear a bikini. The stage was floor level, then there was a riser in front of it about two feet high and two feet wide, and it ran the whole length in front of the bandstand. The girls would get up there and dance on this in front of the band. Instead of a dance floor, there were pillows and cushions. [Though Stevie was not in this band, the group Bear is shown at The Cellar in the photo. Note the strippers' runway in front of the band.]

"In Fort Worth there was a long stairway down from the street; in Houston and Dallas, there was a long hallway from the door. A guy sat at the door with a clipboard that had a lot of names on it, and they would check it every once in a while: 'Do you have a reservation?' Pat Kirkwood, the owner, had an injunction against the police in each city – they couldn't come in without showing I.D. at the door. After they would pass him at the door, the guy

The Cellar, Dallas, TX. COURTESY JOHN MICHAEL SORIA

would flip a lightswitch that would turn on a blue lightbulb on the ceiling of The Cellar, letting everyone know the police were coming in. So anything that was going down, like if the girls had their tops off (which happened a lot) or someone had alcohol they weren't supposed to have, they would see that blue light and straighten up.

"One night down at the Houston Cellar, we had [undercover] Houston narcotics agents who were dressed as preppies – like college students. And we had Liquor Control Board guys all dressed as cowboys, and neither knew the other was in there. So we had a waitress going to the narcotics officers saying, 'Those cowboys over there said y'all look like a bunch of punks!' And then they'd say something and she'd go over to the LCB guys and say, 'Those college guys said y'all aren't nothin' but a bunch of redneck assholes!' So before the night was over we had the LCB and the narcotics division in a fist fight [laughs], and we just stood there and watched them!

"The Cellar was like a university for musicians. Stevie would go and study guys like Doyle Brashear and Arvel Stricklin, 'Tudy' Taddi, Doug Sahm and all these guys. He would sit right in front of them and watch their fingers, then he'd run over in the corner and sit and play along, not plugged in. He could soak it in so quick.

"Stevie got around by hitchhiking, and he would take his guitar – wear it around his neck and stick his thumb out – and whenever he didn't have his thumb out trying to get a ride, he was practicing on the guitar [laughs]."

STEVE LOWREY: "Steve came down to The Cellar, and I want to say he spent maybe a week with us at the most. We played The Cellar, and then Steve moved on – I think he was trying to get

down to Austin. I think he saw The Cellar as kind of the end of the road, and that there were a lot bigger and better things to do."

JAS STEPHENS: "We were not a guitar band. He didn't care much for the type of music we were doing – Jack Bruce, Neil Young, Buffalo Springfield, Moody Blues. We did what he wanted to for a while, but it just didn't work out. It was only ten days to two weeks. Stevie wanted to play more blues, which was fine with me. I started out playing Freddie King."

December 31: Stevie and Blackbird move to Austin and sign a contract with attorney/agent Charlie Hatchett, who booked dozens of bands.

Some recall the move as late as February 1972, but Hatchett was booking them by the end of January. Stevie wrote for his publicity biography that the band moved on January 1, 1972. In any event, home base was Rolling Hills Country Club off Bee Caves Road. It would later become the Soap Creek Saloon.

Keyboard player MIKE KINDRED: "In those days in Dallas, you either played the hits or you didn't play." Or as Stevie put it, in Dallas "you might as well have a quarter slot in your ear." KINDRED: "So there was kind a mass exodus of blues lovers from Dallas – me, Jimmie, Stevie, Paul Ray. We all eventually came to Austin because the musical climate was so much more open to blues and originals."[30]

Singer CHRISTIAN PLICQUE: "We played [in Austin] all the time. That is why we decided to move there, because it was getting too heavy driving back and forth. The rest of the guys in the band were not working and could easily drive down. I was working at Neiman-Marcus and had to work until 5:30 on Fridays. So I had to rush to Love Field and fly down there and change clothes in the car on the way to the gig at the Waterloo Social Club or wherever we were playing. There was also a very hip place called the South Door, at which we later became the house band, like at the Waterloo, and it was packed all the time.

"So Stevie said he was moving and it was my choice to stay at Neiman-Marcus or gamble on

Blackbird at Lancaster High School, Dallas. COURTESY DOUG MAY

Blackbird. I told Mr. Marcus that I was quitting for the second time and that I wanted a career in music. He said if I left, not to come back again and to be sure that it was what I really wanted. I just wanted to sing, so I left and joined the others in Austin. No regrets. It was the best time of my life. I have never been a good singer, I know that, but the band, as a unit, in those days, we really had something special."

Christian stuck with his decision and has been a successful gospel singer for many years. He now lives in Finland.

STEVIE: "Lots of people have gravitated here. Something's in the air here that makes you want to get on the stick and go. People are more open to let you play your music here, but it's opening up in Dallas again.[31] It was like a circus. The first time I came down here, I couldn't believe it. There were real, full-blown hippies. People were just walking around acting strange, looking strange. I was trying to figure out, hey, what's happening here? How are these people getting away with all this? This is the capital. Where are the police?"[20]

JOHN HOFF: "We tried to play gigs around Dallas, but it was a little too commercial. I think Steve brought up that, 'Jimmie's playing in Austin, and they love blues down there; let's move to Austin.'"

NOEL: "I had a big bread truck, and we could fit all the band's gear and the band in. I have a clear memory of us leaving Austin; Kim stayed at the hotel and the rest of us drove back in the bread truck. We were stopped by the Austin cops, and it was 'Oh, god.' We had just been passing a joint around, so I think one of us ate the rest of it, and we opened the windows to clear the smoke out.

"We finally pulled over and the cop came up. Turned out one was a vice guy, a kind of edgy dude, checking us out. [But] by then we had sort of mastered the art of being cool with cops – don't say anything nasty or inflammatory, be cooperative. They weren't real in-your-face either, at that time. They probably realized we were just a band, maybe these punks might have had a joint, but it wasn't going to yield a major drug bust or anything. I don't think they made us take the gear out. They just looked around with a flashlight and said, 'Okay. See ya later.' [Laughs]

"The bread truck finally died. I left it on the side of the road on I-35 between Waco and Dallas. It sat there for about two months and then vanished. I was driving back to Dallas after Roddy had moved to Austin. My girlfriend and I hadn't found a place in Austin yet."

Bass player DAVID FRAME: "When Blackbird played The Cellar, we could play as much as we wanted, back and forth between Dallas and Fort Worth, but it was hard on us and we weren't getting anywhere. You don't get famous playing at The Cellar, but you do get good! That and Funky Monkey, we probably averaged three or four nights a week.

"The Funky Monkey was a black club, and we just got in there by a fluke – our lead singer was black, Christian Plicque,

that's what got us in the door. As far as they were concerned, we were just a bunch of white boys backing up Christian. We had to prove ourselves, but the crowd started warming up to us. We had some characters there. 'The Reverend' was one guitarist – he was actually an ordained minister, had the gold teeth and everything. It was an all-night gig like The Cellar; play a set, go off for a while and come back."

The Cellar was the opposite of the Funky Monkey. "They didn't allow blacks in there. Christian was allowed in because he was in the band, but we had to be careful. If he came in the front door and other blacks saw that, they'd get mad. The Black Panthers would do drive-bys every once in a while – shoot up the wall – because they couldn't come in. Things are somewhat better today because of the integrated bands back then."

NOEL: "Stevie really believed in living the blues lifestyle, sort of a Spartan lifestyle. I think it's true that Stevie really did want to be black. I remember him saying that. Some things you can't change."

DAVID: "I was the oldest guy, and one night at The Cellar I said, 'Hey. This ain't happenin' here – who wants to go to Austin?' Basically, step across this line, and everybody did. So we migrated to Austin in February '72. We started playing little clubs in Austin. Charlie Hatchett booked us in all the main clubs. It was like a rotating thing – Blackbird, Krackerjack and a few other bands."

RODDY: "We really looked up to [Krackerjack]. Charlie Hatchett was our booking agent, and he called us his two hippie bands. We'd play the gig, I'd collect the money and pay everyone in the band, and hold back whatever we needed for expenses. Every Monday morning I'd head to Charlie's and give him his cut. He'd book us out of town – Victoria, College Station, Huntsville. We were supposed to play a gig in Beaumont; we borrowed Krackerjack's old Chevy panel truck. It broke down in Sugarland and never made it to the gig. So we were on the side of the road, and I had money for expenses for hotel rooms. I said, 'Well, hey. Why don't we just go to a nice restaurant and get a steak? So we all spent about $15 each on a steak, we were high-rollin' it [laughs]! We got home with no money."

STEVIE: "I was considered 'weird' by everyone else. I was already making about $300 a week, so I didn't think that school could teach me that much. I wanted to play."[12]

"I moved into a club called Rolling Hills that a friend of mine owned. I slept on the pool table, the stage, the floor, whatever the weather permitted. And to tell you the truth, it was some of my favorite times. I didn't have a dime, but who cares? I was doing what I wanted and around people I wanted to be around and it was *always* good music."[5]

Former bandmate Eric Tagg recalls Stevie sleeping on the pool table, and Stevie commenting about a new discovery. "Hey, Eric. I finally figured out how to get my hair to do what I want it to do. I don't wash it anymore. Now it sticks wherever I slap it."

Blackbird. COURTESY CHARLIE HATCHETT

2

Early Years
in Austin *1972–1977*

1972

Austin. Stevie leaves Dallas and his high school education behind in order to be part of a more liberal and tolerant community with a marginally better music scene. No more going straight from an all-night gig to school. No one to complain about the length of his hair. Freedom as he has never had it before.

Stevie and David Frame. COURTESY DAVID FRAME

Following in the footsteps of Denny Freeman, Doyle Bramhall and Jimmie Vaughan from Dallas and others from around the Lone Star state, he truly begins a new chapter of his life at the age of seventeen. Dallas would always be his home town, and he would return there for the last years of his life, but after he became successful, Austin would claim him as an adopted son.

He has advanced from talent shows, school gymnasiums and teen dances to the nightclubs with ominous-sounding names like The Cellar, The Fog and the Funky Monkey. Stevie is already a veteran of all-night gigs, with some experience in a recording studio and *the road*. Here, then, is when he gets off the local road and onto the highway of his career. Day by day he lives the life of a bluesman, and night after night he gives his audiences everything he's got.

Jimmie's band Storm was "holding court at the One Knite," as keyboardist MIKE KINDRED recalls. "I may have been the eighth or ninth member of that band – they had two horns, and one of the guys played two saxophones at once. Lewis Cowdrey on harp, Paul Ray on bass, Doyle Bramhall sitting on the drums and

he was the lead vocalist. Paul and Lewis had their vocal parts in the show, but it was really the expanded Doyle and Jimmie thing. It was happening about the same time as Ninth Street, but I was hanging out with Jimmie, and he wanted a piano player who could approximate [long-time Muddy Waters sideman] Otis Spann."

RODDY: "We'd been coming down to Austin and staying at Lew Stokes' house. Mike Kindred lived out at Lew's house, and they would let us crash there on a cot in the living room. People would just find someone to stay with – find a girl, you know – whatever. We played the Rolling Hills Club on Bee Caves Road, and it later turned into Soap Creek – we'd sleep on the dance floor at the

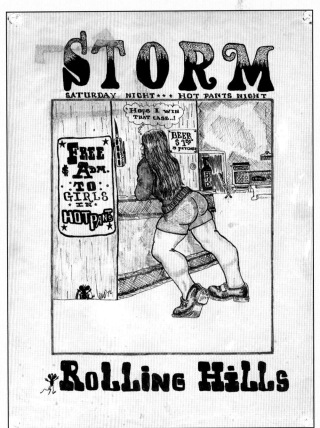

© LEW STOKES

club in sleeping bags. It got to where every weekend we were driving down to play, so we just decided to move. We played Waterloo Social Club on the corner of 7th and Red River, and that became one of our main gigs. We didn't play the One Knite much, but Jimmie did – every Monday night for years. Waterloo Social Club was right down the street, so on the breaks we could go see Jimmie play."

LEW STOKES: "When Stevie came to Austin [in 1971], he was asleep on a pool table at Rolling Hills and I think I was asleep outside. I got up in the morning and came inside and he woke up, got up. I said, 'Man, I know why I didn't make it home; what are you doin' sleeping on the pool table?' And he said, 'Lew, I don't have anywhere to stay here yet.' We talked for a minute and he said, 'Well, this is as good as it gets.'

"Now, he was barely sixteen years old, and that never ceased to amaze me. He had decided he was going to be a professional musician, no matter what it took or what the sacrifices."

BRUCE BOWLAND: "There are stories about him sleeping in the clubs, and I know he did, but I don't think he had to. He had enough friends that would say, 'You can come home with us.' And I'm not saying he *chose* to put himself through those blues, but he did. At that point it was, 'Well, I need to lay my head down; pool table here looks pretty good; I'll see y'all in the morning. Bye.' He never bitched about it."

Stevie's caricature of Bruce Bowland. © STEVIE RAY VAUGHAN, COURTESY BRUCE BOLWAND

The scatalogical drawing by Stevie is of Bruce as a blackbird.

JIMMIE VAUGHAN, on Stevie's move to Austin: "You know how when you don't see your cousins, and then you see them a year later and all of a sudden they're not little kids anymore? That's what happened with Stevie. I noticed he really popped out and he had on a scarf and, you know, he was sort of cool, and he had his guitar. And he was serious – and that was it. He was very checked out. I mean, we both did the same thing – he had heard my records, and so we pretty much knew the same stuff – Bobby Bland and Albert King and B.B. King and Albert Collins. And I was like a blues professor. I mean, that's what I knew about. I didn't know anything else; I didn't know how to live; I didn't know how to be a nice guy; I didn't know how to do anything except play guitar. .... If I don't do that, then I'm in trouble. That means you have to go back to the real world, and who wants to do that?

"There was a while [after Stevie moved to Austin] where he would be at my gigs a lot, so then he met everybody, because I was playing every night. Then he started playing around. He would be on this part of the town, and I'd be over here, and then he'd be in this city and I'd be in this city. I felt like there was just a lot of things that we didn't talk about, but we understood. But all this 'strained relationship' stuff, I didn't notice that. Writers wanted to play up the brother rivalry part. To me, I was me and I was out doing my thing, and that was my little brother. And he was great. If I couldn't get 'em,

Stevie and Glenda, Christmas 1971. COURTESY MARTHA VAUGHAN

he would. It's the way I felt, you know, and together they didn't have a chance, you know, other musicians. People always want to know about it, 'How was the sibling rivalry?' Well, there wasn't any that I knew of."[3]

GLENDA MAPLES, Stevie's girlfriend: "Stevie decided to move to Austin, and he wanted me to go. He went down first, and he wrote me ... I can't tell you how many letters back and forth. He was very tender and had a very sweet way about him. I finally got a transfer [at work] and went down about six months later. I worked and put up the money for an apartment. I even ironed his sheets. We were living on the northwest side when we first moved. I had the weirdest dream one night that Stevie got hurt on that side of town, and I just had to move us immediately. Don't ask me why. We lived with Cutter for a while. We lived with Denny [in 1973].

"We lived just a short period with Jimmie. They had kind of a sibling struggle for a long time. I don't want to hurt Jimmie's feelings, but he constantly tried to put Stevie down, which always made me mad, because I was protective of Stevie. They got into more than one fight about who could play the best. But Jimmie would let Stevie sit in at the One Knite. I think they started to see the light when they started sobering up [years later]."

Jimmie's former bandmate Keith Ferguson later described the sibling situation as Stevie being afraid of Jimmie and Jimmie being pissed off that Stevie was even in Austin.[17]

January 28: Waterloo Social Club, Austin, TX (Blackbird)[32]

February 3: Waterloo Social Club, Austin, TX (Blackbird)

Handbill for a Dallas gig by two of the hottest bands in Austin.
© LEW STOKES

February 5: Studio Texas, Dallas, TX (Blackbird) opening for Krackerjack

February 10: Waterloo Social Club, Austin, TX (Blackbird)

February 17: Waterloo Social Club, Austin, TX (Blackbird)

February 19: Waterloo Social Club, Austin, TX (Blackbird)

February 24: Blackbird signs a contract with Charlie Hatchett. Charlie booked many of the hottest bands in Austin for many years.

February 25: Abraxas, Waco, TX (Blackbird)

February 26: Waterloo Social Club, Austin, TX (Blackbird)

February 29: Waterloo Social Club, Austin, TX (Blackbird)

March 2: Waterloo Social Club, Austin, TX (Blackbird)

March 6: South Door, Austin, TX (Blackbird)

March 7: South Door, Austin, TX (Blackbird)

March 8: South Door, Austin, TX (Blackbird)

March 9: South Door, Austin, TX (Blackbird)

March 10: South Door, Austin, TX (Blackbird)

March 11: South Door, Austin, TX (Blackbird)

MARK POLLOCK: "The first time I saw Stevie play was probably at the South Door. They were *loud*. My god they were loud. I mean, they parted your hair and moved it back! They had Marshall stacks. Christian Plicque was dressed in one of those long silk robes. For a boy from Irving, Texas, it was pretty wild. I was a John Lee Hooker, Muddy Waters, Freddie King guy, and they were doing the Allman Brothers, which to me was the Antichrist. But as a musician, I knew it was good. I probably went to see Kim Davis, who is also from Irving.

"Stevie called me one time, probably from a pay phone, says, 'What're you doing?' I said, 'Nothing.' He says, 'I need help.' I

Stevie's first agency contract. COURTESY CHARLIE HATCHETT

think he and Glenda were living at Paul Ray's house on the couch. Whoever hired Stevie had to feed him and put him up. Stevie had some kind of funky color TV and said, 'Can you take this to the pawn shop?' I drove them over there to a pawn shop on Ben White Boulevard, and they loaned him, like, thirty-five bucks so he could eat and buy guitar strings. Guitar strings number one and food second."

LOIS LOEFFLER: "I was a cocktail waitress at the South Door, and Jimmie and Stevie would come in and play. I met Stevie through Jimmie, who I was dating at the time. What I remember about Stevie as a young man is that he was always very sweet, very polite, and he had a great talent. He really put his heart and soul into his music. He idolized his brother.

"I loved the blues back then, and a lot of what I knew about the blues, I learned from Jimmie. Jimmie would compliment Stevie's playing, at least to me he would, but I think Jimmie still felt he was the best in the room. Stevie put just as much intensity into his music, but Jimmie would say, 'Aww, he's just playing loud.'

"I dated Jimmie a little less than six months. In those days people were pretty promiscuous – free love and all that. When I met Jimmie, he came on pretty strong to me. I know he and Connie were involved back then, but Jimmie had lots of girlfriends. The early seventies were so different. Nowadays I'd probably be shocked if I had a daughter and her behavior was like mine back then. There was more of an innocence to it – a communion. You're young, and you don't think about getting older. It was the hippie generation, and moving to Austin in '69 was the first time I had broken away from home. For me, it was like sowing all my wild oats.

"I never saw Jimmie treat Stevie bad, but he played the big brother role to the hilt. From what Keith Ferguson and others would say, it was kind of like, 'I can talk about my family, but [you can't].' I think that's what the role was like between Jimmie and Stevie – kind of a rough older brother, and Stevie was kind of the adoring younger brother.

"I remember one night at the club Jimmie made a comment about Stevie and his girlfriend [Glenda] that 'Well, he might as well be married,' because they were so close. They seemed like first loves, you know.

"Stevie and I became friends when I lived in Austin. He lived on Thornton Road in South Austin – the rent was about $85. He was moving out and knew I was looking for a place, so he got the landlord to rent it to me. He left some pans and things in the house and said those were my housewarming gifts! He was so sweet.

"I think Stevie wanted to make it big time, but I don't know if Stevie thought about a mansion and wanting this, that and the other. I know Jimmie said all he wanted was to be able to play whenever he wanted, to drive old cars, and he wanted me in a white fox outfit sitting next to him in this old car that he could drive around [laughs].

"I never heard Stevie say anything like that. I think Stevie wanted to play for people and to make his brother and family proud of him. When he thought about success, I think success was more of an emotional thing, not just financial freedom or having nice clothes and a great car, have a good-looking girl by your side. I think there were other things that meant success to Stevie."

March 12: University of Texas Department of Comm., Austin, TX (Blackbird)

March 14: Waterloo Social Club, Austin, TX (Blackbird)

March 16: Waterloo Social Club, Austin, TX (Blackbird)

March 17: Texas A&M University, College Station, TX (Blackbird)

March 23: Waterloo Social Club, Austin, TX (Blackbird)

March 24: Rolling Hills Country Club, Austin, TX (Blackbird)

March 25: Waterloo Social Club, Austin, TX (Blackbird)

March 30: Waterloo Social Club, Austin, TX (Blackbird)

At one of the gigs at Waterloo, Noel recalls that Stevie broke a string early in the gig, and they had to send Cutter out to scare up a replacement guitar string because, true to form, neither Stevie nor Kim had an extra set of strings. Club management was none too thrilled at the extra-long break while the band waited for a string to arrive! These were the days when Stevie would stop by Ray Hennig's Heart of Texas Music and ask Ray if he could "borrow" a set of strings for that night's gig. Ray would pitch him the strings and say, "Pay me when you can."

March 31: Rolling Hills Country Club, Austin, TX (Blackbird)

📖 **Spring:** Lancaster High School yearbook contains a photo of Stevie and one of the drummers as Blackbird performed for a school dance. See page 54.

April 1: Rolling Hills Country Club, Austin, TX (Blackbird)

April 6: Waterloo Social Club, Austin, TX (Blackbird)

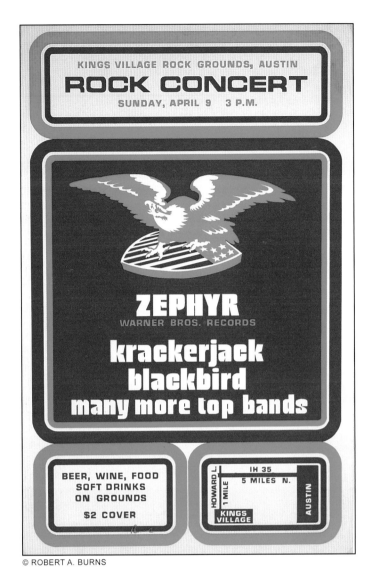

© ROBERT A. BURNS

April 7: private party (Mrs. Wallace Scott) (Blackbird)

April 8: Dobie Center, Austin, TX (Blackbird)

April 9: Kings Village Rock Grounds, Austin, TX (Blackbird).

On April 9 Blackbird, along with Krackerjack, opened for Zephyr featuring Tommy Bolin, who would later join The James Gang and Deep Purple. NOEL DEIS: "I remember Krackerjack and Blackbird did a double-header gig, something that was orchestrated by the booking agents of the time – sort of a poor man's, low-budget pop festival. We were the last act before the main act [Zephyr]. Tommy Bolin was the guitarist. But it had rained, and it was a spot in the middle of a field, basically. It was just a sea of mud." The venue was known to musicians as Rat Flats.

JIM TRIMMIER: "I moved to Austin in '72. This was when Krackerjack was ruling Austin – they were *it*. I remember seeing them many times with John Staehely. Stevie would get us to go

out and see them at the South Door a lot or the Waterloo Social Club. Stevie was living with Tommy Shannon in a house on 16th Street, and Roddy Colonna was there too. Tommy had his little bedroom with Dr. Pepper bottles all over the place – he would sell them. Stevie would just crash on the floor.

"I would follow Blackbird and Krackerjack around, and I remember they played a festival on Howard Lane – Wet Willie was the headliner, and Krackerjack and Blackbird played. Wet Willie walked up to Tommy Shannon, and they went, 'Are you Tommy Shannon? Are you the *real* Tommy Shannon?' They were in awe of Tommy."

MIKE STEELE: "Blackbird was like nothing Austin had seen. It was a big band with a large black guy in a colorful muu-muu and a scarf around his head and big hoop earrings in the early seventies. It was kind of shocking! You had all these other white guys dressed in bell-bottom jeans.

"Christian was very outgoing, very charming; he could really work an audience. He had a whole lot of charisma. He was very articulate and intelligent and a great singer.

"Stevie could do the best version of 'Hideaway,' and that was his signature break song. I used to request it all the time, and

The Burns posters are the earliest known professional, screen printed posters for any of Stevie's bands. © ROBERT A. BURNS

before I could even get it out of my mouth, he'd say, 'I know, I know. I'll play it.' [*Laughs*]"

April 13: Waterloo Social Club, Austin, TX (Blackbird)

April 14: Waterloo Social Club, Austin, TX (Blackbird)

April 20: Waterloo Social Club, Austin, TX (Blackbird)

April 21: Abraxas, Waco, TX (Blackbird)

April 22: venue unknown (Blackbird)

April 27: private party for Susan Woodall (Blackbird)

April 28: private party for Susan Woodall (Blackbird)

April 30: venue unknown (Blackbird)

May 1: South Door, Austin, TX (Blackbird)

May 2: South Door, Austin, TX (Blackbird)

May 3: South Door, Austin, TX (Blackbird)

May 4: South Door, Austin, TX (Blackbird)

May 5: South Door, Austin, TX (Blackbird)

May 6: South Door, Austin, TX (Blackbird)

NOEL: "The South Door was probably our nicest gig, because it had a really good air conditioner [*laughs*]! You could leave that Texas heat in the parking lot. It was a nice club – almost an '80s-style disco decor – kind of slick for a place in Austin at that time. We would hang out there in the afternoon, and one day I was in the pool room and heard a BANG and commotion. I wandered out to see what it was, and Stevie and Kim had burst through the door. Stevie just kind of fell on the floor and they were both laughing and totally drunk. Turned out they had done two Quaaludes each and had been drinking on top of that. You know, people die from that kind of thing. That was the way they lived then."

May 8: Eli's, (Austin?) TX (Blackbird)

May 11: Waterloo Social Club, Austin, TX (Blackbird)

May 12: Mother Earth, Austin, TX (Blackbird)

May 13: Waterloo Social Club, Austin, TX (Blackbird)

May 19: Randolph Air Force Base, near San Antonio, TX (Blackbird)

May 20: Waterloo Social Club, Austin, TX (Blackbird)

May: Blackbird becomes a four-piece, down from seven. Kim and John had moved back to Dallas, David Frame formed Ninth Street with Mike Kindred, Fredde Walden and Jesse Taylor. Tommy Shannon took David's place in Blackbird, joining Stevie and Roddy. Christian Plicque eventually left due to throat problems, probably in the fall, replaced by Bruce Bowland.

DAVID FRAME: "When Blackbird hit town, it seemed like perfect timing. We played to sellout crowds at Mother Earth and The South Door, also Rolling Hills Country Club, which later became the first Soap Creek Saloon.

"Krackerjack broke up in July. At that time, Mike Kindred approached me to start Ninth Street. It was Jesse Taylor on guitar; Mike, keys; me, bass; Fredde Pharoah Walden, drums. I regret leaving Blackbird to this day because I was the oldest in the band and I talked them into moving to Austin, regardless what the books say."

Blackbird showed a lot of promise, but as CHRISTIAN PLICQUE recalls, "There was friction. David wanted to do his own thing. He wanted to sing more in the band, and I wasn't too keen on that idea because that's all I did and felt I would be losing my place. I have never considered myself a great singer, but I love to sing. Technically, David was a better singer than I was. He was moving more into a funk kind of thing as I recall, and Stevie and I weren't ready for that.

"Stevie and Kim had their moments, and we all argued with Noel. Good keyboard player, but from the beginning we teased him for being a pain in the butt. [But] he was well organized and dependable. Roddy,

© ROBERT A. BURNS

Mr. Killer Drummer, was hard to work with at times. Well, let's face it, we were all a pain in the butt, me included!

"It is not true that Stevie didn't like my singing; otherwise we would have never worked together for so many years. Blackbird was a very competitive band. With each other and with other bands. I think that was why we did so well. We had full houses all the time and booked sometimes many months in advance."

RODDY: "I don't think Kim ever liked it much in Austin. He would stay in the apartment all day and then come to the gigs. It never got sour or where they were fighting, but there was less communication and [Stevie and Kim] didn't hook up the sound as well. It started going stale, and one day Kim just said he was moving back to Dallas."

The lineup of Stevie, Bruce, Tommy and Roddy lasted until early December. RODDY: "This other guy tried to join the band – Roy Cox from Houston. He was a bass player and wanted to bump Tommy out of the band [*laughs*]. 'Well, I can play circles around that guy.' He was really obnoxious. He went ahead and just started playing rhythm guitar for a while. He was real flamboyant – looked like Freddy Mercury or something with the cropped top on [*laughs*]!

"That band kind of stumbled around for a while – we were getting some college gigs. Charlie Hatchett was our booking agent. Seems like I fired Roy for driving so reckless I thought we were going to die going to College Station. So it was back to Bruce, Stevie and I and Tommy."

© ROBERT A. BURNS

TOMMY SHANNON: "[Stevie] and I played in a band when he was about sixteen called Blackbird, and then we played together again in Krackerjack. You know, we kind of went our separate ways until we got together again."

RODDY: "Tommy Shannon lived at the big party house, the Krackerjack house. It was a tri-plex over on 16th Street that was 125 years old. Those guys all lived in that place – their road manager Bo, Uncle John, Bruce Bowland and Tommy Shannon. We started going over there a lot. The next year, Uncle John had already left and Bruce had left, and I moved into the middle apartment. It was pretty wild. Stevie and his girlfriend, Glenda

Maples, were having trouble making rent, so they moved in with us. We all lived there for a summer into the fall, experimenting with drugs. The rent was $60 a month, so all Stevie had to come up with was $30. He got to where he couldn't make the rent – but we're making the same exact amount of money. So I just kind of bumped him out of the apartment."

LEW STOKES: "Stevie's humor was very dry and very personal. He was a laugher. He laughed at jokes, but he wasn't a joke teller. When he was living with Glenda Maples, it was like he could go from being a little kid to an old man just walking from the front room to the back room. He was very focused on what his future could hold, but at the same time he was still a kid who hadn't really experienced being a kid. He'd grown up playing in bars, with his dad going with him. That was kind of a big deal that his dad was willing to do that, or he couldn't play."

May 21: Waterloo Social Club, Austin, TX (Blackbird). A headlining gig with former Blackbird members Frame and Kindred opening with their band, Ninth Street.

May 25: Waterloo Social Club, Austin, TX (Blackbird)

May 26: venue unknown (Blackbird)

May 27: Charlie Brown's, (Austin?) TX (Blackbird)

June 1: Waterloo Social Club, Austin, TX (Blackbird)

June 2: Mother Earth, Austin, TX (Blackbird)

June 3: private party for Jack (Orbin?), (Austin?) TX (Blackbird)

June 4: Kings Village Rock Grounds, Austin, TX (Blackbird)

June 4 was a return to "Rat Flats." Again with Krackerjack opening, this time for Sugarloaf, which was riding high on the strength of their debut hit, "Green-Eyed Lady."

The silk-screened Blackbird posters pictured herein were created by Robert A. Burns, who later became the art director for several films, including the classic *Texas Chainsaw Massacre*. He was a world authority on actor Rondo Hatton and a noted genealogist. He took his own life after being diagnosed with terminal cancer at age 60. Burns was known for his wry and irreverent humor, which he displayed when saying goodbye to friends on his website. "I've never understood why people would stay in the theater after it became obvious that the rest of the movie would not be enjoyable," Burns wrote. "Due to physical and psychological reasons too tedious to bore anyone with, it became obvious that the rest of my movie would not be enjoyable, so I left the theater (me and Elvis, you know)."

RODDY COLONNA remembers the posters. "We got together and designed some of those. I think we would get seventy-five for a hundred bucks or something. We would really promote ourselves. We learned that from Uncle John and Krackerjack – they would make posters and distribute them around. They'd buy a keg of beer – 'Free keg of beer,' 'Girls get in free.' We tried all that stuff to get people in. We'd have a packed house."

June 5: The South Door, Austin, TX (Blackbird)

June 6: The South Door, Austin, TX (Blackbird)

June 7: The South Door, Austin, TX (Blackbird)

June 8: The South Door, Austin, TX (Blackbird)

June 9: The South Door, Austin, TX (Blackbird)

June 10: The South Door, Austin, TX (Blackbird)

June 15: Waterloo Social Club, Austin, TX (Blackbird)

June 16: J. Comedy, Austin, TX (Blackbird)

June 17: J. Comedy, Austin, TX (Blackbird)

June 22: Waterloo Social Club, Austin, TX (Blackbird)

June 23: Waterloo Social Club, Austin, TX (Blackbird)

June 24: Waterloo Social Club, Austin, TX (Blackbird)

June 30: Fun Factory, Austin, TX (Blackbird)

July 1: Rolling Hills Country Club, Austin, TX (Blackbird)

July 3: The South Door, Austin, TX (Blackbird)

July 4: The South Door, Austin, TX (Blackbird)

July 5: The South Door, Austin, TX (Blackbird)

July 6: The South Door, Austin, TX (Blackbird)

July 7: The South Door, Austin, TX (Blackbird)

July 8: The South Door, Austin, TX (Blackbird)

July 14: Mother Earth, Austin, TX (Blackbird)

July 15: Rolling Hills Country Club, Austin, TX (Blackbird)

July 21: Mother Earth, Austin, TX (Blackbird)

© ROBERT A. BURNS

© ROBERT A. BURNS, COURTESY STEVE DEAN

© MICHAEL PRIEST

July 26: Waterloo Social Club, Austin, TX (Blackbird)

July 28: Mother Earth, Austin, TX (Blackbird)

July 29: Rolling Hills Country Club, Austin, TX (Blackbird)

August 2: Knights of Columbus Hall, Bryan, TX (Blackbird)

August 3: Rayvell, (Austin?) TX (Blackbird)

August 4: Mother Earth, Austin, TX (Blackbird)

August 5: Galley High, (Austin?) TX (Blackbird)

August 7: The South Door, Austin, TX (Blackbird)

August 8: The South Door, Austin, TX (Blackbird)

August 9: The South Door, Austin, TX (Blackbird)

August 10: The South Door, Austin, TX (Blackbird)

August 11: The South Door, Austin, TX (Blackbird)

August 12: The South Door, Austin, TX (Blackbird)

August 18: private party (Blackbird)

August 19: Waterloo Social Club, Austin, TX (Blackbird)

August 20: King's Village, Austin, TX (Blackbird) opening for Wishbone Ash

Musician and guitar dealer, Tony Dukes: "It was a warm day, the first time I saw Stevie Ray. All you could see was stringy brown locks and a toothy grin over the top of a red Gibson 335 [possibly an Epiphone]. What made you look was *the tone*, a guitar tone that seems to scream and breathe.

"He was playing at King's Village, called by local musicians Rat Flats. Christian Plicque, an avant blues artist, was fronting the band. The music kind of a glam/slam blues-based rock, although there were manly renditions of old blues and soul tunes. I remember the headliner was Wishbone Ash. I left with a promise made to myself to follow both bands.

"One thing that always struck me odd, but identifiable, in my eyes about Stevie – his resilience and his quiet confidence. At the time, Stevie was one step off the main blues guys regiment, from guitars to clothes. When the 'current' blues guys were going

to Strats, Stevie was on a 335 or a weird Rickenbacker. When they were dressing like 'brothers,' Stevie was enjoying colors and absurdities of the time, but with his own concept. In his early days I saw some of the scene discount him and sometimes attempt to ignore him for this, and this is the great, *great* thing about my friend Stevie – he never lost his smile, his energy. I cannot remember him ever dissing or talking bad about someone. Stevie just wanted to smile and check it out and participate. If I were to give him an adjective to describe young Stevie, it would be 'precious.'"

August 24: Rayvell, (Austin?) TX (Blackbird)

August 26: Abraxas, Waco, TX (Blackbird)

August 30: Waterloo Social Club, Austin, TX (Blackbird)

August 31: unknown venue (Blackbird)

September 1: Nickel Keg Saloon, San Marcos, TX (Blackbird)

September 2: private party for Celia Mahan (Blackbird)

September 4: The South Door, Austin, TX (Blackbird)

September 5: The South Door, Austin, TX (Blackbird)

September 6: The South Door, Austin, TX (Blackbird)

September 7: The South Door, Austin, TX (Blackbird)

September 8: The South Door, Austin, TX (Blackbird)

September 9: The South Door, Austin, TX (Blackbird)

September 10: Waterloo Social Club, Austin, TX (Blackbird)

September 14: The South Door, Austin, TX (Blackbird)

September 15: Abraxas, Waco, TX (Blackbird)

September 16: Sabu?, (Austin?) TX (Blackbird)

September 17: Nickel Keg Saloon, San Marcos, TX (Blackbird)

September 18: Nickel Keg Saloon, San Marcos, TX (Blackbird)

September 19: Nickel Keg Saloon, San Marcos, TX (Blackbird)

September 21: private party for Weldon Byrne (Blackbird)

September 22: Crow's Nest, Austin, TX (Blackbird)

September 23: Abraxas, Waco, TX (Blackbird)

September 24: Waterloo Social Club, Austin, TX (Blackbird)

September 27: Mother Earth, Austin, TX (Blackbird)

September 28: Nickel Keg Saloon, San Marcos, TX (Blackbird)

September 29: Nickel Keg Saloon, San Marcos, TX (Blackbird)

September 30: Nickel Keg Saloon, San Marcos, TX (Blackbird)

October 6: The Joint, San Angelo or Conroe, TX (Blackbird)

October 7: The Joint, San Angelo or Conroe, TX (Blackbird)

October 9: The South Door, Austin, TX (Blackbird)

October 10: The South Door, Austin, TX (Blackbird)

October 11: The South Door, Austin, TX (Blackbird)

October 12: The South Door, Austin, TX (Blackbird)

October 13: The South Door, Austin, TX (Blackbird)

October 14: The South Door, Austin, TX (Blackbird)

October 16: Nickel Keg Saloon, San Marcos, TX (Blackbird)

October 17: Nickel Keg Saloon, San Marcos, TX (Blackbird)

October 22: Waterloo Social Club, Austin, TX (Blackbird)

October 28: Waterloo Social Club, Austin, TX (Blackbird)

November 2: Waterloo Social Club, Austin, TX (Blackbird)

November 3: St. Edward's University, Austin, TX (Blackbird)

November 4: private party for Julie Caldwell (Blackbird)

November 9: Waterloo Social Club, Austin, TX (Blackbird)

November 10: Abraxas, Waco, TX (Blackbird)

November 11: Abraxas, Waco, TX (Blackbird)

November 16: Waterloo Social Club, Austin, TX (Blackbird)

November 17: The Joint, San Angelo or Conroe, TX (Blackbird)

November 18: The Joint, San Angelo or Conroe, TX (Blackbird)

November 23: Waterloo Social Club, Austin, TX (Blackbird)

November 30: Waterloo Social Club, Austin, TX (Blackbird)

December 2: Kappa Alpha fraternity, Southwestern University, Georgetown, TX (Blackbird)

December 2 is the last entry for Blackbird in Charlie Hatchett's booking records until December 30-31. It would not be surprising if the band had broken up early in the month but had the 30th and New Year's Eve gigs planned well in advance. Stevie probably moved into Krackerjack at this time.

RODDY: "... Then one day Stevie says, 'Hey, we're getting Uncle John. I felt betrayed and all that. Robin Syler came along and Stevie started playing with that band."

BRUCE BOWLAND: "Me and Uncle John left Krackerjack and moved to Houston to play in a band called Rattlesnake. We had Benny Valerio on guitar. We called him José Hendrix because he was left-handed. The bass player was Roy Cox from Bubble Puppy. Every weekend that we didn't play, I would come back to Austin. That band lasted for the summer, and I moved back to Austin, and Tommy Shannon was already playing with Blackbird. I forget exactly how it took place, but me and Uncle John ended up playing in Blackbird because Krackerjack had dismantled.

"We played at this little-bitty club in San Marcos, right on the river. The stage was that

Krackerjack: Uncle John Turner, Bruce Bowland, Tommy Shannon, Robin Syler, Stevie Vaughan.
© CHERRY RAINS, COURTESY CUTTER BRANDENBURG

tall [indicates a few inches]. I can't remember the name of the club [Nickel Keg Saloon], but when they did the poster, the street was LBJ, spelled El Bee Jay [laughs]. One of those hippie thangs. [There are many streets in Texas named for President Lyndon B. Johnson.]

"We were doing 'Ain't Superstitious,' and for me and Stevie it just seemed to click. That was a magic moment, and at the end of the tune everyone was 'Wooo!' We just looked at each other ... 'That's what it's about.'

"Even offstage, rarely did I see Stevie without his guitar slung over his shoulder. He was one of those guys who just walked around the house and picked. He'd sit there and talk to you and he'd be picking. About the only time he'd take it off is when he'd go to the bathroom. He had a burning desire, not to be famous, but to be good as he possibly could be. Back then everybody had a pat answer to the question, 'What is your goal?' The response was, 'To make it,' and you wanted to be proud of what you were doing.

"I don't recall ever having a cross word with him. He always seemed to be in an up mood. One time, we had played in Houston and were coming back to Austin in my little Fiat station wagon. Roddy, Tommy, Stevie and me, and as much stuff as we could get in the back. The sun wasn't up yet, but it was 3:30 or 4:00 in the morning, and I ran out of gas. I pulled over to the side of the road, and I didn't even have to ask – Stevie volunteered to walk with me.

"I'm not going to say it was summer, but it was warm – we didn't have jackets on. So he said, 'Which way do you want to go?' I said, 'Well, I know there's a town behind us, and I don't know how far the next one is up front, so let's go back.' We walked this little two-lane country road for *hours* – maybe three. It was quiet, and we talked. We covered a lot of subject matter. We got to this little town and this gas station had just opened up. We got some gas in a can and the guy put us in his wrecker and drove us back to the car. We put the gas in, started up, rounded the corner – there's another town [laughs]! Stevie didn't call me stupid or nothin'; he said, 'Well, that's just how it is.' We never discussed philosophy, which was good because I didn't have a philosophy back then! I was just a day-to-day kind of guy. Life was good.

"Cutter used to live with our equipment in a corrugated metal building with his dog Toke. He would lock himself up in this building, and he had this little TV set. The police knew he was there and would come by and check on him. I remember the only time it snowed in Austin, I went by there and he had a little toaster oven that he'd make raison toast with orange marmalade. I would bring some kind of schnapps or something. I'd wake him up at three in the morning and sit in there and have a few drinks and toast, and then I'd go [*laughs*]."

BRUCE: "Blackbird at that point was a four-piece. Roddy was gone. We decided that if we called it Krackerjack (since there were three founding members in the band) we could make more money. When we reformed as Krackerjack, we had two guitarists – Robin Syler and Stevie.

"Blackbird was doing covers, but making them their own, so that they were almost as good as doing originals. At that time, if you went into a club in Austin and said you were a cover band, they'd thumb their noses at you. You had to play original music. So when we reformed as Krackerjack, we played ninety-five percent original music, but I don't recall writing any new material with Stevie and Robin in the band. Mike Kindred had contributed the most, and I wrote some with Mike. 'Chicken Slacks' was a group endeavor, but as the guy who wrote the words, I got half of it.

"We didn't play 100% Krackerjack tunes, but we took what we could work up real good in a short period of time and blended it in with choice R&B covers and tried to make them our own. Krackerjack went through a lot of guitar players – Jesse Taylor, Robin Syler (twice), Stevie, John Staehely – and with every guitar player, they lent their special touch and it made all the songs sound a bit different.

"Krackerjack played The Black Queen, Mother Earth and The South Door primarily. We were really, really popular but never made any records. It was unbelievable. We had been given a record offer, but it was declined by a person in the band who thought we could do better. London Records – good enough."

And so the revolving door of bands and band members had turned again; Krackerjack was now Uncle John Turner (drums), Tommy Shannon (bass), Bruce Bowland (vocal), Stevie and Robin Syler (guitars).

Keyboard player MIKE KINDRED had left Krackerjack by this time but recalls the band's music was very guitar friendly. "Bruce and I had a couple of songs from The Mystics that worked, but we tried some other things in California, and Unc and Tommy were just, 'No, no, don't do that.' So we got back to Austin and started clicking after we came up with the first couple of riff rockers. Primarily Bruce and myself, and some input from Unc – we came up with about twenty tunes that were clearly Krackerjack tunes, all pretty much riff rockers. That's why we were able to replace guitar players without missing a step, because the tunes were so easily played by guitar players – anyone who had that big,

Claptonesque, Hendrixesque style at that time could easily walk in and do the gig."

GLENDA: "That's when we lived in the big house near the Capitol. Tommy had one apartment; Stevie, I, Roddy and Jackie had the middle; and then Uncle John and Jill had the third. It was like a party place where Johnny Winter came and some black guitar player that fell off the stage at the One Knite. The band was harder rock and roll. It was more about the act – it seemed commercialized. I don't think it was really Stevie's style."

December 7: Nickel Keg Saloon, San Marcos, TX (Krackerjack). Free beer from 8:00 to 8:30.

December 8: Nickel Keg Saloon, San Marcos, TX (Krackerjack)

December 9: Nickel Keg Saloon, San Marcos, TX (Krackerjack)

© LEW STOKES

BRUCE: "The jeans everyone was wearing back then didn't have hip pockets – they were Land Lubbers. Stevie carried a VERY thick wallet – his life was in that wallet – and he put it in his left [front] pocket. Even when he had his guitar on, it looked like he had a fuckin' loaf of bread in his pocket! Everyone was on him when we played. 'Stevie! Take your wallet out of your pocket!'

His focus was on the music, and how he looked didn't matter. It became more important later, but it didn't set in early."

December 14: Waterloo Social Club, Austin, TX (Krackerjack)

December 15: Waterloo Social Club, Austin, TX (Krackerjack)

December 16: Waterloo Social Club, Austin, TX (Krackerjack)

December 18: Mother Earth, Austin, TX (Krackerjack)

December 19: Mother Earth, Austin, TX (Krackerjack)

December 20: Mother Earth, Austin, TX (Krackerjack)

December 21: Mother Earth, Austin, TX (Krackerjack)

December 22: Mother Earth, Austin, TX (Krackerjack)

December 23: Mother Earth, Austin, TX (Krackerjack)

December 25: Rayvell, (Austin?) TX (Krackerjack)

December 28: Waterloo Social Club, Austin, TX (Krackerjack)

December 29: Black Queen, Austin, TX (Krackerjack)

December 30: Abraxas, Waco, TX (Blackbird)

Christmas 1972. Jimmie and daughter Tina, Big Jim, Jimmie's wife Donna (center), Stevie, Glenda Maples. COURTESY MARTHA VAUGHAN

December 31: Abraxas, Waco, TX (Blackbird)

Blackbird continued without Stevie at some point (Charlie booked them March 31, 1973, at Abraxas, for example). Stevie probably moved into Krackerjack after the December 2nd gig, and whether he played these two gigs in Waco is unknown. Given that these were year-ending gigs, including New Year's Eve, it is possible the dates were booked well in advance and that Stevie fulfilled the date with Blackbird. However, enough time had elapsed since early December that Blackbird may have picked up another guitarist for these gigs at the end of the year.

A subsequent incarnation of Blackbird formed back in Dallas with Christian singing, Noel playing keyboards, Carter Buschardt on drums and Jack Morgan on guitar, but it was short-lived. They reportedly recorded a single.

1973

January 3: Black Queen, Austin, TX (Krackerjack)

© LEW STOKES

January 7: The Black Queen, Austin, TX (Krackerjack) Storm headlines a benefit for "Freaky" Fredde "Pharoah" Walden, with Krackerjack, Glory, Phoenix and Southern Feelin', the latter featuring W.C. Clark and Angela Strehli.

BRUCE BOWLAND: "We did a benefit for [drummer] Fred Walden because he'd cut his hand and people thought he wasn't going to be able to play again. We all got together and did this day-long thing and raised about $1500 for him." Fredde's hand was in a cast, but he would get it wet and stick the drumstick down inside it so he could play.

January 10: Black Queen, Austin, TX (Krackerjack)

January 12: Abraxas, Waco, TX (Krackerjack)

January 13: Abraxas, Waco, TX (Krackerjack)

January 14: Mother Earth, Austin, TX (Krackerjack)

January 19: The Joint, San Angelo or Conroe, TX (Krackerjack)

January 20: The Joint, San Angelo or Conroe, TX (Krackerjack)

January 21: Rayvell, (Austin?) TX (Krackerjack)

January 24: Black Queen, Austin, TX (Krackerjack)

January 28: Mother Earth, Austin, TX (Krackerjack), with The Werewolves

January 31: Black Queen, Austin, TX (Krackerjack)

It is unclear when Stevie left Krackerjack and joined Stump, but it was probably some time in late January or early February. Some gigs for both bands are listed.

February 3: St. Edward's University, Austin, TX (Krackerjack)

February 4: Black Queen, Austin, TX (Krackerjack), with The Werewolves

February 9: Abraxas, Waco, TX (Krackerjack)

February 10: Abraxas, Waco, TX (Krackerjack)

February 17: Rayvell, (Austin?) TX (Krackerjack)

February 23: Black Queen, Austin, TX (Krackerjack)

© KERRY AWN

February 24: Black Queen, Austin, TX (Krackerjack)

LEW STOKES: "There were so many people that became his mentors – W.C. Clark, specifically. So much of Stevie's understanding of bass guitar and rhythm guitar – that's straight from W.C. Clark as a teacher. Stevie was a sponge. If somebody would teach him, he was ready to say, 'When and where? I'm ready to sit down.' He loved to learn and to innovate."

After a few months, Uncle John brought in Gary Myrick and Mark Stimson to replace Stevie and Robin Syler. TOMMY SHANNON: "It was kind of a Led Zeppelin kind of band – more of a pop rock band, really. We all wore these high-heel boots with these big square toes and bell-bottoms and ruffled shirts. There was some pressure put on [Stevie]. You know, we gotta dress like this and have this image and all that. Everybody had the shag haircuts and he felt uncomfortable with that. It never really was his style, but he tried doing it. He'd come up with some pretty wild outfits sometimes [*laughs*].[3] It became a really good band – we started packing every place we played. Just as things started to get real good, we broke up. We got a record deal and broke up."

© ROBERT A. BURNS

BRUCE: "That version of Krackerjack [with Stevie] didn't last long. We did it to keep playing and make money. Then we got Gary Myrick, and Mark Stimson joined us. Stevie and Doyle went out and played with Marc Benno. The big theory about why Stevie left the band is because he wouldn't wear eye makeup and Uncle John wanted him to. That just wasn't the case. He didn't ask anyone else to wear eye makeup, so why ask Stevie? That's just BS. Stevie had played in Blackbird with Kim Davis, so I don't think it was competition between him and Robin. Either we didn't give it time to gel, or ... they didn't dislike each other, but they didn't hang out together either. I can't tell you why, but it just didn't work."

📷**February 25:** The South Door, Austin, TX. Billed as "Jim and Stevie Vaughan & Friends Jam, plus Mama's Cookin.'"

- shuffle
- Tramp
- Barefootin'
- Lucille
- Lickin' Stick
- Mustang Sally
- Little Bit
- So Long
- Ooh Poo Pah Doo
- For Your Precious Love
- You Upset Me Baby

BRUCE: "It was a Sunday afternoon gig, billed as Jimmie, Stevie and Friends. It was me [vocals], Jimmie, Stevie, David Frame [bass], Mike Kindred [keyboards], Uncle John Turner [drums], Fredde Walden [drums and vocals], Paul Henry Ray [vocals]. And then it just turns into chaos, because it went from noon until midnight.

"The day of the gig, Jimmie came by – his girlfriend had a great big El Dorado convertible – with Keith Ferguson. It was Sunday before noon, and everyone had played the night before. He comes knockin' on the door, 'Y'all need to come down here.' After a little hair of the dog, everybody kind of loosened up. Some of it [was] really good, and some of it really sucks. It turned into such a fiasco that it ceased being 'Jimmie, Stevie and Friends' and turned into whoever walked in and picked up something could get on stage.

"[After the first few songs] Fredde came down and Uncle John played drums. Me and Fredde attempted to do James Brown's 'Lickin' Stick.' The groove is real good and the heart is there, but sometimes the intonation is not so good. You can hear the difference between Stevie and Jimmie.

"I remember we were trying to get levels for the recording, and I was trying to get Stevie to just say 'test' in my microphone. He wouldn't do it. He was petrified. He was that shy. It didn't piss me off, but it irritated me because I was back with the sound man trying to help get levels. Of course, he turned into a fine singer."

MIKE STEELE: "Jimmie was more of a blues purist. Stevie thought the world of Jimmie's guitar playing. He'd tell you, 'Jimmie's a better guitar player than me. He only plays a fraction of what he knows.' And I always said, 'Well, why the hell doesn't he play the rest?' [*Laughs*] Which, occasionally, he does. Someone said, 'I didn't know Jimmie could play like that.' Well, yeah, when he wants to."

Stevie joins the band Stump. The band consisted of former Blackbird bassist David Frame, Jeff Clark (guitar), Tom Holden (drums). After Stevie left, Stump became Too Smooth. March 1 is the first listing for Stump in Charlie Hatchett's book, but the dates Stevie was in the band are not certain.

February 28: Black Queen, Austin, TX (Stump)

March 1: venue unknown (Stump)

March 2: The Joint, city unknown, TX (Stump)

DAVID FRAME: "Stump played originals – a lot of stuff that Jeff Clark had written. Stevie basically had to learn parts. I was writing also: my stuff was more rhythm and blues; Jeff was more rock and roll. That's the way Krackerjack and everybody was – it was kind of Texas rock, it was a southern deal – rock with soul.

Original drawing by Stevie Vaughan from photo of David Frame. © STEVIE RAY VAUGHAN, COURTESY DAVID FRAME

March 7: Black Queen, Austin, TX (Stump)

March 14: Black Queen, Austin, TX (Stump)

© KERRY AWN

TONY DUKES: "I remember seeing Stump's first gig at the Black Queen, and we went out to the pancake house, and that was the most excited I'd ever seen Jeff Clark, because Stevie was there. Before he left, he took syrup and wrote 'Stump' on the table. Stevie went into that gig and just demolished the stage. It was one of the first bands where they really let Stevie loose, and he did everything but tear the paint off the wall."

JEFF CLARK: "Phoenix was a band that Tom Holden and I had together, and when the lead guitarist had an opportunity to go with Michael Murphey and record, then the bass player said, 'I've had enough of this as well.' Tom and I were then looking for a bass player and guitarist to go a different direction. We had heard Blackbird a number of times, Stevie and the other guitarist and David, and had kind of gotten to know each other casually. We approached them about joining us. We may have still been called Phoenix for a while, but we knew it was not the same band at all, and the direction had somewhat changed.

"When I think back to those days, those people [who saw our shows] had no idea who was on that stage. We played a high school party from 2:00 to 4:00 in the morning in Andrews, Texas, up in the panhandle – they had no idea who was on that stage. If there was a picture and they got a magnifying glass, 'Oh my god! That's Stevie Ray Vaughan!'

"I remember one show at Mother Earth where we opened up for John Lee Hooker, and of course Stevie was extra-excited about that. When Hooker was on stage sitting down in a chair, he actually asked Stevie and me to come up and play a song with him. Stevie was excited about that, and I was not so much excited as nervous [*laughs*]. I remember getting up there, and we both took solos. It was the only time I can remember Stevie outwardly complimenting me in the time we were together.

"I don't think Stevie was fully equipped at the time. He used one of my spare Marshall heads, and I know he had a guitar, but he liked one of my guitars. I knew the guy had great talent and potential. Tom and I had started writing our own music, not near as blues as what David and Stevie had, so we kind of had a slight conflict of influences and styles. We got over that and played some of this and some of that.

"I remember Marc Benno being the guy who enticed Stevie away from us, and it was not a communicated departure – he just didn't show up for a gig. He didn't call or anything. Put ol' Jeff on the spot. It was an outdoor one-day festival out south of town near Dripping Springs or Wimberley."

TOM HOLDEN: I think Stevie played with us less than a month, but I really don't remember how long it was. It was obvious he'd rather play with a blues band than a rock and roll band. It was pretty much like the Too Smooth rock and roll. Mostly originals; I don't think we were covering much back then. He was pretty amazing, even back then. He had magic fingers – he always had."

"There's [an item of] Stevie's artwork of him drawing me, and it says 'France Stump,' and [he signed it] 'Skeeter Ray.' Skeeter was kind of his nickname between a few of us – he was still going by Little Stevie. France was a reference to me wearing a French tam, and they called me France. Stump was together probably two or three months. Stevie left with Doyle to join Marc Benno and went to California.

"Ninth Street was together until the fall of 1972. Mike and Fredde went to Storm, Jimmie Vaughan's band. I joined Phoenix, which later became Too Smooth, a hot rock band in Austin. Between Phoenix and Too Smooth was a band called Stump – me, bass; Stevie, guitar; Jeff Clark, guitar; Tom Holden, drums. This group only lasted a short period. I believe it was from February to April, when Marc Benno came into town and picked up Stevie and Doyle Bramhall for The Nightcrawlers. Stump was a rock band, and Stevie was getting weary of rock. He really wanted to go towards the blues at this time. I vividly remember he invited me, Tom Holden, Jeff Clark over. He had something to tell us. That was it – joining the Nightcrawlers."

March 14: Marc Benno and the Nightcrawlers forms. Guitarist Charlie Freeman had overdosed on heroin before recording began, so the band was Benno, vocals and guitar; Stevie, guitar; Doyle Bramhall, vocals and drums; Billy Etheridge, keyboards; and Tommy McClure, bass.

Marc Benno, a Dallas native, had worked with Leon Russell, The Doors and Rita Coolidge. Jimmie Vaughan declined Benno's request to join the band but suggested Stevie.

MARC: "Jimmie was truly a purist, and they were doing things that were absolutely authentic in covering old tunes, and they were great at it. So my stuff to him was almost like pop music. It was not going to be pure blues. It's all a matter of timing. I had started when I was very young and had already been to Hollywood and had some success, and by that time I was already into, 'Okay, let's create some original hits here.' I didn't need to be doing anybody else's music anymore. We were in two different places at the time."

DOYLE: "Benno had called Jimmie about joining the band, and Jimmie said, 'No thanks, but my brother might like to do it.' Stevie approached me and said, 'Marc has a tour lined up and he has an opportunity to record an album.' Neither one of us had been in the studio that much. Except for a few gigs, we had barely even played music out of Texas."

MARC: "Being around Stevie was like being around a basketball star with a basketball. He would walk around the house with the guitar. Whatever he was doing, whatever little chore, he had the guitar. I went through a phase where I slept with my guitar, but

Poster from what may have been Stevie's first gig with Marc Benno and the Nightcrawlers. © RAM

never like him. The things he could do with a guitar – he was like an acrobat."[33]

March 16: Flight 505, Austin, TX (Stump)

March 17: Black Queen, Austin, TX (Stump)

March 18: South Door, Austin, TX (Nightcrawlers). Probably Stevie's first gig with the Nightcrawlers.

March 21: Black Queen, Austin, TX (Stump)

March 25: outside Dripping Springs, TX (Stump) opening for Nitzinger. This is probably the gig Jeff Clark recalls when Stevie had quit the band and didn't show up.

Glenda Maples recalls that for the first time in a while, there was money. "The record company put up some money – Stevie thought he was rich. I think he got $1200 and an airfare out there. It was like we were millionaires.

"All the other guys were taking their old ladies or their wives. I didn't say anything at first; I was just going to let Stevie deal with it. They were getting ready to leave and he goes, 'Okay. I'm giving you this money – I want you to get on an airplane and meet me out there. And it took just about all the money to get me out there, and we only had about $100 left for eight days while they were recording out there. We were just watching everybody eating. We'd take five dollars here and five dollars there to eat [*laughs*].

"But it was fun. One of the Monkees, Mickey [Dolenz] picked us up at the airport! We went all around L.A., but we were in the studio most of the time. There was anything you wanted in the studio. It was fun watching them put it together, but then it was never released. It turned out to be more about Doyle and Stevie than a Marc Benno album."

April 2: The Nightcrawlers begin recording, Sunset Sound studios, Hollywood, California for A&M Records. Marc Benno (vocal, guitar), Doyle Bramhall (vocal, drums), Stevie (guitar), Billy Etheridge (B-3 organ), Tommy McClure (bass); Plas Johnson added on sax. Gordon DeWitty played on one session.

– Dirty Pool (April 4 session)
– Coffee Cup (April 10 session)
– 8 Ball
– Take Me Down Easy
– Love is Turning Green (April 4 session)
– Hot Shoe Blues (April 10 session)
– Mellow Monday
– Crawlin'
– Last Train

Several years later, Stevie would note that these sessions produced his first two efforts at writing songs – "Dirty Pool" and "Crawlin'." With the exception of "Boiler Maker" in 1975, there is no record of Stevie doing much more writing until 1978, after he had started his own band.

DOYLE: "For me it was kind of interesting, because it was a Benno record, and I remember singing most of the songs.[1] During [the recording sessions] there was a lot of drinking. In our [contract] rider, besides the sandwiches and whatever, there was a case of quarts of Tanqueray gin. Every day that was what they brought us from the liquor store down the street. And that did not even include the beer that they brought in. I remember being there one night and Kris Kristofferson came in, and that was during his wild period too. He ended up leaving because we were so out of it."[3]

There has been some conflict regarding song writing credit for "Dirty Pool." Stevie and Doyle maintain that they wrote it together. Benno has claimed at least partial credit. The liner notes for his album state, "All songs written by Marc Benno / Marc Benno and the Nightcrawlers." Glenda Maples recalls that Stevie and Doyle wrote it.

MARC: "The 'Dirty Pool' thing was kind of a mix-up. Stevie contributed to that song originally by adding a lead guitar lick, which I considered arrangement, not writing. I considered that Doyle and I had written that song. I guess he never forgave me for that, and I should have just given him credit, but the way I see it, the song was all about the progression and the lyrics. So later he just took everything out of the song that I wrote and did a couple of verses written by Doyle, but those verses were written by Doyle and I.

"Crawlin' was Stevie's deal – he had that lick. I think the band came up with that '*I'm down, I'm crawlin', no use in hollerin'*,' where we all sang along. That was just a great instrumental that he had come up with.

"We couldn't get anyone to sing on it; everybody was real intimidated besides me and Doyle. Nobody else in the band would sing. We had to keep moving the mic around until, finally, the only place that they were comfortable was where we couldn't see them. So we took a hundred-foot mic cable out into the street on Sunset Boulevard. We had it strung down the hallway, but we could still see them.

"It was really a case of them being real shy, and it shows you how far Stevie came to being such a powerful singer. It was a deep secret that he was working on, and when he did display this talent, I was blown away. I loved his voice."

The experience in Hollywood paid dividends for the emerging musician. Stevie was a guitarist but was beginning to learn how to sing from Doyle. Benno sees it as Stevie stockpiling his talent until he could burst onto the scene with his first record years later. "Everybody played great, but it wasn't my sound at all. I think he

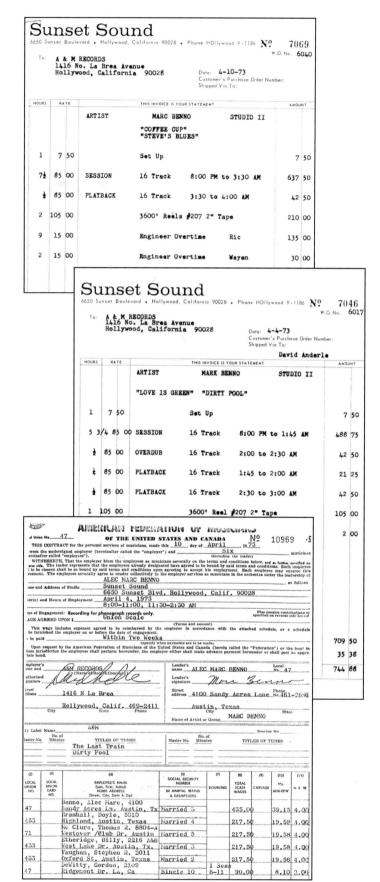

Studio billing and wage reports from The Nightcrawlers' sessions. COURTESY TEXAS STATE UNIVERSITY SOUTHWESTERN WRITERS COLLECTION

saw what was going on and thought, 'No. I'm not doing anything until I've got it down pat. Once we walk into [the studio], you won't be able to take it away from us.' He learned a lot from what was going on. He saw how engineers and producers could take away your sound, and once you got under contract you kind of had to work with them. You couldn't tell them you didn't want any of it. In frustration, you would let them have their way at the cost of the sound of the music.

"Stevie got to see big touring, full-blown recording. A lot of that helps when you step out on the stage [as a band leader] for the first time – you're not starting from Austin. He was not born in a club in Austin and discovered. He had that Hollywood experience and took it back to Austin with all the soul he had, but he had some business

At Sunset Sound recording what would have been his first album, had it been released.
© BOB JENKINS, COURTESY MARC BENNO

experience too. My experience came through Leon Russell, and Leon was really one of the first southern guys to ever go to Hollywood in the early sixties, and he carved a niche for others to come across the desert and make it."

RODDY COLONNA: "I remember Stevie calling me from a pay phone in Hollywood, 'Hey man, you'll never believe this. Chuck Berry just drove by!' [*Laughs*]"

DOYLE: "We were in Studio A, and it was when Ringo [Starr] was doing the *Ringo* album. People were in and out – Mickey Dolenz was one of the many background singers on 'I'm Crawlin'.' In studio B, we knew John Lennon, George Harrison, Ringo and Jim Keltner were back there. I went back and looked though the window in the door, and they were all sitting around with guitars and drums.

"The next day we got a call from David Anderle, the producer. 'Y'all need to come up to the office; someone wants to meet you.' Of course we were busy being idiots. He called about three times and said, 'You guys ... you missed him.' We said, 'What?' He said, 'George Harrison was up here and he stayed thirty minutes thinking y'all were coming up.'"

BILLY: "I walked in the can and was standing there taking a leak; looked over and there was Ringo Starr! Over at the sink was George Harrison. I said, 'Well, shit, man! You're Ringo fuckin' Starr!' [*Laughs*] We snorted a little coke with them, and down the way we went.

"Al Kooper was out there, and I never had any respect for him. Back in those days I was a heinous little bastard, and people I didn't respect I fucked with. I had some White Crosses (the equivalent of real dense aspirin), and of course cocaine was big out there at that time. I smashed up these White Crosses and told him it was cocaine. He snorted a ton of it and was trying to be cool, but it must have hurt like hell – like snorting dirt."

DOYLE: "Andy Williams came to the session with his wife or girlfriend – the one that killed a guy in Aspen a few years later. [Claudine Longet was convicted of criminal negligence in the shooting of champion skier "Spider" Sabich.] They were in the studio, and Andy was real drunk and passed out. [Billy adds that Andy was drunk on Uzo.]

"Rita Coolidge and Kris Kristofferson came in one day, and Bonnie Bramlett came in and helped sing backup. There were people in and out all the time. It was the old Charlie Chaplin studio, and there was a big room where they used to do the filming, and there were basketball goals at each end. Around the walls were all these road cases with 'Billy Preston and the God Squad' on the sides.

"The studio was right off Sunset Boulevard, and the hotel was across the street from the Playboy Club. I remember waking up one day, and I had a little balcony, opened the curtains and couldn't see but barely past the balcony because the smog was so bad. You couldn't see the Playboy Club across the street, and it was a ten-story building or whatever. That was probably at the peak of L.A.'s smog problem.

"We went to Barney's Beanery down the street, a famous place where musicians would go and eat and hang out. But as far as recording, we were serious. We were partying a lot, but there was some good music being made in there.

"I remember being in the hotel elevator one night after recording. We're in ragged jeans and T-shirts, and these guys get on, and they're definitely more upscale than we were. One of them said something, and they were English, and Billy said something – I thought we were going to get into with these guys on the elevator. Come to find out it was two or three of the Moody Blues."

BILLY ETHERIDGE: "We were all cocky and gunslingers. Nobody was intimidated or nervous, but we were optimistic and hopeful. It was a real good chance for us. We didn't work in the daytime. We'd have a late dinner and go in about nine and put in our order each night. [One of us] always wanted five or six cases of beer, I'd always have a fifth of Tanqueray – they ordered all of our alcohol and drugs and had it brought in. It was like Mardi Gras at our session. A lot of powder. We'd spend a few hours getting lubed up and then start rolling the tapes and work all night."

DOYLE: "I think we went out there a couple of tunes short. I wrote the music to 'Coffee Cup,' and Benno wrote the words. We did a tune called 'Crawlin'' and couldn't get the sound the way we wanted it. Stevie came up with the lick, and we just played with it. We didn't have any words, so we just started hollerin', and within a few minutes, we had what it is. We went into the bathroom to try to get the vocal sound we wanted – that didn't work; it echoed like hell. We all ended up outside the studio on the sidewalk doing the vocal parts of the tune. We were all outside yellin' and screamin'. We got people on the street to join in, 'I'm down, I'm crawlin', no use in hollerin'. David Anderle said, 'I should have known this shit was going to wind up on the street.'"

The sessions were important to the guys, and they were bitterly disappointed when the album was shelved. DOYLE: "We wanted to go to that next level, whatever that was. We worked real hard on the songs, and when we found out even before we finished the project that A&M didn't want anything to do with it, we were disappointed. We ended up coming back to Austin and within probably a month Marc Benno and the Nightcrawlers broke up for a couple of months."[3]

BILLY: "The story I got from the producer, David Anderle, was that he thought it was a terrific album, and after having heard it, the tapes were good but probably needed mixing. We got back to Austin, looking forward to money and a tour, and apparently Marc had walked into Jerry Moss's office [the "M" in A&M Records] and Moss wanted to do some things with the album – add some horns and whatever. Marc told him no, and from what Anderle told me, Moss said, 'Well, Marc, it's been nice doing business with you,' and that was that."

May 2: South Door, Austin, TX (Stump)

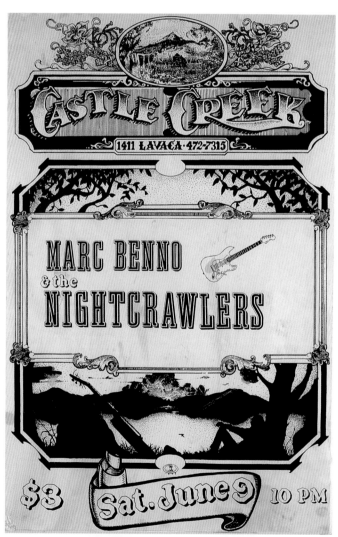

COLLECTION OF CRAIG HOPKINS

May 3: South Door, Austin, TX (Stump)

May 4: South Door, Austin, TX (Stump)

The above three Stump dates are included on the chance that Stevie played with that band after returning from California and before The Nightcrawlers went on tour with Humble Pie, but it is unlikely he did.

June 9: Castle Creek, Austin, TX (Nightcrawlers)

Summer: Hollywood, FL (Nightcrawlers) opening on tour for J. Geils Band and Humble Pie

Summer: Brooklyn Academy of Music, Brooklyn, NY (Nightcrawlers) opening for B.B. King and Humble Pie

(date unknown): Flight 505, Austin, TX (Marc Benno and the Nightcrawlers)

MARC: "Bill Campbell came to the gig, and he was a very tough player. He always called Stevie 'Little Magic Man.' He kept telling me [in gruff voice], '*I'm* the blues player – can I sit in, Benno?' I said, 'Yeah, you can sit in,' because I didn't want him to beat the hell out of me! Stevie says, 'Well, he's not using *my* guitar.'

"So halfway through one of the tunes in the last set I heard this unbelievable racket that was kind of weird. I finally turned around to see what's going on back there – is that some kind of new reverb effect or something? I could hear reverb springs and all kinds of shit. It was Bill *wrestling* the guitar off of Stevie! He was standing behind him over his shoulder and trying to pull the guitar up over his head. Stevie was fighting him and finally he wrestled the guitar off of him and Stevie got really mad. 'I told you I didn't want him to sit in.'

"So the stage was about ten feet off the dance floor, and instead of taking the steps down the side, in a rage he just kind of walked straight off the stage, but he hit the P.A. [speaker] column, and the column stopped him from walking off the front of the stage. It fell about ten feet and landed on this little co-ed girl's knee, and I mean it cut her up.

"Stevie went running around the side of the stage and started paying medical attention to her, and it was really kind of a sweet scene. Bill was screaming at the top of his lungs, no P.A. or nothing, and you could hear him all over the club, 'STEVIE! STEVIE! DAMN IT, STEVIE! ...' Finally, Stevie turns around [and says in an exasperated tone], 'What??' Bill says, 'Everything okay?' 'Yeah, she's gonna be all right.' Bill says, 'Fuck her, I'm talking about the P.A.' Stevie looked at me like, "See what I meant?' That just kind of shows you the personalities that were going on there."

GLENDA recalls going out to the Bennos' home on Lake Austin: "They had a boat and took Stevie out to ski. He came back with rope burns on his legs and was in dire pain. His thighs were bleeding. [On other occasions] Kris Kristofferson and Rita Coolidge would come out there. That's also when the heavier drugs started showing up too."

Stevie and niece Tina.
COURTESY MARTHA VAUGHAN

MARC: "Stevie used to walk around the house doing those figure eights and things, playin' the guitar behind his back, practicing balancing while standing on top of it. He never seemed to put it down – he'd be talking on the phone with the guitar, eating dinner with the guitar on. Never took it off.

"One of the things he would say was, 'I've got to hurry; I'll never make it to age 30.' I said, 'Man, you don't want to say that – what are you sayin' that for?' He said, ' 'Cuz I'm never gonna make it past age 30. I've already seen that.'

"[The tour] was right up until the summer – probably about two months. One tour with Humble Pie and J. Geils; we went on their American tour."

TONY DUKES: "By this time Stevie was a force to be reckoned with. His cutting chops and improved, showy appearance demanded attention from the audience, and he got it, and they loved it."

Summer: After probably less than ten gigs with Marc Benno, the band breaks up and Stevie and Doyle go back to Austin and form the "new" Nightcrawlers: SRV, Doyle Bramhall (drums, vocal), Bruce Miller (bass), Billy Etheridge (keyboards), and later, Ronnie Bramhall (B-3) and Drew Pennington (harp). They hold down the Tuesday night gigs at the One Knite in Austin.

BILLY: "We were blowing people away at our gigs around Austin, and we played Mother Blues in Dallas all the time. But we were staying too wasted."

DOYLE: "Ronnie played organ off and on for about two months and a handful of gigs. Maybe through the summer."

LEW STOKES: "People don't really get it that into the early seventies, making $60-$65 a week was what you got at a straight job. The One Knite was pass-the-hat, and if you made ten, twelve, fifteen bucks for two sets, that was a pretty good deal. A $200-night split four or five ways was pretty much as good as it got for a good-sized club. So if you made forty bucks and you go out to eat after the gig, spend $5, you just spent an eighth of your take!

"If you were at a club that didn't give a bar tab to the band, when the gig's over you *owe* money. That was not unusual. That was a real shocker. 'We just drove here, paid for gas, played our butts off and now we gotta pay *you*?' There's something wrong with this picture!"

Stevie's copy of "Texas Flood" showing extreme wear.
COLLECTION OF CRAIG HOPKINS

DENNY FREEMAN: "Hardly anybody had much money, especially musicians. It was a totally different time, and when you're younger you mainly just want to have a good time. We just wanted to be in a band and earn our money. We didn't make much money, but most people had roommates or girlfriends. When Stevie and Glenda lived with us, it was my girlfriend's house. It was big enough for two couples. Back then houses were cheap enough … I mean, everybody I knew lived in a rent house. Rent was probably $70 to $100. My girlfriend had a regular job, and Glenda probably did, and Stevie and I were playing. He was in the Nightcrawlers.

"One time, I wanted to strangle him. We were living together with Stevie and Glenda, and this was kind of typical of Stevie. He was just a kid and kind of irresponsible. I'd gone out that day to some thrift stores, and I came home with a 78 of 'Lonely Nights' by Johnny Guitar Watson. I was real happy, and we were listening to it. Maybe I had a gig that night and he didn't, but I remember coming in by myself late at night. I came in the house and everybody else had already gone to bed … walking across the living room to find a lamp to turn on. I turn on a lamp and look down at my feet, and there's that 78 of 'Lonely Nights' laying in the middle of the floor of a darkened room.

"Another time, I loaned him that song 'I Tried' – Larry Davis. It was the flip side of 'Texas Flood.' I think Keith Ferguson had given me that record for my birthday. Stevie wanted to learn it,

so he borrowed it. When he returned it to me, it was cracked. Loaning Stevie records was kind of a risky thing to do. But it was hard to get mad at him."

DOYLE: "We were getting more into soul and funk kind of music and jazz. We were going over to Denny Freeman's house and listening to all these great jazz records. Band-wise, we were starting to work more on dynamics – bringing the song up and coming down real quiet with it, where before it might have been more, 'Let's turn the amps on and blow.' It was also the period of time Stevie started messing with singing – backup singing. We would set a microphone in the general vicinity of Stevie and just say, 'If you feel like singing, you know, just help yourself.' Slowly but surely he started coming up and doing backup singing. He wasn't comfortable with it.

"We weren't just experimenting with the music. There was a lot of drinking, there was tons of cocaine everywhere, and we seemed to be going as far as we could with that. It seems like we had this thought that in order to play the blues, you also had to live the blues. And we thought in order to live the blues, you have to really be down. So we missed the boat. We didn't think about who we were stepping on or who we were hurting or how people cared about us.

"Our main focus was if we had ten dollars or five dollars, it wasn't, 'well, we need to get some food.' It was, 'do we have enough beer or wine or drugs for tonight or today?' Eating was secondary. I remember Old Milwaukee beer was three quarts for a dollar. So we had enough money from when we played the night before to get three quarts of Old Milwaukee apiece, and we'd buy a loaf of bread. This was every day. And buy Campbell's chunky soup. That was our lifestyle – drinking, drugging and we had just enough money to eat on."[3]

Summer: Chateau Club, Nacogdoches, TX (Nightcrawlers) This is the "new" Nightcrawlers without Marc Benno. Scott Phares, Stevie's former band mate from Liberation, sits in on guitar.

NOEL DEIS: "I remember going over to Stevie and Glenda's house, and he played Albert King's 'Born Under a Bad Sign' until the grooves were about worn out. Then those signature Albert licks would show up in the lexicon of Stevie's music. He listened to B.B.'s 'The Thrill Is Gone' a zillion times too, but it wasn't until The Nightcrawlers that he really embraced purist blues."

JIM TRIMMIER: "Bruce Miller came in on bass when The Nightcrawlers reformed in Texas. He was sort of financially backing The Nightcrawlers and had a house for them to play at. That's when I started roadieing for them, after Benno left. I remember Bruce Miller would just give me money whenever I needed it to gas the truck or take the equipment somewhere. And Bruce had a lot of guitars that Stevie would play.

"This was when Stevie started playing some jazz – octaves like Wes Montgomery – and started really playing blues instead of rock. Blackbird and Krackerjack were rock bands. The Nightcrawlers was the first one where he didn't play with a Marshall sound anymore; he played with either a [Fender] Twin Reverb or Super Reverb – he still played real loud! He was doing 'Texas Flood' back then.

"I was roadieing for them and would play sax on one set. We were doing a gig on Lemmon Avenue [in Dallas], and that was where Billy Etheridge told me, 'Play [your solo] as loud as you can, or I'm going to hit you with this stick!' I would just blow as

hard as I could even though I didn't know what I was doing. I had about two licks, and my ear was fair."

BILLY: "Stevie had the sweetest spirit. He had a real innocence about him. Stevie never did anything but play the guitar. You could throw a football at him, and he'd just look at it hit him. We got in a fight at Mother Blues one time. There were a bunch of not real big Mexican guys, and they were wasted and started messing around with our wives and girlfriends. So during the break we went down and sort of tapped one on the shoulder and said, 'Hey, you guys gotta stop this.' One of them bucked up and that's all it took and the fight was on.

"Doyle and Bruce and I tore these guys up all over the club. We had Mexicans flying all over. Stevie got up in the corner at one of the padded booths and got as far away from it as he could and just watched. The cops came. Bruce elbowed one in the chin and they took him to jail – not for that, but because he didn't identify himself. They had so many cops in there it looked like the Keystone Cops. They loaded up all the Mexicans because they started it and had dope on them and Bruce because he had an alias ticket. He got back in time for us to play the next set [*laughs*]."

Cobras sax player JOE SUBLETT: "We went out to this place in Austin called La Cucaracha to see Stevie play in the Nightcrawlers. This was before Keith Ferguson joined. Stevie was fully realized as a guitar player then, I have to say. We were bowled over by him. He had the B.B. King in there, some Kenny Burrell; he hadn't quite latched onto the Albert King stuff as much as he later did."

The summer of 1973 was the first time Stevie saw his idol, Albert King, perform. "I had a gig somewhere else that night," Stevie recalled. "After a quick set I got on the microphone and said, 'Ladies and gentlemen, I don't know about you, but I'm gonna go see Albert King, and if you have any brains you will too.' Then I just packed up and left."[13]

Stevie in the Nightcrawlers at Armadillo World Headquarters, Austin, TX. © KATHY MURRAY

July 4: Willie Nelson's first Fourth of July picnic, Dripping Springs, TX (Marc Benno and the Nightcrawlers). A photograph taken by noted music photographer Jim Marshall shows Stevie backstage at this event standing next to the "Silver Fox," Charlie Rich.

© GARY OLLIVER

Willie's picnic may have been a reunion of the band with Marc, because it came after the Humble Pie tour and the rest of the band's return to Texas as simply The Nightcrawlers.

MARC BENNO: "That was an unbelievable event. We got so into it when we started playing, I don't know if we even broke inbetween songs. We played for an hour and half – I think we were supposed to do about twenty minutes. We played until all of a sudden we thought there was some kind of technical problem. The mics weren't working, and the only thing that stopped us was that our amps went dead. Somebody said, 'Willie Nelson personally went over there and cut the power off so you guys would quit.' I was like, 'God almighty! You could have said something!' And they said, 'No, nobody could say anything to you guys. We were waving at you and telling you to stop. It was like you were blind.' I never saw anybody say anything. We were in the zone! It was pretty good, but there was some funky stuff that went down after the gig. Doyle got in a fight with some cowboy because he was, I don't know, pickin' on Stevie or something. It was a wild deal that day [*laughs*]. Long live the picnic."

Doyle's memory is *much* different from Marc's. DOYLE: "The reason we got that gig was Benno's persistence. His girlfriend was Rita Coolidge for a while. He knew her and Kristofferson

and a lot of the band members from L.A. After two songs, Willie pulled the plug on us. We were the only band like us there. He just pulled the plug."

One could argue that Stevie's first work as a session musician or hired gun was the Cast of Thousands session in 1970. We know he was a session player on W.C. Clark's record in 1979, but it may be that Stevie was called upon as early as 1973.

JOE SUBLETT: "I believe Stevie told me he had been asked and I think did a session with Bobby Womack. If memory serves, he played on the session, because he said the bass player was Wilton Felder, who was the sax player for the Crusaders. Stevie said, 'Man, this guy Wilton is a great player, and when we're inbetween songs, he sits over on the side away from everybody and reads the Bible,' and that just fascinated him. He didn't know what to think about that."

By the fall of 1973, The Nightcrawlers were Stevie, Doyle and Keith Ferguson. Bill Ham, ZZ Top's manager, got interested in the Nightcrawlers. MARK POLLOCK recalls being there when the contract was signed: "Me and Stevie and Doyle jumped in my 1970 Maverick in the worst rain storm I think I've ever driven in, to Houston, stopping at every liquor store on the way. They went into his office, and I sat out and flirted with the receptionist."

BILLY ETHERIDGE: "Ham had seen Stevie somewhere and wanted him to play with this left-handed guitar player that he had in another band, just for the visual of two lead guitar players slugging it out all night. He was like a Colonel Tom Parker."

DOYLE: "[Ham] only wanted me and Stevie, so we went down to Houston to Ham's office. He [had this thing about] secrecy; he didn't want us both in the office at the same time. Stevie went in first, and Stevie and I had already agreed that we were going to sign. He came back out and I said, 'Did you sign it?' He said, 'Yeah.' I went, 'Man, I've been thinking about it – I'm not going to sign it.' He really couldn't believe it. I was joking with him [*laughs*].

"I went in and signed, and that's when Ham put together this little tour and booked us in Little Rock. It was going to be four nights at this little club. Glenda rented this U-Haul truck for us. We all had greasy, long hair, scraggly. We looked like nightcrawlers. We were all riding in this U-Haul truck with equipment in it. A cop passed us going the other way, and Drew was driving and said, 'I've got to pull over. Somebody with a license or an I.D. has to drive.

"We knew Keith didn't have a license because he never drove. Stevie goes, 'Well, I don't have a driver's license,' and I didn't either. Nobody had a driver's license or an I.D. – nothing that said who we were! Here we were, driving through the South, greasy, long hair with equipment in the back and nothing to prove who we were.

"So we get to this place and look for the place to load in. The guy looked at us like we were crazy. Come to find out, the club had changed to a country and western place about four months earlier, but Ham didn't know that. We drove all the way there for nothing.

"We had another couple of dates somewhere else, and it ended up being a huge mess. Drew and I hitchhiked home. Stevie and Keith stayed with the truck, and someone in the Ham organization flew in and drove them back. We didn't have any money, but we found this mom-and-pop place, and they let us stay until we got things straightened out.

"We were there about three days. Keith never slept. I mean, he slept, but when everyone else was sleeping, he always thought somebody had to be up. You could wake up any time in the night, and he would just walk, pacing the floor, looking out the window. That's who he was.

"We went out and opened a couple of shows for Kiss on their first tour. We opened for Charlie Daniels on a couple of shows; played Atlanta and opened for E.L.O. That was Bill Ham's doing. He was friends with all these promoters in the South. Of course, we didn't make any money."

Summer: The Nightcrawlers also reportedly open for ZZ Top in Houston.

Summer: Fox Theater, Atlanta, GA (Nightcrawlers) opening for E.L.O

Summer: Cobo Hall, Detroit, MI (Nightcrawlers) opening for E.L.O.

August 27-September 2: Flight 505, Austin, TX (Krackerjack). This series of concerts at Flight 505 was billed as celebrating the "liberation of the 18-year-old drinker." The lowering of the legal drinking age contributed to the rise of the Austin music scene. This is included here only because Stevie kept a poster from this gig in his personal collection. Whether he sat in with the band for these shows is not known but is also not unlikely. It would explain how he came by the poster.

📷**October:** Stevie sits in for a one-night reunion of the band Ninth Street at St. Edwards University: Stevie (guitar), former Blackbird and Stump member David Frame (bass), Mike Kindred (keyboards), Fredde Walden (drums). Kindred recalls this gig happening in October '72, but it more likely occurred in '73, as per David Frame's recollection.

– Walkin' The Dawg
– I Can't Sleep
– Shake, Rattle, and Roll
– My Baby
– Barefootin'

While Stevie was on the road, Glenda was waiting for him back home. GLENDA: "Stevie's mother was very kind to me, but I did

kind of make her angry ... well, *I* didn't do it [*laughs*]. After we had moved to Austin, Stevie had asked me to marry him several times, and I kept saying no. I was raised in an unpredictable-type family and I didn't think marriage was a very healthy thing. I was just never going to get married. So finally he asked me again and he took me to get the blood work and license. I kind of wanted to and then I was scared. He was trying to convince me to go in, and I locked all four car doors and wouldn't open them. I just couldn't make myself do it – I was *so* young.

"We were coming to Dallas to do a gig, and the only way we could stay together in his parents' home was if we were married. So Stevie called her and told her we were married. I really think he did because he thought we were going to get married. So we did go to their house and stayed together. I regret [deceiving Martha] now; I feel bad about it."

SMOKIN' JOE KUBEK recalls his friend Stevie from the early seventies: "He was struggling back then, because there just wasn't anywhere to play blues. We were all struggling. I remember feeling his guitar: he had a white Strat back then with two B strings on there. He had a 16 for a little E and a 16 B string. [*Laughter*] And I thought, man, this guy's stout! He must have hands like Hercules, which he did. It didn't seem to phase him a bit. Coming from Irving, Texas, all the guitar players from there were using big strings. It was one of those deals where when you bumped into one of those guys, 'What kind of strings are you using?' If you said, 'I'm using an eleven,' they'd say, 'Well, *I'm* using a *twelve.*' [*Laughs*] So I guess over the years I got comfortable using the thirteen."

© LEOLA

GLENDA MAPLES: "There were records all over the living room. I heard Jimi Hendrix a thousand times, but I didn't care because I loved it. You could walk into the house, and the living room was constantly covered in albums, and he played guitar. That was our fun – that and going out to see him play or seeing W.C. Clark play and have barbecue or going to the One Knite to see The Storm on Monday nights. He loved Mexican food, and he loved my cooking. Stevie wasn't into movies and things like that – he was definitely focused. I would go out to Lake Travis with the 'old ladies' and swim while the boys practiced. He just wouldn't put that guitar down, but that was okay.

"Stevie was always trying to challenge himself to the next thing and the next thing. He was so focused that when he got up on stage is when he had the most fun, and when he got off he had a tendency to beat himself up a little more than he probably should have: 'Oh, I didn't hit that lick right ...' He did worry a lot about his music. You could see that he was putting his heart and soul into it, and that, to me, was a turn on. You know, if he can put that much into that baby ... [*laughs*]. That and his little grin and laugh were cute."

DOYLE: "Stevie was always sitting around with his record player on, lifting the needle up, putting it back. He'd slow it down to 33 and listen, because you can hear certain things you can't hear at 45. If you play them at 78 you can hear things you can't hear at 45. Stevie was the kind of person that wanted to know what he could get out of 33, what he could get out of 45, what he could get out of 78. It was fun to watch, because he would take a song, learn it not only note for note, but he would have the tone. He would try to get as close to the tone as the record, which, if that meant putting certain speakers in amplifiers, then that's what he would do. To watch Stevie inspired others to

want to be better, and when you're playing, that's what you're looking for. You want to play with people who are better than you."[3]

Doyle and his family lived in a house in South Austin on Armadillo Road, and Stevie lived next door. DOYLE: "At the time it was in way South Austin, pretty much out in the country. There were only four, five houses, and our house was [at the] dead end into this wooded area. Stevie had a setup in his garage, and we could go in there and play. We'd play clubs in Austin, go back out there and play 'til five or six o'clock in the morning. We wouldn't disturb anyone because it was out in the country. We did a lot of playing back then.

"[His guitar] was always his first wife. It was something you could always count on. You could always pick up your guitar – she wasn't going to talk back, she wasn't going to leave you – she was going to be complete support. Stevie could always go in his room, grab his guitar, and it would be the comfort zone. It grounded Stevie."[3]

"The Garage Sale." (l-r) Keith Ferguson, Glenda Maples, Doyle's brother-in-law, Doyle's wife Linda, Stevie, Doyle II (in mouse ears), Doyle Bramhall, Fredde Walden (tallest), little girl is Georgia Bramhall, Jimmie's wife Connie Crouch is partially hidden between him and Fredde, and Paul Ray next to Jimmie. Others include Jane Steves, Candy Truelove, Larry Trout and "Mouse." COURTESY GLENDA MAPLES

1974

February (weekend of 22nd): The Warehouse, New Orleans, LA (Nightcrawlers) opening for J.J. Cale, Quicksilver Messenger Service

📖 **April 11:** *Rolling Stone*, "Austin: The Hucksters Are Coming," issue #158

📖 **May 9:** *Rolling Stone*, mention of SRV in letter from Shirley Dimmick to the editor about Austin music

May 10: Arrest for Class C misdemeanor theft for shoplifting steaks. A Class C misdemeanor is the same level as traffic offenses like a speeding ticket. Stevie is described on the arrest card as 5'9" and 135 pounds.

The times weren't easy for Stevie and GLENDA: "We'd been starving for a long time. Poor little Stevie and Cutter had to sell Coke bottles for us to eat for a while when I wasn't working. I'd buy a bag of red beans and cook 'em, and that was it – we didn't even have salt or cornbread!

"There was one time Stevie went into a grocery store, and he told me, 'I'm just bound and determined to go get us a steak.' I said, 'Oh, Stevie, be careful.' So he goes to the store and picks out two t-bone steaks and he sticks them down his pants. The minute he's walking out he gets busted. They haul him off in handcuffs. Jimmie had to come get him out of jail for two t-bone steaks [*laughs*]! Bless his heart, I felt so bad. We didn't really care though."

MARY BETH GREENWOOD: "Stevie ended up stealing some meat, which at that time was a felony. There was a brief period where meat became scarce. Somehow, [Bill] Ham's people made it go away, but he always held it over Stevie's head."

August 29: Mother Blue's, Dallas, TX (Nightcrawlers)

August?: Cheech Wizard, Corpus Christi, TX (Nightcrawlers)

JOE SUBLETT: "We had a band in Corpus Christi [Crawdaddy] playing six nights a week for several months, and we were going crazy for some time off. We begged the guy that owned the place to let us take the week off, and we suggested The Nightcrawlers. We called them up and said, 'Hey. You guys want to do a week in Corpus?'

"So they came down to spell us for a week. We were trying to get out of the club because we were tired of it, and we ended up at the club every night watching these guys play because they were so good! [Plus] we had a big jam over at our band house when the guys first came into town.

New Orleans, February 1974. © PAUL F. PRICE

"Some of the guys, maybe all three of them, had gone down to North Beach to get tattoos [from Old Man Shaw]. Stevie got the peacock tattoo from this old, funky guy who really hurt him. Stevie told me the guy was pushing on his chest so hard with the tattoo needle that he was lifting the chair off the floor [*laughs*]. He said there was blood running down his chest, and it ended up being a bad tattoo – it didn't look anything like a peacock.

"Flashing forward a few years to when we were playing in the Cobras at some place in southern Louisiana, we went into this restaurant and this little Cajun waitress came up, saw the tattoo and said [in a Cajun accent], 'Is that a *chicken*?' Everybody cracked up laughing! Man, he hated that tattoo."

JIM TRIMMIER was also in Crawdaddy when The Nightcrawlers came in. "They were wearing these kind of dashiki things and stunk to high heaven! They played a weekend at the Cheech Wizard playing blues, and the crowd hated them – except for my friends [who] liked it. Stevie stayed at my house, and that's when he got the peacock tattoo. In my opinion, it was not good art. People kind of made fun of it. He loved it – he thought it was the greatest thing."

DOYLE: "Probably a year earlier, Jimmie and I got tattoos, and Stevie always talked about getting a tattoo. I wanted to get another one too, so we went to this guy – crusty old sailor-type guy. I remember it being under a bridge. His cigarette smoke was going up in his face. I got one in the middle of my chest. You're supposed to take breaks every fifteen or twenty seconds to give the person a little break from the hurting, but he was one of those guys who would push it to the limit – just kept going.

"I thought I was a tough guy, and didn't let on like it hurt, but it did. Of course Stevie asked me, and I said, 'Oh, it hurt a little, but not much.' I thought if I told him how bad it hurt, he wouldn't get it. While I was getting mine, he was looking on the walls at all the tattoos. They had basic stuff – eagles and that kind of stuff. Stevie picked one out [for his chest] and didn't find out until after it was done that it was really an arm tattoo.

"I was sitting there with a bandage on my chest, watching Stevie. I could feel the pain on Stevie every second. The cigarette smoke was going up in the guy's face, and he looked at Stevie and said [in his crustiest accent], 'I bet that hurts, don't it?' It was all Stevie could do to get that thing. I mean, you don't have any meat there in the middle of your chest."

GLENDA: "I remember when he came back with that peacock … I could have whopped all of them. He came back and he was like [imitates Stevie moving stiffly so as not to move the skin on his chest]. I had to doctor that thing for weeks to keep it from getting infected."

Keith Ferguson was not there to goad Stevie on with the tattoo but did have an impact on Stevie's clothing sense. "I had to get him out of T-shirts. I mean, you don't want the front man to look like the roadies."[17]

According to Keith, Stevie and Doyle got drunk and decided to hire Drew Pennington, and that "made Bill Ham drop us like a hot rock." They ended up on a Bible Belt tour with no reservations, and some clubs weren't even open when they got there. They paid their own way, and Drew's girlfriend rescued them by sending money. Stevie and Keith ended up driving the equipment back to Texas from Mississippi in an "illegal U-Haul truck." They got back home and played a couple of gigs, and at the Armadillo, Keith quit half-way through the gig. Drew played "Taps," and that was the end of the Nightcrawlers.[17]

September 1: Mother Blue's, Dallas, TX (Nightcrawlers)

MARY BETH GREENWOOD: "He wasn't real happy about his days with Bill Ham. I remember him upset about Bill quite a bit; he would get real emotional when he would talk about Bill Ham. He felt like Ham was kind of shelving him – sent him on a bum tour."

Benno says that Stevie didn't like Bill Ham, who was accustomed to giving orders as if he was an Army drill sergeant. Not only did Ham leave the band stranded in Mississippi, but Ham insisted that Stevie pay him back for the equipment he had purchased for him.[17]

According to Roddy Colonna and Cutter, Stevie had to "chill" for a while after the split with the Nightcrawlers because of contractual entanglements with Bill Ham.[17]

MIKE STEELE: "Stevie was in and out of bands, playing here and there with people. I don't remember him having a regular band between the Nightcrawlers and the Cobras. I remember the Texas Sheiks, which was Uncle John Turner on drums, Keith

The Nightcrawlers: Doyle, Bruce, Stevie and Billy. COURTESY DENNY FREEMAN

Ferguson on bass, Jack Morgan on guitar and Bruce Bowland on vocals. They played at a club on Sixth Street – this was way before Sixth Street got rejuvenated. Back then it was nothing but hookers, transvestites, drunks, winos and long hairs. The Lamplight Saloon was a great club – a lot of bands played there, including the Texas Sheiks. They played every Sunday night and Stevie would sit in."

Keith Ferguson, Stevie, unidentified woman (probably Lou Ann Barton). COURTESY BRUCE BOWLAND

BRUCE BOWLAND: "That was just a real hard time for everybody in Austin, because all of us who thought we were going to do good, didn't. We all thought we were bulletproof, that no one could touch us, and then this movement called Progressive Country came out and was kicking our ass. Although rock and roll was still happening, it wasn't happening as big. It was disheartening because Krackerjack kind of set the stage for everybody to play original music, we thought. There were other original bands like Shiva's Headband, but that was like hippie music. It was like the wheels just fell off of everything."

In addition to the tattoo, 1974 brings another permanent addition to Stevie's life when he obtains the beat-up Fender Stratocaster® that would be known as Number One, a.k.a. First Wife, from Ray Hennig at Heart of Texas Music in Austin.

RAY HENNIG: "Stevie was kind of my pet, 'cause he never had fifteen cents on him! The little dude was always broke. But he had one good thing – he knew I didn't mind. Most music dealers would run off the long-haired musicians. I didn't mind, so he always felt at home. He knew he could take all day to play on instruments, say 'Bye' and leave. This was true with a lot of 'em, not just Stevie – the Sexton brothers, Eric Johnson ... I kind of considered them part of my family. I dealt with them all the same way – 'Hey, the store's yours, get after it. You ain't got no money, so I ain't gonna sell you anything anyway, so I ain't gonna worry with you.'

"Quite truthfully, the music they played wasn't my thing. I'm just an old country guy. Let me tell you how Stevie would get my attention. Stevie was always kind of quiet. He'd grab an acoustic guitar and hit a lick of 'Wildwood Flower' – a real popular country lick. I would look up and then he'd ask me a question: 'Hey, Ray ...?' Then he'd go back to [mimics fast guitar picking]. What I'm trying to tell you is that I could care less about what Stevie played; his music wasn't what made him to me. *Stevie* was what I looked at. I look at the person. Stevie was just this little, gentle guy that wasn't a hell raiser. He'd come by and hook a guitar into an amplifier – hit that lick of 'Wildwood Flower' – 'Hey, Ray, can I listen to this guitar?'

"It was the latter part of '74 when he found that old junker guitar all of you know as Number One. It was probably in September of '74. Most of the stuff Stevie picked up, I loaned it to him and he'd bring it back. I trusted the little guy – where was he going? [The guitar] had hung all over that wall, 'cause who wanted it? Everybody knows what it looks like. Well, that's the way it looked the day I gave it to him.

"Now, you say, 'You gave it to him ...' Yeah. When he came in, like every other day, we had a long row of guitars. And he wouldn't take them off the hook. He'd simply walk down and feel them and look at them and move on to the next one. If he wanted to play one, first he'd hit that lick of 'Wildwood Flower' – 'Hey, Ray...?' He was always respectful. If I had customers, he would turn his amplifier down low. That wasn't always the case with a lot of people. I respected him for that.

"Then came the day he traded for this old junker guitar, his old Number One. He stood there and looked at that old thing, and I thought, 'Oh, no.' Then he reached down and felt of it, just like he did always. He didn't take it off the hook, he just looked at it, and then he felt of it. And then he took it off the hook, hitting some licks on it. Then he hit a little 'Wildwood Flower.' He said, 'Ray, where'd you get this?' I said, 'Stevie, you have got to have picked the biggest junker on the wall. What in the world are you gonna do with that thing?' He said, 'Well, I like the way it feels.' He said, 'I want to listen to it,' and I said 'Go hook the thing up – do it.'

"And the old guitar actually worked – you can't hardly tear a Fender up. He must have sat back there a couple of hours and then came and said, 'Hey, Ray. How much you want for it?' – like he had money to buy it. I said, 'Stevie, that one's pretty bad.' He said, 'Why don't I give you that one I've got for it?' Well, the one he had was mine anyway! It was a blue Stratocaster as

I recall, but it was a nice one. I'd let him use them a few days and he'd bring them back and pick something else out. And so I thought, 'Oh, boy! I'm coming out a winner this time!' He can take this old trashed-out Strat, and I got this beautiful blue new Strat, which was mine too!"[34] The musician who traded "that old junker" guitar to Ray? Chris Geppert. Most people know him now as Christopher Cross.

TONY DUKES: "Every time Ray got a cool, old piece with the magic to it, he always called me and Stevie. Ray had called and left me a message that he had a guitar or two I might want. I was a day late getting in from a road gig; called Ray and he said to come today after work. He said, 'I called your pal Stevie, as I hadn't heard from you.'

"I rolled up just after closing and walked in to the familiar warm face of Ray Hennig and his hearty handshake. Lights were off in the room with guitars and amps but lit up well by the daylight, and there sat Stevie on a Fender Twin, back to me, lightly playing dizzy licks on a Les Paul.

"I didn't bother Stevie but went up to Ray, who said, 'I know you were down for the Gibson, but since I didn't hear back from you Stevie asked to see it. I also got an old Strat, but you probably won't like it because it's a rosewood neck.'

"Ray and I, propped on the counter, listened to Stevie's fingers dance across the immaculate Les Paul. Damn I wanted it. It had a odd attachment – a palm pedal, an extension of the Tunamatic. Stevie wasn't messing with that. His eyes were closed. He wasn't there – he was in the guitar.

"He put the guitar down, still looking at it with appreciation and more, something only a guitarist can understand. He looked at us, smiling, God love him, always smiling. I know Stevie felt the power of each guitar. The Strat would take more work and would have more options. It was also the guitar *de jour* of the blues guys, but such never influenced Stevie anyway. What I remember is the fact that the Les Paul was more than Stevie

could or wanted to afford. The Strat was a few hundred; the Les Paul I gave $1,900 for.

"I remember Stevie closing up the case, thanking Ray, and Ray had given both us off some space on the books to leave with those guitars. Giving me some word of kindness and enthusiasm and disappearing out the door.

"I thought the Strat was rough and ugly, and get out of here with a rosewood neck, and it looked dirty. Stevie saw and felt the magic in it, and Stevie didn't care what anyone else thought because Stevie found value in what was there, not what others saw. Often they – and I – were not capable of such insight."

DOYLE: "Stevie and I went with Doug Sahm for two months. Johnny Perez hated that Stevie was in the band, but he especially hated that I was in the band – double drums. We played in Dallas several times. The club on Greenville Avenue, we played there four or five nights. Doug was notorious for not paying, so he didn't pay us but about a tenth of what we were supposed to get, saying he'd pay us later. So we quit after about two months."

Sahm's recollection was that he had two weeks of gigs lined up in Houston, Dallas and Austin (Liberty Hall) and that Johnny Winter sat in at The Ritz in Austin. The lineup was probably Doug, Stevie, Doyle and Johnny Perez on drums and Jack Barber on bass.[17] A few months later, Doyle moved back to Dallas "because I felt that if I stayed any longer I was going to die."[3]

October 19: The Ritz, Austin, TX. Storm plays the grand opening weekend; it is believed Stevie sat in with Paul Ray and the Cobras.

By this time, Paul Ray had left Storm and Denny Freeman and Alex Napier had left Southern Feeling (which had included Angela Strehli and W.C. Clark). PAUL recalls: "Denny and Alex said, 'Hey, you're not doing anything. Do you want to get a band together?' And Doyle was not doing anything because that band had just busted up too. So that was the original Paul Ray and the Cobras. The hardest thing was getting a name. We were calling ourselves all sorts of things – Alex and the Blackouts, Denny and the Corals. The funniest one we came up with, we said nobody will show up, we'll make a bet: Paul and Doyle and the Dallasites! And nobody showed. So they said, 'Okay, now it's your turn.' So I said, 'Doyle, what was your first band's name?' and he said 'Cobras.' I said there's our band, Paul Ray and the Cobras."

DOYLE: "Paul asked me, and I said, 'My first band was the Cobras,' which was me and my brother and some other guys in high school."

Stevie, Connie, Jimmie, Tina. COURTESY MARTHA VAUGHAN

October: Jimmie Vaughan and Kim Wilson form The Fabulous Thunderbirds, though Kim did not move to Texas for a while, and the band did not officially debut until May 1975. Lou Ann Barton is an early member of the band, before later forming Triple Threat Revue with Stevie and W.C. Clark. Over thirty years later, Lou Ann continues to perform often with Jimmie Vaughan.

Steve and Lindi Bethel. © MARY BETH GREENWOOD

The long relationship with Glenda Maples was winding down about this time, while Stevie was in California for several weeks. GLENDA: "My drinking got a little bit heavier, and my jealousy got a little bit more. I didn't want to leave him to his own devices [*laughs*]. I tried my best to take care of Stevie and did for a long time. But I wanted the one-on-one thing. I didn't like my man messin' around.

"Stevie was going to California to listen to and learn from someone that Jimmie knew. He was going to be out there from six weeks to three months. We were losing the big house that everybody lived in, and I didn't really have anywhere to go, and that's when I hooked 'em back to Dallas.

"He told me he would contact me when he got back in Dallas. It was really weird because he didn't call me hardly any from California, and I started getting wigged out about it. Then all of a sudden I got a phone call, and he says, 'I'm back in Dallas and I'm coming to get you.' At that point I was tired of going hungry, and I had a job. Doyle and him knocked on the door; I told him I loved him and said, 'Can I see you when I'm forty?' And they left."

Soon thereafter, Stevie had a new girlfriend – Lindi Bethel. She recalls meeting Stevie as early as 1973, but she steered a wide berth around him for a couple of years. LINDI: "He was really intense and made me very nervous. I kind of stayed away from him. A lot of my friends were always trying to pick him up; you know, he was the talk of the town. I was like, 'Ugh. Certainly want to stay clear of him.'

"I thought he was intense, and his eyes were deep brown eyes that when he looked at you, it was like he was looking right into your soul. I knew he was a real soulful person, no bullshit kind of guy. I don't know; he just made me extremely nervous.

"It was one night at Soap Creek when he was with the Cobras, and Storm were playing. The gig was over and I was sitting at the table waiting for my friends to come and find me, 'cause it was my car everyone was going in. Stevie came and sat down and put his head on the table. I was like, 'Are you all right?' He goes, 'I'm just tired.' That was it, because he made me really nervous. I got up and left [*laughs*].

"I had a flat tire, and everyone was leaving Soap Creek. I saw Jimmie get in his car and said, 'Can you give us a ride?' He said sure. We were going probably five miles an hour, the door opened and in jumped Stevie. They dropped everybody off, and when it came time for me to be dropped off, Stevie goes, 'Well, there's a party at Jimmie's house. Are you tired? Do you want to go to the party?' And I said, 'Yeah! I'll go to the party.'

"The relationship developed probably a little too fast. We dated off and on for about a month. He was still having his flings with other women, and then the next thing I know we're living together. I had moved to a place on West Mary, and I don't think I really wanted him to live with me, but he needed a place to stay and we were madly in love.

"I guess what attracted me to him ... he was very soft-spoken, fabulous listener and very complimentary. We just clicked and felt like we had been together forever. He was intelligent, deep and real *cool*. Music was everything. But he was romantic and sensuous. If we hadn't moved right in with each other so early, we probably would have had a better relationship. We just didn't really get to know each other.

"We had a good time together, but when it got to be a little too much I'd get my own place, and the next thing I know he'd be living with me again. It was like we couldn't live together and we couldn't live apart. We both considered each other soulmates. He was very honest, sometimes way too honest.

"We spent a lot of time at the greenbelt [along Town Lake], swimming and going to movies. We went to the Paramount almost every Saturday when they started showing the old movies. We didn't own a TV, so we entertained ourselves. We'd go for long walks, and he loved to eat out. We didn't have a lot of money, but when we did, we ate really well. When he was off, we'd go hear bands he liked. He did his thing with the guys in the band, but I never really hung around. I think they thought I was too weird."

Lindi was a waitress and needed new shoes quite often, plus she loved to shop, regardless. "I paid the rent, so when I went out shopping, he went with me. He would buy me shoes and clothes, and he would just sit and didn't get uptight or irritated. It seemed like he enjoyed it, which is really bizarre to me. Most men don't like to shop [*laughs*]!

"We didn't have a car then, so we walked to Highland Mall and went to this shoe store. I had tried on a million pairs of shoes. The salesman went into the back to get something else and Stevie goes, 'You're not gonna get anything, are you? You're overwhelmed.' And I go, 'You're right.' He said, 'I can't face that poor guy – let's leave.' And we split. That's how sweet he was. That poor salesman.

"We used to have a lot of fights because he was sort of controlling and very, very jealous. That was probably the worst thing, and there was no reason for him to be jealous at all. At Soap Creek with the Cobras, I was dancing with all my friends; it was packed that night. I guess I wasn't paying any attention, but this guy was about to grab me. Stevie had been watching, and he hit him in the back with his guitar and knocked the crap out of him! I felt really horrible because I had created this situation, even though I was just dancing."

Lindi's roommate MARY BETH GREENWOOD: "We would eat at Pecan Street Cafe and have salads because we were so poor. Sometimes we'd split a salad. We also went to LaReyna – Stevie would pick the Mexican restaurants. He'd eat chorizo and he'd get 'em to spice it up, and I've never seen anyone sweat like that to this day! He said it was for a hangover. He also took us to the original Jorge's, and they had this great blues jukebox. He'd constantly be putting coins in there.

"We did simple things together, like doing our laundry, or go to the park, or go for walk. He'd give me a ride to school in Lindi's Volkswagon almost every day for a long time after someone hit my car.

If we'd go to Antone's or Soap Creek, we'd just walk in with him for free. Never paid anything – nobody had any money. Well, I had a job as a photographer in the Astronomy and Physics department that paid four dollars an hour, and I was the one with all the money! I had a little bit of parent money; they didn't. Whenever there was a bill they couldn't pay, I paid it.

"Stevie played every other night, if not every night, and there were some gigs that really paid, and he'd take us out. Every single time he got a paycheck, we blew it. He made things a lot of fun with his money.

"We always had a lot of fun. We did these Chinese fire drills at stop signs [no offense intended to our Chinese friends]. We were always kind of giddy – we were twenty and real excitable. He was really bright, charismatic and a sweetheart. Just going out to lunch was fun with Stevie. He'd have that [black] lingo. We'd imitate him.

"He did a lot of funny things. It still cracks me up when I think about coming home and finding Stevie with clothespins on his ears like earrings. I said, 'Why are you doing that?' and he said, 'Because that's the acupressure point for teeth.' Everybody is doing acupressure now, but Stevie was into it long ago."

December: Just before Christmas, Stevie, Marc Benno and drummer Johnny Perez (Sir Douglas Quintet) attempt another recording for A&M Records, supported by Lee Sklar on bass and Russ Kunkel on drums.

- Friends
- Whole Thang
- Slammer Jammer
- World Keep Spinnin'
- Long Ride Home

MARC BENNO: "I think Stevie and Doyle had gone back to Texas [after the spring '73 tour], and did another Nightcrawlers project. Then I called Stevie back to California because I had convinced A&M to let me finish a solo project. I was living in Marin County, and believe it or not, I had rented Neil Young's house without knowing it was his house. I had this little rent house I rented from this lady who was going to Europe for the summer, and after I moved I found out she's Neil Young's ex-wife."

(date unknown): Lion's Share, San Anselmo, CA.

MARC: "Stevie came and lived with me there, and we did some gigs out there. We played at a place called the Lion's Share where Janis Joplin had played, and kinda got hangin' out a little bit with Jerry Garcia and that scene up there. Jerry just loved to hang out. He loved that Texas guitar sound. He came over one time by himself. In fact I didn't even let him in the house – I didn't know who he was! Very sweet guy, and he did jam with us. We had that rent house in Bolinas, California, and had some awesome jams over there.

"I think I brought in Chris Etheridge to play bass on the live gigs; Johnny Perez played drums, a guy on saxophone – Martin Fierro – he's tremendous."

Everyone knows Stevie put a lot of feeling into his guitar playing, as Marc recalls: "I think Stevie was always having to prove himself, though I don't know who he had to prove himself to. But I always thought he saw himself as an underdog player. He came from a position where he was in the shadow of Jimmie. So he was never content or laid-back with it; he was always trying to achieve more. I think he picked up on a lot of Jimmie's early intensity and ran with it.

"I guess a lot of people were very surprised when he was the guy that emerged as the solo talent. I mean, his vocal and songwriting talent just happened all of a sudden."

Benno went through some personal tragedies about this time, and the resulting bad vibes led Stevie and Perez back to Texas without finishing the sessions.[17]

December 31: Taco Flats (possibly Adobe Flats), Dallas, TX. The Nightcrawlers open for Paul Ray and the Cobras and then split up again.

The Cobras at Antone's, Austin. (l-r) Denny Freeman, Paul Ray, Rodney Craig, Alex Napier, Stevie Vaughan. An early photo of Stevie playing "Number One." © WATT CASEY, JR.

PAUL RAY: "It was like a flip of a coin who was going to open [the New Year's Eve show], and they opened and we played the last set. Stevie played with them, and then asked if he could play with us. I said sure, 'cause he was going to jump up there anyway!" Asked why The Nightcrawlers were breaking up, Paul said, "I think they were all trying to get away from [manager] Bill Ham, 'cause if he gets a fingerprint on you, he's got you. He said, 'My dream of a lifetime is to have Jimmie and Stevie in the same band.' Jimmie was having no part of that."

DENNY FREEMAN: "I had played with Jimmie for about six months, and then Paul Ray and I tried to put a band together, and we couldn't find a bass player and drummer. Paul started playing bass with Storm, and so there I was back on my own, and that's when Alex and me and Andy Miller put together this band that ended up being Southern Feeling with Angela and W.C. Then Alex and I quit that and hooked up with Paul again, and we *still* couldn't find a drummer.

"Stevie and Doyle actually played the first Paul Ray and the Cobras gigs, just so we could play some gigs. They were in The Nightcrawlers. We finally got John Henry Alexander for a while, and Doyle and Fredde Pharoah for a while, and then ended up with Rodney Craig. There just wasn't hardly any good players in Austin wanting to play blues.

"For whatever reason, The Nightcrawlers were going to break up, and Stevie approached Paul about playing with us. I was the Cobras' sole guitar player before Stevie joined, so I had mixed feelings about it. I wouldn't have minded having a keyboard player, but we couldn't find one. I didn't really want to do battle with another guitar player, but it was also really exciting to play with him. He was always really nice to me and treated me with a lot of respect.

"Stevie turned out to be a really good guitar player, but at the time he wasn't a very good rhythm guitar player. I could offer him more help than he could offer me, I think. But we had a lot of fun."

So Stevie debuted as a member of Paul Ray and the Cobras and didn't leave for almost three years! Paul Ray (vocals), Denny Freeman (guitar), Alex Napier (bass), Rodney Craig (drums). Stevie would later bring Jim Trimmier to the band (sax). In late 1976 Joe Sublett took Jim's place.

1975

A new era in Stevie's career begins in 1975 – Paul Ray and the Cobras had become one of the most popular bands in Austin. Sax player JOHNNY RENO: "Back then, the Cobras kind of ruled the roost, and rightfully so. They were a fabulous band." The band was still doing popular reunion shows at the time of this writing (2009).

DENNY: "Stevie was younger than the rest of us, and he could be frustrating to deal with. Like, say we were getting ready to drive to Lubbock for a gig, and we're supposed to meet at the drummer's house by noon. By 12:30, everyone's there except for Stevie.

"Someone tries to call him, but his phone's cut off. So you say, 'Somebody ought to drive by and get Stevie.' So you go by his house, knock on the door, he answers and – he just got out of bed. 'Hey, let me take a shower,' he says. So you wait, then he comes out to the car and goes, 'Hey, can we take my girlfriend home?' 'Okay, Stevie.' So we drop her off and start back, when he says, 'Anyone need to go to the music store?' 'No, Stevie, we've all been there.' 'Well, could we stop by because I need to get some strings.'

"Then we're on the way, and he'll go, 'Hey, have y'all eaten?' 'Yes, Stevie, we've all eaten.' 'Well, could we run into Dan's Hamburgers so I can grab me a few?' Then we'd get there and it would be, 'Could someone lend me five dollars?' [Laughs] He was a little irresponsible like a lot of people are when they're 20, so we would get frustrated. But it was really difficult to get mad at Stevie and harder to stay mad at him because he was sweet and funny and nice. And he kept that sweetness throughout his life; he was always a very nice person."

Stevie's friend, JAMES ELWELL: "I was fifteen and the drinking age was eighteen. Rodney Craig, a friend of my brother's, was playing drums, and I would go to Antone's and say Rodney was my legal guardian, and they'd let me in. That's where I met Stevie. I don't know why we clicked, but we both played guitar. After a while we grew closer, but it took a while – I was a kid, he was a young man.

"We would often compare Denny and Stevie – it wasn't hard to do. Denny was the *dirty* guitar player, and Stevie was the *clean* guitar player, and man, did they complement each other! It was quite a contrast, but at the same time it was kick-ass."

Band leader Paul Ray was cognizant of the potential for conflict between two guitar players of the caliber of Denny and Stevie. PAUL: "I would never have said yes [to Stevie joining] if Denny hadn't said it was okay. I've been in two-guitar bands, and I know how that works – it's like having two drummers. But I knew that we needed another instrument, and Denny did too because he

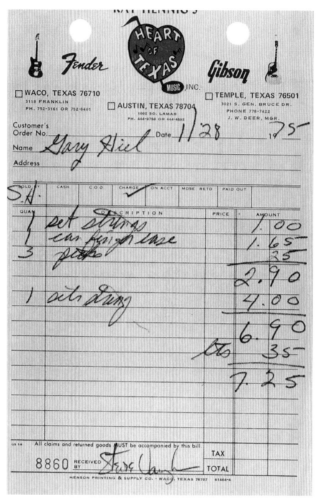

Receipt for supplies signed by Stevie on Cobras manager Gary Heil's account. COLLECTION OF CRAIG HOPKINS

was having to carry that whole load, which he could do, but it made it a lot easier. Stevie was such a quick study and was so into it and knew those songs.

"Stevie was twenty when he joined the Cobras and was very respectful of any elders. He was a quiet guy, but he was funnier than hell! Everybody in the Cobras was just a bunch of funny guys, and Stevie fell right in with it. Like the hamburger eating contest we had. I noticed that Stevie and Gerald took [snaps fingers] that long to eat a burger. It's gone. We were driving down the highway in our potato chip truck, going to Lubbock, I guess, and we stopped at some little town at a hamburger joint. I was going to have to buy them something anyway because neither one of them had any money. I said, 'Okay, we're going to have a contest to see who could eat the fastest,' and I'd never seen anything like it. Gulp, gulp.

"Stevie was very funny. He had all these alter-ego things he would go into, and it was hilarious. Everybody in the band was like that – it was a bunch of smart-asses. It was fun.

"Stevie was shy, but he was very serious about the music. He was a quick study and he copied the right people [*laughs*] ... sings like Doyle and plays like Hendrix!" Paul's wife Diana: "Stevie was shy, but he wouldn't lack for girls. He would have a covey; Paul had his covey. We had really pretty women following the Cobras around, and that worked really well for the band." Paul: "Yeah, [poster artist] Jim Franklin made the statement that the blues boys had the best-looking women, and that got around because it was true." Diana: "We were there for the music." Paul: "He had a girlfriend named Glenda [Maples]. She was a sweetheart. She took care of Stevie. Cutter claims he took care of him, but Glenda took care of Stevie."

Songwriting, for the most part, was still in Stevie's future, though he did bring some original instrumentals to the Cobras. PAUL: "They were Grant Green type things." DIANA RAY: "At his home he had instruments of all kinds, from toys to serious things, and he would play everything. There'd be a keyboard and a bass guitar." PAUL: "He'd also do something that I thought was really neat – I'd only seen one other guy do this. He'd look at a guitar and figure out what kind of music ought to be coming out of it and then pick it up and play it. So if he saw a guitar and thought it was hillbilly, he'd go, 'This is what ought to come out of this guitar,' and do it."

© KERRY AWN

Over time, the Cobras' weekly performances at Soap Creek Saloon became the place to be. The crowds grew from sparse to "wall to wall," as Paul recalls. "It was a honky-tonk. It had been a party barn that was rented to fraternities and sororities for hayrides, picnics – get drunk, keg parties. Alex Napier and Kathy Crabtree came down from Dallas and they leased it and opened it and called it Rolling Hills Country Club. We played out there, drank all his beer and made him go broke, so he joined Denny's band. He wanted to be a bass player, and we drank him dry.

"It had a wooden floor and a stage in the corner." DIANA RAY: "The music would rock the floor up and down." The driveway was referred to as Mars or a moonscape. "You could lose your car in a pothole," Diana remembers. "Travis County was different then. We'd be standing around in a circle in the parking lot and look over and there'd be the sheriff saying, 'Don't worry; I'm just here for the music.'"

The primary source for the Cobras' gigs was the *Austin Sun* newspaper. However, the Cobras were very popular and traveled around Texas quite a bit, so the gig list is incomplete, there being no practical source of gig info available to the author. PAUL RAY: "We went to a bunch of places – Lubbock, Corpus Christi, Huntsville, the Chili Parlor [in Dallas], Abraxas in Waco, College Station, Beaumont, Houston. I accepted every gig anybody offered us. We played anywhere someone would ask us and anywhere we thought we could make some money, especially if they had an ad in the paper, because getting our name in the paper every day, no matter where it was, people kept seeing 'Paul Ray and the Cobras.'"

March 18: Soap Creek Saloon, Austin, TX, opening for John Lee Hooker (Cobras)

March 19: Soap Creek Saloon, Austin, TX, opening for John Lee Hooker (Cobras)

March 20: The Ritz, Austin, TX, opening for John Lee Hooker (Cobras)

March 26: One Knite, Austin, TX

April 2: One Knite, Austin, TX (Cobras)

April 16: One Knite, Austin, TX (Cobras)

May 7: One Knite, Austin, TX (Cobras)

May 8: Soap Creek Saloon, Austin, TX (Cobras)

May 13: Soap Creek Saloon, Austin, TX (Cobras)

May 14: One Knite, Austin, TX (Cobras)

May 21: One Knite, Austin, TX (Cobras)

May 28: One Knite, Austin, TX (Cobras)

© MARY BETH GREENWOOD

June 3: Soap Creek Saloon, Austin, TX (Cobras)

June 4: One Knite, Austin, TX (Cobras)

June 10: Soap Creek Saloon, Austin, TX (Cobras)

June 17: Soap Creek Saloon, Austin, TX (Cobras)

June 21: Soap Creek Saloon, Austin, TX (Cobras)

June 24: Soap Creek Saloon, Austin, TX (Cobras)

July 8: Soap Creek Saloon, Austin, TX (Cobras)

July 9: Soap Creek Saloon, Austin, TX (Cobras)

July 15: Soap Creek Saloon, Austin, TX (Cobras)

While Stevie was playing Soap Creek this night, twenty-five-year-old Clifford Antone, born in Port Arthur, Texas, opened Antone's nightclub at East Sixth Street and Brazos in Austin. The club gained international renown as "Austin's Home of the Blues." In addition to many blues legends, Antone's became a regular venue for the Vaughan brothers and other local blues players. Jimmie's new band, The Fabulous Thunderbirds, was one of the first Antone's house bands.

TOMMY SHANNON: "When Clifford opened his club, it really gave the younger Austin musicians like Stevie [and] Jimmie Vaughan a chance to meet these guys, talk to them, play with them. I think that really gave them an advantage [in how they] developed as musicians, because they were right there in front of the masters."[3]

STEVIE: "I was able to play with so many of my idols at Antone's – Buddy Guy, Otis Rush, Hubert Sumlin, B.B. King, Jimmy Rogers, Lightnin' Hopkins and – the biggest thrill for me – Muddy Waters. At Antone's, I've jammed with everyone from my favorite 'unknown' player, Denny Freeman, to Bono and The Edge from U2. Howlin' Wolf was scheduled to play at Antone's, but he died a week before. That broke my heart."[10]

STEVE DEAN: "Stevie hung out a lot at Antone's back in the early days. The first [location of] Antone's was far and away better than all the rest. People [forget] that Angela [Strehli] did a lot of the booking back then, and she was the one who started this whole movement, because she had a lot more blues knowledge than most of the folks, including Clifford. She'd bring all these legends, so in the beginning there wasn't very big crowds, and it was really the blues nerds and the roots nerds and the record collectors and the musicians. Those were the ones that were there every night. The general populace was off seeing Jerry Jeff

Walker or something because ... the cosmic cowboy thing was happening. Most of the times, because of Clifford's generosity, if you were one of [the Antone's regulars], you didn't pay, you just went in and were part of the thing. I'm sure those people that had money spent money at the bar and helped make it a scene."

Austin was full of musicians because, as CHRIS LAYTON explained, "It was one of the cheapest places [to live.] You could rent places real cheap. It was an easy place to be broke. A lot of musicians – there was a lot of broke people all hangin' out, having fun together [*laughs*]. The clubs were spread out all over town. You could go up north and east and west and south, and you could hear all different kinds of things going on."[3] TOMMY added, "If you wanted to play, you'd go over there and hear some other bands you knew and sit in with them. Everybody knew each other, and it wasn't so much a competitive thing going on as it was just everybody was really absorbed in what was going on here in Austin."[3]

JIMMIE: "You got an amp and a guitar. You play until midnight, and then they change the laws 'til 2:00 and you'll play 'til two o'clock. Then you party the rest of the night, and that's what you do every day. I mean, that's basically what he did. It's what everybody did."[3]

Another guitarist making a name for himself in Austin was Eric Johnson. In 1975 his band, The Electromagnets, released its first record. Eric's music was much more jazz oriented, tending toward jazz fusion.

ERIC JOHNSON: "The first time I met Stevie was when he came down to Austin with a group called Blackbird, and I just met him in passing, out at Ray Hennig's Heart of Texas Music. Everybody was talking about how great a player he was, so I always kind of had a keen ear, wondering what he sounded like. I guess the first time I heard him play was with Paul Ray and the Cobras. I heard him a number of times with Paul Ray. His girlfriend at the time, Lindi, was best friends with this girl I was seeing, my girlfriend Mary Beth.

"I never knew Stevie really well. We weren't best of friends or anything, but we were acquaintances through Lindi and Mary Beth. They would go to Paul Ray's shows quite a lot, and I would sometimes tag along, and a couple of times sat in with those guys. It was very evident he had a real special thing going on. All that potential was there. [It also takes the right] chemistry, like when Hendrix got with Mitch Mitchell – this *magic* thing happened.

"There was an interesting time where Mary Beth, Stevie, Lindi and I decided to go get a bite to eat after an Antone's show. There was this place called Riverside Cafe, which was open late. We were eating there, and there was this drunk guy next to us, totally passed out. The owner didn't know what to do about it. He finally got sick of it and came out and poured a whole pitcher of water on him!

"The guy woke up in a stupor, really upset, and the first thing he saw was Stevie and I. I guess he thought we were trying to pick a fight with him or something. So he busted the table down and got up and was coming at us.

"It was really a serendipitous thing because we'd come from Antone's, and these two big bouncers from Antone's just happened to be walking in the door at the same time. They kind of came up and stood beside us, like, 'Don't bother these guys.' [*Laughs*] So the guy just got kind of weirded out and walked out of the restaurant."

LINDI BETHEL: "My best friend was Mary Beth Greenwood and she was dating Eric. At first they were rivals. [Stevie acted like] 'Oh, he doesn't play the blues, so I don't want to have anything to do with him,' that kind of stupid, immature stuff. Eric was jazz fusion and Stevie was blues. We kept trying to tell Stevie that Eric was really good.

"Mary Beth finally blew up at him and said, 'We go see you all the time, so you are coming to this gig.' It was at the Armadillo, this big show. Stevie bitched the whole time: 'I don't want to do this.' As soon as Eric got out on the stage and started playing, Stevie flipped out! It was embarrassing, because he was standing on his chair, flipping out. 'We told you!' But he was like, 'What do girls know?' After that Stevie wanted to meet him.

"I was living with Mary Beth, and Stevie was over all the time. They got along really well, but they would fight over who was going to grab the guitar first. We thought, 'God, if they're both going to be here, why don't we hide the guitar.' [*Laughs*] They didn't play together, that I recall, because Stevie never went anywhere without his guitar, and I don't think it was Eric's guitar at Mary Beth's. Stevie would play it, and *if* he put it down, Eric would pick it up."

MARY BETH GREENWOOD: "I think at the beginning Eric wondered, 'Why do you hang around with those blues people?' Now he hangs out with them, but at the time I was kind of the go-between. Then one day Eric's piano player, Steve Barber, went down and saw Kim Wilson, and that's all he could talk about for months; and anything Steve said, they all did. I think Eric was a little jealous of me going down to that club all the time with Lindi and Stevie.

"But after Stevie and Lindi broke up, Eric started getting to be more of friends with Stevie. I remember taking Stevie to see Eric at the Armadillo, and he was running up and down the aisles and jumping on chairs. I was really shocked he was so cool about Eric, because they're such different genres.

"They would play in my living room and fight over the guitar. Eric would play something; Stevie would grab it back and show Eric. I remember that guitar would never hit the ground when they were at my house together. At first it was like a competition, and then it was a friendship."

JOE SUBLETT: "I remember one night Stevie and I went to hear Eric Johnson with the Electromagnets. They played at a little joint on the University of Texas campus [probably the Cactus Cafe]. Eric was one of the first people I met when I moved to Austin. It was a great band. They were doing something [fusion] that was the polar opposite of what we were doing, but there was a mutual admiration between Stevie and Eric. Stevie recognized that Eric was a terrific player and respected the fact that Eric was doing something he wouldn't think to do.

"I remember watching Stevie and Eric play together, and that was something else. What happened was they both moved towards a common ground, which was that Jeff Beck / Eric Clapton sort of vocabulary that they both had in common. Eric played less like a fusion guy and more like a Jeff Beck, and Stevie played more like Jeff Beck meets Eric Clapton. It was something I hadn't heard either one of them do. Not ten people heard what that sounded like that night."

MARY BETH: "Stevie would write lots of birthday cards, and they would be, like, five pages. He had the most beautiful handwriting. He could have been a writing instructor. And he would write stuff like I have a lifetime pass to see all of his shows. We [Lindi, Stevie and I] used to leave notes for each other whenever we left the house."

July 17: Soap Creek Saloon, Austin, TX (Cobras)

July 18: Soap Creek Saloon, Austin, TX (Cobras)

July 22: Soap Creek Saloon, Austin, TX (Cobras)

July 29: Soap Creek Saloon, Austin, TX (Cobras)

August 5: Soap Creek Saloon, Austin, TX (Cobras)

August 9: Soap Creek Saloon, Austin, TX (Cobras)

August 12: Soap Creek Saloon, Austin, TX (Cobras)

August 19: Soap Creek Saloon, Austin, TX (Cobras)

August 26: Soap Creek Saloon, Austin, TX (Cobras)

August 28: Soap Creek Saloon, Austin, TX (Cobras)

August 28: Lakes at Lake Austin, Austin, TX. Stevie sits in with the infamous Uranium Savages during their last set.

September 3: Soap Creek Saloon, Austin, TX (Cobras)

September 5: Soap Creek Saloon, Austin, TX (Cobras)

September 7: Armadillo World Headquarters, Austin, TX (Cobras)

September 9: Soap Creek Saloon, Austin, TX (Cobras)

September 12: Back Room, Austin, TX (Cobras)

September 13: Back Room, Austin, TX (Cobras)

September 13: Hungry Horse, Austin, TX (Cobras)

September 14: Soap Creek Saloon, Austin, TX (Cobras)

September 16: Soap Creek Saloon, Austin, TX (Cobras)

September 20: Hungry Horse, Austin, TX (Cobras)

September 23: Soap Creek Saloon, Austin, TX (Cobras)

September 30: Soap Creek Saloon, Austin, TX (Cobras)

October 4: Soap Creek Saloon, Austin, TX (Cobras)

October 7: Soap Creek Saloon, Austin, TX (Cobras)

October 21: Soap Creek Saloon, Austin, TX (Cobras)

October 28: Soap Creek Saloon, Austin, TX (Cobras)

November 4: Soap Creek Saloon, Austin, TX (Cobras)

November 7: Soap Creek Saloon, Austin, TX (Cobras)

November 8: Soap Creek Saloon, Austin, TX (Cobras)

November 11: Soap Creek Saloon, Austin, TX (Cobras)

November 18: Soap Creek Saloon, Austin, TX (Cobras)

November 25: Soap Creek Saloon, Austin, TX (Cobras)

© DIANA RAY

November 27: Soap Creek Saloon, Austin, TX (Cobras)

November 28: Soap Creek Saloon, Austin, TX (Cobras)

December 1: Soap Creek Saloon, Austin, TX (Cobras)

December 2: Soap Creek Saloon, Austin, TX (Cobras)

December 9: Soap Creek Saloon, Austin, TX (Cobras)

December 16: Soap Creek Saloon, Austin, TX (Cobras)

December 27: Soap Creek Saloon, Austin, TX (Cobras)

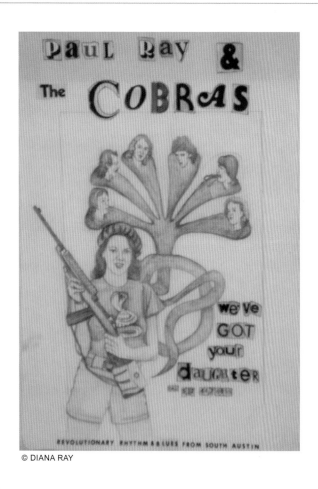

© DIANA RAY

1976

A sampling of songs played by Paul Ray and the Cobras:
- I Tried Pretty Baby
- Boilermaker
- Matter of Fact
- Other Days
- In The Morning
- Cryin' Town

The band had at least one radio broadcast that included:
- Lonely Nights
- St. James Infirmary
- Further On Up The Road
- Thunderbird
- Hambone's Tune

At one of the Cobras' gigs in Austin, a former bandmate of Stevie's, PATRICK McGUIRE, showed up to see his old friend. "Steve didn't know I was coming; walked in and sat down. He'd never seen me with a beard, and it had been at least five years since I'd seen him. He saw me out in the crowd and dedicated a song to me. Photographic memory. We sat and talked later, and it was like no time had passed. It was the last time I saw him."

January 20: Soap Creek Saloon, Austin, TX (Cobras)

January 24: Soap Creek Saloon, Austin, TX (Cobras)

January 27: Soap Creek Saloon, Austin, TX (Cobras)

February 3: Soap Creek Saloon, Austin, TX (Cobras)

February 7: Soap Creek Saloon, Austin, TX (Cobras)

February 10: Soap Creek Saloon, Austin, TX (Cobras)

February 13: Soap Creek Saloon, Austin, TX (Cobras)

February 15: Antone's, Austin, TX (Cobras)

February 17: Soap Creek Saloon, Austin, TX (Cobras)

February 19: Antone's, Austin, TX (Cobras)

February 24: Soap Creek Saloon, Austin, TX (Cobras)

March 2: Soap Creek Saloon, Austin, TX (Cobras)

March 7: Antone's, Austin, TX (Cobras)

March 9: Soap Creek Saloon, Austin, TX (Cobras)

March 12: Boondocks, Austin, TX (Cobras)

March 13: Boondocks, Austin, TX (Cobras)

March 16: Soap Creek Saloon, Austin, TX (Cobras)

March 19: Soap Creek Saloon, Austin, TX (Cobras)

March 23: Soap Creek Saloon, Austin, TX (Cobras)

March 28: Antone's, Austin, TX (Cobras)

March 30: Soap Creek Saloon, Austin, TX (Cobras)

Former Liberation and Nightcrawlers sax man Jim Trimmier joined the Cobras for about six months beginning in the spring of '76. JIM: "Denny would play Fender Rhodes [keyboard] and guitar. Stevie was just balls-to-the-wall lead player. He always played every solo like it was the last solo. Denny was good too, and was a learned guitar player – he knew chords."

© KERRY AWN

April 3: Antone's, Austin, TX (Cobras)

April 6: Soap Creek Saloon, Austin, TX (Cobras)

April 9: Soap Creek Saloon, Austin, TX (Cobras)

April 10: Soap Creek Saloon, Austin, TX (Cobras)

April 20: Soap Creek Saloon, Austin, TX (Cobras)

April 27: Soap Creek Saloon, Austin, TX (Cobras)

April 29: Soap Creek Saloon, Austin, TX (Cobras)

April 30: Soap Creek Saloon, Austin, TX (Cobras)

May 4: Soap Creek Saloon, Austin, TX (Cobras)

May 9: Antone's, Austin, TX (Cobras)

May 11: Soap Creek Saloon, Austin, TX (Cobras)

May 16: Antone's, Austin, TX (Cobras)

May 18: Soap Creek Saloon, Austin, TX (Cobras)

May 21: Soap Creek Saloon, Austin, TX (Cobras)

May 22: Soap Creek Saloon, Austin, TX (Cobras)

May 23: Antone's, Austin, TX (Cobras)

May 25: Soap Creek Saloon, Austin, TX (Cobras)

May 30: Antone's, Austin, TX (Cobras)

June 2: One Knite, Austin, TX (Cobras)

June 3: Soap Creek Saloon, Austin, TX (Cobras)

June 8: Antone's, Austin, TX (Cobras)

June 9: One Knite, Austin, TX (Cobras)

June 10: Boondocks, Austin, TX (Cobras)

June 11: Boondocks, Austin, TX (Cobras)

June 12: Boondocks, Austin, TX (Cobras)

June 15: Soap Creek Saloon, Austin, TX (Cobras)

June 16: One Knite, Austin, TX (Cobras)

June 22: Soap Creek Saloon, Austin, TX (Cobras)

June 23: One Knite, Austin, TX (Cobras)

June 27: Antone's, Austin, TX (Cobras)

June 29: Soap Creek Saloon, Austin, TX (Cobras)

June 30: One Knite, Austin, TX (Cobras) The One Knite closed in July 1976; Stubb's Bar-B-Q is now on the site.

July 4: Antone's, Austin, TX (Cobras)

At Armadillo World Headquarters, Austin. © KATHY MURRAY

At Soap Creek Saloon, Austin. © KATHY MURRAY

week of July 12: Audition with Dallas band Pyramyd

Ever alert to new possibilities, Stevie flew to Dallas to audition with a nine-piece band called Pyramyd that had lost their guitarist, Kenny "Catfish" Renfro, in an automobile accident. Drummer John Bryant recalls that they played most of the afternoon and that Stevie was a great guitar player. However, Stevie was more blues oriented and they had an Earth, Wind and Fire and Tower of Power sound with four horns. Stevie loved the band but was not quite sure about the fit and said, "Let's go get some barbecue and talk about it."

The band's manager, ANGUS WYNNE: "Catfish had a very unique style. He became a real favorite among the players and was killed suddenly in an automobile accident. We were looking all over for a replacement and I thought about Stevie because I had known him since the Nightcrawlers days. I offered to fly him up here to audition. They admired the way he played and he was doing all the right things, but the group was so used to this other guy that it didn't seem to be a match. But it wasn't because of talent at all; they were just trying to replicate a certain sound. He played his ass off, but it just wasn't [Catfish], and I think that had more to do with it than anything else."

In 1990, John Bryant ran into Stevie again in the studio during the Vaughan Brothers sessions in Dallas. Stevie remembered John, who at that time was operating a sound production company. John asked if he could call Stevie sometime to do some work, and Stevie said, "Call any time!" John said he was just as nice as he could be, even though they hadn't seen each other but that one time sixteen years before.

July 23: Soap Creek Saloon, Austin, TX (Cobras)

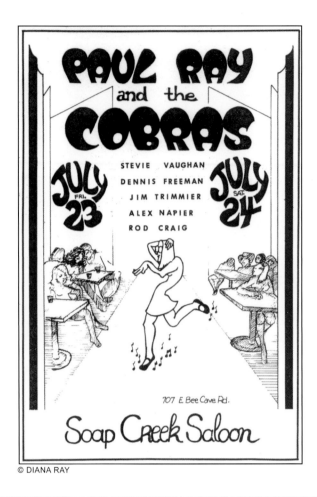

© DIANA RAY

He was always buying and trading guitars with the musicians that came through that club.

"He opened the shop in '76, and it was kind of my home away from home. In fact, when I was on the road with Muddy Waters, James Cotton and all those guys, I didn't even have a house. All my mail went to Charley's. I'd come in every couple of months and pick up my little pile of shitty mail. Disconnection notices and stuff.

"If Charley was your friend, he'd take a bullet for you. If he didn't like you, you were the first to know. I mean, he was the sweetest guy, just like Stevie. But unlike Stevie – I never saw Stevie mad unless he broke a string during a solo or something – Charley was not someone to be trifled with."

August 3: Soap Creek Saloon, Austin, TX (Cobras)

August 8: Antone's, Austin, TX (Cobras)

August 10: Soap Creek Saloon, Austin, TX (Cobras)

📖**September:** *Living Blues*, blurb re Cobras

September 5: Antone's, Austin, TX (Cobras)

September 7: Soap Creek Saloon, Austin, TX (Cobras)

September 14: Soap Creek Saloon, Austin, TX (Cobras)

September 19: Antone's, Austin, TX (Cobras)

September 24: Soap Creek Saloon, Austin, TX (Cobras)

📖**July 23:** *Austin Sun*, large display ad (at left)

July 24: Soap Creek Saloon, Austin, TX (Cobras)

July 25: Antone's, Austin, TX (Cobras)

July 27: Soap Creek Saloon, Austin, TX (Cobras)

In 1976 Charley Wirz opened Charley's Guitar Shop on Harry Hines Boulevard in northwest Dallas. In 1978 he started what may have been the first guitar show in the nation, which continues to this day. When Charley died in 1985, his friend Mark Pollock continued the shop and the Dallas Guitar Show.

MARK: "I met Charley in 1972. He was one of the first people to look at Stevie and say, 'Hey, this is something.' He and Clint Birdwell were trying to find a way to buy him away from Chesley Millikin, buy out his contract. He wanted to put someone in charge of the shop so he could run the guitar show and manage Stevie.

"He was called Teacher Charley because he taught industrial arts (shop) at Pinkston High School – the real rough, urban school. He knew woodworking, metalworking, and he really loved guitars. He was the manager and bartender at a club called Booger's. He had this old panel van that used to be a dry-cleaner van, and he would drive around to pawn shops and buy old Fender amps and guitars.

Stevie and Joe Sublett at Soap Creek Saloon. COURTESY JANNA LEBLANC

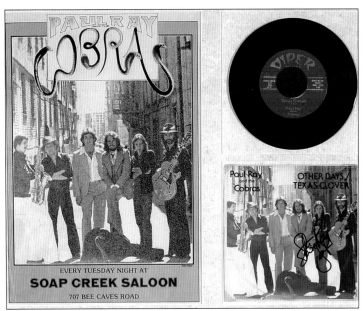

Poster and 45rpm record with sleeve signed by Stevie. COLLECTION OF CRAIG HOPKINS

September 28: Soap Creek Saloon, Austin, TX (Cobras)

October 2: Soap Creek Saloon, Austin, TX (Cobras)

October 3: Antone's, Austin, TX (Cobras) SRV's birthday

October 5: Soap Creek Saloon, Austin, TX (Cobras)

October 12: Soap Creek Saloon, Austin, TX (Cobras)

October 19: Soap Creek Saloon, Austin, TX (Cobras)

October 24:, Antone's, Austin, TX (Cobras)

October 26: Soap Creek Saloon, Austin, TX (Cobras)

📖**October 29:** *Austin Sun*, large ad of Cobras promoting Blatz beer

In September or October, JIM TRIMMIER leaves the Cobras and is replaced by his roommate, Joe Sublett. "Joe had been sitting in, and we had worked up some horn parts for the Cobras. I told Paul I was quitting and recommended Joe for the gig. I moved to Dallas and a month later nothing was happening. I asked Paul for my job back, but Joe was doing well and I didn't get my job back. A couple of weeks later I got a gig with a Vegas show band, and we travelled for eight years, six nights a week, fifty weeks a year."

JOE SUBLETT: "Stevie encouraged me to come out [and play with the Cobras]. Sunday nights were at Antone's, Tuesday nights were at Soap Creek. He liked the two horns – we could do the

Bobby Bland stuff with the two horns. So for about six months, I was just sitting in. Stevie and Denny said, 'Come on down and sit in as much as you like, but we'll pay you.' What a great way to get started in Austin – with a band that already had their thing together.

"Toward the end of the summer, Jim decided he was going to go off on the road with a Top 40 show band. Stevie and Denny came to my door. 'Hey, will you join the band now? Jim's gone.' Stevie said, 'I know you like to do some of those jazz instrumentals – Stanley Turrentine and Grover Washington. We'll do some of that stuff if you'll join the band.' Of course, they didn't have to talk me into it at all. I would have said yes, but they were trying to sweeten the pot. So I said, 'Yeah. I'm on board!'"

In late 1976, the band recorded a single at McAdams Brothers in Austin (released February 7, 1977). PAUL RAY: "We had a friend that was sort of our road manager, without actually doing any work, whose name was Gary Heil. Gary was very responsible with what we were doing. He decided that we could make a record, and he knew these people that were a man and wife who had produced some records. So he got them, and we rented a studio that was in an apartment house in Austin and went in and recorded these two songs – got 'em pressed up at Wakefield. I got my high school band buddy Jeff, who was a commercial artist, and he drew the label and made it look like a good ol' R&B label. We used

Stevie and Jimmie, Christmas 1976 COURTESY MARTHA VAUGHAN

it like business cards. If you had a record, you could ask for more money. It didn't matter if you had put it out and nobody had bought it – you had a record!"

JOE SUBLETT: "We recorded kind of a reggae song called 'Texas Clover,' a song Paul Ray had written. Stevie played the ska-sounding rhythm guitar. Then we did a song called 'Other Days,' and I took a solo and then Stevie took a solo. It was just one day. Gary, if memory serves, paid for the recording.

"There was a time when people didn't just go into a studio unless they had some kind of record deal. People can do a full record now with the digital domain the way it is now – you don't have to go to an expensive recording studio to record. It's not nearly as expensive now. Back then, if you didn't have a record deal, it wasn't easy to get the money together to go into a studio and press it up and do the artwork."

Lindi remembers Gary Heil as "Uncle Gary." "He had lots of money and fed us all. We could be starving for a couple of days and Uncle Gary would come around and take us out to eat. The girls would go over to Uncle Gary's house when we were not at the gigs. Nobody was jealous of him."

DENNY: "We were playing in Lubbock and went to eat. Stevie had this tape player and was freaking out over some tape that he had. He took the tape player into this Mexican restaurant, and you just don't do that, but he couldn't stop listening to this thing, whatever it was. He wanted to play it over and over, and all the people in the restaurant were looking at him ... 'Turn that down!' Once something blew his mind ..."

November 2: Soap Creek Saloon, Austin, TX (Cobras)

November 7: Antone's, Austin, TX (Cobras)

November 9: Soap Creek Saloon, Austin, TX (Cobras)

November 16: Soap Creek Saloon, Austin, TX (Cobras)

November 23: Soap Creek Saloon, Austin, TX (Cobras)

November 26: Soap Creek Saloon, Austin, TX (Cobras)

November 28: Antone's, Austin, TX (Cobras)

November 30: Soap Creek Saloon, Austin, TX (Cobras)

December 7: Soap Creek Saloon, Austin, TX (Cobras)

December 10: Soap Creek Saloon, Austin, TX (Cobras)

December 14: Soap Creek Saloon, Austin, TX (Cobras)

December 21: Soap Creek Saloon, Austin, TX (Cobras)

December 31 Armadillo World Headquarters, Austin, TX (Cobras)

1977

CHRIS LAYTON: "The first time I heard [Stevie] play was [with the Cobras] on a Tuesday night at a place called Soap Creek Saloon in Austin. It was either late '76 or real early '77. When I walked in, they were already playing. Immediately, Stevie caught my ear because of his energy and this feeling from his playing. They were doing Bobby Bland stuff, a couple James Brown things, and a song by Ronnie Laws called 'Always There.'[35]

"I remember that really well. Soap Creek was outside of town, and if it was packed you'd have to park down the hill and walk two or three hundred feet to the club. I remember getting out of my car and walking towards the club, and I heard the band in there playing. And the weird thing about it was you could hear the band like you could hear any band outside a framework building with not real thick walls. I could hear this one guitar player who sounded like he was outside. I thought, 'Isn't that wild. It sounds like this guitar player is outside instead of inside with the band.' It wasn't a volume thing; it was this presence. I walked in and turned the

Paul Ray and the Cobras. © WATT CASEY, JR.

corner where you could see the band, and Stevie was playing a solo, and I was, like, mesmerized.

"It just hit me that I'd never seen, in the concerts I had seen up to that point, anybody [who was] a true master of their instrument. It just has to do with, I don't know, a gift or something – this energy. When I saw him, I couldn't believe anyone plays like that. I never saw Jimi Hendrix. Of course, I heard him and immediately figured he was probably that way as well just by listening. But I thought, this guy is unbelievable. I've thought about that often when I reflect back on that first time. But that's really what it was – he had so much presence, and, I don't know, this undefined energy and charisma. I think it's what accounted for the fact that he was so clear, even when I was outside the building. One of those weird things, almost mystical, that there's no real explanation for them. No real sonic reason why that exists.

"Denny Freeman, of course, was in the band, and he was great too. I guess Stevie just had some kind of star quality. One Tuesday night I went out there to see the band, and Rodney Craig, who was playing drums, had also been doing some sheetrocking during the day and he'd overslept. The place was packed and they needed to start, and they couldn't get a hold of him. Joe said, 'Why don't you let me get my roommate up here and let him play? It would be better than nothing. He doesn't know the material, but he's a good drummer.' So I got up there and played with them for a while. Stevie kept looking back at me, winking and stuff [*laughs*]."

By this time, Jimmie had been in The Fabulous Thunderbirds for well over a year, playing in the same clubs, but on different nights from the Cobras. Asked how much interaction there was between the Vaughan brothers, JOE SUBLETT replied, "Not much. I don't remember seeing them hanging out [together] that much. It seemed to me that Stevie was trying to be Stevie, and not Jimmie's little brother. And Jimmie was ... well, Jimmie.

"Stevie looked up to Jimmie, but there was probably a competition, even if it was unspoken. I don't think there was bad blood between them. They were both hot-shot guitarists. There was the Jimmie camp, and there was the Paul Ray and the Cobras camp.

"Because they were both blues guitar players, there was a comparison that started out as Jimmie was sort of the guitar hero, and Stevie had to overcome that a bit. It wasn't that Jimmie was better or vice-versa – they had completely different styles. Jimmie had that really simple, essential and driving guitar style which everybody loved, and Stevie was this maniac. He was really poring into the Albert King, Stax-Volt stuff. He listened to a lot of Otis Rush and Hendrix, but he didn't really adopt the Hendrix stuff until later. Albert King was his man.

"Stevie and I were the young guys in the band. Paul and Denny were nine or ten years older than me, and I was about a year older than Stevie. I remember one time Stevie and I were probably acting like young jerks, acting silly in a rehearsal, and

[*laughs*] Paul said, 'You know-it-all, smart-aleck young punks!' or something – kind of kiddingly, but it was true. He was into his thirties, and we were early twenties, and probably fairly annoying.

"Because we were the young guys, we hung out a lot and became really good friends. I don't remember Jimmie hanging out with us during that couple-of-years period. We may have gone over to Jimmie's house once or twice to listen to records, but there was definitely a separation."

Stevie was younger than the others, and some of Stevie's fans felt the band treated him as if he were less cool than they were. MARY BETH GREENWOOD: "Denny was real nice to him, but [the others] acted like, 'We're the stars.' Lindi and I had to pump Stevie's ego, saying, 'No, you're the one; you got it.' He was really humble, and he'd always praise everyone but himself. And he would go on and on and on about his brother, almost to the point where it was hard to talk to Jimmie because Stevie had him so built up in our minds."

Mary Beth recalls that the admiration was not necessarily mutual, or at least not demonstrably so. Jimmie's treatment of Stevie was "not always that great. I remember feeling sorry for Stevie on that level sometimes. That's a debatable question, but I don't think he thought as much of Stevie as Stevie thought of him. But Stevie really loved his brother, and it was really sweet."

As usual, Stevie was the youngest in the band again. Going on 23, he was still a bit of a kid at heart. JOE: "Stevie was really funny and could be really goofy. A lot of people don't get that. He was a badass guitar player/gun-slinger and all these things. He got up on stage and had this very severe, commanding and kick-ass way about him. But off stage, he was a very goofy, funny cat. He was very serious about his music once it was time to play and also very serious about sitting around and practicing.

"We had some different characters that we used to do. He had a character that he and I created called Brady [pronounced Bwady]. Brady was kind of a not-so-with-it character that he played.

"On our way to Lubbock to play a gig, we pulled over in a little Texas town to get a Coke. Stevie and I decided we were going to go into the Dairy Freeze, or whatever it was called, and have him act like a young boy who was a few cards short of a full deck. Stevie pulled his pants up to his chest and cinched up his belt, then humped over and did his best goofball, Gomer Pyle rubber-faced grin, practically drooling.

"I held his hand like he was my unfortunate little brother and walked into the place. Stevie walked up to the counter and, grunting and mumbling, tried to order an ice cream cone. The woman behind the counter said (in her strong West Texas accent), 'Well, bless your heart, little feller. Do you want some ice cream?'

"Stevie nodded, drooling and acting like he was shy. The two other women behind the counter came over and started fawning over him. One lady said, 'Isn't he the sweetest thang you ever saw?' The women behind the counter were classic Texas types with the sprayed hair and glasses on clips. They were, like, out of *The Last Picture Show* [*laughs*].

"When we were leaving town, I decided to call his character Bwady because that was the name of the town, or we had passed Brady on the way. Stevie smiled and said he had a cousin named Brady. I don't know if he was pulling my leg or not.

"We had this scenario where he and I and Denny were going to move to this town and open up a head shop and marry the three women behind the counter! Have babies and live in Brady, Texas!

Dare to Dangle! "Bwady" in 1982.
© DON E. OPPERMAN, JR.

"Maybe a year or two later, when Stevie was in Double Trouble, we were partying at Lou Ann and Keith Ferguson's house. They had recently gotten married, and we called them 'mahdow' and 'fahdow,' as in mother and father. Keith decided he was going to adopt all of us and drew up a document written in Spanish in red ink and we all signed it.

"Lou Ann said, 'Joe's my biggest and bestest boy, so he's gonna be Jodo from now on. Stevie's already called Bwady, and Chris – you'll be Hawod,' as in Harold. I don't know where she got that but probably just made it up on the spot. A few years later, Charlie Sexton became our little brother, Chado. Yeah, we were a goofy bunch. The nicknames stuck even though Lou Ann and Keith got a divorce, and we were all now products of a broken home!

"Bwady really stuck as a nickname for Stevie. Goofball Stevie with the rubber face. He could make his face do anything. He claimed he had broken his nose seven times when he was a kid, but none of us believed that. He could stretch his face into almost a mask-type thing. So when he would make that goofy face, that was Bwady. To me, that was Stevie. He wasn't the serious Stevie with the hat. He was a nice, sweet guy – just a regular cat who happened to be extraordinarily talented.

"Chris even named his kid Joseph Brady Layton after me and Stevie. I'm Joseph's godfather. We all got a kick out of it when we realized his initials are J.B.L." [J.B.L. is a famous manufacturer of guitar amplifier speakers and equipment.]

January 1: Soap Creek Saloon, Austin, TX (Cobras)

January 4: Soap Creek Saloon, Austin, TX (Cobras)

January 11: Soap Creek Saloon, Austin, TX (Cobras)

January 14: Texas Tavern, Austin, TX (Cobras)

January 15: Texas Tavern, Austin, TX (Cobras)

January 18: Soap Creek Saloon, Austin, TX (Cobras)

January 25: Soap Creek Saloon, Austin, TX (Cobras)

January 29: Soap Creek Saloon, Austin, TX (Cobras)

February 1: Soap Creek Saloon, Austin, TX (Cobras)

⊙**February 7:** PAUL RAY AND THE COBRAS, "Other Days / Texas Clover," Viper, 30322, 45, with picture sleeve. The 1973 date on the label refers to the copyright date, not release date. SRV plays on both sides, though he is featured more prominently on "Texas Clover." 1000 copies were made.

The mid-1970's was the height of the music phenomenon known as progressive country music, or "cosmic cowboy" – Willie Nelson, Michael Murphey, Jerry Jeff Walker, et al. The Cobras' record sleeve photo (see page 83) was taken in an Austin alley. PAUL: "I kept saying I was tired of all this country music stuff – we play city music! [Photographer] Debbe [Sharpe] was a little nervous because we had this reputation as being these 'blues boys!' I said, 'I know a great-looking alley behind the Paramount,' because I had been out there smoking and drinking and doing whatever you're not supposed to do. We put the guitar case down and Denny holding his guitar. Somebody had the ceramic cobra and put it in front and said, 'Okay – here's your picture.' We were just goofing around."

JOE: "The photograph was taken by a friend of a friend [Debbe Sharpe] in the alley behind the Paramount Theatre [in Austin]. Diana Ray, Paul's wife, did some graphic stuff with the letters.

"I remember it was on a jukebox across town – Casita Jorge – and Stevie and I were drinking margaritas there, and somebody put it on. We didn't know it was on there, and we were very excited, you know – a record that we played on was being played on a jukebox in a restaurant. Big deal, right? But it was a big deal to us."

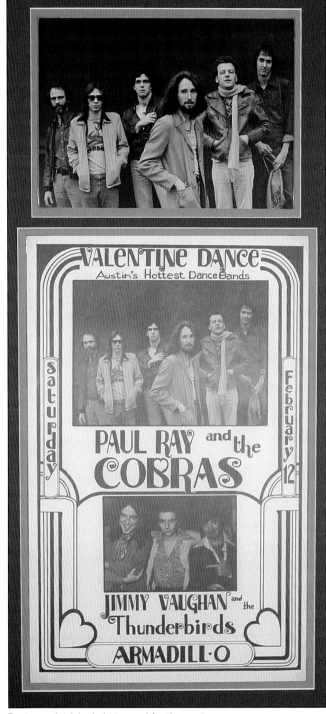

Poster and original photo used for the poster. © WATT CASEY, JR./COLLECTION OF CRAIG HOPKINS

February 8: Soap Creek Saloon, Austin, TX (Cobras)

February 12: Armadillo World Headquarters, Austin, TX, (Cobras) with Fabulous Thunderbirds

---

February 15: Soap Creek Saloon, Austin, TX (Cobras)

February 19: Soap Creek Saloon, Austin, TX (Cobras)

February 22: Soap Creek Saloon, Austin, TX (Cobras)

February 24: Rome Inn, Austin, TX (Cobras)

February 25: Alliance Wagon Yard, Austin, TX (Cobras)

February 26: Alliance Wagon Yard, Austin, TX (Cobras)

March: Paul Ray and the Cobras named Band of the Year in the *Austin Sun* readers' poll. Stevie is listed as "Stevie *Ray* Vaughan, though it does not appear he used his middle name extensively until 1980. (Awards show on May 13)

As a result of winning Band of the Year, the Cobras enjoyed a boost in their careers. PAUL: "It was huge. I mean, the blues bands were spit on before that. We got to play once every two months at the Armadillo if they'd get all three of the bands in there at once and get it over with. Nobody wanted to hear that anymore. 'That's old slave music.'

"We went on salary, had a manager, a truck to travel around in. We got better gigs and didn't have to play pass-the-hat gigs and got guarantees."

The Cobras also went back in the studio. The resulting "Thunderbird" appears on the *SRV* box set released in 2000. JOE SUBLETT: "It was the first session that Stevie ever sang on. Paul sang 'St. James Infirmary'; Stevie sang 'Thunderbird' by The Nightcaps. It was the first time he'd ever fronted a band and sang on a record in the studio.

"One of the things I remember about Stevie was his intensity for learning. He was sort of our *de facto* roommate, me and Chris

Layton. If he didn't have a place to stay, he stayed at our house – a place we called the Blues Palace. He would fall asleep with the guitar in his arms, *with his hands on the fretboard* [*laughs*].

"I would come in some nights and he would be glued to the record player, leaning over listening to certain kinds of bends or a Ray Charles lick that Ray had sung a certain way. He'd say, 'Now listen carefully,' and he'd sing me the lick. Then he'd say, 'Now listen to Ray Charles. Is he singing it like this, or this way?' And I couldn't tell the difference between the two ways, but he was very intense and analytical about it. His hearing was pretty incredible. I think that's what made him such a good guitar player – he heard things that maybe a lot of us didn't hear.

"He was so brilliant, and then I'd have to help him find the Laundromat to do his clothes. Some of the simplest tasks were, like, 'Uh, can you pick me up and take me to the Laundromat?' The simplest tasks were almost beyond him because he was so focused on the music. I don't know what you call someone like that – maybe a genius."

COURTESY JAMES ELWELL AND CUTTER BRANDENBURG

About this time, Stevie became acquainted with a youngster regarded as a musical prodigy – "Little" Charlie Sexton. Stevie's friend, MIKE STEELE: "I remember one night Stevie was playing with someone at the Lamplight, and Charlie Sexton's mother brought Charlie down. He was about nine or ten years old – just a child. He jammed with Stevie and it was amazing. Stevie was just grinning from ear to ear."

Little Charlie had gotten his first guitar at age four and by the age of 13 was in Joe Ely's band. By fifteen he had recorded with Keith Richards and Ron Wood; he released his first album at age sixteen. In 2000 he produced several of the tracks on Double Trouble's first CD, *Been a Long Time*. He became a highly respected guitarist, writer and producer.

March 1: Soap Creek Saloon, Austin, TX (Cobras)

March 4: Too Bitter, Austin, TX (Cobras)

March 5: Rome Inn, Austin, TX (Cobras)

March 6: Steamboat 1874, Austin, TX, (Cobras)

March 8: Soap Creek Saloon, Austin, TX (Cobras)

March 11: Armadillo World Headquarters, Austin, TX (Cobras)

March 15: Soap Creek Saloon, Austin, TX (Cobras)

March 22: Soap Creek Saloon, Austin, TX (Cobras)

March 25: Soap Creek Saloon, Austin, TX (Cobras)

March 26: Soap Creek Saloon, Austin, TX (Cobras)

March 29: Soap Creek Saloon, Austin, TX (Cobras)

March 31: Rome Inn, Austin, TX (Cobras)

April 1: *Austin Sun*, photo of SRV and blurb about April 3 show

April 3: Armadillo World Headquarters, Austin, TX (Cobras), fund-raiser for city council candidate whose platform was legalizing marijuana. [One should not assume band members' opinions on the subject.]

April 5: Soap Creek Saloon, Austin, TX (Cobras)

April 12: Soap Creek Saloon, Austin, TX (Cobras)

April 15: Rome Inn, Austin, TX (Cobras)

April 16: Rome Inn, Austin, TX (Cobras)

April 26: Soap Creek Saloon, Austin, TX (Cobras)

April 29: Soap Creek Saloon, Austin, TX (Cobras)

April 30: Soap Creek Saloon, Austin, TX (Cobras)

May 3: Soap Creek Saloon, Austin, TX (Cobras)

May 10:, Soap Creek Saloon, Austin, TX (Cobras)

📖**May 13:** *Austin Sun*, Cobras Band of the Year article and display ad thanking supporters. The Cobras won the Best Blues Band by a landslide, 40% of the vote, compared to 18% for the second place band and 14% for Jimmie Vaughan and The Fabulous Thunderbirds.

"Whether they're playing Paul Ray originals, dancefloor jazz, or tunes by Bobby Bland, Al Green, James Brown, and Jimmy Cliff, they play hard but smooth, don't talk or waste time between songs, and don't need any stage histrionics. They play for the dancers and the dancers know it.

".... Then there's guitarist Stevie Vaughan, cited by many observers as a man who'll one day take his place among the great Texas blues guitarists. He's a perfectionist. Ask him what he thinks of his own playing and all he says is, 'I sometimes get really disgusted with myself. I'm not where I should be now.'

"Paul Ray and the Cobras have hung on through three very lean years. As recently as last summer, the only gigs were Sunday nights at Antone's and Tuesdays at Soap Creek. Now they play three or four nights a week. .... For a blues band playing honky tonks, there's no more encouraging sign of making it than the time when you don't have to ask club managers to play in their bars any more ... they ask you. That's how it is now for the Cobras in Austin."

JOE SUBLETT: "We did a lot of Bobby Blue Bland and great orchestrated stuff that had big horn sections. I stood between Stevie and Denny. Denny was a great chord guy, as well as a great soloist, so he played a lot of interesting, big, orchestrated-type chords. Stevie would be playing the other horn parts on the guitar with me, and Denny would be doing the Wayne Bennett [Bobby's guitarist] rhythm guitar and fills. We would switch off, and the next song Denny would be doing the horn parts with me. Standing between those guys as a young player was great. You don't stand next to guys like that and not get better.

"Denny would take a solo some nights on 'Lonely, Lonely Nights,' which was a Johnny Guitar Watson song [which Denny must have learned before Stevie left his prized 78 in the middle of the floor], and it was just *nasty* – he'd be bending strings, low-down gritty stuff – totally different than what Stevie would be doing. Stevie would stop playing and hold his nose and stick his tongue out, 'Oh, that's the nastiest, dirtiest stuff I've ever heard!' And then

he'd throw his hands up like, 'I give up,' you know? It was such a tribute to Denny, as a totally different animal on guitar, but a truly valid one. Stevie was very respectful of other players."

May 14: Armadillo World Headquarters, Austin, TX (Cobras)

On a few posters, the band is listed as "Paul Ray and *X-Rated* Cobras." JOE SUBLETT: "Tuesday night was our regular gig at Soap Creek and was called the Cobra Club. Somebody said something about the X-rated Cobras, and I wondered what that was all about – we weren't Lenny Bruce on stage. What I found out was that when the Cobras played on Tuesday nights, every good looking, young girl that you could think of would be out on the dance floor. They would come out and dance with each other. Somebody came in and said that every beautiful, 20-year-old college girl was on that dance floor. Very sexy. And someone said, 'the X-rated Cobras,' and the club owner put it on the calendar. It might have been written in a review in the paper."

COLLECTION OF CRAIG HOPKINS

Told that others had said the blues bands attracted the best-looking girls, Joe said, "Oh yeah. Without a doubt. A lot of it was because they could dance to us, and it wasn't country two-step, it was real sexy – Ray Charles, Bobby Blue Bland, B.B. King and all the good R&B songs. The Cobras were a true R&B band; the Thunderbirds were a blues band. We did blues, but we were R&B, which was different than it is now."

May 17: Soap Creek Saloon, Austin, TX (Cobras)

May 27: Steamboat 1874, Austin, TX (Cobras)

May 28: Steamboat 1874, Austin, TX (Cobras)

June 14: Soap Creek Saloon, Austin, TX (Cobras)

June 23: Soap Creek Saloon, Austin, TX (Cobras)

June 24: Soap Creek Saloon, Austin, TX (Cobras)

© KEN HOGE

JOE SUBLETT: "I picked Stevie up one night to go see Albert King at Antone's. Stevie was dying, *dying* to play with Albert King, but he didn't want to say anything [to him]. He mentioned it to Clifford, and he went up on a break and said, 'You gotta hear Stevie.' Albert wasn't too open to having some kid up there. Clifford was pretty dogged about getting people up on stage. He got me up there with my hero, Junior Walker, one night. Clifford was respected by the artists enough that Albert finally [relented] and brought Stevie up."

CLIFFORD: "The first time we brought Albert King, Stevie was there. And that's the one thing in his life that he wanted was to play with Albert King. And so he asked me if I would go ask Albert King if he could play. Well, you know, I'd never dealt with these guys before. He was a big man, Albert King. And very intimidating, you know. So I didn't know him. This was the first time. It wasn't like later years. So I went up and asked him. I said, 'Sir, I have a friend, this little bitty scrawny boy standing right next to me, and he really wants to play with you. Would it be okay?' He said, 'No.' I said, 'Thank you, sir.' I walked away.

"I told Stevie, 'He said no, man.' Stevie said, 'Oh, please, ask him again.' 'I'm scared, man.' You know, I really was. But I loved Stevie so much I got the courage to go ask him a second time. And so I said, 'Sir, I just want to tell you, we really respect you and we're honored to have you here. And I would never do anything to embarrass you, but I promise you, I promise you this kid can really play.' So, you know, Albert had been through the Fillmore trip and all of that. And I guess to shut me up or something, he said, 'Okay.' And so he got Stevie up there and they started playing. And Stevie almost scared him to death. I mean, he had never seen – he had seen Clapton and Hendrix and everyone else. But he had never seen anything like this kid. Even though Stevie was little, he had those hands that could really bend those strings, man. And he was doing Albert King. And so Albert had to dig into his bag of tricks, man. And it was the best I've ever saw Albert or the best I ever saw Stevie."[36]

June 25: Soap Creek Saloon, Austin, TX (Cobras)

NOTE: The primary resource for researching Austin gigs during this period, the *Austin Sun,* was not published from June 18 to August 3.

July 7-9: Albert King three-night stand at Antone's

It may have been during one of these gigs at Antone's that Stevie finally got to jam with his idol. Clifford encouraged Albert to let Stevie come up, and Albert was understandably reticent but had noticed Stevie at his feet all night.

JIMMIE: "Nobody would sit in with Albert King. You had to be stupid to sit in with Albert King because he would play all this incredible stuff, and then he would make fun of you. I had already been playing with Freddie King, which is about the same thing, you know. But when Stevie sat in with Albert King, Albert would play a line, and then Stevie would play it. I don't know how he did it. Nobody else would even [try]. Albert couldn't believe that this kid could do that because he had never heard anybody do it. You know, [Stevie] could just play the shit out of the guitar, and it was getting better and better, and everybody knew it."[3]

JOE SUBLETT: "Albert gives him a solo and Stevie was tearing it up. You know, Stevie could get on stage with anybody and not be intimidated. He was happy, but he was playing his butt off, and he's doing his version of Albert King! And you could see Albert thinking, 'What's going on with this cat? He's out Albert King-ing me to death!'

"Finally, when it came time for Albert to do his next solo, he turned sideways and was hiding the neck of his guitar, looking at the audience as if to say, 'I know this kid is ripping me off – I'm not going to let him see my fretboard!' Just to let everybody in the place know that this kid was 'borrowing' his stuff [*laughs*]. Everybody got a chuckle out of it, including Stevie. We all just died laughing! 'Man, you're stealing my stuff, and you're kicking my butt with *my stuff*,' but it was a begrudging respect.

"After that, it kind of lightened up, and Stevie was walking on clouds. He was really happy. I think it was a pivotal experience. I mean, we got to play with a lot of great players. The Fabulous Thunderbirds and Paul Ray and the Cobras were the only two bands that played at Antone's except for road blues acts. We got to open for a lot of our heroes and occasionally actually play with our heroes. Stevie got a taste of that, and believe me, he held his own. He showed his Stevie flair even doing Albert King licks.

"I think that kind of opened his mind. It wasn't too much later after that, maybe six or eight months, that he started talking about putting his own band together. We let him sing one song a set, but Stevie hadn't really fronted a band. He'd do 'Texas Flood' or 'Tin Pan Alley.' He'd get one song a set, but it'd be twenty minutes long [*laughs*]! He'd do what seemed like ten choruses before he'd start singing, probably out of being nervous.

"The Cobras did a lot of Ray Charles and Bobby Bland – danceable R&B stuff – and the chicks loved to come out and dance. People hadn't really gotten hip to Stevie's thing yet. When he'd do twenty minutes and these long guitar solos, a lot of people would go outside and smoke a cigarette. It's funny, and you wouldn't think that that would happen, because he could play as well then as he ever could. People weren't ready for it yet. It didn't happen overnight."

JAMES ELWELL: "I remember Stevie [playing with] Albert King at Antone's. He called him out and was just blown away by Stevie – they were trading licks, and I remember Albert just kind of putting his head back, 'Whoa! Who is this kid?' That was quite a big deal." Asked if Stevie talked about it much afterwards, James says, "Well, not a whole lot. Keep in mind he was a very humble man. I don't know if I've ever met anyone who was kinder, with a bigger heart than Stevie. My friends used to accuse me of idolizing the guy. 'There are other things out there, James!' And there are, but I was just blown away with his genuine kindness and not being a bad guitar player either.

"We used to ride around together a lot, throwing his equipment in the back of my mother's '62 Buick or this old pickup I had, and take him down to Rockefeller's. He'd put things in the cassette deck: 'James. Man, dig that guy!' If he got his hands on a stereo, he was always playing with it. It was funny to watch – he was like a little kid. We talked about very little other than music."

Stevie did the same kinds of things other people did for fun. JAMES: "We'd bowl – rather late, or early, whatever you want to call it. Austin Bowl-A-Rama on South Lamar at Barton Springs. That was always a blast because we'd take our own bottles in there – we thought we were sneaking around, getting away with murder! We weren't worth a crap, but we had a blast and were always smiling. You know, I have trouble thinking [of a time] when Stevie wasn't happy. He might be a little disappointed from time to time, but so far as being *unhappy* or truly angry, I can't recall. Which is a pretty significant statement. I never really thought about that until you mentioned it."

July: Paul Ray takes a temporary leave of absence from the Cobras due to a throat problem. Stevie picks up some of the vocal duty. Ray returns on August 12. Whether this brief vocal duty motivated Stevie to start his own band is unknown, but it does seem awfully coincidental that within weeks that is exactly what he did.

MARY BETH GREENWOOD: "We were at Soap Creek Saloon. Stevie and I were sitting in a car with Paul Ray and his wife Diana [after] they got the news that Paul had nodes on his throat. It was a real upsetting night, and we were comforting them. Back then, Stevie wasn't singing, and we talked about him singing. A friend told him to just stay within his range, and he started singing."

GLENDA MAPLES: "He did not sing when I was with him [1970-1974]. Stevie was a preemie, and that's why he had so much trouble with his nose – allergies, asthma – and we didn't have the money to treat it. I think what happened after I left Austin was he went for all the allergy tests and got down to the root of it, and it opened up his vocals."

August 3: *Austin Sun*, Cobras' large ad thanking supporters during Paul Ray's illness and announcing his return on August 23 at Soap Creek Saloon.

August 4: Rome Inn, Austin, TX (Cobras)

August 5: Rome Inn, Austin, TX (Cobras)

August 6: Rome Inn, Austin, TX (Cobras)

PAUL RAY: "I had known Stevie since he was nine or ten years old. We already knew each other, so we didn't have to work any of that out. He was a good kid – smart, funny, great art talent. He could draw really well.

"I encouraged them all to sing – I wanted it to be a revue. I wanted it to be a 1963 Dallas nightclub band that could play just about anything – jazz, R&B, soul music, show tunes – a club band. So I encouraged him, and [Stevie] wanted to sing certain songs. Rodney said, 'I'd like to sing,' so I let Rodney sing – so they were the opening act. Cobras'd come out and do a few songs just like one of those blues revues.

"They'd come out and do one of their jazz instrumentals, one of their hot instrumentals, and Stevie'd just kill with that stuff – Stevie and Denny both. They'd take turns, and then Joe would do a sax thing, Rodney would sing a couple of songs, Stevie'd sing two or three songs. Then I'd come up and do 45 or 50 minutes. That was the show.

"I tell people I can't hear anymore because I had Stevie in one ear and Denny in the other and Rodney's big ol' size thirteen foot behind me on bass drum!"

Clearly, the blues revue scheme rubbed off on Stevie. After cutting his vocal teeth in the Cobras, he decided it was time to start his own band. For a blueprint he used the blues revue, creating Triple Threat Revue with singer Lou Ann Barton and singer/bass player Wesley Curley "W.C." Clark, Mike Kindred (keys) and Fredde "Pharoah" Walden (drums).

STEVIE: "Myself, Lou Ann Barton, Mike Kindred, W.C. Clark, Fredde Pharoah, and Johnny Reno were in a band called Triple Threat Revue, which was another nickname that I'd gotten sitting in at a little barbecue place outside of Austin

called Alexander's. It was a gas station, barbecue, and beer and dancing, bands-on-the-weekends place. I'd been taking turns ... whatever came to mind, playing drums, singing, playing guitar, playing bass – whatever – and somebody started calling me "triple threat." I left a band that I was with called the Cobras and started this band Triple Threat Revue because ... we looked at it as a revue because there were actually five different people in the band doing vocals, doing their little sections of the show. So it was like a revue."[37]

So Triple Threat was not a reference to Stevie, Lou Ann and W.C. at all. Stevie was the triple threat all by himself. Lou Ann and W.C. were part of the revue. In retrospect, perhaps they should have taken the "h" out of "Threat."

August 8: Soap Creek Saloon, Austin, TX (Triple Threat Revue debut?) Stevie said in an interview that this was the debut of Triple Threat Revue, but the author has been unable to confirm this through any other source.

August 19: Toblert's Chili Parlor, Dallas, TX (Cobras)

August 20: Toblert's Chili Parlor, Dallas, TX (Cobras)

Stevie was fulfilling commitments to the Cobras, particularly since Paul had been recuperating, and Mike Kindred had gigs to fulfill at Antone's backing up such folks as Luther Tucker. These situations prevented there being a clean break from the Cobras to Triple Threat. The new band was practicing at Odyssey Studios on 6th Street, possibly as early as the end of June, while Stevie and the others continued with other bands. Paul Ray and others confirm that Stevie did not leave the Cobras until mid-

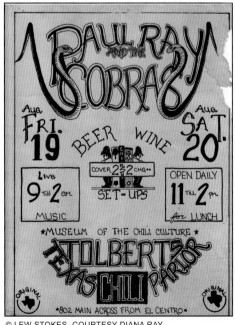

© LEW STOKES, COURTESY DIANA RAY

Triple Threat Revue at Soap Creek, Austin: Stevie, W.C. and Lou Ann. © KEN HOGE

September, and the local newspaper suggests the debut of Triple Threat Revue was September 23rd at After Ours. Mike Kindred recalls the first gig was at After Ours also but that they may have been doing a few gigs in August while Stevie was still playing with the Cobras.

DENNY FREEMAN: "We knew it was inevitable that it would come time for him to go off and do his own thing. We didn't think about it much one way or the other, but then he said he was ready to do his own thing, and we knew that was right and proper. We gave him our blessing and there he went."

JOE SUBLETT: "Stevie had asked me to lead the band with him in '77. But I was digging playing with the Cobras so much that I wasn't ready to leave. It was tempting to go with Stevie, but I didn't know where he was going to go or what he was going to do. You hear all these [great] things about Jimmie and Stevie and Austin and the blues, but back then we were the underground. People weren't really listening to blues at that time in Austin. If it weren't for Antone's, we wouldn't have had a home to learn about this stuff and have a nurturing place to play.

"So Stevie asked if I would play my nights off with Triple Threat as well as playing with the Cobras. He had several regular gigs around town, so I would go out and play with those guys on my nights off.

"Stevie was a very inspiring player, but I kind of knew instinctively when he went out on the road that this was going to be Stevie's thing. At least with the Cobras it was *our* thing. That was probably what made me hang with the Cobras. I would have a lot of influence, and it would be *our* band. Stevie was such a commanding presence as a lead guitar player, you knew it was going to be a Stevie [band] – and it was. It was great."

September 18: Soap Creek Saloon, Austin, TX. According to a note on the back of a photo of the Cobras, this was Stevie's last gig with Paul Ray and the Cobras.

PAUL RAY: "When Stevie quit, he was real sweet about it. He came up to me at rehearsal and said, 'I'm thinking about getting my own band,' and I said, 'Man, you really should – you're a front man now. You don't need to be in somebody else's band.' I was happy for him." Paul had left in July for medical reasons, but Stevie stayed until Paul recovered and was back with the band. Coincidence or another example of Stevie's respectful attitude?

September 23: Tolbert's Texas Chili Parlor, Dallas, TX (Blu-Tex Revue). "Stevie Vaughn's [sic] (formerly with Paul Ray and the Cobras) new band is called the Blu-Tex Revue and has been booked into [Tolbert's Texas] Chili Parlor." *Buddy*, October 1977.

Poster for the earliest confirmed Triple Threat Revue gig. COURTESY MIKE KINDRED

The *Buddy* blurb is the only reference to "Blu-Tex Revue," probably a mistake by the magazine because Mike Kindred does not recall ever using that name, and the poster at Tolbert's advertised "Tripple Threat" [sic]. However, he does recall that it was the first gig where the club owner, of his own accord, advertised as "Triple Threat Revue featuring Stevie Vaughan." MIKE: "I remember we pulled up to Tolbert's and W.C. saw that. 'Mike, what do you think about that?' [*Laughs*] I said, 'Well, man. It's happening of itself. I'm sure Stevie didn't call up here and insist they put his name [on the poster].' Stevie was just so hot. Hell, it just happened, and you can't argue with it."

September 23-24: After Ours, Austin, TX (Triple Threat Revue). The first mention of Triple Threat Revue in the weekly *Austin Sun* newspaper is for these After Ours club gigs. However, they conflict with the Tolbert's gigs in Dallas, and Mike Kindred does not recall doing Dallas and Austin gigs on the same day, two days running. Given that Mike took the poster from the Tolbert's gigs, the After Ours shows were probably cancelled.

W.C. CLARK: "I had a group [in the early seventies] then called Southern Feeling with Angela Strehli, Denny Freeman, Roddy Colonna and Alex Napier. [Later] Stevie was playing with the Cobras. We were all right there in Austin. We were all one big family. A lot of times we didn't even go home – people would just fall asleep at somebody else's house. In those days it was so good; everyone was so friendly in Austin and would wave and speak to you.

"We would get together in the daytime and jam and trade ideas. Stevie was always real interested in the name of chords and how different riffs go together. So we would do things like that at the very beginning, and then I would go hear him play with the Cobras. I knew he was good, but I didn't single him out or anything at the time.

"He then started coming to sit in with me and Southern Feeling. We would play guitars side by side, and I could tell how good he was. After that, things happened with me and I had to go to work. I was doing mechanic work, and he would come down and encourage me. 'Hey man, you shouldn't do stuff like this. Look at all that greasy stuff under your fingernails!' Eventually I took his advice, and that's when me and Mike Kindred, Lou Ann Barton, Fredde Walden [and Stevie] got together Triple Threat."

W.C. wasn't the only musician Stevie pulled out of semi-retirement from the world of automobiles. MIKE KINDRED: "In the summer of '77, Stevie approached me – I was working at the Sigmore Shamrock, pumping gas on South Lamar. He said, 'Come on, man, let's get a band together.' He was scared of me because he thought I would want a scope of repertoire wider than what he would want. I kinda feared him because he might not let me do some of my more imaginative stuff. In reality that is kind of what happened. Triple Threat started out as one thing and almost immediately coalesced into something else.

"I remember Stevie telling me, 'Man, I want you because I think you're the best, but I don't want to play no rock and roll.' I took that to mean he didn't want to play any straight-eight rock beats, and we didn't. I could live with that, 'as long as you have an open mind about some of the jazzier or more Latino things that I'd like to do,' and he agreed to that.

"There was a lot of adventurousness at the start. Everybody in the band sang, and we could put these enormous back-up parts behind whoever was singing. I thought it would be my role to bring different beats to bear. Stevie was so strong on shuffle material, I thought, 'Well, he's got that covered; I'll bring in a two-four beat or a samba or a rumba.'

"We were really pushing the envelope [at the beginning.] At the first gig at After Ours, I asked Lou Ann, 'Are you going to play some keyboards?' She said, 'Yes, I will play some organ.' Well, that night she sat down and played about eight bars of organ, and then got up

and never sat down again [*laughs*]. I was threatening to bring my C-melody saxophone out of the closet – we were just thinking of every wild idea we could.

"But it wasn't long before Stevie started taking objection to a couple of my tunes. The honeymoon didn't really last that long. But we had a lot of fun and had a good following here in town, particularly the Rome Inn and After Ours. With the Thunderbirds, we were considered the hippest acts in town. In those days, whoever was spearheading the local blues movement got the beautiful women!"

Stevie using a wine glass as a slide. © KEN HOGE

Lou Ann was not only one of the first and few white, female rhythm and blues singers, she was arguably the best. JESSE SUBLETT (The Skunks, among other credits): "Lou Ann struck me dead almost the first time I saw her, back in '74, I guess. I had never seen a sexier woman. I still believe she is far and away the best white R&B singer. None of the more recently popular local chick singers can touch her. I mean, she's sexy just reading the phone book."

MIKE KINDRED: "Lou Ann's part of the show was the featured part of the set. She sang more songs than anyone else in the band. We would start off with 'Green Onions' or 'Last Night' on the Hammond B-3, and maybe one other instrumental. Then I would sing two or three and turn it over to Stevie, who was just beginning to sing.

"He learned about vocal projection [in Triple Threat]. There was a W.C. tune on the first recording we did; Lou Ann, Stevie and myself were going to sing back-up vocals. Lou Ann and I, a couple of loud mouths, were, like, *two feet* behind Stevie – Stevie was right up at the mic. Me and Lou Ann were way off from it just to equalize everything!

"Anyway, [for the first set] Lou Ann's part would occur at about the half-way mark, and she would take it almost out, and we'd wind up with an instrumental or two at the end. The second set would go the same way except that W.C. and Fredde Pharoah would supplant mine and Stevie's vocal positions in the set. That way all five members sang. It really was a revue – it was aptly named. Fredde had these marvelous interpretations of Jimmy Reed tunes. He didn't sound like Jimmy Reed, but his own natural voice was perfect for stuff like 'Take Out Some Insurance' and 'Got Me Running, Got Me Hiding' and all that. He would do two or three of those in a row and the crowd just loved it."

Mike is most remembered in the context of Stevie's career for writing "Cold Shot." MIKE: "I had been doing 'Cold Shot' since 1972, but we had this rehearsal down in this church on Red River here in Austin, and that's when W.C. just supplanted the walking bass line that I had with the now famous [hums the familiar bass line that opens the song now]. He acted like he didn't even hear what I was playing, and it made the whole song coalesce, and I just shut up! 'Man, this is workin' – don't fix anything that ain't broke.' It solidified so well that I said, 'If anything ever happens with this, I'll cut you in,' which, of course, I did." W.C. has a twenty percent credit in the song.

JIMMIE VAUGHAN: "[Triple Threat] was a great band, and it was really powerful. I mean, if Stevie couldn't get you, Lou Ann would, you know. If they played somewhere, they were going to kill the audience; they were gonna make a lot of noise."[3]

Singer ANGELA STREHLI: "I was doing 'Texas Flood' for years, and when [Stevie] decided to start a group, to become a front man, he knew that he really should be singing. And he came to me, said that he always liked 'Texas Flood' and asked if I could teach

him the words, which I did. He needed some encouragement to sing – he was still a little scared. But he took the song and made it so associated with him that I quit doing it, because after a while, everyone thought I was imitating him!"[38]

📖**September 23:** *Austin Sun*, "Stevie Vaughan Exits," Jeff Nightbyrd: "The amazing productive relationship guitarist Stevie Vaughn [sic] enjoyed with Paul Ray and the Cobras has ended, with Stevie leaving to form a new band. The Triple Threat Review [sic] includes: Mike Kindred, formerly with Gypsee Eyes and Storm, keyboards; Freddie [sic] Walden of Storm on drums; W.C. Clark, formerly of Southern Feeling, on bass; and Fort Worth singer Louan Barron [sic], vocalist. They debuted at Austin's new and much needed after-hours club, called After Ours.

"Meanwhile the Cobras, who won the 1977 Sun Readers Poll as Band of the Year, plan to move Denny Freeman full-time into Stevie's guitar slot .... The reason for the split appears to be that Paul Ray's moving in a more mainstream direction while Stevie wants to play blues; also, Stevie Vaughn [sic] lately has been recognized as a star in his own right, and he wants his own band."

September 24: Tolbert's Texas Chili Parlor, Dallas, TX (Triple Threat Revue)

Angela Strehli (1971). © VAN BROOKS

October 2: Rome Inn, Austin, TX (Triple Threat Revue)

JAMES ELWELL: "My brother Scott [who was closer to Stevie's age] arranged a surprise birthday party for Stevie – had all the Antone's bartenders there, Alvin Crow came, Asleep at the Wheel's Ray Benson, Jimmie made a [brief appearance], other musicians too.

"How we got Stevie to the house was David Smith and his wife Kathy told Stevie, 'James just bought a new guitar and wants you to come over and take a look at it and see if it's worth a damn.' This is before cell phones, but David called from the house and said, 'We're on our way.' Everybody got quiet – it was amazing how we kept everybody quiet – it was quite a rowdy bunch, and we'd already been into the pre-game festivities!

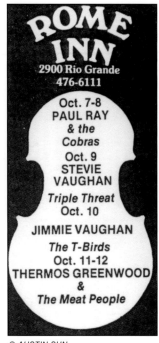

© AUSTIN SUN

"Stevie shows up – surprised the livin' crap out of him. He could not believe it: 'You got me!' Stevie was poor back then. We gave him a stereo system – nothing fancy, one of those receivers with a turntable and speakers to the side. He was out of his mind crazy – could not believe it. Kathy made a guitar cake that looked like a Stratocaster. I got the impression nobody'd ever done anything like that for him before. He was smiling ear to ear all night long. We all had a blast.

"Stevie couldn't believe someone would throw a party for him – he was that humble. At that time, he knew he could play guitar, but I don't think he knew of his potential greatness, whereas a lot of us did: this guy, with some exposure, is going places."

📖**October 7:** *Austin Sun*, "Triple Threat Review," Margaret Moser: "Triple Threat Revue's first week of performances promises to give Austin's blues bands serious competition. Fort Worth chanteuse Miss Lou Ann Barton decided Austin was ready for her once again, and with that in mind, skimmed the cream of the crop of Austin's rhythm and blues musicians. Besides Miss Lou Ann's cat scratch vocals, she hand-picked Freddie [sic] Walden and Mike Kindred, who thundered their way through Storm, on drums and keyboards respectively; W.C. Clark, bass and former lead guitarist for Southern Feeling; and the whiplash guitar of Stevie Vaughan, who just retired from a two-year tenure with Paul Ray and the Cobras. That ain't no empty threat."

COURTESY MIKE STEELE

COLLECTION OF CRAIG HOPKINS

Ms. Moser's report is suspect, missing the band's debut by a couple of weeks and suggesting Lou Ann put the band together. W.C. Clark has steadfastly maintained that it was Stevie who brought him back from working in an auto repair shop, and virtually all the contemporaneous press features focused on Stevie, not Lou Ann.

October 9: Rome Inn, Austin, TX (Triple Threat Revue)

October 20: After Ours, Austin, TX (Triple Threat Revue)

October 21: After Ours, Austin, TX (Triple Threat Revue)

October 22: After Ours, Austin, TX (Triple Threat Revue)

October 23: Rome Inn, Austin, TX (Triple Threat Revue)

November 3: Soap Creek Saloon, Austin, TX (Triple Threat Revue)

November 4: Soap Creek Saloon, Austin, TX (Triple Threat Revue)

November 5: Armadillo World Headquarters, Austin, TX (Triple Threat Revue) opening for Spirit

November 9: White Rabbit, Lubbock, TX (Triple Threat Revue)

November 10: White Rabbit, Lubbock, TX (Triple Threat Revue)

November 11: White Rabbit, Lubbock, TX (Triple Threat Revue)

November 12: White Rabbit, Lubbock, TX (Triple Threat Revue)

November 17: Rome Inn, Austin, TX (Triple Threat Revue)

November 18: Rome Inn, Austin, TX (Triple Threat Revue)

November 19: Rome Inn, Austin, TX (Triple Threat Revue)

December 4: Rome Inn, Austin, TX (Triple Threat Revue)

LEW STOKES: "Triple Threat was a band that should have exploded internationally. It was just mind boggling. Lou Ann never sounded that way with anyone else; Stevie and Kindred together was unbelievable; and W.C. was a true front man. Everyone revolved around – it wasn't just three singers, you had three front men. To watch Stevie play bass guitar and W.C. play lead guitar was really extraordinary. Stevie Vaughan was a *massive* bass guitar player when he wanted to be. W.C. told him that he

© KERRY AWN

needed to understand bass guitar. For all his bizarre take on blues – it's really just rock and roll – comes out of W.C. Clark and his teaching of the bass and rhythm guitar, where you do all three at the same time (including lead guitar)."

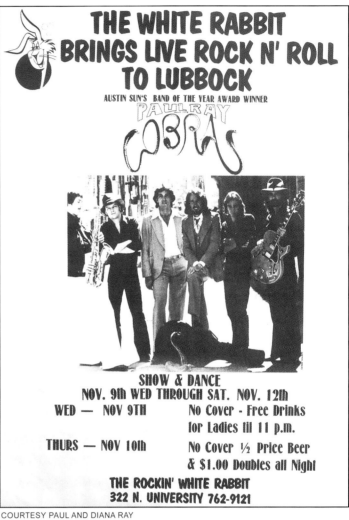

COURTESY PAUL AND DIANA RAY

MARY BETH GREENWOOD: "When he would play at Rome Inn, Billy Gibbons came by on Monday nights [sometimes with Tony Dukes]. It was like a happening, but very few people in the crowd. Gibbons wrote that song, 'Low Down In the Streets'":

Well there comes Lola, out of control-a:
She just loves those rhythm and blues.
And Miss Ivy will be arriving;
In leopard skin tights she's willing to cruise.
It's a fiend scene and it happens 'bout once a week.
So for some bread come do your head
And get lowdown in the street.

There's Jimmie and Jojo, there's Kim and Keith,
Way outside the eyes of cool.
And Sweet M.B., and there's Little G.B.
Everybody wants to be their fool. ... [41]

MARY BETH: "Jimmie is of course Jimmie Vaughan, Jojo is Joe Nick Patoski, Kim Wilson, Keith Ferguson. Sweet MB was me, and Little GB was his girlfriend at the time, Gretchen Barber, and that was kind of late in the scene – Billy was coming along before Gretchen was around. Later, he would get us a limo to go see Stevie, and it was a dollar to get in. Of course Billy paid it for us.

"I was dating Eric Johnson – we had an on again, off again thing for quite a while, but mostly on. There was some little breakup, they usually lasted a couple of weeks, and Billy would get me a limo and have some girls come over and dress me, and we'd all go see Stevie. It was a lot of fun.

"I'm not sure who 'Lola' was. Miss Ivy was a hooker. They kinda had this seedy, side scene. Ivy wanted to learn photography, so I met with her and gave her a book. The whole band cracked up, rolling on the floor. They didn't want me to be friends with her, and I found out later she was a prostitute."

Lola was Lois Loeffler, a member of the "Whorellas," a group of Rome Inn waitresses.

Mary Beth and Lindi visiting the studio. © MARY BETH GREENWOOD

TONY DUKES: "Billy and I had a real appreciation for Jimmie and Stevie, and Billy would come up to the Rome Inn. Billy liked it because he could get away where no one knew him [this was before the long beard]. The first four or five times we went up there, there were literally eight or ten people – Stevie, Ray Benson, Miss Ivy, who was kind of a well known prostitute, and a few other people. Then Billy got the idea of chartering a blues cruise, so he rented a bus and took people up from Houston. That kind of helped break the T-Birds.

"Anyway, before all that happened, Stevie was up there playing that Rickenbacker that he later gave to Hubert Sumlin. Of course, Billy wanted to see it, so he walks up there and turns around with this horrible expression on his face. The strings were so high and so big, he couldn't make a note on it. He was amazed that Stevie could play it."

Word about Jimmie and the Thunderbirds was spreading, but Stevie was just getting started with his own band after two years in the Cobras. Tony remembers several occasions when fans of Jimmie learned he had a guitar-playing little brother. "I was filling in for The Romantics' bass player in Austin, and they wanted to go see the Thunderbirds. So we went and saw them, and afterwards they asked if there was anybody else to see. I said, 'His little brother is playing across the street,' and they said, "He has a little brother?' Like, 'There's *another one*?' We went over and at the break I asked if they were ready to go back, and they said, 'Oh hell no, we're not going back. We've never heard anything like this in our lives.'

"We were at Rome Inn one night after closing. Billy Gibbons, Stevie, Keith Ferguson and Jimmie sitting at a table. I asked Stevie, because Stevie would always talk to you, more than Jimmie, if he cared if I put mailbox letters on my guitar like he did with his initials, just for one club gig. Stevie said, 'Sure;

Triple Threat Revue at the Armadillo: Mike Kindred, W.C. Clark, Lou Ann Barton, Fredde Walden, Stevie. © KEN HOGE

I stole it from Jimmie.' Then I was on the spot. I turned to Jimmie and asked him. He said, 'Go ahead, it's not my idea; I stole it from a [black guy].'"

Later, Tony and Keith were back in Houston: "Keith Ferguson was there one night at Rockefeller's, and we opened for them. Keith was staying with Little Junior, and I lived right next door. [Freddie Cisneros was known as Little Junior One Hand.] He said, 'Dukes, you got all weird about that sticker stuff. Let's go look at some stuff.' We found this applique paper, and Keith bought this roll of stuff that looked like a brick wall. He cut it out and put it on his Telecaster that night, so it looked like he was playing a brick Telecaster! Keith was always a slouch, and it really looked like he was weighted down with bricks. He took it off at the end of the night and handed it to me and said, 'Now, don't you want to use that too?' And I said, 'Yeah, I kinda do.'"

JAMES ELWELL: "The Rome Inn was one of Triple Threat's main venues. I remember taking my father to see Stevie for the first time; didn't know if he would dig it or not, but ... 'Man, that boy can play guitar.' [Laughs] I mean, he was recognized by all generations."

JIMMIE VAUGHAN recalls those slower years: "You'd go to see Triple Threat, or you'd go see Double Trouble, or you'd go see the Thunderbirds or whatever, and there'd be twenty people on Saturday night. And the band would be up there burnin' – just smokin.' There'd be people sitting around taking it for granted because it wasn't the popular thing. It wasn't on the radio, you know. So there's a lot of years when you're just playing hard, and just a few people really knew what was going on, musically speaking.

"[But] you gotta understand – we had everything. If you had a gig and a good band, you didn't know that you didn't have a million dollars. You had $1400 in your pocket – cash – and you had a girlfriend. What more could you want?"[3]

December 3: Armadillo World Headquarters, Austin, TX (Triple Threat Revue) opening for Eric Johnson

---

December 18: Rome Inn, Austin, TX (Triple Threat Revue)

December 21: Soap Creek Saloon, Austin, TX (Triple Threat Revue)

📖 Edentata Press, *Burton's Book Of The Blues: A Decade Of American Music 67-77*, Burton Wilson

3

Triple Threat to Double Trouble 1978–1980

1978

Not having been a frontman for long, and not having done much singing, Stevie had not worked much on lyrics. The only major composition prior to 1978 was "Dirty Pool," written in 1973 with Doyle Bramhall, and Doyle had a lot more to do with the lyrics than Stevie.

MUSICIANS PROFILE

NAME STEVIE VAUGHAN ADDRESS 407 W 43RD AUSTIN TX 78751

TELEPHONE 451 0463

What is your principal instrument? GUITAR

What other instruments do you play with professional competence? (List only those instruments which you own or have readily available for possible work)

What type(s) of music do you prefer to play? R&B, BLUES, SOUL, JAZZY BLUES

Do you read music? NO Are you a proficient sight reader? NO

Are you a present member of a working group? YES Name of group STEVIE VAUGHAN & THE TRIPLE THREAT REVUE Leader of group MY SELF

Do you have recording experience? YES Summarize 2 DEMOS FOR A&M A RECORD WITH THE COBRAS, VARIOUS OTHER STUDIO EXPERIENCE

Are you presently teaching music? NO Seeking students? NO

Summarize Teaching Experience

Are you an arranger, composer, songwriter? (Summarize) HELPED WRITE AND ARRANGE SOME OF THE MATERIAL ON THE A&M TAPES AND FOR MYSELF TO BE RECORDED LATER

(Leaders Only) What is the usual instrumentation of your group? GUITAR, BASS DRUMS AND KEYBOARDS

Are you under contract, obligation to a manager or agent? (Name) NO

Are you available for work? YES Describe type of work sought and limitations of your schedule, if any CLUB, CONCERT, STUDIO, ROADWORK / NONE

Summarize your recent experience listing groups with whom you have worked:

PAUL RAY AND THE COBRAS – MARCH – 75 THRU AUGUST – 77 THE NIGHTCRAWLERS

STUDIO WORK WITH PLAS JOHNSON, TOMMY MCLURE, RUSS KUNKEL, LEE SKLARR, MIKE UTLEY MARC BENNO GORDON DEWITTY

COMMENTS:

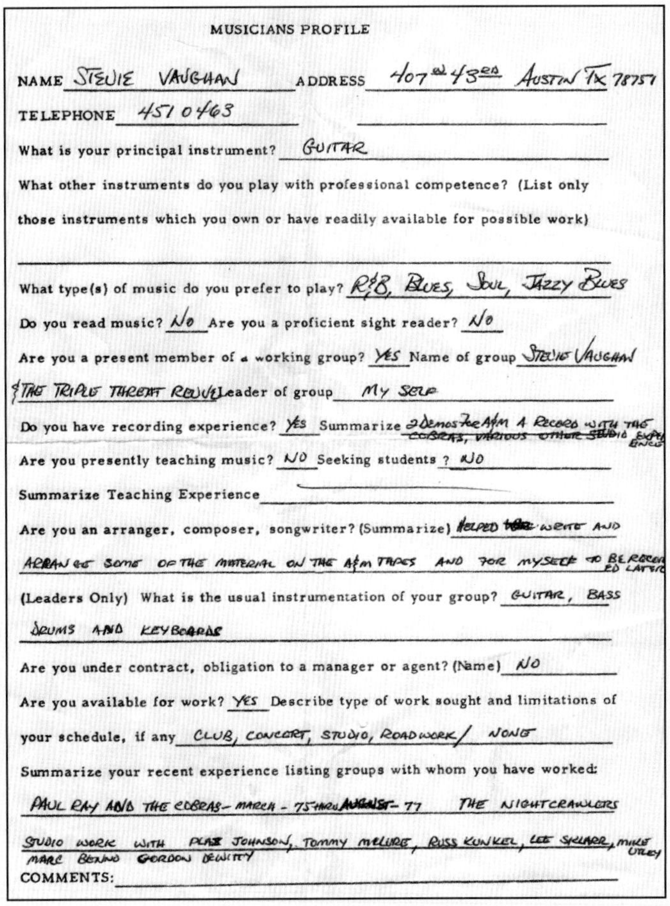

Form completed by Stevie. COURTESY MIKE STEELE

Now that he is part of the quintuple-headed vox machine known merely as *Triple* Threat, Stevie begins to write, starting with "Pride and Joy" and "I'm Cryin'" for his girlfriend, Lindi Bethel. Not bad for essentially the first ride out of the chute. Of course, the two songs are musical twins, but the lyrics reveal opposite perspectives of their rollercoaster relationship.

STEVIE: "'Pride and Joy' was kind of funny. I'd written the song in the studio, recorded it right then and brought it home to the girlfriend that I'd had at the time. I don't know what the problem was, but she didn't think it was really about her, and we got into this big argument. So I got back in the car and went back into the studio and rewrote some words to the song – 'I'm Cryin'' – and brought this home and went, 'Here.'"[5]

Stevie did not record with Double Trouble until July 1978 but he recorded in Hole studios with Triple Threat Revue in January 1978, including "I'm Cryin'". The existence of the Hole recordings in 1978-79 was not public knowledge until thirty years later, so there is always a chance more recordings will surface.

January 10: Hole Sound Recording studios, Austin, TX (Triple Threat Revue) about thrity minutes; only known studio recording of the band

– Tears Come Down Like Rain (I Tried)
– I'm Cryin'
– Reap What You Sew (W.C. Clark vocal)
– Cold, Cold, Cold

LINDI: "The only song I know of that he wrote when I was with him was that – I think he titled it 'Sweet Little Thing,' but they changed it – 'Pride and Joy.' It was late at night and we were already in bed. Then I realized he wasn't in bed, and I thought something was wrong. I got up to go check on him, and he was in the dark with the window open. I guess the moon was shining in because he was just kneeling down. He didn't have any clothes on, but he had his *hat* on [*laughs*]. I go, 'What are you doing?' He said, 'Oh. I just got this idea, so I'm writing a song.'

"He changed it when he married Lenny, whatever that lyric when he puts her name in it ["Well I love my Lenny, she's long and lean ..."]. He used to put my name, and I would be embarrassed.

I said, 'Stevie, I don't think you need to do that.' I didn't like [him using my name]. He may have said he wrote it for Lenny, but I was living with him at that time, and I don't think he had met her." By 1986, he had taken Lenny's name out too.

January 24: Opera House, Austin, TX (Triple Threat Revue)

Beginning in February 1978 Stevie was a fairly regular session player at Hole Sound Recording in Austin, owned by Perry and Patty Patterson. Perry was also a singer and songwriter. Most of the recordings in 1978 featured singer Lynnann Gandy of the band The Stallions, but also included on occasion W.C. Clark, Chris Layton and David Roach. The sessions are noted below, scattered from February 1978 to February 1979. Session personnel are noted where identified from session log sheets. The sessions were often named in a comical or random fashion, such as the "Lou Ann Session" below, which doesn't appear to have anything to do with anyone named Lou Ann.

February 8: Hole Sound Recording, Austin, TX. "Lou Ann Session" with David Nueman, Charlie Sauer, Mike Kindred, SRV and David Roach.
  – Softly Like
  – Gift of My Heart
  – The Memories

© JIM FRANKLIN

February 9: Armadillo World Headquarters, Austin, TX (Triple Threat Revue) opening for Toots and The Maytals

---

MIKE KINDRED: "We played a couple of big shows at the Armadillo, one with Toots and the Maytals, that was recorded, but the tape was lost. That's really sad, because we all listened to it the night we did it, and we just surrendered it into the hands of this hippie guy – I never will forget what bad b.o. he had. We called him Stinky. Then he disappeared. The show was just magic. We went over every bit as big as Toots did. The place was packed – sold out. It was one of the magical Austin nights in the seventies. There's no way to describe the joyful vibe that was going down, man."

© HENRY GONZALEZ, COURTESY MIKE KINDRED

Mike recalls some "very fine moments" with Stevie although they didn't become really tight. "I remember the late nights coming back from Lubbock or wherever, and we'd be the only ones awake in the van besides W.C., who was driving. Lou Ann'd be stretched out bodily across the three of us. And the times he'd come over to my house wanting to talk about philosophy and spirituality – reincarnation, Buddhist precepts, meditation, basic New Age stuff. Everybody was reading the Eastern stuff – that's what hippies read. Like a lot of geniuses, he communicated better with music than he did with words.

"We were travelling around in W.C.'s van. He mounted some speakers on the ceiling of the van, and everybody was always knocking the hell out of their head getting in and out of the van with all those damn speakers. So we found some football helmets in a pawn shop one day and bought 'em, and got in the van before W.C. When he got in the van and looked in the back, he saw these helmeted band members [laughs]."

February 16: Rome Inn, Austin, TX (Triple Threat Revue)

February 17: Rome Inn, Austin, TX (Triple Threat Revue)

February 18: Rome Inn, Austin, TX (Triple Threat Revue)

February 21: Steamboat 1874, Austin, TX (Triple Threat Revue)

February 22: Steamboat 1874, Austin, TX (Triple Threat Revue)

February 23: Steamboat 1874, Austin, TX (Triple Threat Revue)

February 23: Hole Sound Recording, Austin, TX. "Madhouse Session" with Lynnann Gandy, Bill Gandy, Bob Gray, Skip Olsen, Charlie Prichard and SRV.

– Jam/Stevie
– Kathleen
– Outlaw Sunrise
– Foster's (?) Blues
– Get Off That Bottle Daddy
– You Drive
– Lord Have Mercy
– Push King
– Feelin' Like
– Hey You
– Somebody

February 24: Hole Sound Recording, Austin, TX. "Amazing Shit Session" with Lynnann Gandy, Bill Gandy, Bob Gray, Skip Olsen, Charlie Prichard, Perry Patterson and SRV.

– Big Daddy Rock & Roll
– Jail Song
– Drunkard's Salute
– Cold Train
– Too Long
– Outlaw Sunrise
– Hard Luck Girl
– Push King
– Hard Luck Girl
– Cold Train
– Somebody
– Flying Machine / Hey You
– Too Long

February 24: Raul's, Austin, TX (Triple Threat Revue)

JOHNNY RENO sits in on sax during March/April. "I wasn't quite sure what the dynamic was, whether [Kindred and Clark] weren't into what Stevie wanted to do. There was a lot of free-flowing, cross-pollination of bands in Austin. Maybe W.C. wanted to be in a soul band more, and Kindred wanted to be in a rock band more, so they just went on and found other people to play with."

© DIANA RAY

It was also around this time that keyboardist REESE WYNANS saw Stevie perform. Reese worked with Jerry Jeff Walker from 1975 to 1980 and then with Delbert McClinton. "Seeing Stevie in Triple Threat, I thought that he was a great player – had a little work to do on his singing – but had a really good feel for the blues. I liked his blues playing better than I liked his rock playing." Reese would become a member of Double Trouble seven years later.

March 2: Soap Creek Saloon, Austin, TX (Triple Threat Revue)

March 4: Love Field Inn Ballroom, Dallas, TX (Triple Threat Revue)

March 10: Rome Inn, Austin, TX (Triple Threat Revue)

March 11: Rome Inn, Austin, TX (Triple Threat Revue)

© LEW STOKES

119

© KERRY AWN

© HENRY GONZALES

© KERRY AWN

© DILLO/TREY YANCY, COURTESY MIKE KINDRED

March 17: Cotton Club, Lubbock, TX (Triple Threat Revue)

March 18: Cotton Club, Lubbock, TX (Triple Threat Revue)

  – Shake For Me
  – You Done Lost Your Good Thing Now
  – May I Have A Talk With You
  – Tin Pan Alley
  – Howling For My Darling

© KEN HOGE

March 19: Rome Inn, Austin, TX (Triple Threat Revue)

March 24: Raul's, Austin, TX (Triple Threat Revue)

March 26: Rome Inn, Austin, TX (Triple Threat Revue)

March 27: Raul's, Austin, TX (Triple Threat Revue)

March 30: Soap Creek Saloon, Austin, TX (Triple Threat Revue)

March 31: Soap Creek Saloon, Austin, TX (Triple Threat Revue)

April: *Guitar Player*, "Pro's Reply: Doug Sahm," by Dan Forte. The legendary Texas musician Doug Sahm (Sir Douglas Quintet) mentions Stevie as a rising star.

April: *Texas Monthly*, "Play That Funky Music, White Boys," Joe Nick Patoski. "Austin's blues revival is .... led by two recklessly brilliant guitar-playing brothers – Jimmie and Stevie Vaughan from Dallas. Twenty-three-year-old Stevie is the cornerstone of the relatively new Triple Threat Revue, a democratically run five-piece outfit. Each member takes a turn singing. .... The real pyrotechnics are reserved, though, for when Stevie indulges in an old personal favorite like 'Texas Flood,' singing with the resonance of a 45-year-old Mississippi Delta farmhand and playing thick, slurring guitar notes rooted in the groove of Louisiana's legendary Lazy Lester." Note that Patoski was among the first to write about the Vaughans in a regional magazine and, with Bill Crawford, wrote the first biography of Stevie in 1993, *Caught in the Crossfire* [highly recommended].

Vaughan brothers. © KEN HOGE

– Kansas City (Barton)
– I'm a Good Woman (Barton)
– Will My Man Be Home Tonight? (Barton)
– Albert's Alley (instrumental)
– (instrumental)
– (instrumental)
– Raise Your Window (Kindred)
– Shake & Rock 'n' Roll (Kindred)
– Hey Girl (Kindred)
– Every Day I Have the Blues (Clark)
– Sweet Little Angel (Clark)
– I Tried Pretty Baby (SRV)
– Don't You Lie To Me (SRV)
– Texas Flood (SRV)
– You Done Lost Your Good Thing Now (SRV)
– I'm Cryin' (SRV)
– (instrumental)
– (instrumental)
– There's a Place Up the Street (Kindred)
– Roll With It (Kindred)
– Honest I Do (Kindred)
– Lucille (Kindred)
– (instrumental)
– (instrumental)
– Go Easy on Me, Baby (Kindred)
– I Don't Know (Kindred)
– You're Stone Cold (Kindred)
– Part Time Lover (Clark)
– Next Time You See Me (Clark)
– Done Got Over It (Clark)
– Have You Ever Been Mistreated? (Clark)

April 10: Hole Sound Recording, Austin, TX. "Dolores Session" with W.C. Clark, Perry Patterson, Skip Olsen, Charlie Prichard and SRV on drums!
– River Song
– Doin' For You
– Whatever Is Necessary

April 12: Stubb's Bar-B-Q, Lubbock, TX (Triple Threat Revue)

April 13: Stubb's Bar-B-Q, Lubbock, TX (Triple Threat Revue)

A sample set list from a Stubb's show by Triple Threat (vocalist):
– Theme from Peter Gunn (instrumental)
– Natural Born Lover (Barton)
– Tell Me Why (Barton)
– All Through the Night (Barton)
– Te Ni Nee Ni Nu (Barton)
– St. James Infirmary (Barton)

April 14: Stubb's Bar-B-Q, Lubbock, TX (Triple Threat Revue)

April 15: Cotton Club, Lubbock, TX (Triple Threat Revue)

April 19: Soap Creek Saloon, Austin, TX (Triple Threat Revue)

April 21: Rome Inn, Austin, TX (Triple Threat Revue)

April 22: Rome Inn, Austin, TX (Triple Threat Revue)

April 23: Rome Inn, Austin, TX (Triple Threat Revue)

April 26: Soap Creek Saloon, Austin, TX (Triple Threat Revue)

April 28: After Ours, Austin, TX (Triple Threat Revue)

📖**April 28:** *Austin Sun*, "The Vaughans – Mainline Blues," Bill Bentley. First cover story to include Stevie.

Stevie made a habit of remembering those who paved the road for his success. Years later, Stevie inscribed a copy of *Texas Flood* to Bill Bentley, the author of the above article, "To one of the best friends anyone can ever have! All the love."

Asked what reward he gets from playing, Stevie responds, "There's a lot of them, but one stands out. When you're playing and all of a sudden you realize your toes are ... just ... tightened up, and you get a chill all the way up your back because of what you just gave somebody, and they gave it back. That's probably the biggest thrill. Or you're playing someplace and you hit a note and people start screaming – that's it. You gave them a thrill, or you soothed them. That's what the blues do to me. If people tell me they don't want to hear a blues band because it brings them down, they're not paying attention at all."

As BENTLEY commented in the *Austin Sun* article: "Though not actually the leader of Triple Threat – the other two-thirds of the Threat are singer Miss Lou Ann and bassist W.C. Clarke [sic] – Stevie is the one who keeps the fire burning. And, as Jimmy [sic] is sometimes known to point out in explaining the brothers' difference, 'Stevie sings.'"

Jimmie's comment fails to cover the full scope of brother Stevie's talents. On at least one occasion when bass player Keith Ferguson was out of the Thunderbirds lineup, Stevie merely took Keith's left-handed bass and played it upside down. Another time, Stevie sat in on drums.

April 29: After Ours, Austin, TX (Triple Threat Revue)

📖**May:** *Living Blues*, blurb re concert

May 3: "Bach's Lunch," Symphony Square (noon), Austin, TX. Soap Creek Saloon, Austin, TX (Triple Threat Revue)

May 5:, Soap Creek Saloon, Austin, TX (Triple Threat Revue) with George Thorogood

May 6: Soap Creek Saloon, Austin, TX (Triple Threat Revue) with George Thorogood

May 8: Rome Inn, Austin, TX (Triple Threat Revue) with Fabulous Thunderbirds

May 10: Soap Creek Saloon, Austin, TX (Triple Threat Revue)

May 13: Soap Creek Saloon, Austin, TX (Triple Threat Revue)

© KERRY AWN

MIKE KINDRED: "I had finally been introduced to Clifford Antone. I had heard things when the club first got started about club policy and about him that I did not like. I did not join the rush that most of the blues crowd made to run down there and ingratiate themselves before the emperor Antone. I finally made peace with him – I went down and jammed and he liked it or something, so he says, 'Would you be one of our utility band leaders and get cats together to back up certain acts?'

"Clifford had an excellent funk band along the lines of Earth, Wind and Fire in there one night. I had never seen an act like

Austin Sun

that – they were just funkin' the place down! I went to Clifford laughing and said, 'Wow. Dig this!' Clifford was all dejected. He hated it."

Antone's was temporarily out of the picture for Stevie and the band. But it wasn't Triple Threat's music that Antone objected to. Mike continues: "Angela Strehli became Clifford's paramour and the hostess of Antone's – house vocalist. Angela had been with W.C. in Southern Feeling [before Triple Threat], in the biblical sense as well as in the same band. That's why Antone's wouldn't hire Triple Threat. W.C. came in the 6th Street door one night and three of the biggest bouncers in the place came right towards us. W.C. says, 'Aw, now, are we gonna fight?' I weighed about 140 pounds and was thinking, 'Oh, shit.' W.C.'s in fighting stance and here comes Clifford to defuse the thing, and we got in. I recall us playing Antone's only one time."

Double Trouble: Lou Ann and Stevie at Antone's. © KEN HOGE

Contracts in Stevie's handwriting.
COURTESY MIKE STEELE

MIKE: "Stevie was just so dynamic, so as his power grew, he began to exert it more and I felt pushed around a little, so not long after the first of the year I gave notice. 'This is not going the way I thought it would.' Stevie said, 'Give it a month; don't tell me that now.' I did wait another month, but I was out by the middle of May. W.C. was out right around that same time."

One of the things Mike recalls most about Stevie was … "his style. Any blues lick you've ever heard, he did it twice as big as you'd ever heard it done before. He was that intense – like the Gustav Mahler of blues rock. Everything came through Stevie bigger. He was very competitive on stage without being blatant about it. It was like being on stage with Wyatt Earp, and you knew that he would use his guns, and you better have yours loaded! You want to play with guys like that.

"He could crack me up unexpectedly. One night we were at Stubb's up in Lubbock and there was a local blues guitar player opening. Stevie was sitting with his back to the guy, and the guy was clearly trying to impress us and Stevie. He made some kind of crack, 'Now we're going to do a really low-down blues,' and Stevie goes [very sarcastically] 'Oooooo!' and threw up his hands [laughs mightily]. You'd have had to have seen it, but it was hilarious.

At odd moments like that he could really split my sides with his humor."

It was a bit unfair to call it *Triple* Threat, given that Mike and Fredde also contributed lead vocals, and Mike was probably the best songwriter at the time. MIKE: "The thing about Triple Threat was you were dealing with five chiefs. There wasn't a servant in the crowd. It's a wonder it lasted ten months. W.C. and myself split over more or less musical principles, but Stevie and Lou Ann Barton – strong personalities – are you kidding [*laughs*]? They made it happen until they decided, 'Well, I'm not going to be charged with attempted murder here or something.' They were both strong as hell. They each had their ideas about

Stevie with Hubert Sumlin at Antone's; Stevie playing the Rickenbacker guitar he later gave to Hubert.
© KEN HOGE

what they wanted the band to be. So the five chiefs were pared down to two. Still, it's hard to make that work sometimes."

mid-May: Johnny Reno (sax) and Jackie Newhouse (bass) join Stevie, Lou Ann Barton (vocals) and Fredde "Pharoah" Walden (drums) to form Double Trouble, taking their name from the Otis Rush song. Print ads continue to advertise Triple Threat Revue until June 23.

STEVIE: "[In Triple Threat] we had too many leaders. It went off into a bunch of different bands. Lou Ann and I stayed together and the obvious thing to do was to call it instead of Triple Threat Revue, call it Double Trouble, because we were both trouble and there was just two of us [*laughs*]. And at the same time, my favorite song was "Double Trouble" by Otis Rush. Man ... it just made sense."[37]

CHRIS LAYTON: "Triple Threat more or less turned into Double Trouble. A bunch of people left, and the whole band just kind of completely reconfigured. It was basically just Stevie and Lou Ann left, so they thought, 'Well, let's call the band Double Trouble.'" [Andy Aledort: "From what I've heard, it actually was 'double trouble' the way those two got along."] CHRIS: "It was kind of like quadruple trouble."[35] "It was kind of a volatile relationship; they had a great respect for one another and they butted heads a lot, but they did good work together."[3]

New in Stevie's musical life is bass player JACK NEWHOUSE. "I met Stevie in May of '78 when Lou Ann called me and said they needed a bass player. We'd known each other in Fort Worth for years. I came down and met him the day of the first gig we did together at the Rome Inn. I hadn't seen or heard his music, but I knew who he was.

"I think it was really an audition. Johnny Reno and Lou Ann were with Triple Threat. W.C. had decided to form his own band. I played that first night with them and fit right in. At the time, I was living in Fort Worth and playing with the Juke Jumpers. I really enjoyed that, but I needed a change. I'd been thinking about getting out of Fort Worth for a while, so when the opportunity came, I took it."

Johnny Reno, who had cut his sax teeth at the Bluebird club in Fort Worth, recalls that the first gigs for Double Trouble were at Soap Creek Saloon, and they shortly began doing Tuesday nights at Rome Inn. JOHNNY: "The T-Birds had Monday nights (blues night), and we started doing the regular thing on Tuesday nights and scuffling around town trying to get gigs. We played Antone's quite often; we'd open for somebody. The first guys to get the gig at Antone's would be the T-Birds, like if Muddy was in town, Clifton [Chenier] or whoever, and they would open the show or be part of the band to back up [the headliner]. But the T-Birds were gone a lot, so if they weren't doing it, we got the call. And we might do a Wednesday night, or if someone cancelled, we might get the whole night on a Friday or Saturday.

"Lou Ann was pretty happening at that time, and Stevie was still trying to get his frontman chops together. It was kind of tough for him to play the guitar the way he did and sing at the same time. For the first six months or so, there were a lot of times where Stevie would stop playing and sing, leave those spaces while he was trying to figure out how to play that rhythmic style that he did.

"That was part of the reason he wanted the sax or a keyboard. I was known for being more of a rhythmic saxophone player; I wasn't a great soloist at that time. I was into the bands where the horns riffed all the time – they played what a keyboard player would play or a second guitar player – real Chicago style, not so much solos. Although, I played a bunch of solos and got my abilities up, because Stevie was pretty generous with stage time.

"The other thing was that he really dug my sound. I had a real gritty sax sound going. Not a lot of other guys were playing like that; it wasn't a popular style. Joe Sublett played kind of like that with the Cobras. In the seventies, R&B – there was only a small group of people that really liked that stuff – [was] not nearly as popular as it is now."

Double Trouble carried over a bit of the revue format of Triple Threat, with the band warming up the audience before Lou Ann came out. JOHNNY: "We would come out and do two or three instrumentals and just *work out* – things that turned into 'Rude Mood' as a blues shuffle. We might play one of those for seven or eight minutes! Stevie would really work out, and then I would work out. That's where I started getting really good at my horn, because I had a lot of time to play. It was unstructured. I didn't have to play horn parts like if I'd been in the Cobras.

"I had the *sound*, but I wasn't a trained saxophone player. One night, an older black guy that played in Bobby Bland's band was off the road – I could never get that sound, but he had it – and I finally asked him, 'Man, how do you get that sound?' He said, 'You just hum the note while you're blowing it,' and that was the trade secret.

"We would do at least thirty minutes before Lou Ann came out. If we were at Rome Inn and knew we had a long night, we'd probably do three-fourths of the set, and then she'd come out and sing three or four songs, and then we'd take a break. The next set, we'd just do one or two instrumentals and bring Lou Ann up. She'd be the big feature of the middle of the night. For the third set, we'd bring her up again pretty quick, she'd sing for a while and she'd be done. We'd play for the rest of the night.

"Stevie and Lou Ann sounded *great* together – really cool R&B songs with a guy and a gal vocal [sings "I Need Your Lovin' Every Day"] – they sounded so great together. I thought, 'Man, no one else is doing this,' and wished we would get a recording deal."

CLIFFORD ANTONE: "Stevie and Doyle just had a beautiful relationship. I was lucky enough to get to jam with them before I had a club. You know, some nights I'd get to play bass with just Doyle and Stevie and me. And I got to know how much they both loved each other. And just together, musically, they were so beautiful. But we've always known, just like Stevie was great, we knew Doyle Bramhall was great. We knew he was a great singer and a great drummer. Always. It just took the world a long time to find out about these things. But we knew it from Day One. And there is nobody can play drums and sing better than Doyle Bramhall."[36] NOTE: Doyle was nominated for a Grammy award in 2008.

May 17: Soap Creek Saloon, Austin, TX

May 18: Faces, Dallas, TX

May 24: Soap Creek Saloon, Austin, TX

May 26: After Ours, Austin, TX

May 27: After Ours, Austin, TX

May 31: Soap Creek Saloon, Austin, TX

June 1: Stubb's Bar-B-Q, Lubbock, TX

June 2: Stubb's Bar-B-Q, Lubbock, TX

June 3: Stubb's Bar-B-Q, Lubbock, TX

The poster for the June 3 show reveals Stevie's nickname, "Hurricane," said by James Elwell to have been bestowed on Stevie by his friend in Lubbock, David Smith.

MIKE BURK: "Stevie played Stubb's so much that you'd get to where you'd wish there was a little different entertainment there sometimes. Stevie Ray played Stubb's just about every Sunday night for about a year."[39]

June 7: Soap Creek Saloon, Austin, TX

June 9: Soap Creek Saloon, Austin, TX

June 10: Soap Creek Saloon, Austin, TX

June 14: Soap Creek Saloon, Austin, TX

June 19: Juneteenth Blues Festival, Miller Outdoor Theatre, Houston, TX

June 19 is the first known Double Trouble concert for a significantly large crowd. JOHNNY RENO: "That was the first event where we went over really big. We all looked at each other – 'Well, that's kind of interesting. We're not really doing anything different than when we play in Austin and people don't go crazy.' When we finished that gig we thought, 'Wow. I think we're a band now.' And Stevie was into that. It wasn't The Stevie Ray Vaughan Show, it was the band."

JACK NEWHOUSE: "The Juneteenth show was a lot of fun. It was the first time we had played in front of a large crowd. We shared the venue with so many great people – Buddy Guy, Junior Wells, Big Mama Thornton, Albert Collins. To be accepted by the audience and the other artists was a big thrill for all of us."

COLLECTION OF CRAIG HOPKINS

MARY BETH GREENWOOD: "Stevie and Lindi went to Juneteenth, and Stevie picked a fight with some black guy, and they were the only white people there. But the way he talked [like a black person], she was like, 'We're gonna be murdered!' Somebody pissed him off and he went after the guy, and no other white people would have done that at that time. I guess it was just because of the way he acts – I mean, he was a black person in my book for the longest time. I went to Oak Cliff one time and stopped for gas, and I could hear all these people that talked exactly like Stevie. So I got it that day."

Stevie's universe was all about the music. A lot of people search for "meaning" or a connection to a higher plane in their lives, and for Stevie it was music. JOHNNY RENO: "He was kind of off into strange ideas of how music had healing power, it's good for their souls. He'd talk about 'Music is colors' ... that kind of thing."

June 21: Soap Creek Saloon, Austin, TX

June 23: After Ours, Austin, TX

📖June 23: *Austin Sun*, probably the first print ad listing a Double Trouble gig

June 24: After Ours, Austin, TX

At some point during the year, Stevie had broken up with Lindi Bethel. Asked if they ever talked about getting married, LINDI replied, "No, never. We were in our twenties, and I didn't want to get married at that age. I remember his affairs; our relationship was a bit of a double standard. That was kind of hard, but I always took him back. When I decided to get with him, I knew what to expect. Back then, all the clubs' girls' bathrooms had things people had written about Stevie. He was kind of a bad boy."

MARY BETH GREENWOOD: "As he started partying more, he got more promiscuous, and it was hard on Lindi. Every time we'd leave to go shopping – he was kind of jealous – Stevie'd go, 'Be good.' We never left his sight without those two words: 'Be good.' And he was saying don't flirt with anybody else. He kind of tried to keep me in his fold too; it wasn't just her. If I was having trouble with Eric, he would want me to go out with Denny Freeman."

June 27: Faces, Dallas, TX

June 28: Faces, Dallas, TX

June 29: Faces, Dallas, TX

June 30: Faces, Dallas, TX

July 1: Faces, Dallas, TX

The Faces dates above are unconfirmed, but Stevie did prepare a contract for the gigs and did play Faces some time in July. Whether the contract was accepted by the club is unknown.

Stevie and Vicki Virnelson, July 1978.
COURTESY VICKI VIRNELSON

Nine years previously, Stevie had been dating Vicki Virnelson in Dallas. On his return to his home town in July, they ran into each other again. "One thing led to another and we started dating again. Connie [Trent, Stevie's cousin] and I made several trips down to Austin, but it was not going to work." (Dallas is 200 miles from Austin.)

July: Fredde Pharoah quits and is replaced by Jack Moore (drums) July through September.

"Quits" may be a generous characterization of Fredde's departure. More than one person has suggested that Fredde may have had some difficulty with his parole. Johnny Reno recalls, "He was a cool guy, but he lived a hard life. When he was straight and in the pocket, he was really good. There's a place in the backbeat of music, especially for the style that we were playing, where there's kind of a pocket. Doyle Bramhall is *really* excellent at it,

© KERRY AWN

and Fredde played that kind of pocket. It made all the difference in the world the way Stevie was doing the string pulls, rhythmic guitar thing. The only way that works is if the drummer is putting the backbeat in the right pocket. When it clicks, it's great."

JACK NEWHOUSE: "Fredde was commuting from Dallas to Austin, and he wasn't able to do all the gigs. We were having to use other drummers – Andy Miller and Jack Moore. Fredde got tired of driving from Dallas to Austin; he had other things going on up there as well. He had a day job roofing houses, making good money, I think."

Fredde lost his battle with cancer in April 2000.

JOHNNY: "We went through several different drummers right there after Fredde had to go away: a different drummer almost every gig for six weeks, and it was really hard.

"Jack Moore was from Boston and had shown up in Austin with some friends. He said he'd make the gigs, but he couldn't hit that pocket. It was southern style, and if you hadn't studied it or hadn't grown up listening to the backbeat of Texas rhythm and blues, it's a hard thing to educate someone to. Guys like Doyle and Fredde and Rodney [Craig] that played with the Cobras – that white band in Dallas that was such a big influence on Jimmie and Doyle, The Nightcaps, their drummer totally got it. They could do a Jimmy Reed shuffle or an uptempo Chicago shuffle. People would say, 'Can you play like Doyle Bramhall? You're hired!' [*Laughs*]"

📖**July:** *Living Blues*, Juneteenth, Houston concert review by Jim Jasso

---

July: Faces, Dallas, TX

July: Stubb's Bar-B-Q, Lubbock, TX (several dates)

July 2: Soap Creek Saloon, Austin, TX

July 5: Soap Creek Saloon, Austin, TX

Stevie started seeing Lenora Darlene Bailey, who went by "Lenny." She said that July 5th was their "Love Struck Day," the day Stevie wrote the song and said it was for her.[17] JIMMIE VAUGHAN: "They were really in love, and she was real cute. They just had a ball whenever they were together. Once they hooked up, they were together like *that*. Where you see one, you'd see the other."[3]

LENNY: "Sometimes I'd just have to say, 'Hold your guitar and talk to me,' and with his guitar in his hands he could speak a little better. We talked about having kids, but realistically, if a man's not gonna give you a refrigerator in six years, what is he gonna give your kids? We had to get ice at the store because we didn't have a refrigerator."[17]

July 10: Rome Inn, Austin, TX

July 11: Soap Creek Saloon, Austin, TX

July 14: Rome Inn, Austin, TX

July 15: Rome Inn, Austin, TX

July 16: Rome Inn, Austin, TX

July 17: Hole Sound Recording, Austin, TX. Session with Lynnann Gandy, Lindy Barger (sax), Skip Olsen (bass), Chris Layton (drums), Perry Patterson (vocal), Charlie Prichard and SRV (guitars).

– Too Long
– Upbeat Boogie

July 17: Hole Sound Recording, Austin, TX. Earliest known studio recordings of Double Trouble. SRV, Lou Ann Barton, Jackie Newhouse (bass), Johnny Reno (sax) and Jack Moore (drums). The session log sheet indicates the tape "may not be useable," and as of this writing it is not know whether the tape survives at all. The song titles below are as they appear on the log.

– Hawaiian Eye [should be Hawaiian Isle]
– I Tried
– Tin Pan Alley
– I Love You (Hug You Squeeze You)
– Tell Me
– I Gets Evil
– I'm Cryin'
– Rude Mood
– Combo Monbo
– Black Cat
– Hideaway
– Shake For Me
– Don't Mess With My Man
– Tinineninou [Te Ni Nee Ni Nu]
– Oh Yeah
– Maybe
– UHH
– Some Fun / Slipin' and Slidin'
– Shake A Hand
– What Is Wrong
– Through the Night
– Instrumental

July 17: Rome Inn, Austin, TX

July 17: Soap Creek Saloon, Austin, TX

July 26: Soap Creek Saloon, Austin, TX

July 28: After Ours, Austin, TX

July 28: *Austin Sun*, photo of SRV wearing applejack hat and bell-bottom pants in concert calendar

July 29: After Ours, Austin, TX

July 30: Kenny Acosta's Gumbo Boil, Armadillo World Headquarters, Austin, TX (probably an early set)

July 30: Rome Inn, Austin, TX

At one of the Rome Inn gigs in 1978, Stevie met his long time hero, LONNIE MACK (born Lonnie McIntosh), who recalls, "We was in Texas looking for pickers, and we went out to see the T-Birds. Jimmie was saying, 'Man, you gotta hear my little brother. He plays all your [songs].' He was playing a little place called the Rome Inn, and we went over there and checked him out. As it would be, when I walked in the door, he was playing 'Wham!' And I said, 'Dadgum.' He was playing it right. I'd been playing it wrong for a long time and needed to go back and listen to my original record. That was in '78, I believe.

"So we had that studio up there with the *South* band, and we was real impressed with Stevie. We even ended up spending a couple of days with him, partying out, listening to records and carrying on to where when we got our project finished, we wanted to bring him up there and produce an album on him."

As things turned out, Stevie ended up co-producing Lonnie's first record on Alligator in 1985.

July 30: *Lubbock Avalanche-Journal*, "Audience Hypnotized by Stevie Vaughn [sic]," by Bob Claypool: "His red Rickenbacker has such heavy strings that few people can play it for more than a minute or two, and he declines to pick up an ordinary guitar because regular strings break like thread under his fingers. The index finger on his left hand is crooked from playing so much, and both of his hands are so muscular that they would look more in place on a football linebacker."

This article continues with barbecue restaurant owner C. B. "STUBBS" STUBBLEFIELD: "I don't see how a man could be only 23 years old [and] have that much music in him." In a post-show interview, VAUGHAN says, "What's fun is when you play two or three chords in a row that you never played before and they work and give somebody a thrill. .... I'm trying more and more to get to the point where you can hit one note and make people scream instead of having to hit 100 notes to get there. .... When I'm playing, it's my life. I better get intense with it. It's a gift, and I better take it as far as I can go."

Johnny Reno: "That summer of '78, he became the Stevie Vaughan that everybody really dug. Before that, he was known as a side man. But from my point of view, being on stage with him that summer, he really got his Stevie Ray Vaughan artistry. You know, if you were there when they invented the atomic bomb, you kind of went, 'Uh oh. Look out!' [*Laughs.*]"

Stevie loved soul food – chitlins, ham hocks, collard greens. He ate quite a bit on the east side of Austin at the Southern Dinette when he wasn't eating barbecue or Mexican food. When asked if he even knew what chitlins were, Stevie responded, "Yeah. I made them tell me."

Steve Dean: "We were all living that lifestyle, sleeping 'til noon or one and then go get Mexican food or whatever. And then start building the day from there – 'Who're we gonna call, what's going on tonight?'

"We would go to the Southern Dinette, and he got ham hocks. He loved ham hocks. We could never understand it, because on a ham hock, there's just not a whole lot on it. But Stevie'd be down there sucking on that ham hock to get that gristle and that meat out of the middle of it! A lasting image of Stevie!

"When I had the AusTex, with musicians I always had free weenies and sausages. You could tell about one o'clock [in the afternoon] when everyone was waking up, most of the guys were down there wanting a sausage sandwich or something. A lot of those guys couldn't afford to eat, and that was including Stevie. Then we'd end up running off and drinking beer and all that other stuff once the sun went down."

Early draft of "Love Struck Baby". COURTESY DOBBS/JACKSON

Mike Steele had been friends with Stevie since shortly after Blackbird had arrived in 1972. "We used to have lunch all the time at a place on East 11th called the Southern Dinette near the old Victory Grill. It was a soul restaurant, and the old blues guys from Austin frequented the place, and the long-haired white guys could go over there, and girls. They loved Stevie over there. [The east side of Austin had a higher population of minority residents.] We were very welcome on the east side.

"There was a club over there, La Cucaracha. It was a short-lived venue, but it was a good one, and I think Stevie played there some."

It was at La Cucaracha that Lenny recalls meeting Stevie some years before.[17]

Mike: "I hadn't seen Stevie in a while, and we got to talking. I asked him where he was living and for his phone number, and he said, 'Well, I'm not really living anywhere. I'm just staying where I can.' So I offered him a place to stay at 45th and Red River. I had a couch that folded out into a bed. This was '78 – he was just forming Double Trouble, with Jackie Newhouse on bass. Chris lived right up the street on 49th, near Red River. Rent back then was dirt cheap – $75 a month [*laughs*].

"One night I woke up about four o'clock and heard what sounded like an electric drill. I went out into the living room and all the lights were on, the stereo's on, the TV's on with the sound turned down, and there's an extension cord running out the front door. I looked out the front door, and Stevie had pulled his '65 Chrysler New Yorker – two-door, yellow with a black top and black interior, bucket seats – into the front yard. And he's installing speakers in it. I stuck my head in there and yelled, 'HEY!!' and scared the shit out of him [*laughs*]. He turns and looks at me – 'What?' I said, 'What in the hell do you think you're doing? Stevie, it's four o'clock in the morning. My neighbors have to get up and go to work.' 'Oh, okay. I got home from my gig and didn't have anything to do.' [*Laughs*]

"Stevie lived there for a while, and we had some great times. He had a girlfriend at the time, Kelli [after Lindi], and they eventually saved up enough to get a place."

STEVE DEAN: "One night, we'd all been together and went to the trailer that me and Sally lived in. One bedroom was down at one end, and the other bedroom was at the other end of this really long trailer. Stevie and Kelli are off doing their deal, and we're off doing our deal, you know. Kelli had dated this guy Ed, and he'd actually given her an engagement ring. She broke it off with him but never gave the ring back and continued to wear it. She dated Stevie for several weeks – it had been a while, as far as I can remember – but Ed was still hovering around.

"Well, Ed probably got all pilled-up and drunk one night or something, and he'd heard that Kelli was with Stevie, so he decided to come over to the trailer. It didn't take much math to figure out that if Kelli was Sally's best friend, and if Kelli was out somewhere, she was probably with Sally, so let's go over to Sally's place.

"It's about three o'clock in the morning

Stevie outside Steve Dean's OK Records store in Austin. © KEN HOGE

and I heard this BAM! It was the back door, and I'm hearing all this shouting. 'Motherf..., I'll blow your head off!' I get up and I'm half naked and going down to the other end of the trailer, and I see Stevie run out the back door naked. Right behind the trailer was a big field with buffalo grass, or whatever that was, four or five feet tall.

"I think Ed might have had a gun, and he said, 'You see that ring on her finger?' I guess he was claiming he still 'owned' her because of the ring. Stevie didn't want any part of it, so he ran out the back

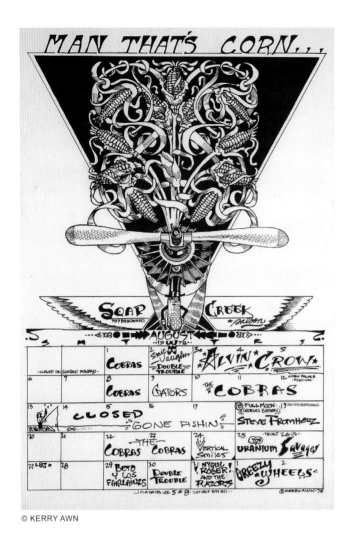

© KERRY AWN

music. Listen to records, or 'parties,' you know ... girls and all that kind of stuff. But I remember a bunch of parties, and if they were playing the hits of the day, he might sneak off. I remember one big party was going on, and Stevie left the main room and went into a bedroom, and he was in there three or four hours playing guitar by himself."

July 31: Soap Creek Saloon, Austin, TX

📖**August:** *Buddy*, "Texas Tornadoes: A Guide To The Heaviest Guitarists ..."

August 2: Soap Creek Saloon, Austin, TX

August 6: Rome Inn, Austin, TX

August 7: Rome Inn, Austin, TX

August 14: Rome Inn, Austin, TX

August 18: Rome Inn, Austin, TX

August 19: Rome Inn, Austin, TX

August 20: Rome Inn, Austin, TX

August 21: Rome Inn, Austin, TX

August 22: Rome Inn, Austin, TX

August 24: Stubbs Bar-B-Q, Lubbock, TX

August 25: Stubbs Bar-B-Q, Lubbock, TX

August 26: Stubbs Bar-B-Q, Lubbock, TX

August 27: Rome Inn, Austin, TX

August 28: Rome Inn, Austin, TX

August 30: Soap Creek Saloon, Austin, TX

door into this buffalo grass in the middle of the field naked. I thought I would just wait until this kind of died down and then go look for Stevie.

"Ed grabs Kelli and takes her off; in the meantime, he picks up a couple of bricks and puts them through the back windshield of Stevie's car. We yelled for Stevie but never could find him, so we left the back door open for him, and I think he probably slipped back in and got his clothes and walked back home.

"That's the thing that was happening back then. Everybody was drinking and partying, and shit happened all the time. Luckily, nobody was seriously hurt. There were always parties at Diamond Joe's, and there are still stories about whether he's alive or dead. He was from money and drove this big Cadillac. He was dating Lenny. Diamond Joe was already a big supporter of Stevie, and Lenny eventually met Stevie and broke it off with Diamond. I think he was frustrated that he wasn't quite the guitar player that Stevie was, so he'd hang out and help Stevie.

"When Lenny made the break from Diamond Joe, she went straight to Stevie, and they were inseparable. Joe felt so betrayed and was bitter forever about Stevie and Lenny. He played the AusTex a lot and I'd hear about it all the time."

When emotions were calmer, Stevie was just a quiet kid. STEVE: "He loved to eat and loved to go and support other people's

JOHNNY RENO: "I can't tell you how many times Stevie blew up guitars and amps. I don't think we had one night where he didn't just fry an amp. The SRV guitar was in the shop constantly. There were nights when he'd play a loaner Rickenbacker, but whatever he played, it sounded like him. Fortunately, he had enough friends that would loan him things. Clifford Antone came to our rescue many, many times, 'cause he had a stock of amps and guitars. Ray Hennig was constantly loaning him stuff.

© 'DILLO/ TREY YANCY

"Sometime in the summer of '78, someone gave Stevie a gigantic '66 yellow Chrysler New Yorker. We went to Lubbock one time with the Chrysler and my Pinto station wagon; all the bass and drums and everything in the two cars. Stevie took a girl with him. So we play the gig and we're on the way back home and Stevie had a flat in the Chrysler out in the middle of nowhere. We pull over and take all the crap out of the trunk, and Stevie goes, 'Where's the spare tire?' And his girlfriend of the moment said, 'Well, I didn't have room enough for my clothes, so I took it out, and it's in Austin.' [*Laughs*]

Stevie visiting Dallas circa fall 1978. COURTESY MARTHA VAUGHAN

"We got in the other car and went down the road to a gas station, waiting for the tire to be fixed. Sunday afternoon about five o'clock on a two-lane road. We're sittin' there and we hear this noise coming, a grinding like someone's pulling a trailer without any wheels on it. It gets louder and louder and this guy comes around the corner really fast and roars into the gas station. He doesn't have a tire on the front right of this old Pontiac station wagon. The rim is grinded down to the brake drum practically – red hot. No hood on the car, the windshield's broken out, the car

is full of stuff, and there's a woman and a man passed out in the front seat with this guy.

"He jumps out and says, 'Hey, man. I need a tire. Can you fix my tire? I gotta get to Florida, man. It's a matter of life and death!' Stevie goes, 'Where's your hood?' And the guy goes, 'Oh man, I lost that in the desert.' [*Laughs*] Somehow we sensed we didn't want to know any more! He got a tire and blasted out of there. I always wondered what happened to that guy. That was one of those Willie the Wimp stories."

September 1: After Ours, Austin, TX

September 2: After Ours, Austin, TX

September 3: Rome Inn, Austin, TX

September 4: Rome Inn, Austin, TX

September 6: Soap Creek Saloon, Austin, TX

September 7: Atzlan Club, Austin, TX

September 8: Atzlan Club, Austin, TX

September 9: Atzlan Club, Austin, TX

September 10: Rome Inn, Austin, TX

According to a calendar in Stevie's handwriting, drummer Chris Layton replaced Jack Moore on September 10, 1978.

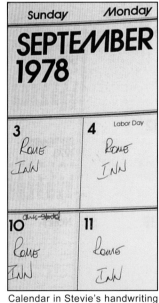

Calendar in Stevie's handwriting showing Chris Layton's first gig with the band. COURTESY DOBBS/ JACKSON

JOE SUBLETT, Chris' roommate and sax player in the Cobras: "Jack Moore was a bass player from Providence, Rhode Island, and had moved down to Texas and decided he wanted to be a drummer. He was a pretty good drummer. Jack decided to go back to the east coast and finish his college education. I saw Stevie at the Rome Inn one night and he said, 'Man, I need a drummer. Do you know anybody?' And I said, 'Hey, man, give my roommate a shot. He's not really a blues drummer, but I'll bet he can learn the stuff.' Stevie said to tell Chris, 'If he will play what I tell him to play, I might give him a shot,' because Stevie knew *exactly* what he wanted a drummer to play like. Stevie was a good drummer. He could sit down and play four or five different kinds of shuffles – double shuffle, a rub shuffle."

JOE PRIESNITZ: "Chris was the drummer for Greezy Wheels, and they worked *a lot*. I was their agent. He came in to tell me. I was befuddled. 'Wow. Chris. You're going to work with Stevie? He's great, but can you make any money doin' that?' [*Laughs*] Money wasn't a factor. It was good chemistry."

"Stingray" Vaughan and Double Trouble. (l-r) Lou Ann, Chris, "Stingray," Johnny, Jack. © K. CUMMINGS

LAYTON grew up on the Texas coast in Corpus Christi. "I was beating around on things ever since I can remember. I guess since I was about three. Beatin' on coffee cans and pots and pans and stuff. I got my first snare drum when I started Band, which was in Mathis, Texas, in seventh grade." Chris recalls the song that got him thinking about playing drums: "It was 'The Twist' by Chubby Checker. I heard that on the radio. It just had a good beat. You know, [hums instrumental intro to the song], that break [just before Chubby starts to sing]. I went, 'Wow, man. That's cool!'

"That just kind of gave me the chicken skin. It kind of, like, switched something on, really. It was right after that I went out and cut some sticks from the oleander bush and started beatin' on the couch with them. My mother came in and got mad at me, because she said it was poisonous and I shouldn't be playing with it [*laughs*]. But that was really it that got me wanting to pick up something and start beating, that I remember."

Chris was in Band in junior high, "which was pretty formal instruction. I had to learn how to read music and play with a group of people. When I got into high school, I actually stopped playing for a while. I got into surfing and hung out at the beach a lot." Chris put the drums away until college, when his high school friend Joe Sublett introduced him to a drummer who rekindled Chris' interest. "I started taking music in college, which had a really good music department. It was real classically oriented. I ended up being the drummer in the stage band, then started a band [Little Mike and the

SRV and Double Trouble. (l-r) Stevie, Lou Ann Barton, Chris Layton, Jack Newhouse, Johnny Reno. © K. CUMMINGS

Lightning Band], and that was when I got my first gigs for money. I got a gig at a place called the Rogues Club, owned by Sam Harrah, who was Freddie Fender's personal manager at the time. It was a real seedy joint. It had been converted from a – how should I say this? – a strip bar to a regular club. It was pretty funky."

Chris had visited his sister at the University of Texas in Austin and made the move from the coast on December 18, 1975. Early bands there were Dan del Santo's Professors of Pleasure, LaPaz and Greezy Wheels.

JOE SUBLETT: "After Stevie said he needed a drummer, I had been playing a lot of Texas blues and Chicago blues records for Chris. We had figured out a way to get the headphones from the living room to the back room where Chris had his drums set up. He was playing along with these records, and Stevie walked in the house and Chris had the headphones on. He tapped Chris on the shoulder and said, 'I'll give you a try if you'll play what I want' – something to that effect.

"Chris was a great student and learned to play that stuff really well and quickly. It was a situation where if Stevie wanted him to play a certain way, he'd sit down and show him."

CHRIS: "Stevie came over to the apartment one day 'cause Joe and I were living together. He walked into my kitchen where I had my drums set up, and I had been playing with the headphones on. Looked down and saw someone standing there with their foot tappin' and it was Stevie. That's how we really met."

The press recognized Chris' contribution to the band: "Layton is a precision artist who, true to a childhood admiration of the recorded works of Krupa and Webb, avoids heavy handedness in favor of fullness via punch-and-withdraw strokes. College-trained (Delmar College's 3 O'Clock Stage Band) Layton helps make Double Trouble output a challenge to the intellect as well as a gut-level stimulus; his application of 6/8 licks to a 4/4 rhythmic context is typical of the treats awaiting the listener who focuses on percussion."[40]

JOHNNY RENO: "When Stevie got Chris in the band, he had to work with him to get him to where he could hit that 'pocket.' He was a really good drummer and a fun kid, no lifestyle problems. When Chris Layton came on, things got really good, 'cause we had a guy that was energetic and young and interested in doing it.

"You could see Stevie's effect on people; I could see it from the stage. What a rocketship that guy was. To have extended [sax] solo opportunities on some songs, Stevie Vaughan playing rhythm guitar behind you, Chris Layton – it was like, 'Man, I sound good [*laughs*]! Holy crap. These guys make me sound really good!'"

Double Trouble. © MARY BETH GREENWOOD

On his September 1978 calendar Stevie wrote, "Try and meet goal of organizing and completing some recordings. Work on Promotion pack etc. Begin booking immediately. Stretch out 2 to 3 months in advance, also possibly several circuits, southwest, east and northern trips."

September 11: Rome Inn, Austin, TX

September 12: Soap Creek Saloon, Austin, TX

September 13: Soap Creek Saloon, Austin, TX

September 14: After Ours, Austin, TX

September 15: Rome Inn, Austin, TX

September 16: Rome Inn, Austin, TX

September 17: Rome Inn, Austin, TX

September 18: Rome Inn, Austin, TX

September 20: Soap Creek Saloon, Austin, TX

September 21: After Ours, Austin, TX

September 22: After Ours, Austin, TX

September 23: After Ours, Austin, TX

September 24: Rome Inn, Austin, TX

September 27: Soap Creek Saloon, Austin, TX

September 28: Fat Dawgs, Lubbock, TX. Private party

September 29: Fat Dawgs, Lubbock, TX. Private party

September 30: Fat Dawgs, Lubbock, TX. Private party

Fat Dawg's owner, Bruce Jaggers: "Stevie Ray just flat would *not* turn down the volume. We'd have eight tables in there and Stevie has got it full-blown – as if there's a full house goin' on! [We] asked him to turn it down a bit and Stevie was like, 'Nope. That's the way I play it, either like it or not.'"[39]

NOTE: The *Austin Sun* ceased publication about this time, and the author has found no comprehensive listings for club dates

through mid-1980. It can be assumed that the band continued a similarly grueling schedule. Among the regular gigs outside Austin were Fat Dawgs in Lubbock, the 5050 Club in San Antonio and Abraxas in Waco.

Stevie and Lou Ann at the Austex Lounge. COURTESY STEVE DEAN

In the early months of Double Trouble, the band didn't even all live in the same town. CHRIS LAYTON: "This was before Tommy was in the band. We had a sax player [Johnny Reno] that lived in Fort Worth, and the bass player [Jack Newhouse] lived up there. We'd all converge and go play gigs. Stevie might call up and say, 'Oh, there's a gig tomorrow.' Or he might call that day and say, 'There's a gig tonight.' A number of times everyone would say, 'Aw, man!' Say it's too late' or even tell him, 'You can't call me at eight o'clock and say we've got a gig in two hours!'

"I remember a couple of times we'd end up playing that song 'Chitlins Con Carne' [by Kenny Burrell] at a little place called the AusTex Lounge, on South Congress. It'd be just Stevie and I. Just guitar and drums, and there'd be like maybe five people out there, sittin' in this little – it was like a bar, you know, a lounge. I remember one night sittin' up there doing that. It's real vivid! There was like four people, and we're playing, just me and Stevie … and they're going, 'God, where's the rest of the band?' [*Laughs*]"[37]

AusTex Lounge owner Steve Dean, who used to help C-Boy at the Rome Inn, recalls that there was no guaranteed money for Stevie and Double Trouble in their early months. STEVE: "At Rome Inn, [Double Trouble] was working for the door. The Thunderbirds were packing the Rome Inn at the time, and it took Stevie a good bit longer to get it going. W.C. Clark was doing my Wednesday nights, and things were going great with that. Stevie asked me if he could do something, and I told him what I paid W.C. as a guarantee versus the door – and W.C. far exceeded the guarantee. So Stevie says, 'Well, I don't know if I can get the whole band down here to do that.' So he'd come down and he and Whipper would just play, just the two of them.

"What was neat about that was at the time he was getting into Kenny Burrell a lot, so he would come down and he wouldn't do a 'Stevie set.' He'd sit down and noodle Kenny Burrell all night long. It was almost like a jazz gig, compared to what you usually saw. Being just the two of them, I think I gave them sixty bucks as a guarantee.

"I remember one night when we had stayed up all night at the AusTex and had decided to go back to the house. Stevie owned few things. He owned guitars, a few clothes and his records, and that was it. W.C. had hired a kid as a roadie, and he had epileptic seizures. [There were about six or seven of us] and this kid comes along. Stevie's got all his 78's and 45's out, we're sitting on the floor groovin' out and everything, and the kid goes into a seizure. When he does, records are all over the floor, and he breaks scads of Stevie's records. Stevie was practically in tears. It was probably early Chicago and Cobra sides – really rare shit that Stevie probably hocked everything he had to buy at the time, you know? It was a real downer after that. Stevie was heartbroken, and everyone just kind of sauntered home."

JOHNNY RENO: "There were places like Lubbock and the crowd was really good, and there were a few people that were Stevie fans. For some reason, in San Antonio they just went nuts – they loved every bit of it. 'Louder? Great!' Dallas was always a weird town. We played there all the time, but that town took forever to get going. Houston was good, 'cause they had a vibrant black community music scene there, and the white kids would go out and hear those kinds of acts. They latched onto the T-Birds and Stevie. We played Tuesday night at Rome Inn and there's twenty people; play Saturday night at Fitzgerald's and it was a line around the block!

Note to band in Stevie's handwriting, probably referencing his increased substance abuse.
COURTESY MIKE STEELE

"There was this one hippie-chick dancer – she was there *every* time we played. Hippie garb on, she would dance by herself from the get-go. No one danced back then, unless it was Saturday night, everyone was drunk and it was midnight. Then they'd get on the dancefloor as long as you were playing something hot and rockin.'

But no matter what we were playing, she was out there dancing. I asked her what was the deal, and she said, 'I dig his vibration.'

"There were quite a few young men interested in Lou Ann at that point. It was funny to be in a band where you had a red-hot guitar player, and most of the guys came to see Lou Ann – the hot-looking chick. She was just a piece of work. She was like Lucy and Ethel rolled into one character and would sing her ass off. She was her own gal. One guy she hooked up with who was her equal was Keith Ferguson. He was an excellent, soulful cat and very cool – didn't chase around.

"In order to keep our musician's union dues up, we would play a free gig once a year – a benefit gig. The guy that ran the local union would call and tell Stevie to play a gig and he'd comp the dues. He sent us one time to play at the state mental school in Austin. A total Fellini experience! It was retarded and Down's Syndrome kids. We would go out there and play a lunchtime concert for an hour in the school gym/auditorium. We were on the floor – there's no stage. We'd drag a tiny P.A. out there – not any kind of big deal.

"They would ring a bell and all the kids knew a band was coming. They would come *roaring* into the gymnasium from their classes [*laughs*], a stampede, and they have no protocol. They would walk right up next to us, 'cause there was no stage cordoned off or anything. They were walking between me and Stevie and the drummer. Lou Ann would come up and sing and guys would try to hump her leg while we were playing, like, 'Wow, look at the tits on that girl!'

"We'd just start playing, look at each other and just laugh, 'cause he got such a kick out of these kids! They were just out of their minds and loved music and loved *loud* music. They would stand a foot away from Stevie and watch him play. The guys would go back and lay their heads on Stevie's amplifier! They were screaming, 'YEAH! YEAH!' Steve was really benevolent in that sense – like, people get us on a level we have no idea where their world is. They liked it fast and loud. It really spoke to him."

In early October, Stevie made a connection at the Rome Inn that would eventually lead to significant advancements in his career. Edi Johnson, an accountant at Manor Downs horse racing track near Austin, saw Stevie perform and was quite impressed. It seemed Stevie had everything going for him to be a successful musician except the financial backing to make it happen. Edi decided to approach her employer, Frances Carr, about helping Stevie and volunteered to do the accounting for Stevie for free.

Carr, loaded for bear because of her interests in the famous King Ranch, now 825,000 acres in South Texas. Edi was able to convince Frances to manage Stevie and provide the financial framework to help Stevie advance. About a year later, Frances persuaded her music industry friend, Chesley Millikin, to take over the day-to-day management of Stevie in addition to his responsibilities at Manor Downs.

Stevie was put on a salary, but it would be three or four years before he made any money. He made so little in the club circuit and spent what there was so fast. Edi was a co-signer on Stevie's bank account in order to make sure bills got paid, band salaries were paid and no one was stealing from Stevie.[17]

COURTESY DEB GASPARD

October 5: Stubb's Bar-B-Q, Lubbock, TX

October 6: Stubb's Bar-B-Q, Lubbock, TX

October 7: Cotton Club, Lubbock, TX

October 11: Soap Creek Saloon, Austin, TX

October 14: Walker Auditorium, Waco, TX. Live recording called the North Waco Revue. Recorded by Hole Sound Recording. Lynnann Gandy, W.C. Clark, SRV, Chris Layton, Charlie Prichard, Skip Olsen, Perry Patterson, Carol (last name unknown) (piano).
– Get Off That Bottle Daddy (Lynnann)
– Lord Have Mercy (Lynnann)
– God Bless Our Love (W.C.)
– Too Long (Lynnann)
– Texas Flood (SRV)
– "Stevie" [perhaps an instrumental]
– Take Me to the River (W.C.)
– Belly Side of Life (Perry)
– Messengers (Perry)
– My Song (W.C.)
– Drunkard's Salute (Perry)
– Upbeat Boogie
– Hard Luck Girl (Lynnann & SRV)

October 15: Rome Inn, Austin, TX

October 18: Soap Creek Saloon, Austin, TX

October 19: After Ours, Austin, TX

October 20: Rome Inn, Austin, TX

October 21: Rome Inn, Austin, TX

October 22: Rome Inn, Austin, TX

October 23: Rome Inn, Austin, TX

October 25: Soap Creek Saloon, Austin, TX

October 26: After Ours, Austin, TX

October 29: Rome Inn, Austin, TX

October 30: Rome Inn, Austin, TX

October 31: 5050 Club, San Antonio, TX

November 1: Soap Creek Saloon, Austin, TX

November 2: After Ours, Austin, TX

November 5: Stubb's Bar-B-Q, Lubbock, TX

November 17: Rome Inn, Austin, TX

November 18: Rome Inn, Austin, TX

November 19: Rome Inn, Austin, TX

November 23: After Ours, Austin, TX

November 24: After Ours, Austin, TX

November 27: Rome Inn, Austin, TX

November 28: KRTU, San Antonio, TX

December 1: St. Christopher's, Dallas, TX

December 2: St. Christopher's, Dallas, TX

December 2: Hole Sound Recording, Austin, TX. Studio log sheet indicates Stevie recorded with W.C. Clark, Chris Layton, and Skip Olsen (bass) on this date for what was called the "Pizza Session," but the date conflicts with the Dallas gig. This could very well be the session that resulted in W.C.'s single, released January 19, 1979.
– Rough Edges
– My Song
– Pretty Little Mama

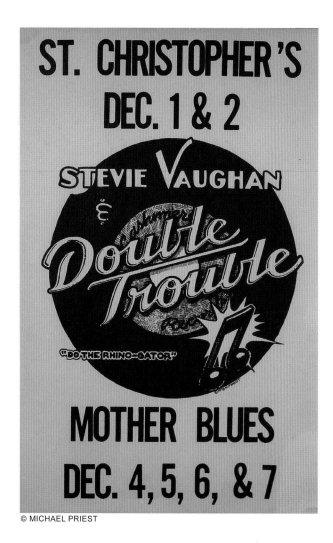

© MICHAEL PRIEST

December 17: Rome Inn, Austin, TX

December 21: LaInza's, Corpus Christi, TX

December 22: LaInza's, Corpus Christi, TX

📷**December 22:** Hole Sound Recording, Austin, TX. Studio log sheet indicates Stevie recorded on this date, but it conflicts with the Corpus gig. "Brady's Bubble Session" is dated this date, and another log sheet that is very similar is undated and called the "Stevie Sauce" session. Both are listed here for lack of better information. There are few vocals on these tapes. Personnel are not noted but assumed to be Double Trouble.

– Woke Up This Morning
– Guitar Slim (Hurricane)
– Albert Shuffle [Te Ni Nee Ni Nu]
– Be Careful
– Shake For Me
– I Tried (To Play This Song)
– Stinghead Sting [Stang's Swang]
– All Your Love
– Tin Pan Alley
– Woke Up This Morning
– I'm Cryin'

December 4: Mother Blue's, Dallas, TX

December 5: Mother Blue's, Dallas, TX

December 6: Mother Blue's, Dallas, TX

December 7: Mother Blue's, Dallas, TX

December 8: Antone's, Austin, TX

December 9: Antone's, Austin, TX

December 10: Rome Inn, Austin, TX

December 12: 5050 Club, San Antonio, TX

December 14: After Ours, Austin, TX

December 15: After Ours, Austin, TX

December 16: After Ours, Austin, TX

© MICHAEL PRIEST

December 23: LaInza's, Corpus Christi, TX

📖 **December 24:** *Lubbock Avalanche-Journal,* "Reel to Reel," William D. Kerns. Article states that the shows at Fat Dawg's later in the week will be recorded for "selective distribution around Texas" to help further the band's career. Whether the recordings were actually made and survive is unknown.

© MICHAEL PRIEST

Johnny Reno and Stevie. COURTESY MARTHA VAUGHAN

Stevie and sister-in-law Donna Vaughan, Christmas 1978. COURTESY MARTHA VAUGHAN

December 29: Fat Dawg's, Lubbock, TX. Recorded?

December 30: Fat Dawg's, Lubbock, TX. Recorded?

December 31: Fat Dawg's, Lubbock, TX. Recorded?

1979

January 1: Fat Dawg's, Lubbock, TX

🔘 **January 10:** Hole Sound Recording, Austin, TX. "Brady's Brother Session" with Stevie, and probably Double Trouble augmented by horns (Joe Sublett?) and piano (David Roach?).

– I'm Cryin'
– Texas Flood
– Guitar Slim
– Howlin' To My Darlin'
– All Your Love (I Miss Lovin')

🔘 **January 11:** Hole Sound Recording, Austin, TX. "Perry Session"; no personnel listed on log sheet, but probably Perry Patterson, Lynnann Gandy.

– Our Old Dance
– Marvel Memory
– Early Morning Hole

January 12: Rome Inn, Austin, TX

January 13: Rome Inn, Austin, TX

January 14: Rome Inn, Austin, TX

⊙ **January 19:** W.C. CLARK, "My Song / Rough Edges," Hole Records, 512, 45rpm. Only 500 copies pressed according to studio co-owner Patty Patterson Dillon. Paul Ray and the Cobras back W.C. Clark on "My Song with Denny Freeman taking lead guitar duty. On "Rough Edges" it is probably Stevie, W.C., Chris Layton and Skip Olsen (bass), possibly from the December 2, 1978 session.

COLLECTION OF CRAIG HOPKINS

January 28: Soap Creek Saloon's Bee Caves Road location closes

February ?: Stubb's Bar-B-Q, Lubbock, TX

February 2: After Ours, Austin, TX

February 3: After Ours, Austin, TX

February 4: Rome Inn, Austin, TX

📖**February 18:** *Lubbock Avalanche-Journal,* "Country Notes." Bob Claypool interviews Lou Ann Barton and notes that at the time she was engaged to Keith Ferguson, bass player for The Fabulous Thunderbirds. Lou Ann opines that she, Angela Strehli of Austin and Sarah Brown of Boston are the only white women singing the blues, but she seems to have conveniently left out Bonnie Raitt and Tracy Nelson, who released albums many years before.

📼**February 27:** Hole Sound Recording, Austin, TX. No personnel listed on log sheet, but probably Double Trouble. This is the last known Hole session for Stevie.

– Love Me Darlin'
– Shake For Me
– Love Me Darlin'

© KATHY MURRAY

📼**March 2:** Soap Creek Saloon, Austin, TX (new N. Lamar St. location)

– Instrumental
– Rude Mood
– Dirty Pool
– I'm Cryin'
– Love Me Darlin'
– Love Struck Baby
– All Your Love I Miss Loving
– Texas Flood
– So Excited (intro for Lou Ann Barton)
– You Can Have My Husband
– Te Ni Nee Ni Nu
– I'll Change
– Scratch My Back
– Sugar Coated Love
– Scuttle Buttin' (outro for Lou Ann)
– Boilermaker
– Empty Arms
– You Done Lost Your Good Thing Now
– Pride and Joy

📼**March:** Joe Gracey records the band in Austin.

– Shake Your Hips
– Oh Yeah
– You Can Have My Husband
– Te Ni Nee Ni Nu
– Will You Be Home Tonight?
– Sugar Coated Love
– Love Struck Baby
– Rude Mood
– Empty Arms
– I'm Cryin'
– Pride and Joy

JACK NEWHOUSE: "Joe Gracey was a DJ in Austin and had an informal studio set up at KOKE on Lamar. It was pretty primitive – a little 4-track board, microphone. We set up in there to record demos."

CHRIS LAYTON: "It was in the basement of the old KOKE-FM radio studios. Joe was Austin's number one DJ for years. He loved Stevie and thought we were cool. We were in a small room, Jack Newhouse, Stevie and I. It wasn't a *studio* – it was just another room in the basement. The cables for the mics ran under the door into the next room, which was like a storage room, into a little quarter-track tape machine.

"Historically, you look back and ask, 'Was that a master session, was it purely for demos ...?' We were just guys going in to record. You think about it now: you could have done that on any day of the week in anybody's house, what we did. It wasn't like [in a very proper and business-like tone] 'We're going in to record now.' It was that innocent. I think the hope was maybe those recordings could lead us somewhere else – a better recording, you know.

"In effect, we *did* do that. [We went] to Nashville and recorded with Clement. [See November 1979.] But the interesting thing about this session, it was the very first recording of 'Love Struck.' I listened to it a few weeks ago on a bootleg. Nobody knows what happened to those original tapes. Those would be the first recordings with me playing with Stevie. It wasn't very good, the performances ... it's not like some holy grail treasure trove. [But] it's actually my favorite version of 'Love Struck.' We played it a whole different way than when we did *Texas Flood*. Somewhat different, rather."

Perhaps the recordings would have been more important had Johnny Reno not left the band a few months later, making the tapes nonrepresentative of the band's sound.

JOE GRACEY: "I was a regular at the Rome Inn, the club where a lot of the better bands were playing then, and it was just down the street from Electric Graceland, the studio in the KOKE basement. Stevie and them were playing there all the time, so I heard them a lot. We never had a contract, just a mutual attempt to get something good on tape and see what we could do with it.

"The basement sessions were great fun because there was no money involved, just my studio and the band in two tiny little rooms. And I had an old Shure SM55 mic that Stevie loved because it sounded so lo-fi on the vocals. We would record for hours and hours just for fun. He and I got to be great friends and our girlfriends ran around together and we became a kind of little family unit, you might say. He wrote "Love Struck Baby" for me and my then-wife, Linda. I'd be at all of his gigs then, just hanging and listening. We got to be like a couple of brothers, just running around having a blast together all over Austin.

"All I had in that studio was a little Teac 4-track 1/4" tape deck and a terrible little cheap mixer and a bunch of cheap, awful mics, but we made some great tapes. Those tapes were destroyed, as I understand it, because I took them to Chesley Millikin and turned them over to him in return for the money John Dyer had loaned us to do the Nashville sessions. I never made a dime out of any of that. In fact, I lost quite a lot of money on Stevie in the end. I think Dyer was the only one who ever got his money back.

"If I hadn't been so dedicated to Stevie and so dutiful in my dealings with him, I would have made a copy of those tapes and hidden it away, which I should have done and wish now that I had done – but I didn't. Stupid, yes, but karmically, the right thing to do, since he didn't want them floating around after he got famous. We all knew he was about to be famous. I knew it all along without any doubt at all. So that's what I did."

It was probably during this time period that Gracey also recorded Stevie for use on The Skunks' unfinished record, later known as *The Black Album*. When Gracey finally released 500 copies of the album, Stevie's solo had not been used. When asked about adding Stevie to The Skunks track, Joe responded: "I don't remember that happening at all. If it did, it would have been at Graceyland, where I was recording The Skunks tracks. I have no copies or memory of that."

JESSE SUBLETT of The Skunks: "I was a fan of Stevie's from the beginning – Krackerjack and Blackbird. Krackerjack was the reason I started playing. The Skunks formed at the end of 1977 and started playing in early '78. I was in The Skunks and The Violators. We started the punk scene; there was a big buzz, and ... mushrooming every week.

"The Skunks played at Soap Creek, and Joe Gracey was there and flipped out and wanted to record us. He had done a Fabulous Thunderbirds single, and we loved the sound of that. We started recording immediately, and it clicked and was fun. At first we were going to do a single and then decided to make an album. We'd only been together about three months – we started in February and were recording in April. We had this album done by the end of [1978], except one lead track was missing. Eddie [Munoz] decided to split and went on tour with Elvis Costello as his roadie.

"Before Jon Dee Graham joined the band, Gracey and Bobby Earl Smith were recording with Stevie. We had given them money to finish the record. They made excuses about what the holdup was, and we never saw them again. One thing that they did after they got the money – they were in Nashville recording with Stevie and had him do a [solo] on one song called 'Something About You Scares Me' – a song about Bela Lugosi. It just had about eight bars where Eddie used to do this really wild, psychedelic, horror movie solo. So Stevie did that, and I saw him a few months later at the Armadillo, and he said, 'Yeah. They said just play as wild as you can,' and he said it was really far out.

"I mentioned it to Gracey a couple of years ago, and I think he said there was something technical wrong with the track, which is why they ended up putting out the album two years later with no solo at all. In a way it's a non-story, but I sure wish I could hear it, even if it was technically messed up."

April 2: Soap Creek Saloon, Austin, TX, with Roomful of Blues

---

April 6: Ricardo's Cadillac, San Antonio, TX

April 7: Ricardo's Cadillac, San Antonio, TX

April 8: Rome Inn, Austin, TX

April 13: "Lake Austin Party" is written on Stevie's calendar, but it is unknown if this is a social or professional event.

April 14?: Austin Blues Fest, Austin, TX
 – Natural Born Lover
 – Te Ni Nee Ni Nu
 – Scratch My Back
 – I'll Change
 – Shake A Hand, Shake A Hand
 – Oh Baby
 – Sugar Coated Love

April 15: Rome Inn, Austin, TX

April 20: Armadillo World Headquarters, Austin, TX, opening for Robert Gordon

Stevie made a lasting impression on a particular member of the audience on April 20: JOE PRIESNITZ of Rock Arts Management. Joe had seen Stevie at the Rome Inn the previous year, but "he made the biggest impression on me when we went to the Armadillo to see Stevie open for Robert Gordon. That was the night that it was, like, 'Wow! That guy's a star!'

"They were hungry. Anybody that would pay attention to them and get them work, they'd listen to them. I think we had a meeting at the Rock Arts office within days of that show and started booking them. We had a small roster – Omar and the Howlers, The Lotions – Stevie was one of the first acts we signed at the agency."

Stevie (with perm) and Johnny Reno at Rome Inn. © DON DAVIS

Stevie rarely worried about fashion trends, but he did experiment with his hairstyle a couple of times in 1979. Don Davis captured Stevie's 1950's greaser look and disco perm. The hairstyles were so fleeting that Don's are the only photographs of these hairdos to have surfaced.

MIKE STEELE: "I think the ones with his hair greased back, he was playing at the Armadillo. Then the perm shots might have been at the Rome Inn. That hairdo was just horrible. That was one I teased him about. If I remember correctly, it

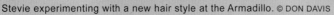

Stevie experimenting with a new hair style at the Armadillo. © DON DAVIS

was a girlfriend that talked him into it [*laughs*]. He couldn't wait for it to grow out. When I first saw him with that, I started laughing. He said, 'Shut up! Don't say a word!'"

April 21: Ricardo's Cadillac, San Antonio, TX

April 22: Rome Inn, Austin, TX

April 27: Fitzgerald's, Houston, TX, opening for Rocky Hill

April 28: Fitzgerald's, Houston, TX, opening for Rocky Hill

© BILL NARUM

The poster for the Fitzgerald's shows above was among the most elaborate of Stevie's career (pictured, with the black background). All the gray areas of the design are covered in glitter! The smaller handbill (also pictured) is much more common than the glitter poster, of which only a handful are known to exist today.

TONY DUKES: "I had moved to Houston to run Parker Music, which would become a home for Billy Gibbons, Rocky Hill and crew, Alan Haynes, and, every time when in town, Eric Johnson and our boy Stevie. It was like heaven, Cutter said, for times were still very rough and thin for Stevie and crew. Knowing this, and having seen my pal Cutter give up his burger money to buy Stevie strings, I had no qualms about restringing all of Stevie's guitars and [throwing in] a half dozen sets of strings with a bunch of extra high E's, which at that time were 13's. I also dipped

© BILL NARUM

into petty cash and made sure Stevie and Cutter and whoever came with them, usually Chris, ate that day – a burger and Orange Julius. It became known as 'Dukes and Burger Day.'"

ALAN HAYNES: "I was fairly popular in Houston at the time, and somebody came up to me one night and said, 'You're my *second*-favorite guitar player.' Then they said Stevie Vaughan, and that may have been the first time I heard about him."

NOTE: If you haven't discovered the music of Alan Haynes, the author suggests you do so immediately. Alan plays regularly in Austin, Houston and the DFW area, and not one of the dozens of people I have taken to see Alan play have been disappointed.

April 29: Rome Inn, Austin, TX

May 8: Soap Creek Saloon, Austin, TX

May 22: Soap Creek Saloon, Austin, TX

Summer: Johnny Reno leaves Double Trouble but continues to sit in with the band on occasion for several months.

© KERRY AWN

JOHNNY: "Basically, Stevie and the band were going toward the trio. The Hendrix stuff was happening. There was no hard feelings. I felt like it was going to happen sooner or later. I was having a ball playing with a guy who has this skill level, but if I was a record producer, I'd go, 'You, know, we don't really need the saxophone guy.' Musically, they were going in more the rock vein, and that wasn't what I was interested in.

"Part of the deal was we were starving, not making any money. We might walk out of the Rome Inn with fifty bucks for the band. Stevie lost the gig money now and then. It was better for someone else to be in charge of the business dynamics. Chris and I had a couple of conversations [about money]. I said, 'I can't hang in here and make a living doing this.' [Chris replied,] 'I'm going to take over stuff; it's going to get better.' I think he did and it was a big improvement. He was a good thing that happened for Stevie.

"The only reason Stevie had to care about money was he had to pay bills just like me and you. But really, he didn't care about it. All he cared about was playing music – that's all he did, all the time.

Stevie, Fredde and Lou Ann at After Ours, Austin, photo signed by W.C. Clark and Fredde Walden. © KATHY MURRAY, COLLECTION OF CRAIG HOPKINS

"I could make more money with these other guys [The Juke Jumpers], and the trio thing was evolving, and the sax wasn't working in that context. It wasn't a big deal, it was just an evolution. More and more it was like, 'Little Wing' at three o'clock in the morning at Rome Inn, and he would stretch out and play it for an hour. It was great, but it was a Stevie concert with a bass player and drummer. That's where Stevie wanted to go, and that's where the response was from people in the business. They weren't interested in a band with a chick singer and a sax player doing R&B covers from Chicago in the 1950's. All of a sudden, Stevie was a rock guitar player. He always was, but he could mix blues in with credibility – some guys can't do that.

"So I was there when he kind of went over that line: 'Oh. This is working too. I can become a rock guitar player with blues stylings and really control my destiny.' That's the kind of stuff people like John Hammond was responding to; the Stones ... guys were starting to hang around – Billy Gibbons was hanging around ... . The word was out.

"It was really fun. I never had any conflicts with Stevie personally. He was a good guy, real genuine good guy. There was some turmoil – he was with Lindi [Bethel] when I came on, then he wasn't with Lindi, then he was with Lindi. We spent a lot of time together because we would crash at Lou Ann's place in South Austin. He didn't have any place to live, and I didn't have any place to live because I still had my apartment in Fort Worth. We sat around playing records, and he practiced a lot.

He was pretty ambitious and dedicated to thinking, 'You know, I'm going to set the world on fire with this guitar.' I thought he had a clearer vision than I did. I didn't have any idea there could ever be a commercial market for what we were doing. But I was also older and more cynical [*laughs*].

"Stevie wasn't a yuk-it-up joke teller kind of guy. He was more ... funny in an aside, or Seinfeld way [*laughs*]. He could do great imitations of people. There was this character that would come into Antone's ... he was always selling weed or some sort of version of weed, and he might have worked at the shoe shine stand. He'd be talking, [affects funny voice] 'Hey 'tevie, man, I got tum really great weed, man, it's da best grass in the world, man. Dis is Bermuda grass, man, Bermuda grass. It's bad.' Stevie could do this guy and just crack you up. He had a keen sense of timing and his ear was real good.

"Stevie was so intense and so fiery. I was fortunate in being in the right place at the right time." As for a lasting memory, "Probably one of those Rome Inn nights that wasn't particularly special, when no one was there at ten o'clock when we started playing. There were a couple of nights when there were only three or four people there, and Stevie always just threw down!

"I went, 'A guy that is that passionate about what he's doing. There's nobody here, but he just wants to *and can*.' His integrity served him well. It was like having a hot race car and taking it out on the blacktop and putting the pedal down and letting it go do what it does!

"Whether anybody's in the room or not, he's always good. He was never not good. Every night I got on stage with him, he was *burnin'*."

June: Joe Gracey takes the band to Jack Clement's studio in Nashville for three days to record.

– You Can Have My Husband (Lou Ann vocal)
– Rude Mood
– Pride and Joy
– Oh, Yeah (Lou Ann vocal)
– Love Struck Baby
– Te Ni Nee Ni Nu (Lou Ann vocal)
– Empty Arms
– Will My Man Be Home Tonight? (Lou Ann vocals, Stevie on slide guitar)
– I'm Cryin'
– Sugar Coated Love (Lou Ann vocal)

JOE GRACEY: "John Dyer came in as an investor in Stevie and the band, and so I got him to give us enough money to finance the Nashville sessions. After that, when Chesley came into the picture and I bowed out, I think Dyer started demanding his money back, and that's when I took my tapes and the Nashville tapes to Chesley, who in turn paid Dyer back his money [in 1983]. I think at one point Dyer actually had somebody slash the tires on Stevie's van at a gig in Dallas, just to make his point about wanting his money back. By then I was out of the whole thing; I just heard about it.

"The Nashville sessions were much more complicated [than the KOKE sessions] because suddenly we had this investor, and I had to get them all to Nashville, house them and feed them and keep them all happy. I also had to keep Jack Clement happy, which wasn't all that easy since he became worried about a blues band blasting his neighbors to death at 11p.m. One day I came up to the studio to find him hammering 3/4" plywood panels over the windows in the studio (it was in his attic), which was his way of telling me they were playing too fucking loud, but there was nothing I could do about it.

"Unfortunately, the band had gotten a hold of some crank, and a lot of the tempos to those tracks were too fast because of it, but all in all they sounded great. The engineer made Chris tune his snare head down so that it was more like an L.A. or Nashville snare, which was a mistake, but so it goes. Those tracks ended up being mastered by me on my last day in Nashville. There were only two copies, one for me and one for Stevie, and somehow, somebody sold those tracks to some bootleggers, so you can hear them now. I didn't do it.

"We kept on recording [in Austin], using what little money I had, for a while after that. I pitched our tapes to Rounder and all of the small labels that I had access to and they all turned it down, so I was at a dead end, except to release them on my own label. He didn't want that, which I respected, so our thing ended. I loved him and as far as I was concerned, I had taken him as far as I could. All I cared about, literally, was what was best for Stevie."

JACK NEWHOUSE: "I think we had gone in hoping to get something out of the Nashville session to put out. I remember at the time we didn't like the overall quality of it, but it sounds pretty good today. The performances were good – probably the best thing that survived from back then. [But] it wasn't done in a professional studio; it was more of a demo-quality studio in Jack's house."

CHRIS LAYTON: "We recorded at the Cowboy Arms Hotel, Recording Studio and Spa. It was a big, ol' Tudor-looking house in Nashville. We didn't really record with [Jack Clement]; we went to his place. Joe was there, and we just set up in the attic of that place and ran through the songs, pretty much [like we had at KOKE that spring]. It was a little more ambitious than just packing your stuff into a

The Cowboy Arms, Nashville.

Stevie's handwritten drafts of songs including "Honey Bee".
COURTESY DOBBS/JACKSON

storage room at a radio station in Austin, but when you're that young and you get a chance, you think, 'Maybe this could be something.'

"I do remember thinking, 'Wow. Jack Clement. That's cool.' But we only saw him a couple of times. It was hot; and a window AC unit that kept the attic cool. When we were recording, we had to turn the window unit off – it was right behind me. Downstairs there was a console and an actual studio, but we were up in the attic. There wasn't any huge deal being made out of all this. History does that. We just went there because we could."

JOE PRIESNITZ: "Stevie was really picky about what we sent out as a demo. We would ask for tapes to send out to solicit bookings, and they might bring four or five. And as I recall, it was mostly the Joe Gracey tapes." When it was suggested that Stevie didn't like the production quality of those tapes, Joe responded, "I don't think he did. He didn't want a lot of them out there. We didn't have much until that KLBJ broadcast [April 1, 1980, which became *In the Beginning*].

📖**June:** *Texas Nickelodeon.* "The Austin-based band, Double Trouble, recently recorded tapes at Jack Clement's studio in Nashville. With Stevie Vaughn [sic] playing sizzling lead guitar, and Lou Ann Barton melting hearts with her vocals, bassist Jack Newhouse and drummer Chris Layton provide a solid bottom to sessions that should be on wax soon. Watch for this band to begin frequent area engagements soon."

June 3: Rome Inn, Austin, TX

June 7: Reed's Red Derby, San Antonio, TX

June 8: Reed's Red Derby, San Antonio, TX

June 9: Reed's Red Derby, San Antonio, TX

June 10: Rome Inn, Austin, TX

June 11: Rome Inn, Austin, TX

June 14: The Rox, Lubbock, TX

June 15: The Rox, Lubbock, TX

June 16: The Rox, Lubbock, TX

📷**June 18:** Juneteenth Blues Festival, Houston, TX
  – Dirty Pool
  – Empty Arms
  – Love Struck Baby
  – Pride and Joy
  – You Can Have My Husband
  – Te Ni Nee Ni Nu
  – Scratch My Back
  – Oh Yeah
  – Long Tall Sally/Tutti-Frutti
  – Collins' Shuffle

June 19: Stevie probably stayed for the Thunderbirds' gig at the Juneteenth Festival, as it is written on his calendar.

June 28: Reference on Stevie's calendar, "E.J.'s dad party"; unknown if this is a social or professional event or whether this is a reference to Eric Johnson.

June 29: After Ours, Austin, TX

June 30: After Ours, Austin, TX

📖**Summer:** *Living Blues,* Juneteenth, Houston concert review by Jim Jasso

📖**July:** *Texas Nickelodeon,* Austin blues article mentions SRV and the temporary closing of Antone's nightclub. After almost four years on 6th Street in Austin, the club moved into North Austin, where it would remain in various locations until moving back downtown in the 1990's.

July 3: Fannie Ann's, Dallas, TX

July 6: Rome Inn, Austin, TX

July 7: Rome Inn, Austin, TX

July 8: Rome Inn, Austin, TX

July 12: Reed's Red Derby, San Antonio, TX

July 13: Reed's Red Derby, San Antonio, TX

July 14: Reed's Red Derby, San Antonio, TX

July 15: Rome Inn, Austin, TX

Interestingly, Stevie wrote on his personal calendar that July 15 was a tentative release date for the album recorded by Joe Gracey. The band later paid several thousand dollars for it *not* to be released.

July 20: Steamboat 1874, Austin, TX

July 21: Steamboat 1874, Austin, TX

Steamboat was a long narrow club on Sixth Street. When you walked in the door, the stage was directly in front of you, but it was facing the far end of the club. You could either walk past the stage into the street level of the club or you could walk up some stairs to the right to an upstairs narrow balcony that ran lengthwise down the wall.

MIKE STEELE: "I was standing behind Stevie [behind the stage], and he just happened to be playing slide guitar. George Thorogood had played the Opera House, and he came in and was standing next to me. Stevie finished the song and turned around to put his slide down and saw me and waved. I kind of motioned like, 'Look who's next to me.' He saw George and invited him up, but George didn't want to [*laughs*], and I don't blame him!"

July 22: Rome Inn, Austin, TX

July 25: Miranda's, College Station, TX

July 26: Miranda's, College Station, TX. One of these two shows was recorded by an audience member with Stevie's permission. "I remember during the break Stevie huddling back by the drum set with a soldering iron trying to fix his guitar (#1). A friend I was with was a guitar player and offered his guitar to Stevie, but he said, "Naw man. I'll be all right."[42]
  – You Done Lost Your Good Thing Now
  – Woke Up This Morning – instrumental
  – Dirty Pool
  – Rude Mood
  – Hideaway

July 27: Armadillo, Austin, TX, opening for Randy Hansen

July 27: Steamboat 1874, Austin, TX (cancelled)

July 28: Steamboat 1874, Austin, TX (cancelled)

July 29: Rome Inn, Austin, TX

TONIGHT.....
STEP INTO THE DANGER ZONE

jack newhouse, bass   stevie vaughan, guitar   chris layton, drums
                        and vocals
**Stevie Vaughan & Double Trouble
from Austin, Texas**

"Santa Cruz had never swung with such intensity. Double Trouble leader and guitarist Stevie Vaughan is just amazing. Making like a 'new wave' blues band, Double Trouble mixes vintage blues stylings with fresh, modern rock arrangements. Vaughan, undoubtedly one of the finest guitarists Santa Cruz will ever see, had super back-up help from solemn bassist Jack Newhouse and hard-hitting drummer Chris Layton."
            Greg Beebe
            Santa Cruz Sentinel
            Santa Cruz, California
            August, 19, 1979

"And when he plays that big red guitar with the heavy strings, they don't just watch him, they are hypnotized by him."
            Bob Campbell
            Lubbock Avalanche Journal
            Lubbock, Texas
            July 30, 1978

"Double Trouble shook the show out of the doldrums by cranking up the electric blues all the way to its modern progeny, Rock & Roll—boasting the hottest guitarist of the evening."
            Dale Adamson
            Houston Chronicle
            Houston, Texas
            June 19, 1979
            Juneteenth Blues Festival

Possibly the first publicity flyer prepared for Double Trouble, circa early 1980.
COLLECTION OF CRAIG HOPKINS

August: *Buddy*, "Texas Tornados: A Guide to the heaviest guitars in the Lone Star State, Kirby Warnock

August 2: The Rox, Lubbock, TX

August 3: The Rox, Lubbock, TX

August 4: The Rox, Lubbock, TX

August 6: Opry House, San Antonio, TX

August 7: Opry House, San Antonio, TX

August 10: Iron Horse

August 11: Coffee Gallery, San Francisco, CA (not on agent's calendar; Festival appearance may have been moved to 11th)

August 12: San Francisco Blues Festival, San Francisco, CA. One of the first important out-of-state gigs. On this afternoon of the two-day festival, Double Trouble shares the bill with Louis Myers, Jimmy Rogers, Luther Tucker, Robert Cray, Mel Brown, Paul Delay, Blue Sax All Stars and J.J. "Bad Boy" Jones.
  – Instrumental
  – Rude Mood
  – You Can Have My Husband
  – Te Ni Nee Ni Nu
  – I'll Change

August 12: Keystone, Berkeley, CA (evening)

August 17: High Country, Santa Cruz, CA, with Ron Thompson Band

August 18: High Country, Santa Cruz, CA, with Robert Cray Band

August 20: Keystone, Palo Alto, CA, Fat Fry show for KFAT-FM, with Robert Cray (guitar) and Curtis Salgado (harmonica)

August 23: Steamboat 1874, Austin, TX

August 24: Steamboat 1874, Austin, TX

August 25: Steamboat 1874, Austin, TX

August 26: Rome Inn, Austin, TX

August 27: Rockefeller's, Houston, TX. Attendance: 49

August 28: Rockefeller's, Houston, TX. Attendance: 88

August 30: Fat Dawg's, Lubbock, TX

August 31: Fat Dawg's, Lubbock, TX

September 1: Fat Dawg's, Lubbock, TX

September 5: Steamboat 1874, Austin, TX (cancelled)

September 7: Crazy Bob's, Austin, TX (Austin Opera House cancelled)

September 8: Crazy Bob's, Austin, TX (Austin Opera House cancelled)

September 10: Rome Inn, Austin, TX

September 12: Miranda's, College Station, TX

September 13: Miranda's, College Station, TX

September 14: Antone's, Austin, TX

September 15: Antone's, Austin, TX

September 18: Rockefeller's, Houston, TX

September 19: Rockefeller's, Houston, TX

September 21: Steamboat 1874, Austin, TX

September 22: Steamboat 1874, Austin, TX

September 23: Rome Inn, Austin, TX

September 28: Fast Eddie's, Fort Worth, TX

September 29: Fast Eddie's, Fort Worth, TX

September 30: New Bluebird, Fort Worth, TX. Ft. Worth blues great Robert Ealey sits in on songs marked *.
- Hideaway
- instrumental
- Rude Mood
- Dirty Pool
- Guitar Hurricane
- All Your Love I Miss Loving
- You Done Lost Your Good Thing Now
- Woke Up This Morning
- Collins' Shuffle
- I'm Just A Man *
- Thrill Is Gone *
- I'll Take You There(?) (long jam with saxophone)*
- Don't Lose Your Cool *

Autumn: *Living Blues*, San Francisco Blues Fest review by Richard Cohen mentions Double Trouble

October 1: Rome Inn, Austin, TX (cancelled)

October 4: Skipwilly's, San Antonio, TX

October 5: Rome Inn, Austin, TX

October 6: Rome Inn, Austin, TX

October 7: Rome Inn, Austin, TX

COLLECTION OF CRAIG HOPKINS

MIKE STEELE: "Stevie was playing one night at the Rome Inn, and they were filming that movie *Honeysuckle Rose* in Austin. It was Willie Nelson and Dyan Cannon. Stevie took a break and came down off the stage, and I was standing at the far end of the bar. He came over and got a drink and said, 'Did you see who's standing at the other end of the bar?' I looked down and there was Willie, Dyan Cannon and several others. They were just hanging out listening to Stevie.

"What amazed me, Dyan Cannon – what a knockout she was – was wearing these skintight white bell-bottoms and a white halter top, you know, with her stomach exposed. She was *built*; oh my god! Anyway, she danced with every guy in the club that asked her. Some of these drunks didn't even know who she was; they just knew she was beautiful and would dance [*laughs*]!"

October 10: Tipitina's, New Orleans, LA

October 11: Tipitina's, New Orleans, LA

© BILL NARUM

October 12: Hattiesburg, MS

October 13: Hattiesburg, MS

October 14: Solomon Alfred's, Memphis TN

October 15: Solomon Alfred's, Memphis TN

October 16: Solomon Alfred's, Memphis TN

October 17: Solomon Alfred's, Memphis TN

October 18: Atlanta, GA, with Albert Collins

October 20: Atlanta, GA (with White Face Capri?)

October 24: Brother's, Birmingham, AL

October 25: Brother's, Birmingham, AL, with Delbert McClinton

October 26: Brother's, Birmingham, AL, with Amazing Rhythm Aces

October 27: Brother's, Birmingham, AL, with Amazing Rhythm Aces

October 28: Double Door Inn, Charlotte, NC

October 29: Double Door Inn, Charlotte, NC

October 31: Cabaret (PA?)

November 2: Depot, West Virginia

November 3: Depot, West Virginia

November 5: University of South Carolina

November 6: University of South Carolina

November 9: Desperado's, Washington, D.C.

November 10: Desperado's, Washington, D.C. Note that it appears Lou Ann only sang two songs, presaging her imminent departure from the band.

- Dirty Pool
- I Tried Pretty Baby
- All Your Love I Miss Loving
- You Done Lost Your Good Thing Now
- Don't Lose Your Cool
- Collins' Shuffle
- In the Open
- instrumental
- Rude Mood
- Drivin' South
- Natural Born Lover (Lou Ann vocal)
- Tell Me Why (Lou Ann vocal)
- Stang's Swang
- instrumental
- Love Struck Baby
- Tin Pan Alley
- Hug You Squeeze You
- Guitar Hurricane
- Empty Arms
- Savoy Shuffle
- Hideaway

November 12: Washington, D.C. – unknown whether Stevie played in support of, or merely attended, B.B. King's show

November 13: Lone Star Cafe, New York, NY

November 14: Lone Star Cafe, New York, NY

CLEVE HATTERSLEY, who booked Double Trouble into the Lone Star Cafe: "We booked them for $100. They drove all the way up from Austin and crashed on friends' couches. The gig went all right, but afterward, Lou Ann kind of got out of hand. She was real drunk and threw beer glasses and screamed at the waitresses. Stevie, of course, was upset. That was the final gig that band ever had together."[13] Actually, Lou Ann finished the tour.

November 16: Stanhope, NJ

November 17: Stanhope, NJ

November 18: Salisbury, MD

November 21: Washington, D.C.

November 22: Knickerbocker Cafe, Westerly, RI.

– Dirty Pool
– Pride and Joy
– Love Struck Baby
– Hideaway
– In The Open
– Rude Mood
– The Sky Is Crying
– Love Me Darlin'
– So Excited (intro for Lou Ann Barton)
– You Can Have My Husband
– Te Ni Nee Ni Nu
– I'll Change
– Oh, Yeah
– Natural Born Lover
– Shake Your Hips
– Don't Lose Your Good Thing
– Collins' Shuffle

CHRIS LAYTON: "There were so many shows, it's hard to remember specific ones. Either it's a good day or it's a bad day, and maybe you might remember something because of a specific incident that was out of the ordinary, like the truck blew an engine and you had to sit by the side of the road for four hours. We played at the Knickerbocker on Thanksgiving, and the motel didn't have a restaurant. We got in the van and we drove until we saw this little storefront, and we went in and we sat there. It was cold and it was raining, and we just sat at the counter, eating this horrible turkey and dressing.

"And I remember that because I thought, 'God, I'd really like to be home in a warm house with my family and not out here sitting in this horrible little diner, eating this steam-table prison food.' It's kind of hard, trying to find that balance between living out of a suitcase and all the hardship that comes from eating crappy food and not being able to sleep in good beds sometimes, and try to combine that with inspirational playing and feeling healthy and rested – when you don't feel either one. In my book, that was probably the toughest trick of all."[35]

Speaking of living out of a suitcase, Stevie's friend JAMES ELWELL was often called upon to help Stevie move. "He moved about every six months, and I helped him move all those boxes." When asked what was in the boxes, the answer was simple: "Records."

STEVIE, on his record collection: "I don't get the chance to get home very often 'cause we're on the road a lot. I'll walk in the house and I'll *look* at my records. I'll just thumb through them, and I don't even necessarily have to put them on at first. Just looking at the covers, I can remember all the feelings. It's like, 'Okay, I'm home. Here's my books, and here's my roots.' And then I'll put something on and it's like being rejuvenated."[74]

Stevie's friend DONNA JOHNSTON: "Stevie and I had a conversation one time about our respective record collections. I expressed concern about what was going to happen to mine when I died, and Stevie told me that his was going to the Smithsonian! This was probably in late '85 or early '86, so he may have been joking, but I didn't get that impression."

November 24: Lupo's Heartbreak Hotel, Providence, RI

– Dirty Pool
– I'm Cryin'
– So Exited (intro for Lou Ann Barton)
– You Can Have My Husband
– Te Ni Nee Ni Nu
– I'll Change
– Sugar Coated Love
– Natural Born Lover
– Shake Your Hips
– Collins' Shuffle
– instrumental
– The Sky Is Crying
– Love Struck Baby
– May I Have A Talk With You
– Don't Lose Your Good Thing
– My Baby's Gone
– Stang's Swang
– instrumental

Lupo's was the final show for Lou Ann Barton as a member of Double Trouble. She joined Roomful of Blues, which had been on the bill with Double Trouble for some of the shows on the east coast.

Whether Lou Ann was fired or quit probably depends on whom you ask. More than one person close to the band has said that Lou Ann was quite a handful when drunk and that she could out-consume anyone in the band. One of the band recalls that on this east coast swing, "She was not in her best form [*laughs*]." Matters apparently came to a head when she fell down on stage in quite an unbecoming display better left without further description. She allegedly looked up at Stevie and said, "You handle your shit, and I'll handle mine."

It is likely that Stevie's growing confidence to be the sole leader of the band played as much a role in the decision making as Lou Ann's preference for R&B rather than the more rock- and Hendrix-oriented songs that were stirring up crowds when she wasn't on stage.

JACK NEWHOUSE: "We did some shows in Rhode Island with Roomful of Blues. They were losing their vocalist – it may have been right after Duke Robillard left. They were looking for a singer and they asked Lou Ann. She wanted to join them, and we gave her our blessings and thought it would be a great thing for everybody."

CHRIS LAYTON: "All in all, I think there was really only room for one chief in Double Trouble. Part of the band wanted to go in one direction, and part of the band wanted to go another direction."[3]

Agent JOE PRIESNITZ: "We put him out on the road. We had a pretty good circuit through the southeast. I can't remember if it was the first or second little run that we put him on that Lou Ann quit [in the northeast]. I don't think Lou Ann and Stevie were getting along. I know there was a continuing hot and cold artistic relationship. They came home, and we had twelve or twenty dates booked for them. So we were wondering what we were going to do – 'We're minus a singer.'

"They were assuring us they were going to keep playing and everything was going to be fine. I said, 'Hey, I'm sure we can play, but who's going to sing?' And Stevie said, '*I am*,' and gave me this look like, 'I am, you asshole.' [*Laughs*] Like, 'How dare you even ask?' I mean, *she* was the vocalist. I think I might have heard Stevie sing two or three songs before that, and it wasn't the high point of the show."

CHRIS LAYTON: "[After Lou Ann] the band had become very essential. It was a power trio and the focus was there. There was one direction, and I think a whole different style of music grew out of that. Like I said, it was very focused and things were pretty clear at that point [that] wherever [Stevie] was gonna go is where the band was gonna go. .... He was always a very determined person, very strong-willed and kind of like a dog to a bone. Once he made up his mind to try to go do something, that's what he set his sights on, he went and did it.

"We started doing some Hendrix-type stuff, and his guitar playing got a lot more wild. He started playing behind his head and between his legs and behind his back and just kind of a lot more stage antics. It was all in fun, it was all real honest, but we kind of moved away from being an R&B blues approach to just, 'Hey, whatever we come up with will be what our thing is."[3]

Hendrix was a hot-button topic for the media, of course, some saying it was sacrilege for anyone to try to do Hendrix that closely, and arguments surfaced over whose version was better. Tommy Shannon: "Early on [Stevie] just played blues. It was later he became less afraid [to play Hendrix]. He wasn't trying to copy Jimi Hendrix; it was more like a tribute to Jimi and [to] honor him."[3]

November 30: Antone's, Austin, TX

December 1: Antone's, Austin, TX

December 2: Rome Inn, Austin, TX

December 5: Palace, Houston, TX (with Muddy Waters)

On December 5, Stevie and Lenny are busted for cocaine in Houston. The arrest card shows Stevie at 5'9", 140 pounds.

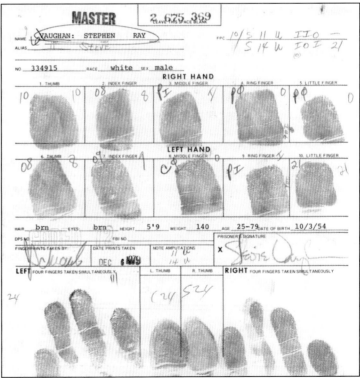

Houston police fingerprint card. COLLECTION OF CRAIG HOPKINS

AGENT JOE PRIESNITZ: "He was playing a show in Houston and got busted backstage while doing cocaine in front of the picture window. I got the call early in the morning, 'Stevie's in jail. What are we going to do?' We had to wire money down to bail him out, but they made the next show."

December 6: Lubbock, TX (cancelled)

December 7: Lubbock, TX

December 8: Lubbock, TX

December 14: Rockefeller's, Houston, TX

December 15: Rockefeller's, Houston, TX

December 16: Rome Inn, Austin, TX

December 19: Fast Eddie's, Fort Worth, TX (cancelled)

December 21: Skipwilly's, San Antonio, TX

December 22: Antone's, Austin, TX

December 23: Rome Inn, Austin, TX. Stevie marries Lenora Darlene Bailey upstairs at the club.

The story goes that Stevie decided to marry Lenny after having a dream in which she was sitting on Howlin' Wolf's knee. In attendance at the wedding were Chris Layton, Jack Newhouse,

Lenny and Stevie opening wedding gifts at Rome Inn.
© MARY BETH GREENWOOD

Cutter and Peggy Brandenburg, Keith Ferguson of the Thunderbirds and Mary Beth Greenwood, among others.

Lenny recalls they decided to get married at seven o'clock that evening. C-Boy Parks had a preacher at the club by eleven; they got to the Driskill Hotel around four in the morning and had to check out by eleven.[17] Joe Priesnitz recalls getting a call about the wedding earlier in the afternoon, but in any event, there wasn't much notice. The Driskill Hotel opened at the corner of what is now Brazos and 6th Streets in 1886, the same year construction began on the State Capitol a few blocks away.

Newlyweds Stevie and Lenny. COURTESY MARTHA VAUGHAN

MARY BETH: "Stevie called me at Pecan Street Cafe to announce that he's going to marry Lenny that night and he wanted me there. He said not many people were invited. The room [upstairs at Rome Inn] was a cracker box – broken beer bottles. I couldn't believe he was doing it. I let Lenny wear the silk shirt I had on because she had a pink, polyester, button-down, kind of a men's shirt-looking thing. I was shocked they were getting married so loosely, and then he went downstairs and played.

"I noticed right away that he flipped the songs that he had written for or dedicated to Lindi every night to Lenny. A week or two before he got married, he'd asked me to marry him, so this guy just wanted to get married to someone he liked."

COURTESY MARTHA VAUGHAN

CHRIS: "Everybody had been partying beforehand. We were all pretty drunk. It was a night of celebration. It wasn't like there was invitations sent out or a certain group of people attended – it was just whoever was there was hanging around. Stevie didn't have rings, so he had these two pieces of wire that he wrapped around his finger and hers and kind of twisted together. It was right before we started playing."[3]

JACK NEWHOUSE: "It was a pretty bizarre night, to say the least. It happened so fast, between sets at the Rome Inn; it seemed like everything was made up on the spot."

MIKE STEELE: "I was at the club that night and Stevie told me he was going to marry Lenny at the break. I thought he was kidding. He came back down after the break and had some twisted wire on his finger. I still thought it was a joke, but someone said it was true. Lenny and Stevie had been kind of off and on. He and Lenny broke up, and then he went out with Kelly, and then got back together with Lenny and got married."

LINDI BETHEL: "I moved back home to Corpus Christi to get back on my feet financially and didn't tell anybody I was moving. Stevie wrote me a letter, and we started back our relationship, got hot and heavy again. He was always wanting to know when we were going to get back together, when I was going to move back. The next thing I know, a friend of mine calls me and goes, 'I just want to say congratulations!' I said, 'Congratulations for what?' He says, 'Well, I just heard you and Stevie got married.' 'WHAT?!' Talk about a blow. How did that happen? I was hurt when I found out he had married Lenny." Lindi's recollection is that Stevie had been trying to get back together with her only a few weeks before.

As for Stevie's relationship with Lenny, Chris says it was "pretty excitable. Let me reach in my bag of euphemisms here. You know, they were pretty passionate. They did all kinds of wild things together – they chased around town and did their skirmishing like other couples might do."[3]

December 28: Rome Inn, Austin, TX (possibly cancelled due to "honeymoon")

December 29: Rome Inn, Austin, TX (possibly cancelled due to "honeymoon")

December 31: Antone's, Austin, TX

1980

The new year brings Stevie a new set of challenges. Without the triple or double threat of singers W.C. Clark and Lou Ann Barton, the vocal responsibilities fall solely on him. In his personal life, he is married and facing the consequences of a drug arrest. The departure of Lou Ann was actually liberating, for without her the band was now free to play any music Stevie wanted. This

immediately brought a louder, rock feel to their sets. Hendrix's music was featured more prominently as well. STEVIE: "With the Cobras and Triple Threat, we'd been playing straight blues. I got to stretch out more in Double Trouble, and that's one reason Lou Ann and I didn't get along. She didn't like my Hendrix stuff."[18]

CHRIS LAYTON: "We had a sax player and a featured singer, Lou Ann Barton. At that point we were playing stuff that sounded like R&B-type blues. It's not that Stevie was playing more reserved then; it's that he was playing more blues/R&B stuff. [When we became a trio,] the only thing that guided our music was whether we were moved by it. If we weren't moved by it, then we weren't moving in the right direction."[43]

DOYLE BRAMHALL: "There was a time when Stevie would play three hours solid, and he wouldn't say one word to the audience. But that wasn't because he was trying to be standoffish; it was because he was not comfortable with that. What he was comfortable with was playing music. His road manager, Cutter Brandenburg, would talk to Stevie about, 'You need to start talking to the audience!' Cutter would take him to these gigs – Rod Stewart, B.B. or whoever happened to be in town – to watch them and see how they interacted with the audience. Not just their music, but with speaking. So Stevie slowly started getting more comfortable with that."[3]

Back with the band as roadie is Cutter Brandenburg, who would stay with the band into September 1983. Among all the other work he did for the band, Cutter would occasionally make sure Stevie had his favorite candy, Goodart's Peanut Patties.

In 1980, the band's gross receipts each night varied widely from $150 in places like New York City, where they had yet to establish a following, to $750-$900 per night in Austin and Houston, with the overall average right at $500 per night for the second half of the year.

In early 1980, Chesley Millikin becomes Stevie's manager, doing business as Classic Management. Charles Comer takes over as publicist.

Chesley Millikin had been Epic Records' general manager in Europe and was now the general manager of a horse racing track called Manor Downs, in Manor, Texas, outside Austin. It was owned by Frances Carr, who was the first to offer Stevie's band financial support. Her accountant, Edi Johnson, had brought Stevie to Frances' attention. They both believed Stevie had a great amount of talent and that he could go places if he had someone to help him with the business of being a successful musician.

Carr had asked Chesley to help turn Manor Downs around and suggested managing Stevie to keep Chesley from getting bored.[17]

Chesley was adamant that Stevie not be sold as a bluesman. He instructed publicist Charles Comer, "For God's sake, whatever you do, do not call him a blues guitar player." Comer delivered, and by the mid-eighties the tandem moved Stevie well beyond the paltry sales figures most blues artists were realizing – by hundreds of thousands of records.

He was not interested in having Stevie sign a deal with Alligator Records because it was only blues. Elektra Records wanted Stevie. Hammond Music Enterprises didn't have the money to handle Stevie's potential. Greg Geller at Epic signed Stevie to the label.[17]

Roadie Cutter Brandenburg is credited by Chesley for wanting the band called "Stevie Ray Vaughan *and Double Trouble*." Chesley didn't want Double Trouble's name on anything. Stevie was the irreplaceable talent, and as a businessman, he preferred not to have any entanglements with the band that might limit Stevie's flexibility and progress.[17]

Sharks and hustlers had been circling for a while, and Chesley had a good eye for them. Edi recalls one occasion when someone was trying to surreptitiously record a conversation with Stevie backstage. He circled the guy a couple of times, checking him out, and then grabbed his lapel, revealing the recording device.[17]

Chesley Millikin, manager 1980-1985.
© BYRON BARR

Among the first requests from new manager Chesley Millikin is that Stevie provide autobiographical notes for use in publicity. STEVIE's handwritten response:

"Stephen Ray Vaughan (Stevie Ray). Born Oct. 3rd 1954 in Dallas, TX. Grew up mainly in Oak Cliff (South Side Dallas) and began playing guitar in late '61 – early '62 at 7 to 8 years of age. Began playing in my first bands around 12 years of age. Continued to play (Dallas-Ft. Worth local) clubs, USO's, parks, etc. for several years.

"While in Dallas formed a band known as Blackbird that began to receive considerable recognition over a fairly large area (statewide). The band moved to Austin January 1, 1972, where we based out of until disbanding a year or so later. By that time Tommy Shannon had been playing bass in Blackbird along with Bruce Bowlin [sic]. Both of a previous form of Krackerjack.

"I joined up with Tommy, Bruce, Robin Syler and John Turner to reform the band Krackerjack in late '72. which disbanded 6 or so months later. In spring of '73 I joined Doyle Bramhall, Tommy McClure and Bill Etheridge as the Nightcrawlers who were then backing Marc Benno. We soon (12 days later) went to L.A. to do some studio work for A&M. The tapes, though never released, included 2 of my songs. My first attempts at writing.

"The band came back to Austin and continued on our own without Benno and replacing Tommy McClure on bass with Bruce Miller. The band continued for a year and a half touring with various bands until disbanding.

"I returned to L.A. for more studio work (3 months) before moving back to Austin to stay and join the Cobras. We were voted by public opinion "Band of the Year" as well as "Best R&B Band" in the *Texas* [sic – should be *Austin*] *Sun* Music Poll in mid '76.

"I went on to form Triple Threat Revue with W.C.

Charles Comer, publicist 1980-1990. © DAVID BETITO

First publicity portrait under Chesley's management. COLLECTION OF CRAIG HOPKINS

Clark, Mike Kindred, Fredde Pharoah and Lou Ann Barton. April 15, 1979 [sic – should be 1978] I formed Double Trouble, once again with Barton, Jackie Newhouse on bass, later adding Chris Layton on drums. Newhouse since replaced by my bassman Tommy Shannon of Johnny Winter, Edgar Winter, Krackerjack notoriety. Lou Ann and I have gone separate ways for mutual benefits since early '80."

Stevie then listed his main influences as: "Jimi Hendrix, Albert King, B.B. King, Freddie King, Albert Collins, Lonnie Mack, Johnny Guitar Watson, Robert Lewis Stephenson, Carl Perkins, Buddy Guy, Howlin' Wolf, Bobby Bland, James Brown, Larry Davis, Buster Benton, Hubert Sumlin, Junior Walker, Les Paul, Django Reinhardt, Otis Rush, Guitar Slim, Ray Charles, Muddy Waters, Big Mama Thornton, Gatemouth Brown, Lowell Fulson, Jimmy Smith, Johnny Smith, Grant Green, Wes Montgomery, Kenny Burrell, Barney Kessel, Howard Roberts, George Benson, Horace Silver, Denny Freeman, Bill Etheridge, Doyle Bramhall. And of course Jimmie Vaughan."

January 3: Skipwilly's, San Antonio, TX

January 4: Antone's, Austin, TX

January 5: Antone's, Austin TX

January 6: Rome Inn, Austin, TX

January 9: Rockefeller's, Houston, TX

January 10: Rockefeller's, Houston, TX

January 11: After Ours, Austin, TX

January 12: Skipwilly's, San Antonio, TX

January 13: Rome Inn, Austin, TX

January 16: Court date for drug bust

January 17: Skipwilly's, San Antonio, TX (cancelled)

January 18: The Rox, Lubbock, TX

January 19: The Rox, Lubbock, TX

January 20: Antone's, Austin, TX

📷**January 23:** Steamboat 1874, Austin, TX. Radio broadcast in Austin (probably KLBJ-FM)

January 24: Skipwilly's, San Antonio, TX (cancelled)

January 25: Fitzgerald's, Houston, TX

January 26: Fitzgerald's, Houston, TX

January 27: Rome Inn, Austin, TX

February 1: After Ours, Austin, TX (cancelled)

February 2: After Ours, Austin, TX (cancelled)

February 5: Chief's, Baton Rouge, LA

February 6: Chief's, Baton Rouge, LA

February 8: Agora, Atlanta, GA

February 9: Double Door, Charlotte, NC

📷**February 12:** Desperado's, Washington, D.C.
- Drivin' South
- Third Stone From the Sun
- Hideaway
- In the Open
- The Sky Is Crying
- Pride and Joy
- Love In Vain
- Tin Pan Alley
- Crosscut Saw
- Wham!
- I'm Leaving You
- Manic Depression

February 13: Desperado's, Washington, D.C.

February 15: No Fish Today, Baltimore, MD

February 16: No Fish Today, Baltimore, MD

After the gigs in Baltimore, Chesley cancelled a west coast tour because, in his opinion, the band was getting too drunk. He didn't want them to screw up in front of VIP's on the west coast.[17]

February 21: Elbow Room, Harrisonburg, VA

February 22: Mancini's, Pittsburgh, PA

February 23: Evergreen, Pittsburgh, PA

February 25: Downtown Cafe, Atlanta, GA

February 26: Downtown Cafe, Atlanta, GA

February 29: Fitzgerald's, Houston, TX. Omar and the Howlers open. There is some evidence the band also played Rome Inn before going to Houston. Stevie had a court date this morning regarding the cocaine bust.

© R. LUCKETT

March?: Holiday Inn, Groton, CT
- Love Struck Baby
- Love Me Darlin'
- Tin Pan Alley
- Shake For Me
- Wham!
- Come On, Part III
- Dirty Pool
- I'm Cryin'
- A Letter To My Girlfriend
- I Tried
- Little Wing
- Drivin' South / Third Stone From The Sun
- Rude Mood
- Close To You
- You'll Be Mine
- Empty Arms
- Boilermaker

March 1: Fitzgerald's, Houston, TX. Omar and the Howlers open

March 2: Continental Club, Austin, TX

Former bandmate JIM TRIMMIER: "I saw Stevie at Fitzgerald's with Jackie Newhouse on bass. There was about fifteen people there, and Stevie was playing 'til 2:30 in the morning, and the fifteen people were just *screaming*."

JOE SUBLETT: "Stevie was goofy and came up with this nickname for Jack, Globe-head McNally, because he always insisted on driving and always swore he knew where he was going and got the band lost. He'd never look at a map [*laughs*]." Of course, "McNally" is a reference to the famous map publisher Rand-McNally.

March 7: Rome Inn, Austin, TX

March 8: Rome Inn, Austin, TX

March 9: Rome Inn, Austin, TX

March 14: Antone's, Austin, TX

March 15: Antone's, Austin, TX

March 16: Rome Inn, Austin, TX

March 18: Stephen F. Austin State University, Nacogdoches, TX

COLLECTION OF CRAIG HOPKINS

March 20: Steamboat 1874, Austin, TX

March 21: Fitzgerald's, Houston, TX

March 22: Fitzgerald's, Houston, TX

March 27: The Rox, Lubbock, TX

March 28: The Rox, Lubbock, TX

March 29: The Rox, Lubbock, TX

April 1: Steamboat 1874, Austin, TX. The concert is broadcast on KLBJ-FM radio and posthumously released as the *In The Beginning* CD. For this gig on a Tuesday night, the band received $500 vs. 90% of the door.
- In The Open
- Slide Thing
- They Call Me Guitar Hurricane
- The Sky Is Crying
- I'm Leaving You

– All Your Love I Miss Loving
– Tin Pan Alley
– Love Struck Baby
– Tell Me
– Shake For Me
– Little Wing
– Collins' Shuffle
– I'm Cryin'
– Texas Flood
– I Tried
– Hideaway

This recording and broadcast for KLBJ have always been listed as April 1. However, booking agent Joe Priesnitz's calendar indicates "KLBJ" on May 13, not April 1. It would not be the first time a tape box was mismarked.

April 4: Steamboat 1874, Austin, TX. This Friday night gig was worth $600 vs. 90% of the door, compared to $500 for the Tuesday show.

April 5: Rome Inn, Austin, TX

April 7: Rome Inn, Austin, TX, with the T-Birds

April 10: Rockefeller's, Houston, TX

April 11: T.J.'s, College Station, TX

April 12: T.J.'s, College Station, TX

April 17: Stevie is sentenced to 2 years probation (Lenny gets 5) for the cocaine possession charge from December 1979. He is ordered not to leave Texas. Frances Carr has a lawyer get Stevie's probation changed (and gets him a new probation officer) to allow him to work outside Texas.

April 18: Rome Inn, Austin, TX

April 19: Fitzgerald's, Houston, TX

🎙️ 📷 **April 24:** Rome Inn, Austin TX. Double bill with The Fabulous Thunderbirds on the closing night of the Rome Inn. The owner of the club filmed part of the show, which is the earliest known video of Stevie performing. A few seconds of the film appears in the 1997 VH-1 documentary *Legends: Stevie Ray Vaughan*. The video of Stevie at the Rome Inn is approximately thirteen minutes in length. There is a bootleg audio purported to be from this show containing these songs:

– Shake For Me
– You Done Lost Your Good Thing Now
– May I Have A Talk With You
– Tin Pan Alley
– Howlin' For My Darlin'
From another source:
– Hideaway
– I'm Leaving You (Commit A Crime) (video)
– The Sky Is Crying (video)
– Love Struck Baby (video)
– I'm Cryin'
– Little Wing
– My Baby's Gone (Oh, Yeah) (with Lou Ann Barton)
– Shake Your Hips (with LouAnn)
– Collins' Shuffle

MELODY WILSON: "I remember Stevie stole the Rome Inn sign off the top of the building [after it closed] [*laughs*], and they put it in the truck. I came around the next day and there it was in the back yard. Lenny was laughing and telling me about it. It was a great big, huge white plastic sign. He must have carried that thing with him for years, because every time you saw it, it would be broken more."

Melody had been running into Stevie since the days of the Cobras in 1974, when one night she actually tripped over Stevie, who was sitting in the audience at a San Antonio show. "I looked at him and said, 'I'm going to know you someday,' and he just looked at me. I didn't know who he was right off. Then I saw him again in Dallas about '76 or '77, and said, 'I know you …' [*Laughs*] As the years progressed, I kept running into him and saying, 'I'm going to know you.'

"It was 1980. A friend of mine, Kathy Smith, had met Lenny. I lived in South Austin off Bluebonnet, and Stevie lived on Ashby in a place that was so small, the living room, bedroom and kitchen were all in one. Kathy took me over, and there was equipment everywhere – you couldn't move. Stevie looked up and said, 'I know you.' [*Laughs*] I couldn't believe this.

"From that day on, Lenny and I became really, really good friends. Stevie was always out of town, so I would see Lenny more than Stevie. Lenny would come to me for psychic readings. That's what I did for years. I would give her little readings, and I would try not to do too much because Lenny would put too much into it and get it all confused.

"They never lived in one place very long. Lenny was always moving; she just felt like that was the thing for her to do. She wanted to keep Stevie away from town and away from friends and people. She wanted him to come home and rest; she wanted to cook. She had this idea to keep Stevie healthy, but of course nobody was healthy at that time. Stevie would get up in the middle of the night and leave, or he'd be gone in the morning, or he wouldn't even come home. He was always hanging with his

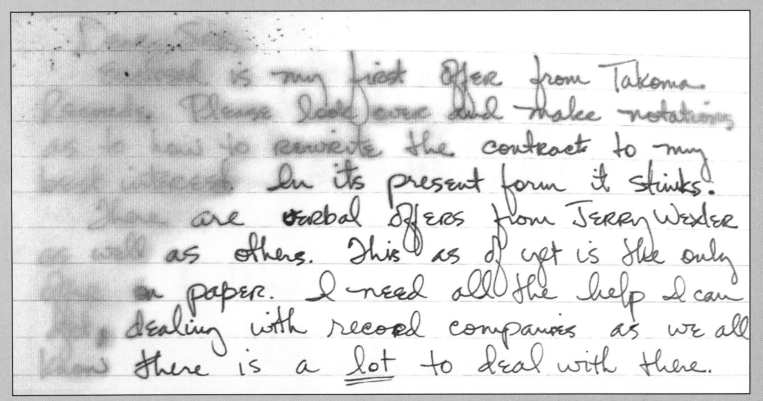

Takoma was among the first to offer Stevie a record deal. Stevie's handwritten note requesting assistance negotiating a record deal. COURTESY DOBBS/JACKSON

buddies. Jimmie was always sitting somewhere like a bump on a log with his sunglasses on.

"Lenny told me about a house she had found out in Volente. I had been in the house when it was a restaurant years before, but I didn't recognize it from the outside because it was all grown up. It was way out a winding road and was probably the last place they lived that was big. I was always there because I did chiropractic, and I'd always give him chiropractic. I'd massage his feet and his hands all the time.

"Because the place used to be a restaurant, it had a pay phone in it that had never been removed. They had another phone, but Lenny had a habit of throwing them and breaking them because she'd get mad at Stevie or whoever else was on the phone. They'd hang up on her, and here'd go the phone flying across the room. In Volente, Stevie put a round table and a stool by the payphone, and a bucket of quarters on the table [*laughs*]. He'd be putting quarters in the phone whether it was New York or California, interviews … The phone would get so full that Stevie would bang on it and quarters would fall out. It was hysterical.

"Stevie would walk down the street to the store barefoot, with his hat on, and no shirt." Apparently he found a place that didn't say, "No shirt, no shoes, no service."

"Stevie would always say, 'Melody, don't you ever lie to me, 'cuz if I find out you lied to me, that's the end of our friendship.' And Lenny would say the same thing, 'Melody, don't you lie to me.' Well, there were times I had to tell a white lie, because Stevie would be off with this person and Lenny would be off with that person. Stevie would call me and ask where Lenny was, and I'd say, 'I don't know.' But I did know, because Lenny always

made sure I knew where she was. They were both jealous, and when they fought, it was like cats and dogs. I never saw anything physical, though.

"Lenny knew Stevie was going out with other girls, but it wasn't two weeks with someone, it was one night here or there. I know that for a fact, because I knew some of the girls. One girl's family was very famous in L.A. She lived north, and I'd been over to her house many times. Her family are the ones that started the 'elevator music,' Muzak. And her uncle was Jack Nicholson, the actor. I got to meet him in California through her. Same eyes, and she was even crazier than he was.

"But Stevie really loved Lenny. He was the sweetest, most kind man I have ever met. His heart was so big, and he cared about people. There would be times he'd be sitting and playing the guitar, playing 'Lenny' or something else, and tears would just be rolling down his cheeks.

"He talked and would sing in his sleep. He would ramble and ramble for thirty or forty minutes, snoring in between. And he'd talk and talk, and at the same time, both his hands were playing an air guitar. One night Lenny said, 'Come here,' and I walked in and he was snoring, and he started singing and playing air guitar. You couldn't understand a word he was saying. That was very weird."

April 25: Steamboat 1874, Austin, TX

April 26: private party (possibly San Antonio, TX)

April 28: Rockefeller's, Houston, TX

April 29: Steamboat 1874, Austin, TX

April 30: house party, Austin, TX, for artist Bill Narum

May: Takoma Records (label home of The Fabulous Thunderbirds) offers the band a record deal, but Stevie is advised to turn it down by Chesley. (See Stevie's note, pictured.)

May 3: Splash Day, Manor Downs, Manor, TX

May 5: South Austin Rec. (afternoon?); Steamboat 1874, Austin, TX

May 8: Fat Dawg's, Lubbock, TX

May 9: Fat Dawg's, Lubbock, TX

May 10: Fat Dawg's, Lubbock, TX

May 11: Tornado Jam, Lubbock, TX. 6:15 A daylight, outdoor gig filmed with a hand-held camera. Not to be confused with the next year's Tornado Jam in Austin, from which there is about 30 minutes of video.

    – instrumental (incomplete – 1:00)
    – Little Wing (incomplete – last 10 seconds)
    – Collins' Shuffle (4:00)

May 13: Steamboat 1874, Austin, TX. This may actually be the date of the *In the Beginning* recording, rather than April 1 as commonly cited.

May 21: Wintergarden Ballroom, Dallas, TX with Albert Collins, Syler-Bramhall Band

May 23: Fitzgerald's, Houston, TX

May 24: Fitzgerald's, Houston, TX

May 30: Fat Dawg's, Lubbock, TX

May 31: Fat Dawg's, Lubbock, TX

While living on Rabb Road in Austin with Lenny, Stevie's name appears in a phone book for the first time.

June 1: Steamboat 1874, Austin, TX, benefit

© BILL NARUM

June 2: Rockefeller's, Houston, TX

June 6: Steamboat 1874, Austin, TX

On June 6, 1980, Stevie signs a management contract with Chesley Millikin, effective through September 5, 1981. Chesley secures an option to renew for two years. Chesley is to earn a fifteen percent commission.

June 8: benefit for C-Boy, Austin, TX

June 18: Opera House, Austin, TX, opening for Randy Hansen's Hendrix tribute

RANDY HANSEN is credited by some as perhaps the first serious tribute act: "I used to wear [an afro] wig for the Hendrix show, and Stevie put the wig on. We were walking through the streets of Austin and going to a pizza parlor. We wandered in to where his brother was playing; his brother took one look at him and, like, disowned him [*laughs*]. We left there and went back to his place and played guitars all night.

"He came to my show one time, and I was walking around the crowd playing

COURTESY ANDREW
HENTRICH

with a wireless, and Stevie was sitting there. I threw my guitar in his lap, and he played a few licks and threw it back. I think we were doing 'Voodoo Chile.' That was at Willie Nelson's place [Austin Opera House]. We never really got on stage and jammed together though."

Asked what he thought of Stevie's versions of Hendrix tunes, Randy replied, "I thought it was really cool. He kind of put his own stamp on it, which is not easy to do. His stamp was on everything he did, so it's easy to tell when you're listening to him. That may be one of my biggest problems, because I sound like another guy [*laughs*]!"

JAMES ELWELL: "It was a full crowd, and most of them came to see Randy Hansen. Stevie opens up and just tears the place apart, playing his own stuff. Well, he closes with 'Little Wing,' and I remember hearing people around me, 'I can't believe he's doing that.' Kind of pissed off. He burned it up, and by the end of the tune people were, like, 'Whoa!' The non-believers were surprised. So Randy comes out and … you don't let Stevie open for you, because what are you going to follow with?"

STEVE DEAN: "I remember when Randy Hansen came to town. We went over to Rome Inn afterwards and they just kind of took over. I don't know whose gig it was. Stevie had such a good sense of humor. That Randy Hansen kid would dress with an afro wig to try to be Hendrix. They all got in a car and went over to the Rome Inn, and I remember Stevie getting up, and he was wearing the afro wig, which would have been great if

we'd gotten a picture. I think he might've even had a flowing, Hendrix-like shirt on. They played, the two of them, traded licks for a good while – just kind of took over the place."

Obviously, memories differ about that night after the Opera House gig. Randy and Steve both recall being at Rome Inn, and both recall Stevie wearing the afro wig. Randy does not recall actually playing at the club but does remember playing all night at Stevie's house. Coinsidering that Steve was the owner of Rome Inn and not present with Stevie and Randy anywhere else that night, it seems more likely that Randy has forgotten the stage jam than that Steve would make up something that didn't happen at all.

June 20: Rockefeller's, Houston, TX. The set list below is believed to be from a Houston gig during this time period.
- Little Wing
- Drivin' South
- instrumental with segue into Dirty Pool
- Dirty Pool
- Letter To My Girlfriend
- All Your Love I Miss Loving
- Shake For Me
- Love In Vain
- You Done Lost Your Good Thing Now
- Don't Lose Your Cool
- Rude Mood
- Manic Depression

June 21: Rockefeller's, Houston, TX

June 22: Agora Ballroom, Dallas, TX. "Double Trouble opened for the Thunderbirds, and they were met with ecstatic applause and good reviews in the morning papers. At 25 he is the 'baby' of the guitar brothers, but many feel that his time is coming."[99]

BRUCE BOWLAND, formerly of Krackerjack, would sing with the band when they came through Dallas. "[Stevie] still wasn't singing much back then. He'd sing a verse, play guitar for ten or fifteen minutes, sing another verse, and that'd be the tune. Cutter was the roadie and told me that he was trying to get me into the band, and the people who were funding him didn't want to spend another two hundred dollars a week. But I never had to ask to sit in. I'd get up and do a whole set with them."

June 23: St. Christopher's, Dallas, TX

June 24: D.J.'s, Dallas, TX

Delores Nilsey Proudly Presents
STEVIE VAUGHAN
WITH
DOUBLE TROUBLE
TUESDAY
JUNE 24TH
DJ's
2000 GREENVILLE ✕ 827-3967

COLLECTION OF CRAIG HOPKINS

June 30: Chief's, Baton Rouge, LA

July 1: Chief's, Baton Rouge, LA

July 4: Brothers, Jacksonville, AL

July 5: Brothers, Jacksonville, AL

July 9: Double Door Inn, Charlotte, NC

July 11: Elbow Room, Harrisonburg, VA

July 12: Hideaway

July 14: Lone Star, New York, NY

Texas Blues Bash

STEVIE VAUGHAN & DOUBLE TROUBLE

OMAR AND THE HOWLERS

from Austin, Texas THURSDAY, JULY 17, 1980
The Psyche Delly 4846 Cordell Avenue Bethesda, Md: 654•6611

COLLECTION OF CRAIG HOPKINS

July 15: Lone Star, New York, NY

July 16: Heat Club

July 17: Psyche Deli, Bethesda, MD

July 18: No Fish Today, Baltimore, MD

July 19: No Fish Today, Baltimore, MD

July 21: Mine Shaft

July 22: King's Head Inn, Norfolk, VA
- Hideaway
- Love Me Darlin'
- Tin Pan Alley
- Love Struck Baby
- I'm Cryin'
- Texas Flood
- I'm Leaving You (Commit A Crime)
- Little Wing
- instrumental variation of Drivin' South
- Don't Lose Your Cool
- Tell Me
- The Sky Is Crying
- Guitar Hurricane
- Slide Thing
- Crosscut Saw
- Love in Vain
- Dirty Pool
- Shake For Me

July 24: Desperado's, Washington, D.C.

CESAR DIAZ, later Stevie's amp technician: "I have this vivid memory of seeing him play at a club called Desperado's. The air conditioner hung right above the stage and dripped on top of the guitar player. I remember watching him move around to avoid being hit by the drops of water."[63]

July 25: Evergreen, Pittsburgh, PA

July 26: Mancini's, Pittsburgh, PA

August: *Buddy*, "Texas Tornados: A Guide to the Heaviest Guitars in the Lone Star State," Kirby Warnock: "Catch [Stevie and Jimmie Vaughan] on a good night and you could have a religious experience."

August: *Buddy*, "Living the Blues," K. Warnock: "Stevie is the wilder of the two [brothers] onstage, jumping around more, hitting wilder licks, and taking the spotlight. Jimmie is content to be a part of the band and 'fill in the holes.' His days of being the hot, young guitarist have passed, and he is into a more restrained groove, although he still lets some of the old flash emerge on certain nights. It's like Stevie is following in Jimmie's footsteps, but the footprints don't quite match."

August 1-21: vacation

August 22: Fitzgerald's, Houston, TX

August 23:, Fitzgerald's, Houston, TX

August 28: Steamboat 1874, Austin, TX

August 29: Steamboat 1874, Austin, TX

August 30: Steamboat 1874, Austin, TX

August 31: Steamboat 1874, Austin, TX

September 1-4: Joe Priesnitz's calendar says "Studio"

September 5: Bottom Line, Austin, TX

September 6: Bottom Line, Austin, TX

September 8: Rockefeller's, Houston, TX

September 12: St. Christopher's, Dallas, TX

September 13: St. Christopher's, Dallas, TX

"St. Christopher's has definitely been where it's happening .... Stevie Vaughan and Double Trouble smoked the stage to a cinder."[64]

September 14: Zeros, Fort Worth, TX

September 16: Agora, Dallas, TX

September 18: Fat Dawg's, Lubbock, TX

September 19: Fat Dawg's, Lubbock, TX

September 20: Fat Dawg's, Lubbock, TX

"Tour blank" and mailer had facsimile stamp on the back of Stevie's face; poster signed by the band. COLLECTION OF CRAIG HOPKINS

September 22: Antone's, Austin, TX, with Ruben Ramos and the Mexican Revolution, Miss Lou Ann and the Flip Tops. There is some evidence Stevie's appearance was cancelled.

September 23: St. Christopher's, Dallas, TX

September 24: St. Christopher's, Dallas, TX

September 25: Crossroads, Nacogdoches, TX

September 26: Fitzgerald's, Houston, TX

September 27: Fitzgerald's, Houston, TX

October 3: Christopher Moon, Dallas, TX

October 4: Christopher Moon, Dallas, TX

BYRON BARR, who would later become one of Stevie's roadies: "I saw him one time at a place on Greenville [Avenue] called Christopher Moon, in front of about ... nobody. The band considered not playing. Five people – literally."

Stevie and Lenny, October 1980. COURTESY MARTHA VAUGHAN

October 5: Armadillo World Headquarters, Austin, TX, opening for James Cotton

October 6: Rockefeller's, Houston, TX

October 10: Steamboat 1874, Austin, TX

October 11: Steamboat 1874, Austin, TX

October 13: Rockefeller's, Houston, TX (cancelled)

October 14: Tipitina's, New Orleans, LA (cancelled)

October 15: Fatty's, Ruston, LA (cancelled)

October 17: Bottom Line, Austin, TX

October 18: Bottom Line, Austin, TX

October 20: Rockefeller's, Houston, TX

October 21: Christopher Moon, Dallas, TX

October 22: Christopher Moon, Dallas, TX

October 23: Fat Dawg's, Lubbock, TX

October 24: Fat Dawg's, Lubbock, TX

October 25: Fat Dawg's, Lubbock, TX

October 27: Rockefeller's, Houston, TX

TOMMY SHANNON heard Stevie was playing at Rockefeller's: "I went down there that night, and I'll never forget this: it was like, when I walked in the door and I heard them playing, it was like a revelation – 'That's where I want to be; that's where I belong, right there.' During the break I went up to Stevie and told him that. I didn't try to sneak around and hide it from the bass player – I didn't know if he was listening or not. I just really wanted to be in that band.

"I sat in that night and it sounded great. I guess maybe two weeks later they came back in town. I had had a tooth pulled and I'd taken some pain pills, so I was kind of, you know, wasn't quite all there. They had the deli tray backstage, and I picked up some broccoli and put it in this dip and dropped it right in his lap! He had on this nice suit and everything, you know, nice clothes. So I remember I went home that night and thought, 'Well, I blew it. He'll never call me now.'"[3]

October 30: Tootsie's, Fort Worth, TX

October 31: Christopher Moon, Dallas, TX (see photo at left with Lenny)

November 1: Tootsie's, Fort Worth, TX

November 7: Third Coast, Austin, TX

November 8: Third Coast, Austin, TX, with Dixie Dregs

November 12: Crossroads, Nacogdoches, TX

LAYTON, on the origin of his nickname, Whipper: "Cutter Brandenburg gave it to me. Old Dallas boy who was our first road manager. He knew Stevie way back in senior high. He came off the road working with the Bee Gees and started working with us. We got into this argument one night in the Nacogdoches Holiday Inn; we started a bunch of name calling. I said some things to him, and he jumped on me and wrestled me to the ground. But he was really big and kind of slower than I was. I kind of jumped all around the room, he never could catch me, and I kind of wore him out. He made some comment that I was a real whippersnapper, and the first part of it just stuck. As the fight went on, everyone was calling, "Whipper!" I've been called that ever since [*laughs*]. I'm one of those guys that all through my life I've always had a lot of nicknames. People called me one thing and another but rarely by my actual name [*laughs*]! This is the one that stuck the longest."

November 13: Fatty's, Ruston, LA

November 14: Fatty's, Ruston, LA

November 15: St. Christopher's, Dallas, TX

November 21: Third Coast, Austin, TX

November 22: St. Christopher's, Dallas, TX

November 24: Opera House, Austin, TX, opening for Savoy Brown

November 28: Fitzgerald's, Houston, TX

November 29: Fitzgerald's, Houston, TX

December 4: Nick's Uptown, Dallas, TX, with Joe Ely

December 5: Nick's Uptown, Dallas, TX, with Joe Ely

December 6: Nick's Uptown, Dallas, TX, with Joe Ely. Priesnitz' notes indicate a video simulcast.

December 11: Cheatham Street Warehouse, San Marcos, TX

December 12: Tootsie's, Fort Worth, TX

December 13: St. Christopher's, Dallas, TX

December 18: Steamboat 1874, Austin, TX

December 19: Steamboat 1874, Austin, TX

December 20: Steamboat 1874, Austin, TX

December 21: Bottom Line, Austin, TX

December 22: Bottom Line, Austin, TX

December 26: Steamboat, Houston, TX

December 27: Steamboat, Houston, TX

December 31: Opera House, Austin, TX. On this night, Tommy Shannon is playing his last gig with Alan Haynes' band in Houston.

© WATT CASEY, JR.

Power Trio

1981–1982

1981

The new year brings a significant change to Double Trouble—the bottom end will now be provided by Thomas Lafitte Shannon. Most observers thought Jack Newhouse was doing a fine job but Tommy adds that indefinable symbiotic quality that the most successful bands share. The trio is now set for the next four years. They will soon experience an amazing progression of events that will establish the band as one of the best blues-rock trios of the era.

Preston Hubbard, who had been the bass player with Roomful of Blues, recalls that Stevie called him to play bass for Double Trouble, but Preston declined due to being settled in Atlanta.[45] He later served in The Fabulous Thunderbirds from 1984 to 1994. Stevie then called his former bandmate, Tommy Shannon.

In 1981, the band's gross receipts averaged $700 per night, up from an average of $500 the year before. Understandably, the band continued to make two to five times more per night at their regular gigs at Steamboat in Austin and Fitzgerald's in Houston than in other parts of the state.

© TONY RODRIGUEZ

January 1: Skipwilly's, San Antonio, TX

January 2: Skipwilly's, San Antonio, TX

January 3: Skipwilly's, San Antonio, TX. Jack Newhouse's last gig as a member of Double Trouble.

JACK: "Everybody knew [Stevie] was going to go somewhere, and it was an honor and privilege to play with him. Stevie was a gentle and sweet person for the most part."

Fan HUNTER HARRISON: "I saw SRV and Double Trouble play one night at Skipwilly's. Me and my friend were the only two people other than the staff in the place! A four-hour gig just for us! They played like there was a whole room full of people there."

January 4: Tommy Shannon replaces Jackie Newhouse on bass.

Tommy Shannon. COURTESY BRUCE BOWLAND

167

Shannon was born Thomas Lafitte Smedley in Tucson, Arizona, but soon moved to the Texas panhandle. TOMMY: "Where I was, there wasn't really any blues. In Dumas [pronounced doo-mus], Texas, back then there wasn't one black person in town. So there weren't any black radio stations, and it was mostly just Top 40 stuff. A few things made it through, like Sam Cooke, Fats Domino, guys who had a big hit. I really didn't know anything about the real blues until I got with Johnny Winter. He's the one who educated me about that."

Tommy started playing guitar at age 14, joined his first band, The Avengers, at 16 and started playing bass at about age 21. The Avengers "used to set up at the drive-in theatre. In fact, I still have a poster of it. We used to set up between drive-in movies at the snack bar. We would play anywhere that they would let us!"

Tommy got his first recording experience as a member of The Echoes in high school, and then it was on to Dallas, where he started The New Breed, featuring drummer Uncle John Turner. "We had a regular soul band. Back then, you know, bands in clubs dressed alike – they'd wear a suit and tie – and play five nights a week or sometimes two weeks in a club. And then you'd go across town and play another club and do the same thing. It was a lot different than it is now."

In 1968 a series of events transpired that would lead Tommy out of the small clubs of North Texas to Max Yasgur's farm in New York. "Uncle John had quit and moved to Houston. He had known Johnny Winter since childhood because they were both from Beaumont. He started playing with Johnny, and we stayed real close friends. I was playing in Dallas in a soul band in this club called The Fog. What's strange is that's the same place I met Stevie. One night [Uncle John] and Johnny came in and sat in, just the three of us, and it sounded great. He asked me to play, so I did. I was making good money in Dallas, and I was sleeping on floors and being broke all the time with Johnny for a while."

It wasn't long before Winter was recording his first albums with Shannon and Turner and participating in perhaps the most significant rock performance scene ever. "1969 was the year of all the pop festivals. Every major city would have a giant festival, and they would have 100,000 or 150,000 people. It was great getting up in front of that many people." The biggest of them all was Woodstock, with an estimated attendance of 400,000. "We had to come in by helicopter because there was no way to get there by any kind of automobile, truck or otherwise. I remember from the sky seeing this ocean of people. Incredible. It went on and on and on."

Regarding Tommy's musical history and age, Stevie often said, "He was on the original Moses tour!" While Tommy says he joined on January 2nd, he also confirmed that his first gig with Double Trouble was in Dallas. Joe Priesnitz' notes confirm Tommy joining on January 4, followed by several days of rehearsal before playing in Dallas on the 9th. The agreement between Stevie and Tommy may have been made on the 2nd, but Jackie played through the 3rd. Double Trouble's lineup would only change one more time – in 1985 when Reese Wynans joined on keyboards.

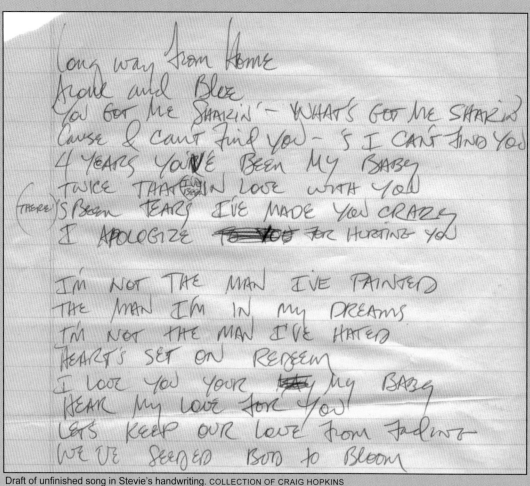

Draft of unfinished song in Stevie's handwriting. COLLECTION OF CRAIG HOPKINS

Tommy recalls his motivation for joining Double Trouble: "The potential that I could see there – it was obvious there was no other guitar player around that I'd heard anywhere close to him. He had developed and grown into something completely new; there had been several years I hadn't even seen him. He was singing and he seemed real confident on stage, and he was dressing really good. He had a real good image going, and it seems like we really started evolving then. When I first got in the band, we'd go to rehearsal and we'd work up a couple of Hendrix songs, and the rest were straight blues by some old blues guys. Then we started evolving ... more into the heavier blues/rock thing – that's when things really started taking off for us."[3]

ERIC JOHNSON had seen Stevie's potential years earlier when Stevie was with the Cobras. "I saw that potential. All the fire was there, but it was more contained. When he got with Tommy Shannon, it was like the magic unleashed. Not that he wasn't playing great before that, but there was that magic chemistry with Chris Layton and Tommy Shannon and Stevie that all of sudden ... I remember seeing that, and it was like a complete shift. You could tell there was something really heavy and profound happening. It was a combination of Stevie coming into his own focus, and [getting] with Tommy and Chris. When you get with the right people, there's that alchemy which produces that special thing.

"I appreciate his singing as much as his guitar playing. I think he was a phenomenal singer. He really didn't sing that much [when I first met him]; then all of a sudden he started fronting his band and singing. Most people take years to develop their voice, but for all those years he played guitar and someone else was singing. Then the next week he becomes a singer, and he's great [laughs]!

"[His guitar tone] was awesome. I especially liked it when he first got the amp made by Alexander Dumble. He had a real simple rig; he just used the Dumble and a couple of Fender Vibroverbs and an Ibanez Tube Screamer. To me, that was the real crest of his sound. Sometimes when it gets more and more stuff, it gets too complex. His sound was always great, but that was probably my favorite tone, like you hear on those first couple of records.

"He was a very nice guy. The times I hung around with Stevie, he was always a very sweet guy, very cordial, seemed to love life, smiled a lot and was passionate about everything, especially his music. Just a nice guy. That sounds clichéd, but he was just a very affable, sweet person."

"Bassist Shannon is the connector between Layton and Vaughan. His bass line 'walks' in classic danceable tradition – distinct note changes with each on-the-count beat – but it also is engagingly offbeat in both the literal and figurative senses. While providing a constant bottom, Shannon adds immeasurably to the choral quality of the sound, adding two and often three harmonies to the complexities Vaughan cranks out."[40]

CHRIS: "We would travel around in this old milk truck which had a couch behind the two front seats and a sliding bed above the equipment in the back. We travelled all over the U.S., making two hundred bucks a week and nobody knew who we were."[46]

The old milk truck was known as the African Queen and was, of course, regularly in need of some type of mechanical attention. JAMES ELWELL: "I remember one time Stevie came by the bike shop where I worked and said, 'Man, the auxiliary fuel tank switch isn't working or something. Do you think you can help us out? We're about to go on the road.'

"So I rode down to his house with some tools, and I'm underneath the truck. He stretches out this long extension cord from his house out by the truck, brings his Twin Reverb amp out there, sits down on it and starts playing Jimi Hendrix tunes. He asked me, 'James, do you think this is intruding, or do you think people would go for this?' And man, I was underneath that truck just rockin' out! Not only was it on-the-money, it kind of sounded ... *better*. Cleaner."

The bike shop in Austin is also where Stevie picked up the "Custom" sticker that adorned Number One.

January 9: St. Christopher's, Dallas, TX. First gig with the power trio of Stevie, Tommy and Chris.

January 10: St. Christopher's, Dallas, TX

January 11: Agora, Houston, TX

January 12: private party

January 16: Steamboat 1874, Austin, TX

January 17: Steamboat 1874, Austin, TX

January 22: University of Houston, (afternoon?); Fitzgerald's, Houston, TX

January 23: Fitzgerald's, Houston, TX

January 24: Fitzgerald's, Houston, TX. Helpinstill Blues Band opens.

January 26: *Houston Post*, "Music: SRV," Nanette Fodell DeCreny: "The raw power that escapes from Vaughan's beat-up guitar is authentic. .... He chokes and growls notes from his 'ax' that provoke his audiences to riotous behavior. .... I suppose there *could* be a national revival of blues great enough to warrant his stardom, but he will most likely continue travelling the circuit of clubs like Fitzgerald's – and in those clubs, he is king."

The best evidence available to the author at this time suggests that Stevie started wearing wide-brimmed black hats from Texas

Hatters in early 1981 (hat size 6 3/4). Bassist Jack Newhouse does not recall Stevie wearing the bolero-style hats when he was in Double Trouble. Photographs from 1979-1980 are not plentiful, and the earliest photos in the author's collection that show Stevie wearing the now famous black hat are from early 1981.

Cutter Brandenburg recalls that Stevie wore his big black cowboy hat one night, and people thought it looked good on him. Lenny had an inexpensive bolero-style hat that Stevie wore one night soon thereafter. Of course, Lenny's hat bore a resemblance to one that Jimi Hendrix wore, and Stevie often took style cues from Hendrix. Cutter, the band and Lenny convinced management to give Stevie a gift certificate to Texas Hatters for his birthday, and Stevie selected a quality, custom hat called the "Plateau."

STEVIE: "The crown is called a "high roller" crown, and it's a flat brim. It's just what I thought a hat oughta look like if I wore one [laughs]. However, actually, when I first got it, it reminded me of Hendrix's hat. [So] that was the first reasoning behind me wearing a hat."[4]

JIMMIE: "He was real cocky. He was just like his hat. I mean, Stevie would put on these getups, and he would go out. Rednecks would want to kill him. 'Who is this weird guy, and why is he dressed like that?' He would always have the weirdest stuff on and walk around in public."[3]

The rest, as they say, is history. Martha Vaughan recalls that years later when she and Stevie went shopping at the mall, Stevie told her he wished that fans would not interrupt their family time by asking for autographs. Martha coolly retorted that if he wasn't wearing that black hat, maybe fewer people would recognize him!

January 28: Cheatham Street Warehouse, San Marcos, TX

January 29: Tootsie's, Fort Worth, TX

January 30: St. Christopher's, Dallas, TX

January 31: Third Coast, Austin, TX

February 6: Crossroads, Nacogdoches, TX

February 7: Crossroads, Nacogdoches, TX

February 13: St. Christopher's, Dallas, TX

February 14: St. Christopher's, Dallas, TX

One of the early 1981 gigs at St. Christopher's was the last time sax player Jim Trimmier saw his old friend. They had known each other and played in several bands together all the way back to 1970. "Tommy Shannon had just joined a few weeks earlier, and my immediate reaction when I heard them was, 'They're going to make it.' They sounded badass and big time – huge. Tommy was the right bass player Stevie was meant to play with.

"Stevie had me sit in with the band, and they were already tuning their instruments down a half step, and I couldn't find anything – partly because I was blind drunk and probably stoned too. I just couldn't find the notes. I sounded terrible.

"After the gig, Stevie was real drunk and asked me to join the band. I said, 'I'll have to think about it,' but I knew it wasn't in the cards. Luckily, they didn't really hear me play that night because they were so loud I couldn't be heard. I knew I was no match for this – I couldn't do it.

"Stevie, from the first time I ever heard him, was the best guitar player I ever heard and the first person I ever met that played every note like he meant it. He knew he was special, but he never got a big head about it."

February 17: Cheatham Street Warehouse, San Marcos, TX

February 18: Skipwilly's, San Antonio, TX

One of the first concert posters to use Stevie's full name. © DANNY GARRETT

COURTESY JANNA LEBLANC

February 19: Skipwilly's, San Antonio, TX

February 20: Steamboat 1874, Austin, TX

February 21: Steamboat 1874, Austin, TX

"After seeing Stevie Vaughan and Double Trouble's set last month at Austin's Steamboat Springs [sic], old Bullfeather has to come out and say that Stevie may be the best guitarist playing anywhere in the country. With the addition of bassist Tommy Shannon, Double Trouble has become a virtual blues machine, while Stevie is leaning more and more toward a blues-Hendrix style. If you close your eyes, you can believe that it is Jimi Hendrix on stage and not this smoking white boy. Get out and see this band just as soon as you can because they will be breaking *big* soon."[48]

February 22: Nick's Uptown, Dallas, TX with Albert Collins (cancelled)

February 24: Cheatham Street Warehouse, San Marcos, TX

February 25: Skipwilly's, San Antonio, TX (cancelled)

February 27: Fitzgerald's, Houston, TX

February 28: Fitzgerald's, Houston, TX

TONY DUKES: "Albert Collins used to park the bus right outside the door, and they'd locked the keys in it. They were trying to figure out how to get in. There's Little Junior and Stevie and us standing out there, and using my, uh, *talents*, I credit-carded the little vent door open and got Cutter to lift me up and went in and opened it up. I remember everybody was kidding, and Stevie said, 'Only a bass player could've done that.' Albert Collins thought that was so funny!

"Albert and those guys looked at Stevie like he was a little puppy in the room. They really admired him, but he was like a child or puppy – he just fascinated them. It was always like a fraternal appreciation – Albert Collins loved Stevie."

TONY, regarding Texas Tom's Music store in Houston: "I can see Stevie, God love him, he would come in every time, smiling, making all feel good, then disappear. Then you would hear him [playing] some guitar and amp he had never seen and 'meet them.' He did so privately. He never played loud in the store. He took the time and opportunity to get knowledge of the gear.

"Of course, he often drew a crowd. In the countless times that Stevie came in a guitar store I ran, he always responded to all, from idiots, to novices, all with a smile and a complete reply. This is part of his wonderful legacy – a sense of anonymous giving that has spoken louder to me as time passes."

March 2: Continental Club, Austin, TX

March 3: Cheatham Street Warehouse, San Marcos, TX

March 4-7: Band is grounded because of truck repairs.

March 10: Cheatham Street Warehouse, San Marcos, TX

March 11: Skipwilly's, San Antonio, TX

March 12: Skipwilly's, San Antonio, TX

March 13: Al's Bamboo, Dallas, TX

March 14: Al's Bamboo, Dallas, TX

March 20: Steamboat 1874, Austin, TX

March 21: Steamboat 1874, Austin, TX

March 23: Austin Opera House, Austin, TX, opening for George Thorogood

March 24: Cheatham Street Warehouse, San Marcos, TX

March 25: Skipwilly's, San Antonio, TX

March 27: Friendly Club, Fort Worth, TX

COLLECTION OF CRAIG HOPKINS

March 28: St. Christopher's, Dallas, TX

📖 ⏱ **April:** *Buddy*, SRV wins 1981 Texas Music Awards Critics' Choice for Best Blues Band; display ad from band with thanks. (T-Birds won the fan voting.)

April 3: Cheatham Street Warehouse, San Marcos, TX. Fourteen-year-old Charlie Sexton sitting in on some songs, with Stevie moving to baritone or 6-string bass guitar.

– instrumental
– Dirty Pool
– I'm Cryin'
– All Your Love I Miss Loving
– Love In Vain
– Little Wing
– Drivin' South
– Third Stone From the Sun
– Rude Mood
– Slide Thing
– Tin Pan Alley
– Crosscut Saw
– instrumentals

JAMES ELWELL: "I remember telling Stevie, 'I met this kid, Charlie Sexton, from Wimberley. He said he was going to be the baddest guitar player of all time!' Stevie laughed about it and thought, 'What an ambitious kid.' Double Trouble would be playing at Steamboat, and Charlie and Will would stand up by the stage at the end of the night – now mind you, these are little kids, it's two o'clock in the morning – like little kids waiting for Santa Claus!

© FLATHEAD

"Sure enough, at the end of the night they'd jump up on stage. Stevie'd hand Charlie his guitar, Will would get Jackie's bass. Will was so small he had to lay the bass across his knees to be able to play it – he couldn't hold the damn thing up. Stevie would jump back on drums, and they'd play – Charlie going nuts with his 'tingy-tingy-tingy' thing and put the guitar behind his head. That was always fun to watch."

CHRIS LAYTON: "There was one night when we were doing 'Third Stone From The Sun,' and Stevie was getting all this feedback, and he would have the body of the guitar on the stage, the guitar facing him, and he would jump up on the horns of the guitar and grab the headstock and somehow he was balancing. It was a real

Stevie presents a guitar pin to Muddy Waters. COURTESY PAUL THE VAN HALEN GUY

wild-looking thing. It almost looked like a circus act, and all these really wild sounds were coming out of the guitar while he just balanced there. Then he kicked one foot off and then the other, and he jumped back onto the stage and the guitar went spinning like a top. All these wild sounds came out that I'd never heard come out before. It was almost like trick stuff, but it was also so spur-of-the-moment, so inspirational and non-rehearsed. Energy of the moment."[44]

April 4: Third Coast, Austin, TX

April 5: Paramount Theatre, Austin, TX, opening for Fabulous Thunderbirds

April 6: Nick's Uptown, Dallas, TX, opening for Muddy Waters. "Stevie Vaughan was simply phenomenal as the opening act for Muddy Waters' birthday show at Nick's Uptown and, as a special gift, Stevie presented Muddy with a custom-made guitar pin that even had real strings and miniature tuning knobs."[49]

April 7: Cheatham Street Warehouse, San Marcos, TX

April 9: Nick's Uptown, Dallas, TX

April 10: Fitzgerald's, Houston, TX

April 11: Fitzgerald's, Houston, TX

April 12: Beaumont, TX (unconfirmed)

April 14: Cheatham Street Warehouse, San Marcos, TX

April 17: Steamboat 1874, Austin, TX

April 18: Steamboat 1874, Austin, TX

April 21: Cheatham Street Warehouse, San Marcos, TX

April 23: Fat Dawg's, Lubbock, TX

April 24: Fat Dawg's, Lubbock, TX

April 25: Fat Dawg's, Lubbock, TX

COURTESY STEVE DEAN

The exact date is unknown, but during one of the 1981 gigs in Lubbock, Number One was broken. STEVIE: "Have you ever seen Jimmie throw his guitar? I learned this trick from him, except his guitar never broke! I was playing in Lubbock back in '81, and when I threw it, it hit this paneled wall, catching it up by the headstock, snapping the wood. It laid there on the ground, and some of the strings went up [in tone], and some of the strings went down. It was doing all this 'BLUBGBBNGBG!' by itself, and I was standing there going, 'Yeah!' It happened during 'Third Stone From The Sun,' and it sounded fine, like it was supposed to be there. But I cried later."[47]

April 27: Continental Club, Austin, TX

April 28: Cheatham Street Warehouse, San Marcos, TX

April 30: Easy Street, Padre Island, TX (cancelled)

📖**May:** *Buddy*, display ad for Freddie King memorial concert starring SRV; photo of SRV and Muddy Waters

May 1: Easy Street, Padre Island, TX (cancelled)

May 2: Third Coast, Austin, TX

May 3: The Ark Co-op, Austin, TX (advertised as a "60's Party," also known as Mothers' Day Party)

May 7: Blossom's, Fort Worth, TX

May 8: Al's Bamboo, Dallas, TX

May 9: Al's Bamboo, Dallas, TX

May 10: Lee Park, Dallas, TX (afternoon)

"Several thousand people packed Lee Park for *Buddy*'s Freddie King Memorial Concert to see knock-out performances by Stevie Vaughan and Double Trouble, Vintage, and the Buddy Brothers .... Stevie Vaughan and Double Trouble cut loose with some hot rockin' blues after finishing a SRO weekend gig at Al's Bamboo, showing the crowd why they received the Critic's Choice award as the Best Blues Band in Texas."[50]

The promoter recalls: "I asked Stevie if he could play for a Freddie King Memorial Concert that *Buddy* would be hosting in Lee Park one Sunday. Stevie said that he would be playing Al's Bamboo the night before and would stay over on Sunday to play our gig – *for free*. That Sunday afternoon I saw him and his band put on just as good a show for free as they had done the night before when they were being paid. When the show was over, Stevie and crew threw their amps and guitars in an old van and left for Austin, where they had another gig that night."[51]

Lee Park, Dallas. © BRUCE HAND

May 10, 1981. © BRUCE HAND

📼**May 10:** private party for Jeff Newman, Austin, TX
– Tell Me
– Texas Flood
– Crosscut Saw
– Thunderbird
– Come On (Part III)
– I'm Cryin'
– Love Struck Baby
– Hug You Squeeze You
– Little Wing
– Drivin' South

"Come On (Part III)" is Stevie's version of the classic Earl King song, "Come On." Hendrix called his own version "Part II," and Stevie followed suit, paying tribute to both men.

May 15: Steamboat 1874, Austin, TX

May 16: Steamboat 1874, Austin, TX

May 20: Humphrey's, Shreveport, LA

May 21: Humphrey's, Shreveport, LA

May 22: Tavern, Opelousa, LA. Scott Thistlethwaite, bar owner's brother: "There were only 30 people there that night, but he still played as though there were thousands listening."

May 10, 1981. © BRUCE HAND

May 23: Chief's, Baton Rouge, LA

May 24: Tipitina's, New Orleans, LA

May 26: Beaumont, TX

May 29: Fitzgerald's, Houston, TX

May 30: Fitzgerald's, Houston, TX

June 3: Auditorium Shores, Austin, TX

June 5: Al's Bamboo, Dallas, TX

June 6: Al's Bamboo, Dallas, TX

June 12: Steamboat 1874, Austin, TX)

June 13: Steamboat 1874, Austin, TX)

June 17: Club Foot, Austin, TX, opening for Delbert McClinton

June 18: Club Foot, Austin, TX, opening for Delbert McClinton

June 22: Tulsa, OK

June 23: Tulsa, OK

June 24: Lawrence Opry, Lawrence, KS

June 26: Jawbone, Chicago, IL (possibly Tut's also)

June 27: Hyatt Regency, Chicago, IL with Albert Collins

Stevie played for *Musician* magazine's private party as part of the NAMM convention in Chicago. "Young Stevie Ray Vaughan instantly pumped up the evening's energy level with a torrid, if slightly clichéd, set of blues and rock 'n' roll standards. Fronting his Texas trio Double Trouble, Stevie Ray Vaughan pushed his vintage Strat ('aged' in the glorious Rory Gallagher tradition) to the limits: squeezing, bending and literally shaking notes out of the guitar. His gruff, sympathetic vocal style, compact, rhythm-based guitar playing and total commitment to the blues form (with frequent nods to Hendrix) bode well for Vaughan in the future."[6]

At the time Stevie played the NAMM convention, Mindy Giles was with Alligator Records and pushed Bruce Iglauer to sign Stevie. He passed because Alligator had yet to start signing any white artists, and Stevie was doing standard blues fare and developing as a singer. He felt Stevie was not charismatic enough. Mindy set up a gig at Jaw Bones, but Iglauer thought Stevie was too loud.[17]

Agent JOE PRIESNITZ: "Nobody'd sign him because he was 'just a blues band.' Chesley waved that stick too. 'Oh, Junior, he's just going to die playing the blues. He's not going to change.' I pretty much stood my ground – he's phenomenal, whether he plays blues or whatever – that's what he does. Let's not try to change it; let's just work with it.

"Chesley wanted things to progress quicker. I remember they would spend weeks bringing in singers to audition with him, to try to find another element to add to the band – make it more commercial or more appealing. They auditioned Lydia Pense, I think. There were two or three pretty famous female singers that they brought in."

Lenny Vaughan. COURTESY MARTHA VAUGHAN

June 28: Tut's, Chicago, IL

June 30: Union Bar, St. Paul, MN

📖**July:** *Buddy*, "Stevie Vaughan"

July 1: Minneapolis, MN

July 2: B & B Tap, Oshgosh, WI

July 3: Fitzgerald's, Chicago, IL

👀**July 4:** Harling's Upstairs, Kansas City, MO
– You'll Be Mine
– Little Wing
– Drivin' South
– Third Stone From the Sun
– Albert Collins medley
– Shake For Me
– Letter To My Girlfriend
– They Call Me Guitar Hurricane
– Texas Flood
– Love In Vain
– All Your Love I Miss Loving
– Manic Depression
– I'm Leaving You (Commit A Crime)
– Hideaway
– In the Open
– The Sky Is Crying
– Tell Me
– Crosscut Saw
– Love Struck Baby
– Close to You
– May I Have A Talk With You
– You Done Lost Your Good Thing Now
– Oh Yeah (My Baby's Gone)
– Wham
– Collins' Shuffle
– Come On (Part III)
– Look At Little Sister
– Thunderbird
– Tin Pan Alley

July 7: Boston Avenue Market, Tulsa, OK

July 8: Boston Avenue Market, Tulsa, OK

July 9: New Bamboo, Dallas, TX (cancelled)

July 10: New Bamboo, Dallas, TX (cancelled)

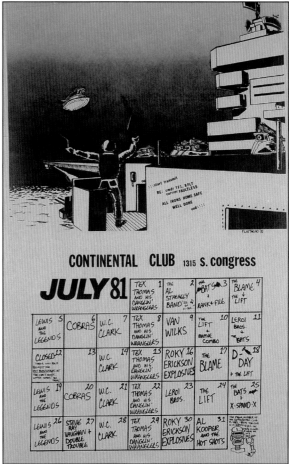
© FLATHEAD

🎸**July 11:** Manor Downs, Manor, TX, Joe Ely's South Texas Tornado Jam. 57:30. (afternoon show)
– Collins' Shuffle
– Come On (Part III)
– Look At Little Sister
– Dirty Pool
– Love Struck Baby

The July 11 concert is filmed for what was proposed as a series of television shows. Despite some post-production work to ready the film for broadcast, the series was not picked up by a network. This is believed to be the earliest professional video of Stevie.

One may wonder why the earliest known, professionally filmed performance of Stevie Ray Vaughan, lasting approximately thirty minutes, has never been commercially released. Regrettably, a tangled web of ownership, Internal Revenue Service claims and death has conspired to prevent the release to date. Attempts were made to secure a license to use some of the footage in both the VH-1 documentary *Legends* in 1997 and in Sony Music's *SRV* box set in 2000. Unfortunately, attorneys and rights clearance personnel for the interested parties could not be satisfied as to who actually owns the rights.

From contemporaneous correspondence provided by the son of the original investor in the film, here is one version of the circumstances. The investor is referred to herein simply as

"George." The bottom line is that George maintains he made a genuine investment in the tapes, but the IRS alleged it was an illegal tax-avoidance scam.

According to George, in 1981, at the age of 56, he was looking to make an investment to provide an income stream for his retirement years. His firm had voted to terminate its investment trust, and he needed to find an alternative for the funds he was about to receive from the trust.

He became interested in a project suggested by a Dallas broker involving live performance tapes that could be marketed in a retail setting or as a series of television shows. The twenty-six, half-hour master tapes were being sold for $160,000 each and included not only Stevie, but also The Fabulous Thunderbirds, Joe Ely, Ray Wylie Hubbard, Marcia Ball and other popular Texas bands of the day.

Stevie and Doyle Bramhall in the studio. © LINDA LOU BRITT

George was familiar with the music of many of these performers and believed it was a good investment, as several were likely to become stars. (Turns out he was right.) He felt he could get in on the ground floor of a new technology – home video tapes. The new phenomenon was still pitting VHS against Beta formats. News media were reporting that companies were forming to open retail video stores. Digital video discs were also being discussed as a new format, and cable television was in the midst of great expansion.

The research George conducted and the appeal of the musical performances led him to purchase eighteen of the twenty-six master tapes, including Stevie Ray Vaughan and Double Trouble. The down payment was $225,000, with promissory notes totalling over two-and-a-half million dollars due in ten years, but he believed he would make both short- and long-term profits from the investment. This was the crux of the dispute with the IRS.

Just as George was trying to get a production and distribution plan going for the tapes, the whole situation was roped into an existing IRS investigation of someone else's scheme to market audio tapes. This action by the IRS essentially tied George's hands, but he spent another $120,000 in the last half of the 1980's to keep the marketing effort alive.

Twelve years later, after George had filed bankruptcy, the IRS concluded, in a decision that was not appealable, that George had no profit motive and never intended to pay the promissory notes: it was a scam. Consequently, he was ordered to pay over five million dollars in back taxes, penalties and interest, disallowing all the tax deductions he had taken since 1981.

Recording "Too Sorry" with Doyle Bramhall. © LINDA LOU BRITT

The single question before the tax court was whether George had a legitimate profit motive in the tapes, and this question was answered by the tax court judge, not a jury. He supposedly relied on the opinion of an appraiser who concluded the value of the tapes in 1981 was negligible. Here are the reviewer's comments regarding Stevie's performance:

It features a typical Rock [sic] group, led by Stevie Vaughn [sic] whose somewhat dull voice was relieved by his pyrotechnical performance on the guitar. Mr. Vaughn, for example, was able to relieve the tedium produced by the comparatively dull repetition of his Rock themes by placing his guitar behind the back of his neck and playing it over his head. An audience reaction shot edited into the program at this point, reflected only mild interest in these acrobatics. The program ended with the playing of numerous choruses of a song entitled 'Let the Good Times Roll,' which bore no relationship to the 1974 movie of the same name.

To which summary, dear readers, you might inquire whether the reviewer was watching the correct tape. And if you think he was harsh on Stevie, you should see what he wrote about Kim Wilson of the T-Birds! He didn't even bother to get his name right, calling him "Ken Lewis."

The evaluation of the programs concluded with this pearl of business judgment:

'Tornado Jam' was apparently never offered to an experienced national television distributor, and it is just as well, because no such businessman would handle it. .... In 1981, the 'commercial value' of the owner's interest in the taped series was $35,750. Its value as tested by a projected arms-length sale, pursuant to the willing buyer-willing seller theory, was zero.

Add to this horror story for George a suggestion that Chesley Millikin later claimed to own the tapes, though on what basis he asserted such ownership is not known. Access to files that might reveal such basis was denied to the author. It would seem ownership by George is clearly established in the tax court findings.

In late 2007, according to George's son, George was 82 years old, and the IRS was still trying to seize what few assets he has left, including his house. George's son is still willing to market the tape but says Jimmie Vaughan has threatened to fight any release of the performance.

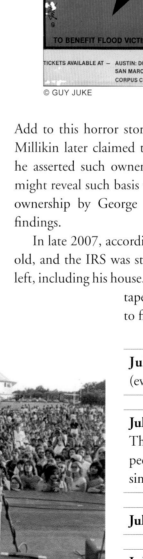

Auditorium Shores, Austin. The Stevie Ray Vaughan Memorial, erected in 1993, stands a few yards from where the Auditorium Shores stage was located. © WATT CASEY, JR.

July 11: New Bamboo, Dallas, TX (evening show)

July 15: Auditorium Shores, Austin, TX. The show is said to have drawn 12,000 people, more than doubling the record for similar concerts by other performers.[52]

July 17: Club Foot, Austin, TX

July 20: Tipitina's, New Orleans, LA (cancelled)

July 22: Chief's, Baton Rouge, LA

July 23: Fat Dawg's, Beaumont, TX

July 24: Fitzgerald's, Houston, TX

July 25: Fitzgerald's, Houston, TX

"Sometimes at night's end, when the waitresses were picking up empty glasses and soiled napkins and fallen chairs, he would plop alone on the lip of the stage, exhausted, and tap out a sublime instrumental to chase the stragglers home. The stragglers understood. It was church in the honky-tonk, the silence that follows every storm, and it played out forlornly in the humid Gulf Coast night when the rest of the city slept and the restless souls who remained would make their peace, still sweating from ripping up the joint."[99]

July 27: Continental Club, Austin, TX

July 28: Nick's Uptown, Dallas, TX

July 29: Nick's Uptown, Dallas, TX (cancelled)

July 30: Blossom's Downstairs, Fort Worth, TX. Bootleggers erroneously call this recording August 30, 1980. Maybe it was July 30, 1981. There is no record of Stevie playing this club before May 1981.

- Wham!
- Guitar Hurricane
- The Sky Is Crying
- Empty Arms
- I'm Leaving You (Commit A Crime)
- Howlin' For My Darlin'
- Be Careful
- I'm Cryin'
- Collins' Shuffle
- Hideaway
- In The Open
- May I Have A Talk With You
- Tell Me
- Tin Pan Alley
- Love Struck Baby
- Crosscut Saw
- Texas Flood

July 31: New Bamboo, Dallas, TX

August 1: New Bamboo, Dallas, TX

Auditorium Shores, Austin. © WATT CASEY, JR.

August 4: Boston Avenue Market, Tulsa, OK

August 5: Parady Hall, Kansas City, MO. The contract indicates three 60-minute sets between 9:30 and 1:30 for $400 plus 70% of door receipts over $500.

Once Stevie got to the point of being able to have contract riders (requirements beyond the standard performance and fee arrangements), it was stipulated that the venues provide clean socks for Stevie. He would come off stage and his socks would be soaked and foul. It was easier to just throw them away and put on new socks. "We wouldn't let Stevie take his shoes off unless he was in a room by himself," recalls Edi Johnson.[17]

MELODY WILSON: "I'm the one that got him to stop wearing black socks, blue socks, because his feet were a mess. He had the worst feet on earth, from wearing boots – boots that didn't fit, boots that did fit. He lived in boots, and half the time he'd sleep in them. I bought white, cotton socks for that boy. He had callouses and bunions. I'd rub his feet, and he said, 'Melody, if you touch my bunions, I'll slap you silly.' And there was a part of the back of his head that was flat. I said, 'I guess when you were a baby your mother didn't roll you over!' He said, 'No, I think it's from Jimmie hittin' me on top of the head all the time.' [*Laughs*]"

August 7: Chicago, IL (noon show)

August 8: Fitzgerald's, Chicago, IL

August 9: ChicagoFest, Chicago, IL, with T-Birds

August 11: Mason Jar, Rochester, NY, with T-Birds

It is believed that it was around 1981 that Stevie got his dog T-Bone.

MELODY: "I got a call at work one time: 'Melody, it's Stevie. You've got to go to the bank for me. I'll call you back in thirty minutes.' I said, 'Stevie, where are you?' 'I'm in a limo in New York right now.' He calls back and everyone at work just about passes out, 'Melody! It's Stevie Ray for you!'

"I get on the phone and Stevie says, 'Melody. You have to go to the bank and go to the back door. It's down on Congress, and this is the name of the bank ... they're going to let you in the back door.' I went, 'Stevie, are you sure you know what you're talking about?' He says, 'Yeah. Lenny's in trouble.'

"I had already heard from Lenny. She'd been

Boston Avenue Market, Tulsa. Note the small pin of Jimi Hendrix on Stevie's shirt. © BYRON BARR

driving in Dallas, and she didn't turn her blinker on. She drove erratic anyway, 'cuz she was too stoned. They pulled her over, and she had fragments of [stuff] on her. Nothing big, just fragments.

"So Stevie says, 'Now, are you listening to me? You have to do this right. Go to the bank, knock on the back door, and you tell 'em you're Melodic Melody, and T-Bone sent you.' [*Melody laughs.*]

"I said, 'Okay. What're they gonna do?' 'They're going to give you some money, and then you take it down to wire the money to me.' So here I am in my work T-shirt with sticky, oily stuff from making sandwiches, riding my motorcycle. I get to the bank, and here's all these guys in suits looking at me, and I went, 'Uh. I'm Melodic Melody and T-Bone sent me.' And they went, 'Okay. Come on in.'

"I go into the bank, into the vault, and they count out twenty thousand dollars! Counted it three times. They put it in an envelope, and I had to sign all these papers and go out the back door. I'm standing there stunned! I wired it to New York, and I guess that's what he bailed Lenny out of jail with. I couldn't believe what would happen with those two."

From Joe Priesnitz' calendar, it appears all the following gigs through September 3 were cancelled:

August 12: Shorts Bar, Rochester, NY
August 13: Shorts Bar, Rochester, NY
August 14: Long Branch, Buffalo, NY
August 15: Imperial, Niagara Falls, NY
August 18: The Haunt, Ithica, NY
August 20: Sunrise, Hartford, CT
August 21: Lupo's, Providence, RI
August 22: Swing Street, Groton, CT

Al's Bamboo, Dallas. The Marshall amplifier would later be painted black and gray for the David Bowie tour in 1983. It is now in the author's collection. COURTESY MARTHA VAUGHAN

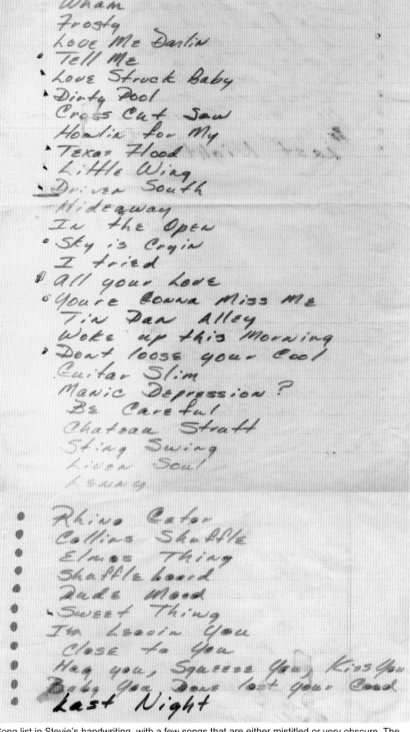

Song list in Stevie's handwriting, with a few songs that are either mistitled or very obscure. The date of the list is probably 1982 or earlier. COURTESY DOBBS/JACKSON

August 23: Pelham Street, Newport, RI
August 26: Showcase East, New Haven, CT
August 27: Showcase East, New Haven, CT
August 28: Hangar One, Hadley, MA
August 29: Stanhope House, Stanhope, NJ
August 31: Desperado's, Washington, D.C.
September 1: Desperado's, Washington, D.C.
September 2: No Fish Today, Baltimore, MD
September 3: The Cave, Virginia Beach, VA

© GARY OLLIVER

August 26: Chesley's management contract would expire the next week if he chose not to renew it. On August 26, he and Stevie agreed to a new contract, in which Chesley reduced his commission from 15% to 10% on the first $500,000 of income and 15% on anything over $500,000 in a one-year period. However, he would be allowed to continue to collect 15% on all income, the extra 5% to be used to pay down the amount Stevie owed Classic Management for loans used to buy equipment, travel expenses and other things.

📖 *Record World*, date unknown: "Guitarist Vaughan and his sturdy rhythm section play straight-ahead rhythm 'n' blues with so much taste, style and sensitivity as to make the current fave-rave practitioner of the art, George Thorogood, look like a lounge act by comparison. Without question, Stevie Vaughan himself is one of the finest white blues guitarists anywhere."

📖 **September:** *Wavelength*, (New Orleans) SRV listed on centerfold Tipitina's calendar

September 4: Crockmeyer's Saloon, Columbia, SC

September 6: Crockmeyer's Saloon, Columbia, SC

Fan TAMI KYRE: "My cousin and a few others in Columbia, SC, claim to have seen Stevie play in a small club called Crockmeyer's Saloon. The story I got was that Stevie left the club that night and spent the night at my cousin's place, where they proceeded to stay up all night partying. The next afternoon when they woke up, my cousin's wife told my cousin to 'tell your friend to go home.' I guess she didn't know she was kicking Stevie Ray Vaughan out of her house!"

September 8: Tipitina's, New Orleans, LA

September 9: Chief's, Baton Rouge, LA
 – Collins' Shuffle
 – In The Open
 – The Sky Is Crying
 – Look at Little Sister
 – Come On (Part III)
 – Dirty Pool
 – Love Struck Baby
 – Little Wing
 – Drivin' South
 – Third Stone From the Sun
 – Hideaway
 – So Excited
 – Love Me Darlin'
 – You'll Be Mine
 – You Done Lost Your Good Thing Now
 – I'm Cryin'
 – Guitar Hurricane
 – Empty Arms
 – I'm Leaving You (Commit A Crime)
 – Slide Thang
 – Manic Depression
 – Boilermaker
 – Don't Lose Your Cool
 – Wham

September 11: Steamboat 1874, Austin, TX

September 12: Steamboat 1874, Austin, TX

September 14: Continental Club, Austin, TX

September 17: Blossom's Downstairs, Fort Worth, TX

September 18: New Bamboo, Dallas, TX

September 19: New Bamboo, Dallas, TX

September 23: Opera House, Austin, TX, opening for Johnny Winter

September 25: Fat Dawg's, Beaumont, TX (cancelled)

September 26: Fitzgerald's, Houston, TX (two shows)

MELODY WILSON: "Lenny would try to make it a home with the cooking and the cleaning, but the drugging and the drinking and all the partying got in the way of it. And I think about '81 is when people started going against Lenny because she was 'interfering' with Stevie, as they thought. That was mostly Chesley Millikin, Edi and all that group. I saw some things that Lenny was talking about, about management, that was really true, and no one else would believe her. Stevie didn't too much believe her, but he really loved her very much. He was pulled by management and by the ring of friends where you could get anything you wanted (drugs, etc.). And management did their best to keep Stevie away from Lenny by keeping him on the road.

"I was in places when Lenny wasn't there, and I heard what management said about her. She would ask for checks to pay the bills, and they would take weeks and weeks before they would send her money, and then it wouldn't be half the right amount for rent and food and things. So, on Lenny's side, she needed money and didn't have any – she'd be eating popcorn. There were times when I had to take the cars and get the flats fixed. She would be *raving* at management, 'Where's the checks? Where's the money?'

"I saw Lenny trying to do the best she could in the situation she was in, when in reality management should have been doing this for Stevie and Lenny. That way there would be no mishandling of things – except by management, because they never wanted to send the money. Stevie knew [Lenny was spending money on drugs] because he was part of that. He couldn't walk away from it because he was in it just as bad as anyone else.

"Lenny was very down to earth, but very demanding. One of her friends told me, 'When Lenny gets mad at you, she won't speak to you for months.' And then when Lenny was ready, she'd call. When she got mad, she'd stomp her foot and pound the table so you'd know she wanted you to hear something. I saw her do the same thing to Stevie. She took care of herself as best she could, but she was always left alone, left behind. Maybe that's why she took to me – I wouldn't put up with her heavy demanding."

Stevie and Lenny. COURTESY MARTHA VAUGHAN

© GARY OLLIVER

October 2: Steamboat 1874, Austin, TX

October 3: Steamboat 1874, Austin, TX, Stevie's 27th birthday. A benefit for the Palmer Drug Abuse Program
- May I Have A Talk With You
- Letter To My Girlfriend
- Tell Me
- Wham
- Manic Depression
- Lenny
- instrumental
- Boilermaker
- Close To You
- You'll Be Mine
- Empty Arms
- Dirty Pool
- Slide Thing
- I'm Leaving You (Commit A Crime)
- Texas Flood
- Drivin' South
- Third Stone From the Sun (end first set)
- Wham!
- Hideaway
- So Excited
- Love In Vain
- The Sky Is Crying
- Love Struck Baby
- May I Have A Talk With You
- Thunderbird
- You Done Lost Your Good Thing Now
- Woke Up This Morning

October 8: Fat Dawg's, Lubbock, TX

October 9: Fat Dawg's, Lubbock, TX

October 10: Fat Dawg's, Lubbock, TX

📖 **October 11:** *Houston Chronicle*, "Stevie Vaughan," Marty Racine: "I'll say it straight away, so we have no misunderstandings: Stevie Ray Vaughan is the most exciting and heartfelt rhythm and blues guitarist I've ever heard in live performance. That, folks, is a lot of blues."

October 13: Continental Club, Austin, TX

📼 **October 14:** Fitzgerald's, Houston, TX. This appears to be a complete setlist, which gives you some idea what a typical show was like in this era. Wow! Imagine sitting in a little club in Houston and having Stevie and Double Trouble deliver these songs with their customary passion and expertise:

– Collins' Shuffle
– In the Open
– Come On (Part III)
– Look At Little Sister
– Thunderbird
– The Sky Is Crying
– I'm Cryin'
– Crosscut Saw
– Shake For Me

Sam's Barbeque, Austin. © WATT CASEY, JR.

– Wham
– Hideaway
– So Excited
– Pride and Joy
– Tin Pan Alley
– Love Struck Baby
– May I Have A Talk With You
– Letter To My Girlfriend
– Little Wing
– Manic Depression
– Boilermaker
– Close To You
– You'll Be Mine
– You Done Lost Your Good Thing Now
– Empty Arms
– Slide Thing
– I'm Leaving You (Commit A Crime)
– Texas Flood
– Rude Mood
– Don't Lose Your Cool

October 15: Fitzgerald's, Houston, TX

October 16: Crossroads, Nacogdoches, TX

October 17: Crossroads, Nacogdoches, TX

October 18: St. Christopher's, Dallas, TX

Tommy Shannon was no different than most Austin musicians when it came to finding a place to live – he stayed with other musicians. "I moved in with [Stevie] when I moved down to Austin. I lived with him and Lenny for a long time, so I saw a lot of crazy things happen. They really loved each other, but they had a lot of conflicts and a lot of arguing and a lot of fighting. It seemed like I did a lot of refereeing, but I loved them both."[3]

COURTESY BRUCE NEWLIN

October 23: New Bamboo, Dallas, TX

October 24: New Bamboo, Dallas, TX

October 30: Cheatham Street Warehouse, San Marcos, TX

October 31: Ark Co-op, Austin, TX

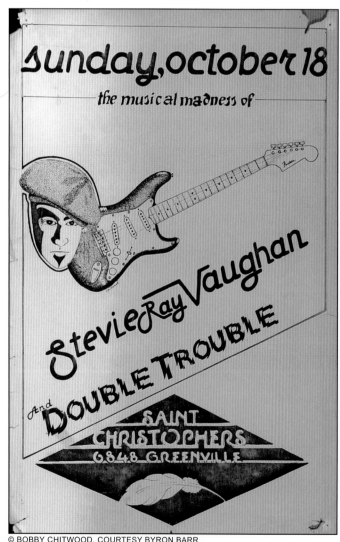
© BOBBY CHITWOOD, COURTESY BYRON BARR

© CORDNER

© GARY OLLIVER

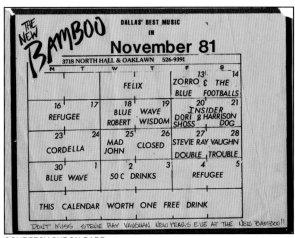

COURTESY BYRON BARR

November: *Sounds Of Austin*, "Stevie Ray Vaughan," no author credit, probably Bruce Newlin. "Undoubtedly, there is a medically scientific explanation for the phenomenon that occurs when the amplified sounds of an electric guitar supercharge the listener's nervous system, causing an uncontrollable urge to get up and dance, or scream at the top of one's lungs, or other shocking behavioral displays, but who cares? There aren't many people around who can make it happen, and Stevie Ray Vaughan is the one who's doing it right here and right now. He says, 'It's my life. I've been gifted with something, and I'm going to take it to its fullest extent.'"

November 4: Scarlett O's, Lake Charles, LA

November 6: Chief's, Baton Rouge, LA

November 7: Chief's, Baton Rouge, LA

November 12: Nick's Uptown, Dallas, TX

November 13: Steamboat 1874, Austin, TX

November 14: Steamboat 1874, Austin, TX

November 19: Fitzgerald's, Houston, TX

November 20: Fitzgerald's, Houston, TX

November 21: Lafayette, LA

November 24: Continental Club, Austin, TX

November 27: New Bamboo, Dallas, TX

November 28: New Bamboo, Dallas, TX

November 30: A.J.'s Midtown (formerly Hondo's Saloon), Austin, TX. On September 3, 1982, this would be the new home of Antone's on Guadalupe Street.

December 3: Crossroads, Nacogdoches, TX

December 4: Touch of Texas, Huntsville, TX

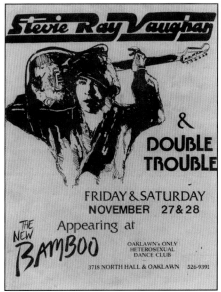

COURTESY BYRON BARR

December 5: Touch of Texas, Huntsville, TX

December 7: Texas Moon Palace, Amarillo, TX, opening for George Thorogood

December 8: University of New Mexico, Albuquerque, NM, opening for George Thorogood

187

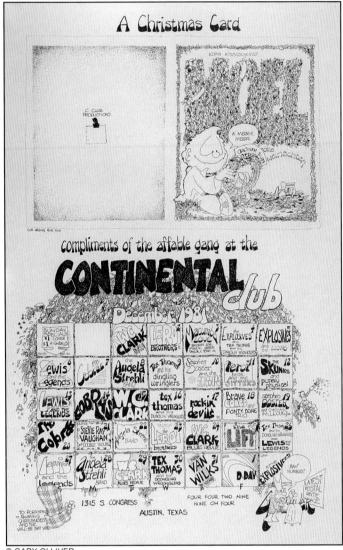

© GARY OLLIVER

December 12: Steamboat 1874, Austin, TX

December 16: Scarlett O's, Lake Charles, LA (cancelled and replaced with Chief's, Baton Rouge, LA?)

December 17: Tupelo Tavern, New Orleans, LA (cancelled?)

December 18: Fitzgerald's, Houston, TX

December 19: Fitzgerald's, Houston, TX

December 21: Continental Club, Austin, TX

December 31: The New Bamboo, Dallas, TX

1982

In 1982, the band's gross receipts for performances averaged $950 per night, up from $700 the year before and from $500 per night in 1980.

January 1: The New Bamboo, Dallas, TX

DON OPPERMAN (shown in the photo below) joins Stevie's crew. "Every weekend was booked solid. We would usually go out on Thursday and come home on Sunday. Austin to Dallas; Austin to

DON OPPERMAN was a friend of roadie Cutter Brandenburg. Don would later become part of Stevie's crew and years later worked for Kenny Wayne Shepherd and Joe Bonamassa. Don first saw Stevie play at the university in Albuquerque. "Stevie was on a George Thorogood tour, which I think lasted maybe ... one gig or two [*laughs*]. It was the tour where George was in the Yellow Cab, and that was his transportation to the gig. Cutter had called me, and they were already on stage starting, and I came in through the front entrance and walked through the door, and I was just floored – just mesmerized from that point on. I think it was like seeing Jimi Hendrix for the first time – that kind of awe. You can hear the records, but until you see him play ..."

Stevie's equipment was rudimentary at the time – not even a pedal board. "Cutter would run out there for 'Voodoo Chile' with the wah-wah and a cable. Stevie would plug into it. It was plugged straight into the amp; they split it with a little splitter [*laughs*]." Stevie would then have to unplug the wah-wah to play the next song.

December 11: Steamboat 1874, Austin, TX

Nick's Uptown, Dallas. That's tech Donnie Opperman behind Stevie.
© BYRON BARR

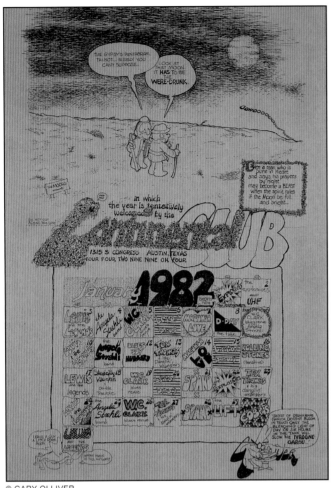

© GARY OLLIVER

Roadie James Arnold and Chris Layton inspect the slashed tires on the African Queen. © BYRON BARR

January 2: The New Bamboo, Dallas, TX

January 8: A.J.'s Midtown, Austin, TX

January 9: A.J.'s Midtown, Austin, TX

January 14: Fitzgerald's, Houston, TX

January 15: Baton Rouge, LA, with the T-Birds

January 16: Tupelo's Tavern, New Orleans, LA

January 18: Continental Club, Austin, TX.

DON OPPERMAN: "We did the Continental on Monday nights once a month. The guitars were out in the alley because there wasn't enough room inside the club to put the guitars, so I stood in the doorway to the alley at the back of the club."

It was very common for Stevie's name to be misspelled on marquees, posters and tickets throughout his career. © BYRON BARR

Houston; Austin to East Texas. We would go in the little cube truck [the African Queen] that they had rigged up with the air conditioners hanging in the back, the couches that fold out into beds. Chris and Tommy had the upper ... you couldn't call it a bunk: it was a ledge with foam on it. [On the road] Chris and Tommy would sleep; Stevie would usually sit between Cutter and I [in the cab], and if he got tired he would fold the couch out and lay down. It did break down a lot. We would get stuck in a garage all day.

"I remember the first time I strung Stevie's guitar, I'd left a string [end sticking] out. I was in a hurry and cut it off instead of pushing [the end] down into the tuning peg and wrapping it around, and it poked a hole in his hand. He was grabbing the head stock when he was getting crazy doing the Hendrix stuff. He showed it to me later and I thought, 'I won't do that again.'

"There were some places we'd set up and after the first set, the guy would go, 'God. You guys are too loud; you're going to have to turn it down.' Pack it up; we're outta there!"

STEVIE VAUGHAN
DOUBLE TROUBLE

(512) 441-5833

Stevie's business card circa 1981 before using his full name full-time.
COLLECTION OF CRAIG HOPKINS

January 20: Scarlett O's, Lake Charles, LA

January 21: Tipitina's, New Orleans, LA

January 22: Grant Street Dance Hall (Lafayette, LA?)

January 23: Baton Rouge, LA

January 27: Nick's Uptown, Dallas, TX

January 28: Nick's Uptown, Dallas, TX

January 29: Blossom's Downstairs, Fort Worth, TX

January 30: Blossom's Downstairs, Fort Worth, TX

📖**February:** *Buddy*, SRV in concert calendar

February 8: Continental Club, Austin, TX

February 11: Nu Blue Club, Arlington, TX

February 12: Boston Ave Market, Tulsa, OK

February 13: Boston Ave Market, Tulsa, OK

February 19: A.J.'s Midtown, Austin, TX

February 20: A.J.'s Midtown, Austin, TX

February 25: Crossroads, Nacogdoches, TX

February 26: Crossroads, Nacogdoches, TX.

Fan M. WEAVER: "At Crossroads they would always have a big happy hour crowd in there on Fridays, and being wasted college kids, we'd usually bail out at 5:30 or 6:00. The owner would have whatever band that was playing that night get up and play a number to entice the crowd to stay. When Stevie got up to play, the looks on people's faces was sheer amazement. Even the sorority girls could tell they were seeing a guitar master."

📷**February 27:** Fitzgerald's, Houston, TX

February 28: A.J.'s Midtown, Austin, TX, Barton Creek Benefit

Charley Wirz and Stevie at the Dallas Guitar Show that Charley founded.
© DON E. OPPERMAN, JR.

February: Millikin gives a videotape of Stevie's 1981 Tornado Jam performance to Mick Jagger when he and his girlfriend, Texan Jerry Hall, visit Manor Downs to look at horses. Chesley had worked with the Stones, so this meeting is not terribly unusual.

CHESLEY: "Mick was up in my office and he was running around saying, 'I love a good blues guitar player, but there just aren't any anymore.' I gave him a videotape that we had made of Stevie, and he took it with him to New York. Then a little bit later, Charlie Watts called me up and said that he was staying with Mick. And then he said, 'By the way, we just looked at that video and we want to know when and where we can see him.'"[20] A gig was set up for April 22.

© GARY OLLIVER

📖**March:** *Buddy*, SRV in concert calendar (three listings); Lou Ann Barton cover and article

March 1: Continental Club, Austin, TX, benefit

Former Double Trouble singer Lou Ann Barton released her first album, *Old Enough*, in early 1982. Atlantic Records producer Jerry Wexler came to Austin in support of her record release and ended up seeing Stevie play at one of the Continental Club gigs. He was duly impressed and contacted Claude Nobs to urge him to find a slot for Double Trouble at the Jazz Festival in Switzerland that summer. Connections made in Montreux would prove to make that gig the most important of Stevie's career. WEXLER: "Seeing him that one time at the Continental Club was almost an out-of-body experience. I couldn't believe it. I called Claude Nobs at Montreux the next morning. I said, 'You gotta book this musician I'm telling you about. There's no time, I have no tapes, no videos, no nothing – just book him.' And he did, on my say-so."[53]

March 4: Sam's Truck Stop, Arlington, TX

March 5: New Bamboo, Dallas, TX

March 6: New Bamboo, Dallas, TX

© BYRON BARR

📼**March 7:** Antone's, Austin, TX, Barton Creek Benefit (*with Kim Wilson and Kent Dykes of Omar and The Howlers)
  – Voodoo Chile (Slight Return)
  – instrumental
  – Pride and Joy
  – Texas Flood
  – Come On (Part III)
  – Love Struck Baby
  – Letter To My Girlfriend
  – Little Wing / Third Stone From The Sun
  – Hideaway/Rude Mood
  – So Excited
  – Know What It's Like *
  – You Don't Have To Go *
  – My Babe*
  – Bad Boy Blues Jam *
  – Sweet Home Chicago / Too Much Whiskey *
  – Lenny
  – Collins' Shuffle

March 8: Continental Club, Austin, TX

March 12: A.J.'s Midtown, Austin, TX

March 13: A.J.'s Midtown, Austin, TX

March 19: Sam's Truck Stop, Arlington, TX

March 20: Sam's Truck Stop, Arlington, TX

March 25: Club Foot, Austin, TX. Don Opperman recalls that Stevie opened a show at Club Foot for James Brown. Whether it was this date is unconfirmed. Priesnitz' calendar says "Legendary Blues Band."

📖**March 25:** *Houston Chronicle*, "Catch Him Now," Marty Racine

March 26: Fitzgerald's, Houston, TX, two shows

March 27: Fitzgerald's, Houston, TX, two shows

March 28: A.J.'s Midtown, Austin, TX

📼**March 28:** Barton Creek Benefit, Luckenbach, TX

April 1: Nu Blue Club, Arlington, TX

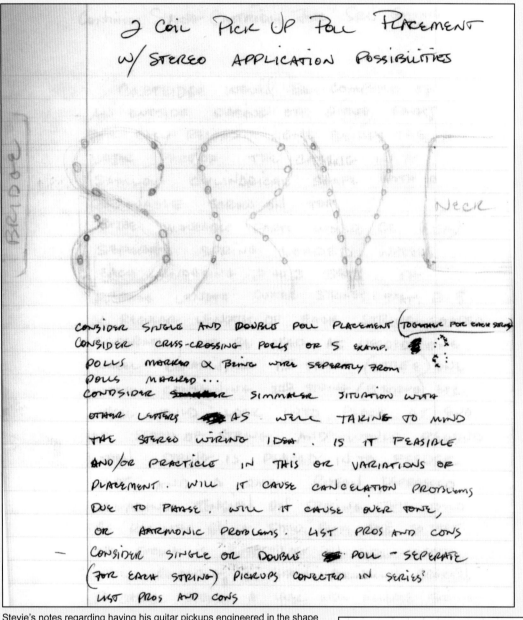

2 Coil Pick Up Poll Placement
w/ Stereo Application Possibilities

CONSIDER SINGLE AND DOUBLE POLL PLACEMENT (TOGETHER FOR EACH STRING)
CONSIDER CRISS-CROSSING POLLS OR S EXAMP.
POLLS MARKED α BEING WIRED SEPERATLY FROM
POLLS MARKED ...
CONSIDER SIMILAR SITUATION WITH
OTHER LETTERS AS WELL TAKING TO MIND
THE STEREO WIRING IDEA. IS IT FEASIBLE
AND/OR PRACTICLE IN THIS OR VARIATIONS OF
PLACEMENT. WILL IT CAUSE CANCELATION PROBLEMS
DUE TO PHASE. WILL IT CAUSE OVER TONE,
OR HARMONIC PROBLEMS. LIST PROS AND CONS
CONSIDER SINGLE OR DOUBLE POLL - SEPERATE
(FOR EACH STRING) PICKUPS CONECTED IN SERIES?
LIST PROS AND CONS

Stevie's notes regarding having his guitar pickups engineered in the shape of his initials. His notes reflect that he was aware that this might not be possible, but the man he was working with on a custom guitar design did follow through and discuss the idea with a major pickup manufacturer. Alas, the design was not technologically feasible, and Stevie continued to apply his initials with stickers on his pickguards. COURTESY DOBBS/JACKSON

Stevie's custom guitar design that he drew in 1982. This design was apparently a favorite of his because years later it became a real guitar. In this book's companion volume, *His Final Years, 1983–1990*, there is a photo of Stevie holding a prototype body at Carnegie Hall (see October 4, 1984), and a photo of him playing the unfinished prototype guitar on stage (see the discussion and photo at April 5, 1988). COURTESY DOBBS/JACKSON

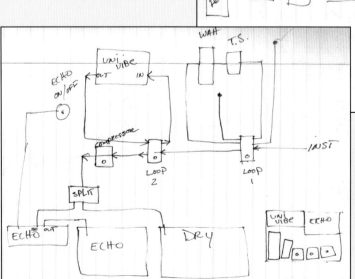

Two pages of Stevie's notes regarding his gear setup, including wah pedal, Tube Screamer, Uni-Vibe, Echoplex, loop selectors and amplifiers, including a Fender Vibratone (Leslie). COURTESY DOBBS/JACKSON

Lou Ann Barton receives a well-deserved, favorable review of her debut album on Asylum Records in the April 1 issue of *Rolling Stone Magazine*.

April 2: Nick's Uptown, Dallas, TX

April 3: Blossom's Downstairs, Fort Worth, TX

April 8: Fitzgerald's, Houston, TX

April 9: A.J.'s Midtown, Austin, TX, with Angela Strehli

April 10: A.J.'s Midtown, Austin, TX, w/ Angela Strehli

April 12: A.J.'s Backstage, Austin, TX

Agent JOE PRIESNITZ: "Someone had brought Mercury Records in to see the band at the Backstage. They saw him play, and it was like every other label that came in: 'Well, it's just a blues band. We can't work with that!' [*Laughs*] It always got me when people would say that because he was so much more. I mean, he was a blues player, but he had charisma and magic.

San Antonio, TX. © DON E. OPPERMAN, JR.

"We were backstage after the show, and someone told Stevie they didn't get [the record deal]. Lou Ann happened to walk in and Stevie wasn't in a good place [emotionally] at the time. She just plopped herself on his lap and had that *Rolling Stone* story and said, 'How 'bout that? *Rolling* fuckin' *Stone*, son of a bitch! What do you think?' And he was just on the edge of tears."

Asked if there was anything difficult about booking Stevie, JOE responded: "I guess the most difficult part was that he was just totally uncompromising. He was, 'Hey, this is what I do,' and we would have to actually turn down shows when the offer was if he would not play as loud. These were places we were trying to rebook him into. We'd get complaints, 'Oh, he was great, but it was just too loud and people were leaving. I'll have him back, but he's going to have to turn down, and I want it in the contract.'

"He'd just say, 'If that's the criteria, I don't need them. I'm not playing there.' It was his art, and that's how he wanted it presented. I respected him for it, but man, it cost us some routing dates. It caused a problem at the time, but it served him well later on."

From the gigs listed herein, the reader can get some sense of how often Stevie played. JOE: "They weren't month-long tours. We might send them out for a week or two at a time, because it was hard booking an original blues-rock act, trying to make ends meet for them out there. I can't tell you how many times they would call the agency just to say, 'Well, we're in San Francisco and we're out of money. Send us some money!' [*Laughs*] But he would play ... like the Marines – any time, any place. He liked to play full moon nights. He thought people reacted better, you know, a bit more lunatics."

Joe's booking calendars really do have "full moon" handwritten on the appropriate dates.

April 13: Danceteria, New York, NY (rescheduled to 22nd)

April 15: Sam's Truck Stop, Arlington, TX

April 16: Fat Dawg's, Lubbock, TX

April 17: Fat Dawg's, Lubbock, TX

April 20: Sam's Truck Stop, Arlington, TX (cancelled)

April 21: Sam's Truck Stop, Arlington, TX (cancelled)

April 22: Danceteria, New York, NY. Chesley's gift to Mick Jagger of the video of Stevie and Double Trouble pays a dividend. Chesley arranged a private party for The Rolling Stones at New York's Danceteria. Stevie makes *Rolling Stone* magazine's Random Notes page on June 10, 1982. Soon

Ronnie Wood of the Rolling Stones focuses intently on Stevie and Double Trouble. © CHUCK PULIN

rumors circulate that the band will sign with Rolling Stones Records and open European tour dates for the Stones. Neither happens.

CHRIS LAYTON: "Chesley knew Mick Jagger, and Mick had seen the tape [of the Tornado Jam show]. Chesley said, 'You've really got to see these guys live.' Mick was into it, and he told Chesley when he'd be in New York. We did all of the work to set up that gig at the Danceteria, and it was all at our own expense. That was a really bizarre gig. Danceteria had different things happening all night, with different bands and constant turnover. For one of those segments, we closed the club off and showcased for the Stones. There were only a few people there – Mick Jagger, Ron Wood and whoever else made their way in. We only played a few songs, met them, the photographers took some shots, and then everyone was gone. It was a 'drive-by' showcase for Mick Jagger."[54]

STEVIE: "We were only supposed to play for 35 minutes or so, but it ended up being close to two hours. [Stevie said on another occasion that it was "three hours."[20]] Every time we'd

At the airport on the way to New York, with Stevie's parents.
© DON E. OPPERMAN, JR.

San Antonio, TX. © TONY RODRIGUEZ

Don Opperman: "We went to New York for the Rolling Stones 'audition.' We didn't really know … we thought we were auditioning for a tour or a record deal. It was basically Stevie's manager and Frances [Carr], who was backing him, getting Stevie some exposure. Nothing really came of it."

There were, however, some interesting moments. Don continues: "When Stevie was playing 'Tin Pan Alley,' Ron Wood sat right in front of him with his mouth open watching him play the whole thing. Also, I remember during that gig, where he turns around with the guitar and unsnaps the strap and then buckles it behind him … he'd pulled the strap button and the screw out of the guitar [laughs], and he was kind of twirling around. He was trying to stick it back in the hole and, of course, couldn't find it. It was pretty comical."

stop, Jagger would say to keep playing, he'd *buy* the bleeping place if he had to! There were all kinds of people, everybody from Johnny Winter to … what's that blond-headed guy, Andy Warhol? I kept seeing this guy jumping up and down, acting like he was playing along. With all those bright lights, you could hardly see, and I thought it was somebody I knew from Texas. Come to find out it was Jagger that I'd been playing to the whole time, and I didn't even know it![24] It was just a big fat party, and we didn't choke. We were nervous, but we didn't let it stop us. Amps were blowing up; most of the equipment didn't work. My guitar strap-holder popped off the guitar."[20]

COLLECTION OF CRAIG HOPKINS

© GARY OLLIVER

Photos of Stevie and Mick together soon made it into *Rolling Stone* magazine, escalating the rumors that the Stones would sign the band to their record label. Chris Layton: "Supposedly, Mick's comment to the guy running their label was, 'I like them, but everybody knows that blues doesn't sell.' So they passed."[54]

The Stones weren't the only celebrities Stevie encountered in the early eighties. Antone's by this time had moved from its original Sixth Street location (to make way for a parking garage in 1979) to North Austin. James Elwell: "Clifford moved over to Anderson Lane, and I remember James Brown playing there, and Stevie met him. James Brown may have known a little bit about him, but not a whole lot. On Stevie's hat James Brown wrote, 'Soul Brother Number One.' Stevie was just flipped out. James was a legend and Stevie was just a humble guitar picker from Texas."

Stevie and Mick Jagger after the "audition." © CHUCK PULIN

April 23: Cooper's, Port Arthur, TX

April 24: Cooper's, Port Arthur, TX

April 26: Continental Club, Austin, TX

April 28: Fitzgerald's, Houston, TX

April 29: Fitzgerald's, Houston, TX

🎸 **April 30:** University of Houston (TX) 32:20. Audience video.

    – instrumental
    – Voodoo Chile (Slight Return)
    – Look At Little Sister
    – Love Struck Baby
    – Pride and Joy
    – Texas Flood

© GARY OLLIVER

May 1: Touch of Texas, Huntsville, TX

May 3: "Rock for the Guac" benefit, Continental Club, Austin, TX

May 5: Nick's Uptown, Dallas, TX

May 6: Nick's Uptown, Dallas, TX

May 7: A.J.'s Midtown, Austin, TX

May 8: A.J.'s Midtown, Austin, TX

© CLIFF CARTER

Austin Blues Heritage Festival, May 9, 1982. © WATT CASEY, JR.

May 9: Austin Blues and Heritage Fest, Auditorium Shores, Austin, TX

May 10: Continental Club, Austin, TX (cancelled?)

May 11: Chesley exercises his option to renew his management contract with Stevie, effective September 5, 1981, and continuing until September 5, 1982.

May 13: Nu Blue Club, Arlington, TX

May 14: Blossom's Downstairs, Fort Worth, TX

May 15: Blossom's Downstairs, Fort Worth, TX

May 18: Club Foot, Austin, TX, opening for The Nighthawks

May 21: Fitzgerald's, Houston, TX

May 22: Fitzgerald's, Houston, TX

TONY DUKES: "Stevie and the guys had gone to New York – Chesley had gotten them that review in front of the Stones. They came back and Cutter had me meet them early at Fitzgerald's and said, 'We can buy Stevie's paper for ten grand or less [becoming Stevie's manager by buying out Chesley]. If you can give me five grand today, I can lock it up.' He said, 'Can't you go to Gibbons or somebody?' But Gibbons was so gun-shy. Any time you touched a Texas band with Bill Ham ... I mean, when ZZ Top played with the Stones in the Astrodome, Bill Ham tried to bump the T-Birds off the bill because he didn't want Texas competition. I was sitting in Louis Messina's office at Pace Concerts when he made the call. Also, early on, Billy was invited to record with several folks – Duane Allman, Mark Knopfler – Ham 86'd it all."

"I negotiated getting ZZ Top on the cover of *Guitar Player* for the first time. I went out and sat with Tom Wheeler. He said, 'Tell them we don't want to discuss it anymore, because every time we talk to Bill Ham, he wants all three guys on the cover.' This is *Guitar Player* magazine, and Ham said, 'You're not breaking up my group.'"

May 23: Highway 16, KISS radio, San Antonio, TX

May 24: Continental Club, Austin, TX (cancelled)

May 28: Pappy's, San Antonio, TX

📖**May 28:** *Austin Chronicle*, "Stevie To Sign With Stones?", Margaret Moser

May 29: A.J.'s Midtown, Austin, TX

May 31: Manor Downs, Manor, TX, opening for Bobby & the Midnites (Bob Weir of the Grateful Dead, Billy Cobham, Dave Garland, Alphonso Jackson, Bobby Cochran)

June 4: A.J.'s Backstage, Austin, TX

June 5: A.J.'s Backstage, Austin, TX

June 7: Austin Opera House, Austin, TX, opening for Dave Edmunds

June 8: Coliseum, Austin, TX, opening for The Clash, a punk rock group

DON OPPERMAN recalls the June 8 gig: "[The crowd] actually booed him. Of course, if you look at the audience and the gender and the music, these kids were ready to see a punk band from England rock 'to the Casbah' or whatever. I remember we were at Ray Hennig's [Heart of Texas Music], and they had this brand new plexi stack, unplayed, really nice. Stevie talked Ray into letting him borrow it for that gig – it was the loudest thing [*laughs*]. It was louder than anything he'd had before, because he had always played through those little Vibroverbs. [The crowd] didn't get it, and Stevie was pretty disgusted. But The Clash was a huge band. Needless to say, they didn't care about some blues guy from Austin."

"'It was traumatic,' recalls Chris Layton about Double Trouble's first-night opening slot for The Clash at the City Coliseum in 1982. 'We were warned that The Clash's audience hated everyone, but we figured, 'Hey, this is good ol' liberal Austin!'"

"Indeed, watching rising star Stevie Ray Vaughan being heckled mercilessly on the Combat Rock tour was depressing and embarrassing, but it was a bad move from the start to book the local blues trio. The Clash cultivated a punk audience who valued passion over precision, and Double Trouble was too slick for their raw standards.

"The Clash rolled into town early to scout opening bands. It was their m.o., a move that won them much respect. The day before the show, management representative Stuart Weintraub sat at the Sheraton Hotel and fielded tapes from local bands vying for the opener – D-Day, the Lift, 5 Spot. That night, The Clash were scoping out reggae bands, dropping by the Opera House to catch Stevie, and sweeping into the Continental Club to see a rockabilly outfit called the Trouble Boys. Double Trouble got the now-infamous gig that began as badly as it ended.

"'To walk out into the lights and see people throwing shit at us and shooting us the rod, yelling 'get fucked' and 'get off the stage' was awful,' remembers Layton. 'At Montreux, there were four or five people booing, and it felt like 400 or 500. I remember [the Coliseum] as being venomous. Stevie was like, 'What is all this shit?'

"Afterward, Stevie thanked Joe [Strummer] and said, 'I guess I don't understand your audience. We're not accustomed to this, and we can't do tomorrow night.' Strummer was real apologetic, a great guy. But I'm surprised they found anyone to open [the second night].'"[55]

June 9: scheduled to open for The Clash at the Coliseum, Austin, TX, but Stevie refuses based on the previous night's experience.

June 10: Miller Outdoor Theater, Houston, TX

📖**June 10:** *Rolling Stone*, "Random Notes," photo of SRV with Mick Jagger at private NYC party

June 11: Fast Lane, Fort Worth, TX

June 12: Fast Lane, Fort Worth, TX

June 15: Crossroads, Nacogdoches, TX

June 16: Crossroads, Nacogdoches, TX

📖**June 17:** *Dallas Times Herald*, "Hot Property – Guitarist Stevie Vaughan Ready to Step Out," Bruce Nixon. "Stevie Ray Vaughan plays the endless boogie .... with a thick, aggressive tone and machine-gun cascades of notes, and the furious wails and screams and breath-swallowing rushes of noise that electric guitars can sometimes make."

STEVIE, commenting on rumors that Double Trouble would open some of the Rolling Stones' European shows and possibly be signed to their record label: "Things are starting to happen. What will come out of all this is yet to be seen, but we're gonna push for whatever we can get. I feel we can do something on our own in Europe even if the Stones thing doesn't happen. We've just worked really hard, and we're breaking out of the United States, is what we're trying to do."

A later unconfirmed report suggested that Double Trouble was actually scheduled to open for the Stones on some European dates that were cancelled due to rioting in Europe.

June 18: Lone Star Bar & Grill, San Antonio, TX

June 19: Lone Star Bar & Grill, San Antonio, TX

June 19: Lee Park, Dallas, TX, Juneteenth celebration with Albert Collins, Koko Taylor, Johnny Copeland (free show). Despite the 300-mile trip, both shows are on Priesnitz' calendar.

June 23: Fitzgerald's, Houston, TX

June 24: Fitzgerald's, Houston, TX

June 25: Blossom's Downstairs, Fort Worth, TX

June 26: Blossom's Downstairs, Fort Worth, TX

June 30: Nick's Uptown, Dallas, TX

July: *The Record*, "Faces & Places," photo of SRV and Mick Jagger at Danceteria and blurb about Double Trouble auditioning for Rolling Stones Records.

July 1: Nick's Uptown, Dallas, TX

July 2: Fat Dawg's, Lubbock, TX

July 3: Fat Dawg's, Lubbock, TX

COLLECTION OF CRAIG HOPKINS

"Stevie Ray Vaughan .... treated his audience to a smoking retrospective of blues/rock guitar ranging from Lonnie Mack and Link Wray to Hound Dog Taylor and Elmore James to Jimi Hendrix and Pete Townshend, all the while insinuating his distinctive interpretations thruout [sic]. Vaughan, the first guitarist .... to ever carry this tradition to a modern-day mainstream context, cares chiefly that his listeners respect the roots while digging the sound."[40]

July 7: Continental Club, Austin, TX. Billed as a "Farewell Show" before Stevie left for Europe. Prophetic, considering the days of playing mainly in small Texas clubs would be over soon as a result of connections made in Montreux in the next two weeks.

July 9: Sam's Truck Stop, Arlington, TX (cancelled)

July 10: Sam's Truck Stop, Arlington, TX (cancelled)

July 15: The band leaves for Europe.

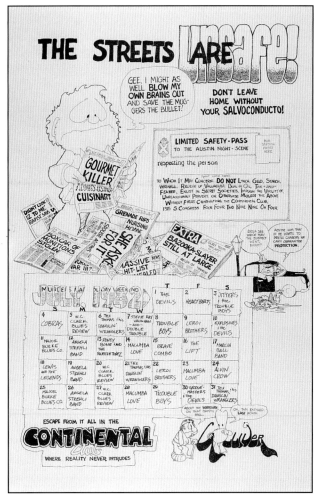

© GARY OLLIVER

July 17: Montreux International Jazz Festival, Montreux, Switzerland, main stage plus after hours in Casino ballroom. Stevie also jammed with harmonica player Sugar Blue (Rolling Stones). The songs with Sugar Blue were probably worked up during sound check, and whether the audience got to hear them is unclear.

- Hideaway / Rude Mood
- Pride and Joy
- Texas Flood
- Love Struck Baby
- Dirty Pool
- Give Me Back My Wig
- Collins' Shuffle

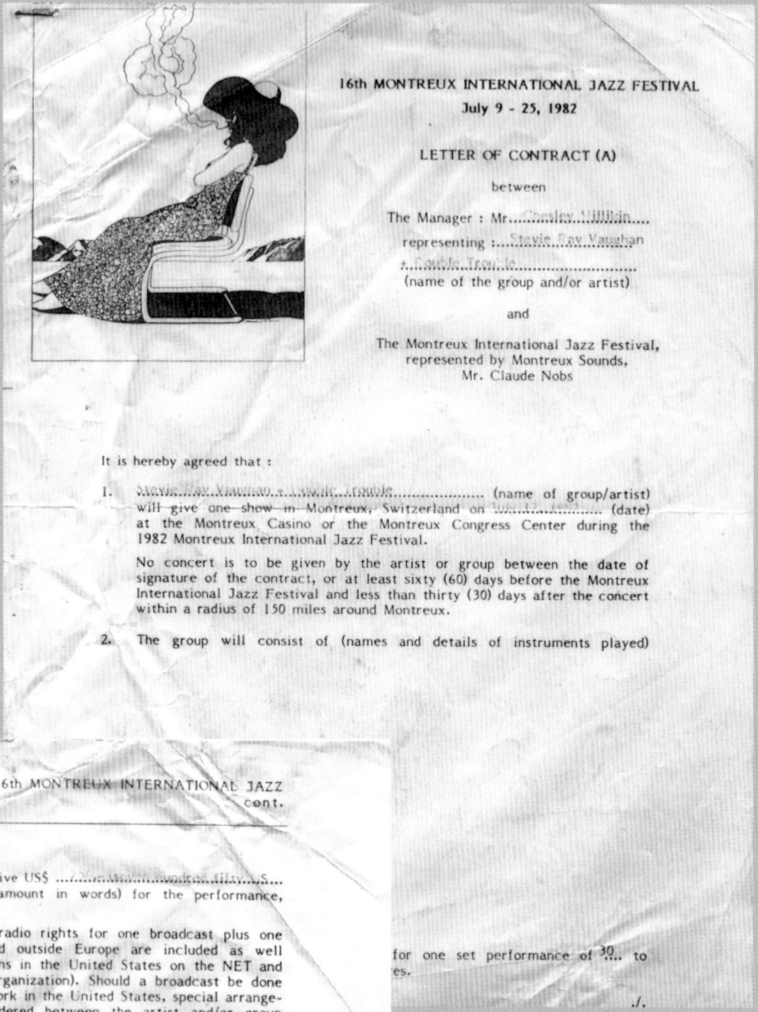

16th MONTREUX INTERNATIONAL JAZZ FESTIVAL
July 9 - 25, 1982

LETTER OF CONTRACT (A)

between

The Manager : Mr. Chesley Millikin
representing : Stevie Ray Vaughan + Double Trouble
(name of the group and/or artist)

and

The Montreux International Jazz Festival,
represented by Montreux Sounds,
Mr. Claude Nobs

It is hereby agreed that :

1. Stevie Ray Vaughan + Double Trouble .... (name of group/artist) will give one show in Montreux, Switzerland on .... (date) at the Montreux Casino or the Montreux Congress Center during the 1982 Montreux International Jazz Festival.

No concert is to be given by the artist or group between the date of signature of the contract, or at least sixty (60) days before the Montreux International Jazz Festival and less than thirty (30) days after the concert within a radius of 150 miles around Montreux.

2. The group will consist of (names and details of instruments played)

... for one set performance of 30... to
...es.

./.

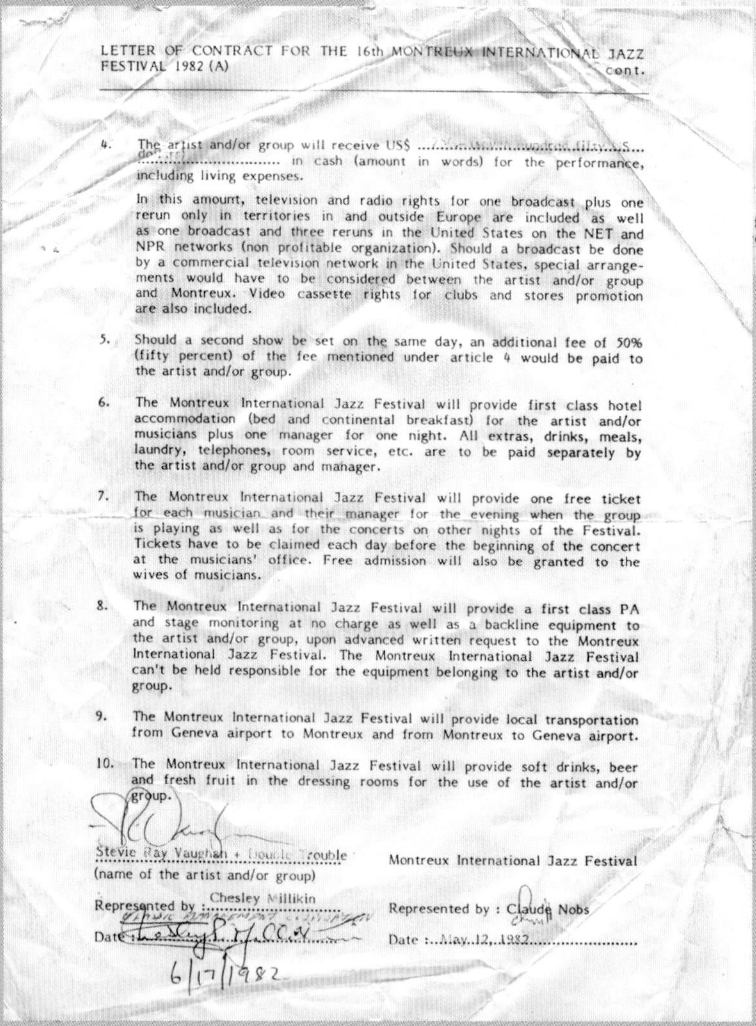

LETTER OF CONTRACT FOR THE 16th MONTREUX INTERNATIONAL JAZZ FESTIVAL 1982 (A)
cont.

4. The artist and/or group will receive US$ .... in cash (amount in words) for the performance, including living expenses.

In this amount, television and radio rights for one broadcast plus one rerun only in territories in and outside Europe are included as well as one broadcast and three reruns in the United States on the NET and NPR networks (non profitable organization). Should a broadcast be done by a commercial television network in the United States, special arrangements would have to be considered between the artist and/or group and Montreux. Video cassette rights for clubs and stores promotion are also included.

5. Should a second show be set on the same day, an additional fee of 50% (fifty percent) of the fee mentioned under article 4 would be paid to the artist and/or group.

6. The Montreux International Jazz Festival will provide first class hotel accommodation (bed and continental breakfast) for the artist and/or musicians plus one manager for one night. All extras, drinks, meals, laundry, telephones, room service, etc. are to be paid separately by the artist and/or group and manager.

7. The Montreux International Jazz Festival will provide one free ticket for each musician and their manager for the evening when the group is playing as well as for the concerts on other nights of the Festival. Tickets have to be claimed each day before the beginning of the concert at the musicians' office. Free admission will also be granted to the wives of musicians.

8. The Montreux International Jazz Festival will provide a first class PA and stage monitoring at no charge as well as a backline equipment to the artist and/or group, upon advanced written request to the Montreux International Jazz Festival. The Montreux International Jazz Festival can't be held responsible for the equipment belonging to the artist and/or group.

9. The Montreux International Jazz Festival will provide local transportation from Geneva airport to Montreux and from Montreux to Geneva airport.

10. The Montreux International Jazz Festival will provide soft drinks, beer and fresh fruit in the dressing rooms for the use of the artist and/or group.

Stevie Ray Vaughan + Double Trouble
(name of the artist and/or group)
Represented by : Chesley Millikin
Date : 6/17/1982

Montreux International Jazz Festival
Represented by : Claude Nobs
Date : May 12, 1982

Stevie's copy of the Montreux contract. COLLECTION OF CRAIG HOPKINS

Stevie and Double Trouble are the first unsigned band to play the Montreux Jazz Festival. A few in the crowd boo the loud band. STEVIE: "It wasn't the whole crowd. It was just a few people sitting right up front. The room there was built for acoustic jazz. When five or six people boo, wow. It sounds like the whole world hates you. They thought we were too loud, but shoot, I had four army blankets folded over my amp, and the volume level was on 2. I'm used to playin' on 10!"[56]

DON OPPERMAN: "The backline was all rented. Stevie had two [Fender] Twins, and they were so loud that everybody was freakin' out. I tipped them back to try to diffuse them somehow – that didn't work. Then I got towels and put over the front of the amps, covering up the entire amp, which helped a little bit. But they were still pretty loud because the sound was going out the back too.

"The way I remember it, the 'ooos' and the 'boos' were mixed together, but Stevie was pretty disappointed. Stevie [had] just handed me his guitar and walked off stage, and I'm like, 'Are you coming back?' There was a doorway back there; the audience couldn't see the guys, but I could. He went back to the dressing room with his head in his hands. I went back there finally, and that was the end of the show.

"Claude [Nobs, the festival producer] came back and just raved and kind of picked up his spirits. Claude just went ape over it. [Stevie] and Lenny, and maybe [engineer] Richard Mullen, went up to

Claude's house, this castle or whatever he lives in – chateau – and played the tapes back from that night's performance and remixed them. Stevie comes back: 'Man, you gotta hear the tapes; the video looks great!'"

"He seemed to come out of nowhere, a Zorro-type figure in a riverboat gambler's hat, roaring into the '82 Montreux festival with a '59 Stratocaster at his hip and two flame-throwing sidekicks he called Double Trouble. He had no album, no record contract, no name, but he reduced the stage to a pile of smoking cinders and, afterward, everyone wanted to know who he was. 'Stevie Ray Vaughan,' he twanged."[57]

David Bowie saw the performance and later met Stevie and the band in the artists' bar.

CHRIS: "He comes back and we spend hours with him talking. He wants to know all about us, the band, Stevie, where we come from, how long we've been together – the whole story."[3]

John Paul Hammond, Tommy, Chris, David Bowie. © DON E. OPPERMAN, JR.

On stage in Montreux. © DON E. OPPERMAN, JR.

DON OPPERMAN: "He was very reserved, very soft spoken. He came in and introduced himself. Chesley was like, 'David's here. Let's get some champagne,' turning it into a big deal. But [Bowie] was very cool. John Hammond, Jr. was there [This reference is to blues singer and guitarist John Paul Hammond, son of the legendary producer John Henry Hammond II; the son is widely, but mistakenly, referred to throughout the industry as John Hammond, Jr.] and Stevie was doing an interview with Swiss radio, and that was a big plug for him. So with all that stuff, wheels were turning pretty quickly. After that show, they had no dates booked in Europe, and all of a sudden they were wanted by club after club after club."

The show in Montreux was to lead to more than just European club bookings. Later in the year, David Bowie would ask Stevie to add guitar work to his *Let's Dance* album and to join his "Serious Moonlight" tour; and John Paul Hammond, who had recorded part of the show, would give a copy of the tape to his father, producer John Hammond. Chesley, knowing that the senior Hammond was responsible for advancing the careers of Charlie Christian, T-Bone Walker, Billie Holliday, Bob Dylan and Bruce Springsteen (among others), would also arrange for him to receive a copy of "Tin Pan Alley" (from

On stage in Montreux. © DON E. OPPERMAN, JR.

the April 1, 1980, Steamboat show) that had been in regular rotation on KLBJ radio in Austin.

"Some people maintain Hammond was the first person to hear Gabriel play. Others simply say he made the first recordings of sticks being pounded together in some bubbling swamp. Either way, when Hammond's name is used in music circles, it is usually with awe, reverence and in breathless tones."[20]

HAMMOND recalled hearing Stevie on the tape his son made: "I first heard Stevie on a tape that had my son playing on it, along with Stevie Ray. Now, I like my son, but Stevie knocked me out."[20]

Knocking out John Hammond with the Montreux tape would eventually lead to a recording contract for Stevie and Double Trouble, and in 1984, they would win a Grammy for their performance of "Texas Flood" at the Montreux festival – despite the boos.

© MTO SWITZERLAND

July 18: Montreux Jazz Festival, Montreux, Switzerland, after hours in the Montreux Casino basement artists' bar

---

CHRIS LAYTON: "The next night we were in Montreux with nothing to do. We could go to the festival. The manager said, 'Well look, I can book y'all in the musicians' lounge, you know, downstairs. Y'all want to go down there and play? There's no money in it, but I thought maybe you might like to play.' Yeah, sure! You know, we were jazzed! So that's when we did that, and it was after Jackson's show that night he came down with the whole band and we all got up and jammed until after daybreak. That might have been the longest I ever played in one sitting."[37]

Pass for the artists' bar.
COLLECTION OF CRAIG HOPKINS

hard for me to even chord. They played 'til the wee hours. Some of Jackson's songs, like 'Mercury Blues,' because he had his band there – Danny Kortchmar, Bob Glaub ..."

STEVIE on playing with Browne's bandmates: "We took one twenty-minute break and played from about 1:15 'til about 8:30 in the morning. We all just had a blast and went nuts. Definitely closed the place down!"[58]

Don Opperman was friends with Jackson Browne's house manager and told him he needed to check Stevie out in the artists' bar after Jackson's set at the festival that night. DON: "One by one the band shows up; finally Jackson's down there watching this guy. 'Where did this guy come from? What's his name?' and all these questions. He didn't believe 'Stevie Ray Vaughan,' so I got Stevie's driver's license and showed it to him. So then it was like, 'I want to play – I want to get up there.' Stevie always tuned down a half step, so Jackson couldn't play down a half step (on the piano). I tuned the guitars up a half step, wondering how Stevie's going to bend the notes. Jackson could hardly play the thing [laughs]. It already had big strings on it, and then tuned up it was

Lenny and Stevie in the airport. © DON E. OPPERMAN, JR.

JACKSON BROWNE: "Montreux is really famous and kind of a high-water mark for musicians – you want to play Montreux. Historically, so many great people have played Montreux, and it was such a bastion of music lovers."

Jackson had known Chesley for a long time. "Chesley was always saying, 'You gotta hear this guy, you gotta hear that guy.' I was doing an interview in a restaurant upstairs from the bar,

Arrival in Europe. Note Stevie's right hand. © DON E. OPPERMAN, JR.

Chris admiring the Swiss landscape. © DON E. OPPERMAN, JR.

and fresh and yet it was still blues, a familiar form completely rethought.

"I didn't play. I just sang some blues lyrics. I may have sung a verse about Stevie [*laughs*]. I just sat in on one song." Donnie Opperman's photos show Jackson at least holding Number One. "I'm pretty sure I didn't play it [*laughs*]. I became aware that he tuned down and used heavy strings."

One of Jackson's band members, guitarist Rick Vito, didn't come down to play at the bar. At the Dallas Guitar Show in 2004, Rick told the author that Bob Glaub had come up to his room and said, "You've got to come down and check out this guitar player in the artists' bar." Rick asked who he was, and Bob said, "He's a blues player – Jimmie Vaughan's little brother." Rick stated that he wasn't interested in going down to play with some Texas blues player's little brother, a decision he later regretted!

Among the others who jammed in the artists' bar with Stevie were bass player Larry Graham (Sly and the Family Stone) and drummer Willie Hayes. The planned jam during Larry's set at

and the guys in my band came upstairs with this wild look in their eyes, saying, 'You've *got* to hear this guy.' We were finished [with our show] and everybody was out loose running around. I finished the interview and went to see him, and it was amazing. "There were probably about fifty people in this room listening to him play. The sheer power and incredible prowess of his playing was just one of those things where you're not expecting that, you know? You think you know blues [*laughs*] and you think you know guitar playing, and here's somebody who's taken it apart and rebuilt it in this ultra-hyper version. It seemed totally new

Richard Mullen driving, Donnie Opperman riding shotgun.
COURTESY DON E. OPPERMAN, JR.

Stevie and Jackson Browne. © DON E. OPPERMAN, JR.

Jackson Browne and his band watching Stevie in the artists' bar after hours in Montreux. © DON E. OPPERMAN, JR.

while we had to have guards because it was a funky part of town. We had Studer machines and a Neotech board – it was kind of rudimentary stuff but the space was incredible. It was huge – a half a block long. It gave amazing ambiance for close micing the drums and having room mics up, and we had worked that out pretty well. So they walked into a pretty cool recording setup. It wasn't a commercial studio – I wouldn't have charged him, and I don't think [the engineer] charged him anything. Maybe I paid him, I don't know.

The band at Dingwall's, London, England. © DON E. OPPERMAN, JR.

the festival was cancelled after Stevie's poor reception during his own set.

Chris recalls Jackson offering the use of his studio to Double Trouble: "He goes, 'I have a studio in Los Angeles. I keep it for my pre-production work and have loaned it out to a number of people for special projects. If you guys are ever in Los Angeles and you want to use it, just let me know in advance and it's yours.'"

JACKSON: "I just said, 'If you want some place to record, come to L.A. and use my studio – I don't use it all the time. He showed up without me knowing he was coming just then. They just got in their car with a U-Haul and drove here from Texas. They called me when they got here: 'We're here!' [*Laughs*] It happened to be the day before Thanksgiving vacation began. I didn't know he was coming, and I had plans. It was perfect timing except that we hadn't made any arrangements for the studio to be operating.

"The studio was on the fifth floor of this building downtown on Broadway, and we could lock it up pretty good, but it took having a presence there to run it. For a

"First I asked Greg Ladanyi if he wanted to record them, but he had Thanksgiving plans too. James Geddes, the second engineer (a great engineer, by the way), stepped up and said, 'I'll do it. I'm not doing anything; I'll be glad to do it.' I think I'd have come back around if I'd realized how great this was going to be [*laughs*].

"As great as I thought his playing was, I think I was of the mind that he had to figure out some way of making this music more accessible, you know? Blues had not been sort of 'resurrected' and Stevie Ray did that. Blues was a long-standing musical pillar in most musicians' life, but it was not something that was going to make any bread. You played blues and you listened to blues, but you didn't form a blues band and go gigging. He sort of resurrected the really deep blues and roots music and took it to the altar and made it a serious thing.

"I've gotta say that I never would have dreamed that his coming and recording the songs that he did would have the effect that it did. *Texas Flood* did really well, and it was one of those really cool surprises. Had I started to try to bend his ear about what to change, it would have been a waste of time because I had no idea. I can't lay any claims to knowing what was about

© *TEXAS JAZZ*

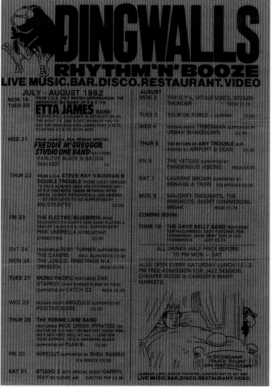

COLLECTION OF CRAIG HOPKINS

to happen. Within a year or two he was playing places like the Universal Amphitheater, and blues was suddenly a force in a lot of people's lives.

"I remember my girlfriend's brother being just a freak for him. Stevie assumed a place of authority that was a good thing for music. [He wasn't] just the guy who played the hot licks on the David Bowie record. To have become the powerhouse and introduced the blues to a whole new generation, that was quite a stunning development."

The two nights in Montreux became the single most important gigs in Stevie's career. Contacts he made those nights served him well indeed. He accepted Bowie's invitation to add guitar to *Let's Dance,* the most popular album of the Chameleon of Pop's career. But he really made headlines when he turned down the opportunity to join Bowie's band for the 1983 world tour. As a result of *not* going on that tour, Stevie received the most publicity of his career.

Another invitation he accepted was Jackson Browne's offer of free studio time, which, as indicated above, led to the recording of what would become the band's first album, *Texas Flood.*

Rounding out the Montreux hat trick were the doors that opened when John Paul Hammond gave his father a tape of the night's performances. When a compilation album featuring one of Stevie's songs was released and won a Grammy, that marked another first in his career. Years later, the Montreux performance would be posthumously released on DVD and CD.

Montreux marked the first time that Stevie and the band performed outside North America. Exposure in Europe, offers for studio work and a world tour with a rock icon, a boatload of publicity, free studio time the band could not otherwise have afforded, an entree to producer John Hammond, a Grammy award, and recordings for a CD and DVD ... not bad for Stevie's first trip to Europe. Stevie's talent, Chesley's connections and fortuitous encounter with Jerry Wexler had combined to knock Stevie's career out of Texas bars and onto the world stage in almost a single movement.

Only three months previously, Lou Ann had been taunting Stevie with her *Rolling Stone* review. Now her record company's executive was responsible for the Montreux trip. It was Stevie's turn to enjoy international recognition far beyond that of a *Rolling Stone* album review.

July (20?): Basel, Switzerland with a German blues band. Attorney Frank Cooksey served as road manager for the rest of the trip, while Chesley went to visit relatives in Ireland.

DON OPPERMAN: "[Stevie] had incredible strength in his hands. We did this little club, that one in Basel, Switzerland, and that day during sound check, he was bending the strings and actually broke the glue joint loose at the nut! So I had to figure out how to glue it back with whatever I could find in Europe – I think it was epoxy [*laughs*], not what I should have used, but I don't think it came off again!"

July 22: Dingwall's, London, England

July 23: The band returns from Europe.

July 29: Nick's Uptown, Dallas, TX

July 30: Pappy's, San Antonio, TX

July 31: Pappy's, San Antonio, TX

📖 **August:** *Texas Jazz,* "Little STEVIE: Coming Of Age," Mike H. Price: "Stevie Ray Vaughan, whose own press release hoopla undersells him, has long been acknowledged in the provinces as the nexus of blues guitar, a joiner of heritage with new directions, with a style which bears both academic and hedonistic scrutiny. Vaughan has an eleven year history of giving a thousand percent, taxing his gifts in public and private as tho [sic] his guitar collection were a Nautilus gym for the forearms."

August 5: Palmer Drug Abuse Program benefit, (Dallas?) TX

At Antone's, Austin, TX. © DON E. OPPERMAN, JR.

August 6: Club Foot, Austin, TX

August 7: Touch of Texas, Huntsville, TX

August 9: Continental Club, Austin, TX

August 20: Fitzgerald's, Houston, TX, with Alan Haynes

August 21: Fitzgerald's, Houston, TX, with Alan Haynes

ALAN HAYNES, one of Texas' best guitarists: "It was a magical thing when he came out on stage. There was a vibe: no matter what was happening in the room, it just went up another level. Before they would walk out, you would hear Stevie Wonder's 'Fingertips.' Then on the first song, Stevie would be smoking in a way that ... very few people can come out and have it *right there* [indicates a high level] – like no one I've ever seen ... besides Johnny Winter. The first song Stevie would play was like the last song that the most popular bands would be playing. That's how much energy it had.

Austin and different places. Apparently he liked my taste in shirts."

At Antone's, Austin, TX. © DON E. OPPERMAN, JR.

The band with Stevie's friend and fellow guitar slinger Alan Haynes © DON E. OPPERMAN, JR.

"He left me a phone message. It's real cool because he made up a song about me. I had a Lightnin' Hopkins-style blues recording on my answering machine. He called twice, and the first time he's in a hotel and you can tell he didn't have anything prepared, but my recording obviously inspired him, and at the end he says, 'Caught me by surprise, motherf....' Then he calls back about five minutes later, and you can tell he's made up some lyrics and tuned up the guitar.

"He starts singing 'The Ace of Threads,' because he wanted me to take him clothes shopping. We'd been shopping together in

STEVIE RAY VAUGHAN
Saturday, September 11
BLOSSOM'S
DOWNSTAIRS

COURTESY BYRON BARR

August 27: Steamboat 1874, Austin, TX

August 28: Fiesta Gardens, San Antonio, TX

📖 **Autumn:** *Living Blues,* Austin Blues Fest review by Hugh Drescher mentions Double Trouble

📖 **September:** *Guitare,* (France) "SRV: Le Nouveau Jimi Hendrix," Alain Dister

September 2: Nick's Uptown, Dallas, TX, with The Juke Jumpers

September 3: Yellow Rose, Austin, TX

September 4: private party; Rick's, San Antonio, TX

September 5: Contract with Chesley technically expires, but see November 10.

September 8: Continental Club, Austin, TX

September 10: Stephen F. Austin Union, Nacogdoches, TX

September 11: Blossom's Downstairs, Fort Worth, TX

© GARY OLLIVER

© GARY OLLIVER

© GARY OLLIVER

September 16: Blossom's Downstairs, Fort Worth, TX

September 17: Sam's Truck Stop, Arlington, TX

September 18: Sam's Truck Stop, Arlington, TX

September 20: Soap Creek Saloon, Austin, TX, benefit for Louis Wheeler (security for SRV, Fabulous Thunderbirds, and the Armadillo)

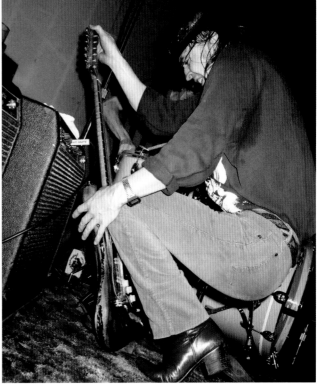

At Sam's Truck Stop, Arlington, TX. © DON E. OPPERMAN, JR.

September 22: Nick's Uptown, Dallas, TX, opening for The Fabulous Thunderbirds

September 23: Nick's Uptown, Dallas, TX, opening for The Fabulous Thunderbirds. "[M]erging the considerable fruits of their individual experiences,... fine sets by each brother's band were capped by a blazing brotherly jam."[58]

At Sam's Truck Stop, Arlington, TX. © DON E. OPPERMAN, JR.

📖 **September 23:** *Dallas Morning News*, "Vaughn [sic] brothers dazzle Nick's Uptown crowd," Nancy Bishop: "It could have been a battle between two of the best rhythm and blues guitarists: Jimmy Vaughn [sic] with The Fabulous Thunderbirds and his brother, Stevie Ray Vaughn [sic], leader of Double Trouble. Instead, they were above such a duel. By the time they blasted the capacity crowd with some of the tastiest guitar playing imaginable, the emphasis was on the music rather than some supposed competition. ... [Stevie] shot out on stage like a restless rodeo bull, restless to dazzle listeners on the first number. Not long after that, he was showing off his favorite stunts: playing guitar behind his back and neck."

September 24: Fat Dawg's, Lubbock, TX

September 25: Fat Dawg's, Lubbock TX

September 26: Amarillo, TX (cancelled)

© BYRON BARR

The Vaughan brothers. © BYRON BARR

At Nick's Uptown, Dallas. © BYRON BARR

At Nick's Uptown, Dallas. © BYRON BARR

San Antonio, TX.
© TONY RODRIGUEZ

© MUSIC CONNECTION

September 29: Fitzgerald's, Houston, TX

▣ September 30: Fitzgerald's, Houston, TX
- instrumental
- instrumental
- Tell Me
- The Things (That) I Used To Do
- Look At Little Sister
- Give Me Back My Wig
- Love Struck Baby
- The Sky Is Crying
- Voodoo Chile (Slight Return)
- Empty Arms
- Wham
- Little Wing
- Third Stone From the Sun
- Drivin' South
- Lenny

📖 October: *Music Connection* (Houston), "SRV," Jo Rae DiMenno

📖 October: *Buddy*, SRV in concert calendar with two small photos with two concert listings

October 1: Antone's, Austin, TX. The band's following in Texas is now strong enough to command $2000 vs. 90% of the door. Out-of-town gigs are still averaging $600-800, except for Lubbock which is on par with Austin.

October 2: Antone's, Austin, TX

"Vaughan pulled out all the stops in sets that ranged from Howlin' Wolf to the obligatory Hendrix numbers. The usual moves on the dance floor took a detour Saturday as Stevie Ray coaxed the audience into a trance state while making love to the Marshall amps with his battered old Fender Stratocaster. After 2 a.m. Vaughan marked his 28th birthday by playing with bassist Roscoe Beck, the audience camped at their feet. Then Layton [sic] came back on and it was into an extended version of 'Third Stone From The Sun' which finally ended near 3 a.m. with Vaughan bending his Stratocaster into paroxysms of feedback. ....

"Stevie Ray climaxed the night with a session that went on until 3:30, with Kim Wilson of the T-Birds standing in on 'Tears Falling Like Rain' and Cobras vocalist Medlow Williams working out on 'Red House.'[59]

© DANNY GARRETT

October 3: Soap Creek Saloon, Austin, TX, second benefit for Louis Wheeler (security for SRV, Fabulous Thunderbirds, and the Armadillo); Stevie's twenty-eighth birthday

October 8: Opera House, Austin, TX, opening for Johnny Winter

October 9: Touch of Texas, Huntsville, TX

October 13: Continental Club, Austin, TX

October 15: Crossroads, Nacogdoches, TX

© DANNY GARRETT

October 16: Crossroads, Nacogdoches, TX

October 17: Antone's, Austin, TX, Cobras Reunion

October 18: Coliseum, Austin, TX, opening for George Thorogood

📼**October 19:** Cullen Auditorium, University of Houston, Houston, TX, opening for George Thorogood
- – Testify
- – So Excited
- – The Things (That) I Used To Do
- – Pride and Joy
- – Love Struck Baby
- – Voodoo Chile (Slight Return)
- – Little Wing
- – Third Stone From the Sun
- – Lenny

October 21: Ritz, Corpus Christi, TX, opening for George Thorogood

October 22: Blossom's Downstairs, Fort Worth, TX

October 23: Austin Opera House, Austin, TX, with the T-Birds

October 29: Fitzgerald's, Houston, TX

📖**October 29:** *Austin Chronicle*, review of Antone's birthday shows, by Greg Stevens

October 30: Fitzgerald's, Houston, TX

At Antone's, Austin, TX. © DON E. OPPERMAN, JR.

Sometime during October, guitar tech/sound man Don Opperman left the crew. Among his recollections of his ten months with Stevie is the time "... he was helping a girl push her Volkswagon Beetle up a hill in Houston, slipped on the concrete (because he always wore those Italian boots and things), hit his tooth on the bumper and cracked it. He had to go to the emergency dentist. [Wait,] it gets better. So the next night during the show, he's doing the Hendrix thing, playing with his teeth, and it caught in the strings, and when he pulled back, it fired out of there like a gunshot! I actually went out and found it on the stage somewhere, and he stuck it back in. Oh, it was hilarious. That wasn't too smart. He turned around and looked at me like snaggletooth [*laughs*]."

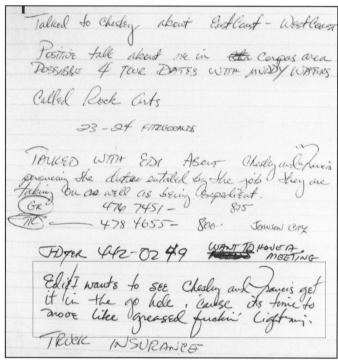

Interesting note regarding Stevie's desire for management to "get it in the go hole." COURTESY DOBBS/JACKSON

Don also recalls that Stevie broke a number of tremolo bars, particularly when he would lay the guitar on the floor and stand on it and flip it around by the bar. "He would do the whammy bar against the stage, the whammy bar breaks off and the guitar just goes off the stage into the audience and hits the floor [*laughs*]! He tortured that guitar."

JIMMIE VAUGHAN: "Nobody had ever seen anybody just abuse a guitar like that on purpose, you know, since Jimi Hendrix."[3]

DON continues: "When I first saw him, he didn't have a guitar tech. He would put extra strings, like the [high] E and B, through the block, and then tape them to the top of the guitar. He could put a string on fast. He had this little [trick] where he could take the string, make a little bend in it and then goes [indicates a snapping or pulling motion with his hands] and it would break in two. He'd stick it in there and wrap it, and tune it while he's talking.

Stevie's band meeting notes regarding possible players and other personnel. He obviously had an eye on the future. This document is circa 1982, and already indicated Reese Wynans as a potential contributor to the band, as well as Denny Freeman, Derek O'Brien and Doyle Bramhall.
COURTESY DOBBS/JACKSON

"One day he calls me up, 'Donnie, gotta come over here and hear this tone.' So I'm thinking he's come up with something really cool. I run over there and he's got guitars and stuff all over the house and amps. He's got two wah-wahs plugged into each other. They're both on, but one's at one tone, and the other at another tone, and it had this really kind of funky, hollow, out-of-phase sound. He's like, 'Man, isn't that cool?' And I'm like, 'Whaaaaat??' I didn't get it [*laughs*]. He would go crazy, alone, you know. By himself, he'd have all the guitars out, just goofing off.

"One time we were in … maybe Lubbock; we found this Vox fuzz-wah at a pawn shop. So I get it, and it's stereo. So Stevie goes, 'Wow, this will be cool. We'll put the Vibroverbs … separate them like stereo and plug the wah-wah in.' Well, what it did was [*laughs*], you push down and the sound would come from over there, and then back off and it would come from [the other amp] over there. It was chaos – it wasn't working! After the first set, we put them back together. Some [of Stevie's ideas] worked, some didn't. Basically, it was the Tube Screamer, the wah-wah and the selector, which just sent the guitar signal straight to the amp and bypassed all the pedals." Don built the first pedal board for Stevie. Previously, Cutter would run out on stage whenever he needed the wah-wah and plug it in.

Asked about his lasting recollections of Stevie, Don replied, "I feel like I was very lucky and blessed to be around a talented person. And at the time nobody really knew – they knew he was special, but I don't think they knew how far it was going to go. Stevie had a heart of gold. He would have given you his last dollar and helped you out in any way he could."

📖**November:** *Buddy*, "Sibling Revelry: Brother Can You Spare Some Blues?" Ray Brooks, SRV/JLV

November 1: Agora Ballroom, Dallas, TX

November 5: Antone's, Austin, TX, with Hubert Sumlin

November 6: Antone's, Austin, TX, with Hubert Sumlin

November 8: Stubbs' Bar-B-Q, Lubbock, TX

November 9: Club West, Santa Fe, NM

November 10: Club West, Santa Fe, NM

Chesley's management contract had expired on September 5, two months earlier, but he "renewed" the contract on November 10 through September 5, 1983. As indicated in later correspondence regarding a contract dispute, it was noted that Chesley was not represented by an attorney. That may explain why Chesley let the contract expire in September. But now, with Stevie heading into the studio the next day to begin recording, Chesley has Stevie sign a "renewal" of the contract through September 5, 1983.

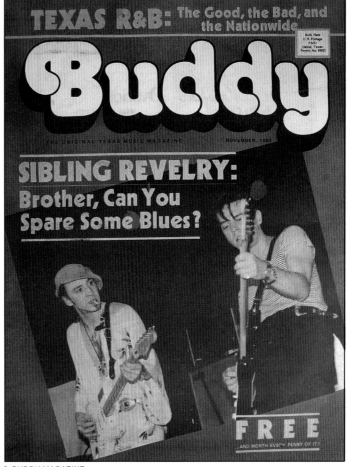

© BUDDY MAGAZINE

© BRIAN CURLEY

November 19: Keystone, Palo Alto, CA, with John Lee Hooker and Elvin Bishop

November 20: Keystone, Berkeley, CA, with John Lee Hooker and Elvin Bishop

November 21: The Stone, San Francisco, CA, with Robby Krieger of The Doors

November 23-25: The band records what would become *Texas Flood* in Jackson Browne's Downtown Studio in Los Angeles. The studio was only available for three days, given that the band had not provided much advance notice they were coming.

CHRIS: "We got there and the studio was also like a production house where you had a bunch of technical people that always were fixing gear and stuff – cable, amps, all kinds of stuff. We show up and they're like, 'Uh, yeah ... well, I guess.' There was kind of this air of like, 'Well, yeah, okay. The room's over there.'

"It's kind of like a warehouse – a few floors up was an open warehouse [with] a little room like a big closet where they had a big console and tape machine. They said, 'You have tape?' We said no. They said, 'Well, we have some used tape.' I think it was

the tapes that he did the *Lawyers in Love* record, pre-production. So we used that and we recorded *Texas Flood* on this used tape.

"We said we've got our [engineer] here – Richard Mullen. They said, 'Well, Greg [Ladanyi] does the work here.' They said he wanted to start the thing off because he ran the operation there. So we did that for a while. I don't even know if he really wanted to be there, because then he decided to leave. Richard stepped in and, in short order the next couple of days, we just played through this stuff just as if we were doing a live show – only we were in a warehouse.

"It was pretty much that simple. We didn't know what we were gonna do with it. There wasn't a record deal at that time."[3]

Stevie's manager, Chesley Millikin, sent Browne a two-year-old horse from his stable at Manor Downs as thanks for Jackson's kindness. As of early 2008, Jackson reported that he still has the horse. "I had visited Chesley at Manor Downs, and he used to go out with my sister. He used to wear a top hat and run the Love-Ins in L.A. – one of those great counter-culture things. Now he was one of these Irish equestrian gentlemen running a stable in Austin [*laughs*]. I hadn't paid that much attention when he said he was managing a band, because he was always involved in bands. He had me play a club he opened in Oxford or Cambridge called the Magic Mushroom."

During the sessions at Downtown Studios, Stevie broke a string on "Testify," and rather than start over, the engineer backed up the tape, let it roll, and the whole band "punched in" right at the moment of the string break and completed the song – a difficult

Recording engineer Richard Mullen. © DON E. OPPERMAN, JR.

thing for one person to do, much less the whole band. They got it fixed on the first try. The fix was so seamless that only those in the studio knew the track was stopped and restarted.

STEVIE: "We set up like we do on stage, without headphones or anything, and I did scratch vocals – we redid them later. We did eight songs one day, two the other, redid the vocals, mixed it in two days. We did master it twice, 'cause we didn't like the sound the first time, or it would have been done in seven days. We didn't do any overdubs at all, except for when I broke a string,

© WATT CASEY, JR.

and then the whole band punched in." When asked about the number of takes per song, Stevie responded with a casual, "One."[60]

RICHARD MULLEN, engineer: "Stevie was a real performer [in the studio] in the sense that he didn't really think too much about the technical things. If he was into it, you'd see him do his little dance steps all over the studio, just like he was playing for 10,000 people.

"My first record with Stevie, *Texas Flood*, only took us two hours to record. It was basically him playing his live set two times straight through. They went through about twelve songs, took a break, and a half-hour later did the whole set again."[61]

JACKSON BROWNE: "When Stevie came to L.A., he started playing this Dumble amp that we had laying around, that we all called the Mother Dumble because it was kind of like the first one Howard Dumble built. I have since sold that to try to buy a tape machine years ago, but it was an amp he continued to borrow when he would come to L.A. He also played this Fender Leslie, and he would call up and ask if he could borrow those for a night when he was playing L.A."

The vocals were recorded a few weeks later at Riverside Studios in Austin. Final mixes were done by Lincoln Clapp at Media Sound in New York.

CHRIS LAYTON: "*Guitar World*" did a cover story on the making of *Texas Flood*. [They wanted to interview me] and I said, 'Okay. But it seems like you're looking for a *Sgt. Pepper* here, and it really wasn't.' It got down to, 'Well, do you remember what kind of mic y'all used? Tell us about all this interesting and ground-breaking stuff.' I said, 'We were just a bunch of guys sitting up in a warehouse running through their show a couple of times, you know?' But now, they have to have a thirty-page story on the process and the making of, and the mystique revealed. [*Derisive chuckle*] Go down to Rome Inn any night and hear the same thing. I'm not trying to discount it, but some of these things are really simple and innocent."

November 26: Blue Lagoon, Marina del Rey, CA

November 27: Cathey de Grande, Los Angeles, CA

December 3: Touch of Texas, Huntsville, TX

December 4: Touch of Texas, Huntsville, TX

December 9: The Cellar, Midland, TX

December 10: Fat Dawg's, Lubbock, TX

December 11: Fat Dawg's, Lubbock, TX

December 12: Big Spring Prison, Big Spring, TX

December 15: Continental Club, Austin, TX

December 16: (Golden Nugget?), Baytown, TX

December 17: Fitzgerald's, Houston, TX

December 18: Fitzgerald's, Houston, TX (* with Johnny Copeland and horns)

- Testify
- So Excited
- Dirty Pool
- Voodoo Chile (Slight Return)
- Little Wing
- Third Stone From the Sun
- Hideaway *
- slow blues instrumental *
- instrumental *

December: Stevie adds guitar work at Austin's Riverside Studios to Vince Bell's "I Don't Wanna Hear It."

Bell is severely injured by a drunk driver on the way home from the studio on December 21, and the album is not finished or released. Miraculously, Bell recovered from near death and massive injuries to record again twelve years later.

VINCE BELL: "In 1982, among the flotilla of guitar wizards in Austin, there were two clearly virtuoso players vying nightly for bragging rights to the live music capital of Texas. One played a Les, one played a Strat. One was precise, considered, and

The one that got away. The yellow guitar was later stolen and never recovered. © BYRON BARR

powerful in his rock: Eric Johnson. The other was Stevie Ray Vaughan, a "whatever it takes" sort of fellow, with big hands and a raw talent for the guitar that had ruled the popular music world since Jimi Hendrix. In those breathless Sixth Street days, it was hard to think of one without thinking of the other.

"Whereas Eric was cool, studied, and methodical in his soaring music, Stevie's genius could raise the hairs on the back of your neck with nothing but a piece of wood and steel. It could've been blues like a sweet singing bird, or 4 by 4 rock 'n' roll like a sledgehammer. He was an inspired musician who wasn't afraid to sweat like a boxer.

"In December of that year Stevie agreed to play on a three-song demo of my songs that I was recording at Herschel Cunningham's Riverside Studio, with Richard Mullen, Tom Taylor, and Andy Salmon producing. The other players invited to the sessions from horns to keys read like a Who's Who of popular Texas music.

"Stevie came into the studio very late in the recordings, after much of the arrangement was done. The excellent sessions had wound down to a spirit of saving some of the best, perhaps, for last. He quietly strode in without fanfare, unpacking his guitar and a cord.

"He never even went into the large studio room littered with musical regalia. Instead, he sat down on a folding chair in the control room next to Richard at the vast recording board like an aircraft carrier of sliders, knobs, and blinking lights. He probably listened to the cut he was to play on only long enough to tune his guitar before he began a signature assault on my song with a slide.

"From note one he smiled understandingly like he had been playing the piece ... for years. And by the time he put his guitar

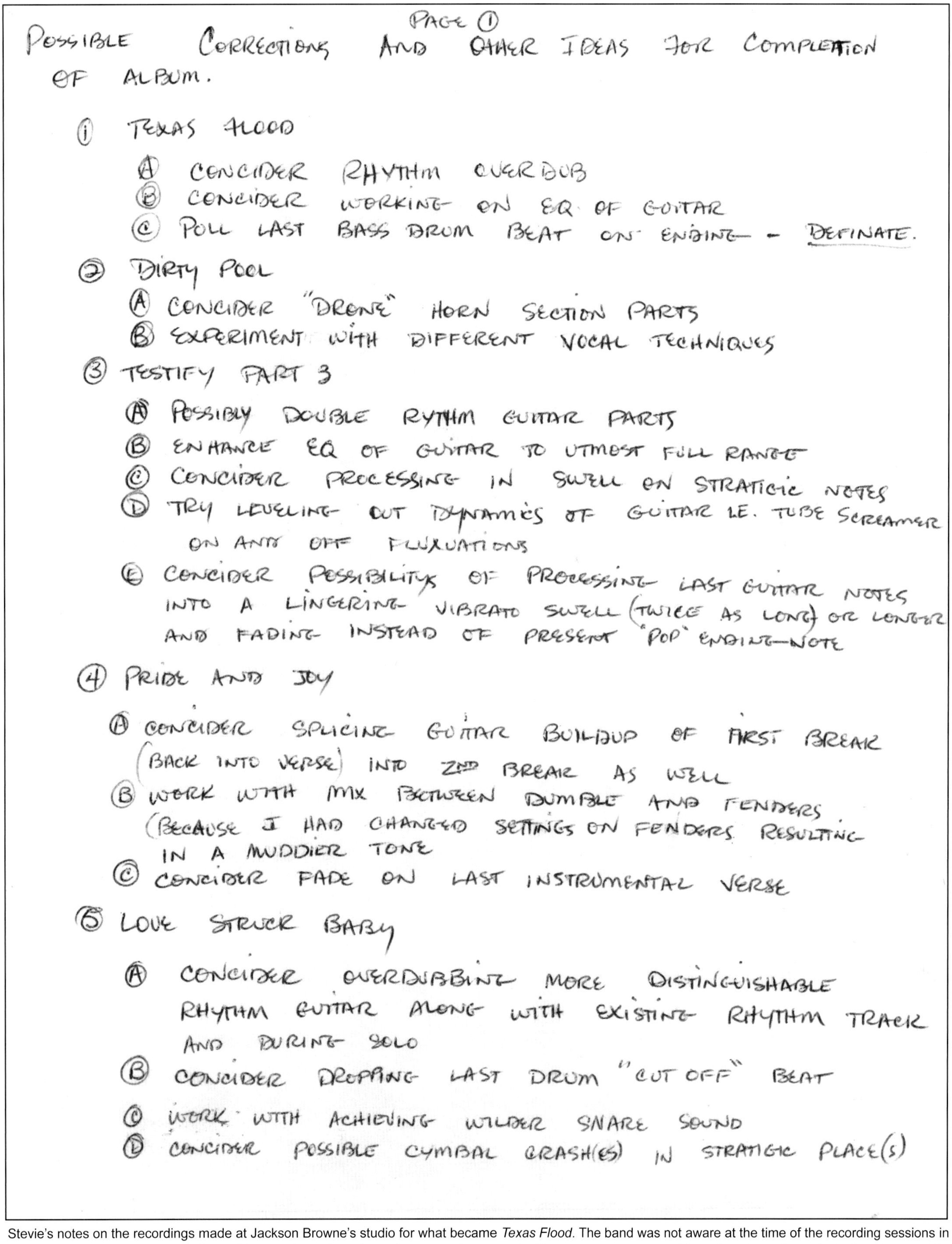

POSSIBLE CORRECTIONS AND OTHER IDEAS FOR COMPLETION OF ALBUM.

PAGE ①

① TEXAS FLOOD

    Ⓐ CONCIDER RHYTHM OVERDUB
    Ⓑ CONCIDER WORKING ON EQ OF GUITAR
    Ⓒ POLL LAST BASS DRUM BEAT ON ENDING — DEFINATE.

② DIRTY POOL

    Ⓐ CONCIDER "DRONE" HORN SECTION PARTS
    Ⓑ EXPERIMENT WITH DIFFERENT VOCAL TECHNIQUES

③ TESTIFY PART 3

    Ⓐ POSSIBLY DOUBLE RYTHM GUITAR PARTS
    Ⓑ ENHANCE EQ OF GUITAR TO UTMOST FULL RANGE
    Ⓒ CONCIDER PROCESSING IN SWELL ON STRATIGIC NOTES
    Ⓓ TRY LEVELING OUT DYNAMICS OF GUITAR I.E. TUBE SCREAMER ON AND OFF FLUXUATIONS
    Ⓔ CONCIDER POSSIBILITY OF PROCESSING LAST GUITAR NOTES INTO A LINGERING VIBRATO SWELL (TWICE AS LONG) OR LONGER AND FADING INSTEAD OF PRESENT "POP" ENDING—NOTE

④ PRIDE AND JOY

    Ⓐ CONCIDER SPLICING GUITAR BUILDUP OF FIRST BREAK (BACK INTO VERSE) INTO 2ND BREAK AS WELL
    Ⓑ WORK WITH MIX BETWEEN DUMBLE AND FENDERS (BECAUSE I HAD CHANGED SETTINGS ON FENDERS RESULTING IN A MUDDIER TONE
    Ⓒ CONCIDER FADE ON LAST INSTRUMENTAL VERSE

⑤ LOVE STRUCK BABY

    Ⓐ CONCIDER OVERDUBBING MORE DISTINGUISHABLE RHYTHM GUITAR ALONG WITH EXISTING RHYTHM TRACK AND DURING SOLO
    Ⓑ CONCIDER DROPPING LAST DRUM "CUT OFF" BEAT
    Ⓒ WORK WITH ACHIEVING WILDER SNARE SOUND
    Ⓓ CONCIDER POSSIBLE CYMBAL CRASH(ES) IN STRATIGIC PLACE(S)

Stevie's notes on the recordings made at Jackson Browne's studio for what became *Texas Flood*. The band was not aware at the time of the recording sessions in Los Angeles that they were actually making an album. As with previous recording opportunities, they were merely taking advantage of any studio time they could get in order to have demo tapes to circulate to club owners, promoters and anyone who might help them get closer to a record deal. As it turned out, the tapes were good enough to be the basis for a deal and the record itself. COURTESY DOBBS/JACKSON

Backstage at Nick's Uptown, Dallas. © DON E. OPPERMAN, JR.

a gentleman, Stevie Ray Vaughan was almost always an asshole. Kinder souls were quick to point out that it wasn't his fault: he had a rampaging drug problem, and drank a lot, too. Mostly, people just preferred to avoid him offstage.

"David Bowie tapped him for his 'Serious Moonlight' tour and at the last moment, Stevie Ray Asshole refused to go, in what was either a colossal blunder, or a carefully thought out bit of strategy."[2]

Ed didn't go into any detail, cite any specific examples (other than the Bowie incident) or quote anyone who agreed with his assessment, nor did he respond to

down, that cut was forever transformed. When he did his tracks that evening, plain and simple, he played notes beyond the fretboard that just don't come with that model Fender."

the author's request to elaborate on the reasons for his opinion. Certainly, few people like to speak ill of the departed, but this is the only harsh criticism of Stevie's personality in the press.

December 20: Waterworks, Waco, TX (cancelled)

December 21: Nick's Uptown, Dallas, TX

December 22: Nick's Uptown, Dallas, TX

December 31: Antone's, Austin, TX

date unknown: Fitzgerald's, Houston TX 19:51. Audience video.
- Voodoo Chile(Slight Return)
- Heart Fixer
- Pride and Joy

In seventeen years of meeting people who knew Stevie, there haven't been many who have had negative things to say about him – Ed Ward is the one exception among media critics. Ed wrote for the Austin daily newspaper, as well as the weekly, more hip paper, and was one of the founders of the South By Southwest music festival. He interviewed Stevie and Jimmie and wrote excellent articles about their careers.

ED: "Blues nerds complained about his alleged Hendrix fixation, and lots of people complained about his personality. Not to put too fine a point on it, where Jimmie was at worst taciturn and at best

INSTRUMENTALS	VOCALS
1 DON'T LOOSE YOUR COOL	TELL ME
2 HIDE AWAY	LOVE ME DARLIN
3 IN THE OPEN	LOVE STRUCK BABY
4 THIS MORNIN'	I'M LEAVEN' YOU
5 COLLIN'S SHUFFLE	I'M CRYIN'
6 STINGS SWING	SWEET THING
7 CHITLINS CON CARNEY	LOST YOUR GOOD THING
8 CHATEAU STRUT	WOKE UP THIS MORNIN
9 LITTLE WING	DIRTY POOL
10 DRIVIN SOUTH	TIN PAN ALLEY
11 ALBERTS ALLEY	SKY IS CRYIN'
12 FROSTY	TEXAS FLOOD
13 RHINO GATOR	CROSS CUT SAW
14 LIVIN SOUL	SHAKE FOR ME
15 BOILERMAKER	HOWLIN' FOR MY DARLIN
16 ELMORE'S THING	BE CAREFUL
17 TANYA	HUG AND SQUEEZE YOU
18 SHUFFLIN' BOARD	EMPTY ARMS
19 LENNY	GUITAR SLIM (HURRICANE)
20 BLUES FROM THE BOTTOM	MAUDIE
21 RUDE MOOD	ALL YOUR LOVE
	KEEP LOVIN ME BABY
	✓ MANIC DEPRESSION

Song list in Stevie's handwriting, circa 1982. COLLECTION OF CRAIG HOPKINS

Continuous String Cartridge for SRV Guitar

CARTRIDGE would be composed of
an outside casing of 2 (two) parts
for easy reloading. one being the
major part of the casing in a
shallow cylindrical shape with a
removable screw on top.
 The moveable parts would be 6 (six)
separate spring loaded wheels,
each encasing 2 to 3 sets of
average length guitar strings. exam. 2-3
x regular lengths of each string loaded
seperately to be used as needed. one
wheel containing 1st string (little E) one
wheel containing 2nd string (B string) etc.
wheel would lock into place at end
of spool of string, and would rewind
when string is placed into feeder
slot and a small button depressed
relaxing tension on spring. this would
be regulated by a fixed "brake pads" so that
the string is never lost in side cartridge
while reloading, or when string is broken.
To change string a lever will release string
from top of guitar body and string
would be pulled through body of guitar

Stevie's notes regarding a device to allow quick string changes. These notes, along with those regarding pickups formed in the shape of his initials, show that Stevie was always thinking about how he could improve and customize his guitars. COURTESY DOBBS/JACKSON

Band Personnel 1965–1990

The following chart is based on months of research and dozens of interviews. These are bands in which Stevie was considered a true member, even if only for a couple of weeks. Memories fade, so many dates are approximate.

Miscellaneous notes: Virtually nothing is known about **Epileptic Marshmallow**. Stevie mentioned the band in an interview, but no one could be found who remembers the band. Stevie didn't just "sit in" with **Texas Storm**. It didn't last long, but he was the bass player. **Cast of Thousands** was a real band, but it only existed, in this incarnation, for the purpose of trying to land a spot on a compilation album. It successfully met the goal and disbanded. The author is not aware of any public performances by Cast of Thousands when Stevie was in the band. Designations "I" "II" and "III" are not part of the band names but denote such a significant change in personnel that it could be considered a distinct band.

THE CHANTONES
summer 1965–1966

Stevie Vaughan	guitar
Jimmy Bowman	vocal, sax
Billy Gable	rhythm guitar - short term
Glenn Anderson	bass
Gerald Mason	drums
Phil Coaster	keyboards - short term

EPILEPTIC MARSHMALLOW
1966 or 1967

Stevie Vaughan	guitar
?	?

THE BROOKLYN UNDERGROUND
1967–1968

Steve Vaughan	guitar
Billy Metcalf	vocal
Paul Kessler	guitar
Randy Martin	bass
Bobby Ragan	drums

THE SOUTHERN DISTRIBUTOR
May 30, 1969 into 1970

Patrick McGuire	guitar, vocals
Steve Vaughan	guitar
Darryl Haynes	bass
Mike Steinbach	drums
Jim Cullum	"guest" guitarist

TEXAS STORM
January–February 1970

Jimmie Vaughan	guitar
Doyle Bramhall	vocals
Stevie Vaughan	bass
Bill Campbell	drums

LIBERATION
spring–summer 1970

Steve Vaughan	guitar
Mike Reames	vocals (short term, original)
Christian Plicque	vocals
Don Tanner	vocals (took Mike's place)
Steve Lowrey	keyboards
Scott Phares	bass (until summer)
Mike Day	drums
Jim Trimmier	sax
Scott Leftwich	trumpet
Wes Johnson	sax
Larry Chapman	trombone
Robert Penhall	bass (took Scott's place)

LINCOLN
late summer 1970

Steve Vaughan	guitar
Christian Plicque	vocals
Don Tanner	vocals
?	keyboards
?	bass
Gabriel Saucedo	drums (original)
Brad Smith	drums

CAST OF THOUSANDS
late summer 1970

Robert Forman	vocals, guitar
Jim Rigby	vocals, guitar
Stevie Vaughan	guitar
Stephen Tobolowsky	vocals
Mike McCullough	bass
Chris Lingwall	drums

PECOS
late 1970–early 1971

John Nixon	guitar
Don Tanner	vocals
Steve Vaughan	guitar
Lynn Fisher	bass
Joe Wilmore	drums

BLACKBIRD "I"
early 1971

Stevie Vaughan	guitar
Christian Plicque	vocals
Jimmy Bowman	saxophone
Bill ?	bass
?	drummer

DERYK JONES PARTY
summer–fall 1971

Ron Hellner	vocals
Adam Palma	guitar, vocals
Stevie Vaughan	guitar
Ken Brooks	keyboards
Eric Tagg	bass, vocals
Roddy Colonna	drums

BLACKBIRD "II"
summer 1971–fall 1972

Stevie Vaughan	guitar, some vocals
Christian Plicque	vocals
Kim Davis	guitar
Noel Deis	organ
David Frame	bass
Roddy Colonna	drums
John Hoff	drums

ORCHRIST
late 1971

Steve Lowrey	keyboards
Mike Harrison	vocals
Steve Vaughan	guitar (guest)
Mike Howell	bass
Jas Stephens	drums

BLACKBIRD "III"
fall 1972–December 1972

Stevie Vaughan	guitar, some vocals
Christian Plicque	vocals
Tommy Shannon	bass
Roddy Colonna	drums
Roy Cox	rhythm guitar (short term)

KRACKERJACK
December 1972–February 1973

Bruce Bowland	vocals
Stevie Vaughan	guitar
Robin Syler	guitar
Tommy Shannon	bass
Uncle John Turner	guitar, vocals

STUMP
March 1973

Stevie Vaughan	guitar
Jeff Clark	guitar
David Frame	bass
Tom Holden	drums

MARC BENNO AND THE NIGHTCRAWLERS
March–summer 1973

Marc Benno	vocals
Stevie Vaughan	guitar
Doyle Bramhall	vocals, drums
Billy Etheridge	keyboards
Tommy McClure	bass

THE NIGHTCRAWLERS "II"
summer 1973–?

Doyle Bramhall	vocals, drums
Stevie Vaughan	guitar
Ronnie Bramhall	keyboards
Drew Pennington	harmonica
Bruce Miller	bass
Jim Trimmier	sax (occasional)

THE NIGHTCRAWLERS "III"
1974

Doyle Bramhall	vocals, drums
Stevie Vaughan	guitar
Keith Ferguson	bass

DOUG SAHM
1974

Doug Sahm	vocals, guitar
Stevie Vaughan	guitar
Doyle Bramhall	drums
Johnny Perez	drums
Jack Barber?	bass

PAUL RAY AND THE COBRAS
March 1975–September 1977

Paul Ray	vocals
Denny Freeman	guitar
Stevie Vaughan	guitar
Alex Napier	bass
Rodney Craig	drums
Jim Trimmier	sax (April–October 1976)
Joe Sublett	sax (October 1976 on)

TRIPLE THREAT REVUE
September 1977–May 1978

Stevie Vaughan	guitar, vocals
Lou Ann Barton	vocals
W.C. Clark	vocals, bass
Fredde Walden	drums, vocals
Mike Kindred	keyboards, vocals
Joe Sublett	guest - sax

STEVIE RAY VAUGHAN AND DOUBLE TROUBLE
May 1978–August 1990

Stevie Ray Vaughan	guitar, vocals
Lou Ann Barton	vocals (1978–79)
Johnny Reno	sax (1978–79)
Jackie Newhouse	bass (1978–80)
Fredde Walden	drums (spring 1978)
Jack Moore	drums (summer 1978)
Chris Layton	drums (1978–1990)
Tommy Shannon	bass (1981–1990)
Reese Wynans	keyboards (1985–1990)

THE VAUGHAN BROTHERS
spring 1990 (studio only)

Stevie Ray Vaughan	guitar, vocals
Jimmie Vaughan	guitar, vocals
Al Berry	bass
Preston Hubbard	bass
Larry Aberman	drums
Doyle Bramhall	drums
Stan Harrison	sax
Steve Elson	sax
Richard Hilton	keyboards

Endnotes

The endnotes in this volume also apply to the companion volume, *His Final Years, 1983–1990*.

[1] Unless otherwise noted, all quotes in the book are from interviews conducted by the author:

Carlos Alomar, April 2007
Rick Alter, January 28, 2008
Geoff Appold, August 30, 2007
Byron Barr, May 7, 2007
Vince Bell, November 29, 2007 (via email)
Marc Benno, August 20, 2007
Lindi Bethel, July 18, 2007
David Betito, summer, 2007
Bruce Bowland, September 28, 2007
Doyle Bramhall, summer 1994; Nov. 2007
Christian Brooks, August 23, 2007
Jackson Browne, January 9, 2008
John Bryant, February 1, 2008
Bob Cady, September 8, 2007
Larry Chapman, December 28, 2007
Jack Chase, August 10, 2007
Jeff Clark, January 2, 2008
W.C. Clark, fall 1994
Roddy Colonna, August 5, 2007
Frank Cooksey, September 8, 2007
Leslie Crowder, December 17, 2007
Jim Cullum, September 16, 2007
Jim Dawson, date unknown; January 21, 2008
Mike Day, April 2007
Steve Dean, October 26, 2007
Noel Deis, July 14, 2007
Chistian dePlicque, spring 1994
Timothy Duckworth, August 23, 2007
Tony Dukes, November-December 2007
Dennis Dullea, October 30, 2007
James Elwell, August 8, 2007
Bill Etheridge, December 11, 2007
Robert Forman, April 2007
David Frame, June 16, 2007
Denny Freeman, November 26, 2007
Anson Funderburgh, January 1997
Manny Gammage, summer 1993
Joe Gracey, December 16, 2007 (via email)
Mary Beth Greenwood, September 6, 2007
Lt. John Hancock, *ca.* 1994

Randy Hansen, December 10, 2007
Mike Harrison, September 8, 2007
Stan Harrison, April 2007
Charlie Hatchett, October 26, 2007
Alan Haynes, October 9, 2007
Ron Hellner, September 13, 2007
Ralph Helmick, July 7, 1993
Ray Hennig, June 1998
Trey Hensley, October 23, 2007
Alex Hodges, October 22, 2007
John Hoff, August 2007
Tom Holden, January 2, 2008
Dan Jackson, Sept. 1997
Eric Johnson, October 28, 2007
Bill Jones, April 2007
Paul Kessler, September 6, 2007
Mike Kindred, July 2007
B.B. King, February 6, 1994
Smokin' Joe Kubek, January 1997
Janna Lapidus-Leblanc, October 23, 2007
Chris Layton, April 19, 1996; Nov. 17, 2007
Lois Loeffler, December 13, 2007
Steve Lowrey, September 8, 2007
Lonnie Mack, October 1995
Glenda Maples, June 27, 2007
Randy Martin, September 8, 2007
Gerald Mason, October 10, 2007
Christopher McGuire, September 17, 2007
Pat McGuire, September 9, 2007
Paul "Rocky" Miller, April 2007
James Moncrief, September 22, 2007
Jack Newhouse, August 3, 2007
Dick Nicholas, September 18, 2007
John Nixon, September 6, 2007
Don Opperman, May 10, 2007
Adam Palma, September 22, 2007
Scott Phares, April 2007
Mark Pollock, October 29, 2007
Smiley N, Pool, October 14, 2009
Joe Priesnitz, November 2, 2007
Bonnie Raitt, November 29, 2007
Paul and Diana Ray, May 21, 2007
Mike Reames, September 9, 2007
Redbeard, October 9, 2007
Johnny Reno, June 2007
Skip Rickert, June 17, 2007

Jim Rigby, April 2007

Carmine Rojas, October 7, 2007

Tommy Shannon, May 1995

Kenny Wayne Shepherd, Sept. 1996

Al Staehely, July 16, 2007

Mike Steele, September 18, 2007

Mike Steinbach, September 6, 2007

Jas Stephens, September 25, 2007

Lew Stokes, September 26, 2007

Jesse Sublett, December 10, 2007

Joe Sublett, September 17, 2007

Eric Tagg, September 22, 2007

Don Tanner, September 29, 2007

Jim Trimmier, August 2007

Stephen Tobolowsky, April 2007 (via email)

Gordon van Ekstrom, June 14, 2007

Martha Vaughan, November 18, 2007

Vicki Virnelson, September 26, 2007

Rick Vito, April 2004

Russell Whitaker, June 7, 2007

David Wilds, September 6, 2007

Melody Wilson, October 17, 2007

Steve Wilson, October 18, 2007

Johnny Winter, October 6, 2007

Reese Wynans, August 2, 2007

Angus Wynne, January 31, 2008

[2] *Musician*, May 1987, "Blues Brothers," Ed Ward

[3] Interviews by Dan Jackson, July 26-27, 1997: Doyle Bramhall, Jimmie Vaughan, Chris Layton, Tommy Shannon

[4] Interview by John Sebastian for *Rock Stars* radio

[5] *Musician*, June 1991, "SRV: Talking With The Master," Timothy White

[6] *Musician*, November 1990, "Lost And Found And Lost Again: SRV In His Own Words," Tony Scherman

[7] *Houston Chronicle*, October 11, 1981, "Stevie Vaughan," Marty Racine

[8] *Guitar World*, "The Sound Of Texas: SRV: Hendrix' White Knight," Bill Milkowski

[9] *Dallas Morning News,* August 28, 1990

[10] *Request* (Musicland store publication), July 10, 1989, "My Guitar Heroes" by Stevie Ray Vaughan

[11] *Guitar For The Practicing Musician*, May 1991, "Now And Forever," Andy Aledort, interview from 1986

[12] *Buddy*, August 1983, "Stevie Ray Vaughan: The Big Time at Last," Kirby F. Warnock

[13] *Guitar World*, Fall 1992, "*Guitar World* Presents Guitar Legends: The Complete Stevie Ray Vaughan"

[14] Joe Cook interview, KERA-TV Dallas, Fall 1996

[15] *Dallas Morning News*, Nov. 16, 1975, Maryln Schwartz

[16] *Buddy*, August 1983, "Sibling Revelry: Brother Can You Spare Some Blues?" Ray Brooks

[17] from interviews by Joe Nick Patoski and Bill Crawford for their book *Caught in the Crossfire*, Little Brown 1993, Southwest Writers' Collection, Texas State University

[18] *Guitar For The Practicing Musician*, November 1983, "Nobody's Sideman," Ed Ward

[19] *Block* magazine (Holland), July 1994, interview of Jimmie Vaughan, Rien Weiss

[20] *Dallas Morning News, Dallas Life Magazine*, March 17, 1985, "Stevie Ray Vaughan"

[21] *Guitar For The Practicing Musician*, Dec. 1990, "So Real: Stevie Ray & Jimmie Lee Vaughan," Andy Aledort

[22] *Lubbock Avalanche-Journal*, July 30, 1978, "Audience Hypnotized by Stevie Vaughn [sic]," by Bob Claypool

[23] *Charlotte Observer,* August 3, 1984, "Stevie Ray Vaughan's Early Guitar Interest Paid Off," Steve Morse

[24] *Dallas Morning News*, April 17, 1983, "Fame the next gig for blues guitarist out of Oak Cliff," Joe Rhodes, "Stevie Ray & the Bowie Tour," Joe Rhodes

[25] *Vintage Guitar Online*, Ralph Heibutzki

[26] *Guitarist* (UK), Sept. 1988, "He's Got the Blues," Tom Nolan

[27] *Relix*, August 1991, "One Year Gone - Remembering SRV," Ted Cogswell, Grateful Dead publication

[28] unedited interview transcript, Ed Ward, probably for *Guitar For The Practicing Musician*, November 1983, "Nobody's Sideman," Ed Ward

[29] *Lance Monthly* (online), October 10, 2002, Dale Smith

[30] *Guitar World*, December 1990, "The Good Texan," Bill Milkowski

[31] *Dallas Times Herald*, June 17, 1982, "Hot Property - Guitarist Stevie Vaughan Ready to Step Out," Bruce Nixon

[32] gig information for 1972, primarily from Charlie Hatchett

[33] *San Antonio Express-News*, July 16, 2006, "Guitarist goes way back with Stevie Ray," Jim Beal, Jr.

[34] Ray Hennig, speaking to the Stevie Ray Vaughan Fan Club, June 1998

[35] *Guitar For The Practicing Musician*, March 1992, "Chris Layton: Remembering Stevie Ray," Andy Aledort

[36] from an interview by Jody Denburg, June 27, 2000, KGSR-FM, Austin, TX

[37] *A Tribute to Stevie Ray Vaughan: An Up Close Extra*, MediaAmerica Radio, 1991, Dan Neer

[38] *Guitar World*, August 1999, "Blue Smoke," Alan Paul

[39] *VirtualLubbock*, May 14, 2000, Chris Ogelsby

[40] *Texas Jazz*, August 1982, "Little Stevie: Coming Of Age," Mike H. Price

[41] Billy Gibbons, Dusty Hill and Frank Beard, "Lowdown in the Street," from the album *Deguello*, ZZ Top

[42] Ron Rawls, posted at srvrocks.com

[43] *Guitar World*, May 2000, "Rise & Shine," Andy Aledort

[44] *Experience Hendrix*, January 1998, "Soul to Soul," Bruce Madden

45 *Austin Chronicle*, Oct. 20, 2000, "Jailbird," Preston Hubbard

46 *Guitar School*, May 1995

47 *Guitar World*, January 1996, "The Heart of Texas: The SRV Interviews," Andy Aledort

48 *Buddy*, March 1981, Belicose Bullfeather

49 *Buddy*, May 1981

50 *Buddy*, June 1981

51 *Buddy*, September 1990

52 *Sounds of Austin*, November 1981

53 *Austin Chronicle*, December 1, 2000, "A Man and a Half: Jerry Wexler," Raoul Hernandez

54 *Guitar World*, August 2000, "Pride and Joy," Andy Aledort; "The Lost Interviews," Andy Aledort

55 *Austin Chronicle*, January 17, 2003, "Revolution Rock," Margaret Moser

56 *Music & Sound Output*, October 1985, "Stratocasting The Blues With A Touch Of Texas," Robert Santelli

57 *People Weekly*, March 25, 1985, "To The Top: You Can Take The Boy Out Of Texas ...," James McBride

58 *Buddy*, November 1983

59 *Austin Chronicle*, October 29, 1982, Greg Stevens

60 *Music* (Central FL), September 1983

61 *Guitar Player*, July 1996, "Double Trouble: Tone Secrets of SRV and Eric Johnson," Ellis/Obrecht

62 *Guitar Player*, Aug. 1983, "Blues To Bowie," Bruce Nixon

63 *Guitar Shop*, "Texas Tone: An Insider Look at the Amp Sound of SRV," Lisa Sharken

64 *Buddy*, August 1980, "Living the Blues," Kirby Warnock

65 *High Fidelity*, August 1983, "Backbeat: Stevie Ray Vaughan," Stephen X. Rea

66 *Washinton Post*, February 19, 1987, "Stevie Ray, Battling His Blues," Mike Joyce

67 *Dallas Morning News*, June 1, 1983, "Vaughan says fine print made him quit Bowie," Joe Rhodes

68 *Dallas Morning News*, June 18, 1983, "Friends do Tango at album party," Nancy Bishop

69 *Austin Chronicle*, July 8, 1983, "Stevie Ray Vaughan," Michael Hall

70 *Guitar World*, June 1999, "Talkin Blues - Remembering SRV," Buddy Guy

71 *Downbeat*, January 1984, "SRV: New Blues Blood," Michael Point

72 *Houston Chronicle*, October 7, 1983, "Stevie Ray Vaughan," Bob Claypool

73 *In The Studio*, Album Network, 1993, Redbeard

74 *Musician*, December 1989, "Praying Through The Guitar: SRV Interviewed by Larry Coryell"

75 *Dallas Times Herald*, June 18, 1984, "Dallas' Stevie Ray strums up a storm on 'Weather' LP," Bruce Nixon; "Vaughan travels long road from Oak Cliff to Fair Park," Russell Smith

76 *Ram* (Australia), Sept. 28, 1984, "Jes' Doin' The Best He Can"

77 *New York Newsday*, 1984, Wayne Robins

78 *Dallas Times Herald*, July 12, 1984, "Stevie Ray still cares," Joe Rhodes

79 *Dallas Times Herald*, July 14, 1984, "Vaughan pleases hometown crowd," Lisa Taylor

80 *The News & Observer*, Aug. 11, 1984, Melanie Sill

81 *Chicago Soundz*, November 1984, "SRV: A Guitarist's Guitarist," Shelly Harris

82 *Dallas Times Herald*, Oct. 6, 1984, "Stevie Ray wows Carnegie crowd," Joe Rhodes

83 *Dallas Times Herald*, Oct. 11, 1984, "Even now, Stevie Ray has to pinch himself," Joe Rhodes

84 *Guitar Presents Guitar Classics XIV*, April 1996, "SRV: Well-Healed," Wolf Marshall

85 *Guitar Player*, Feb. 1990, "SRV & Jeff Beck: Of Meat And Fingers," Resnicoff /Gore

86 *Modern Guitars,* October 29, 1985, Steven Rosen

87 *The Brownsville Herald*, March 11, 1985, "Spring Break! SRV highlights island concert," Linda Kring

88 *Dallas Times Herald*, April 19, 1985, "Stevie Ray getting in tune with success," Bruce Nixon

89 *Blues Chat*, René Martinez, July 26 and September 6, 1995, conducted by Beverly Howell

90 *Blues Chat*, Reese Wynans, August 27, 1995, conducted by Beverly Howell

91 *Atlanta Journal*, Nov. 2, 1985, "SRV: In Double Trouble and the big time," Russ Devault

92 *Albuquerque Journal*, ca. Oct. 19, 1985, "Vaughn, Double Trouble Music Rocks Red-Hot," [sic] Steve Reynolds

93 *Music Express*, Oct. '90, "Austin Blues," Michael Point

94 *News-Sentinel* (Knoxville, TN), Nov. 1, 1985, "Audience gets taste of rock 'n' roll roots," Betsy Pickle

95 *Dallas Observer*, March 26, 1987, "Alive and well: Texas bluesman SRV conquers the urge to splurge," M.Corcoran

96 thanks to Marta Lozano, J.J. Vicars and Rene Carrillo

97 *Music*, November 5, 1987, "Cold Shot To Cold Turkey," Ken Hall

98 *Kerrang*, #193, "Life Without Booze," Steve Joule

99 source unknown

100 *Sounds*, November 10, 1986, "Vaughan to Blues," Neil Perry

101 From an interview for Barnes & Noble by Roberta Penn on May 27, 1989

102 *Dallas Morning News*, January 31, 1987, "Vaughan's return is red hot," Russell Smith

103 *Charlotte Observer*, Feb. 11, 1987, "Stevie Ray Vaughan Gives Audience His All," Kathy Haight

104 *Nine-O-One Network*, October 1987, "Wearing the label," Bill Stuart

105 *Austin American-Statesman*, August 7, 1987, "Vaughan pauses for a breather between projects," John T. Davis

106 *The Music Paper*, December 12, 1989, "Getting In Step," B. Eschenbrenner

107 *Guitar World*, May 1996, "The Dirty Dozen – The 12 Greatest Guitar Sounds Of All Time," DiPerna, et al.

108 *Guitar Player*, Summer 1994, "Best Of *Guitar Player*: SRV," various authors

109 *Evansville Courier*, August 1989, "Double Trouble, Strat Cats strut without clutter," Anthony McLean

110 *Austin Chronicle*, September 17, 2004, "Looking Out My Back Door"

111 *Outer Shell,* Katherine Bessette

112 *Chicago Sun-Times*, November 1989, "Beck, Vaughan put on guitar-playing clinic at Pavilion," Don McLeese

113 *Dallas Morning News*, June 10, 1990, "No More Wild and Crazy Days for This Guitar Guru," Diane Jennings

114 *Austin Chronicle*, "Page Two" (Editor's column), Michael Hall; "The Early Years Of A Voodoo Chile," M. Moser-Malone; "The Coldest Shot Of All," Michael Corcoran

115 *Dallas Morning News*, June 19, 1990, "Stevie Ray, B.B. blister the blues," Jay Brakefield

116 *Guitar World*, October 1990, "Fender Bender," Joe Bosso

117 *Guitar Player*, March 1991, "A Final Interview: Stevie Ray & Jimmy Vaughan," S. Chernikowski

118 *It's Hip*, November 1990, "SRV: Parting Words," Nash & Flowers

119 *Dallas Morning News*, Aug. 28, 1990, "Air crash kills guitarist Stevie Ray Vaughan," Vincente Rodriguez

120 *Milwaukee Sentinel*, date unknown, "Pilots felt fog wasn't a problem," Mary Zahn & Eldon Knoche

121 *Milwaukee Sentinel*, Aug. 28, 1990, "Pilot says he wouldn't have flown," Tom Held

122 *Austin American-Statesman*, Sept. 1, 1990, "Graceful Goodbye," Michael MacCambridge

123 *Interchords*, Epic Records, 1992 promo CD for *The Sky is Crying*

124 *Dallas Observer*, August 6, 1992, "Crossfire: Friends & Family Of SRV Squabble Over New Release," Robert Wilonsky

125 *Guitar World*, Sept. 1995, "Family Ties," Alan Paul

126 *Washington Post*, Sept. 7, 1996, Al Weisel

127 *Austin Chronicle*, Sept. 29, 2000, "Paying the Cost to Be the Boss," Raoul Hernandez

128 *Dallas Morning News*, Sept. 1, 1990, "The Guitar Slinger," Brad Buchholz

129 *Guitar Presents: Hendrix/SRV*, 1992, Jim Fahey

Intermission

At the end of 1982 Stevie Ray Vaughan is now twenty-eight years old. You have seen that for twenty-one of those years the guitar has completely taken over his life. Day by day and night after night he has studied, practiced and performed, honing his craft to such a fine edge that he has already attracted the attention of The Rolling Stones, David Bowie, Jackson Brown and legendary producer John Hammond. Several record companies are courting young Vaughan, and the long-sought record deal is just around the corner.

In *His Final Years, 1983–1990*, the second installment of this two-volume work, you will follow the band's recording career and rise to stardom, but the experience will not be without controversy, severe substance abuse, a near-death episode and, happily, recovery from the excesses of success. In early 1983 Stevie and Double Trouble stand on the threshold of the national and international music scene. By the end of the year, the Texas circuit of small bars and clubs featured in *His Early Years* will be replaced by world tours, and the resulting acclaim will carry them to the stage of Carnegie Hall in 1984 and to festival gigs and sold-out special events throughout the rest of their careers.

His Final Years, 1983–1990 will also take you on Stevie's personal roller coaster ride through the twists and turns of new management, the ups and downs of divorce and a new fiancée, a bold move back to Dallas, and the incredible highs of sharing stages with his idols, who by 1990 will have become his peers. Not only will you trace his steps to recovery (pun intended), but also, regrettably, those fateful steps on the last night of his life. After sharing the stage with Eric Clapton, Buddy Guy, Robert Cray, and his brother Jimmie, Stevie boarded the helicopter that would take him on the final ride of his life. What really happened that night?

The bibliographic and discographic information has been updated to the present in the second volume and also incorporates significant awards and events honoring Stevie's memory. Featured as well in the second volume is an in-depth treatment of his primary guitars, amplifiers and effects.

Please join me in *His Final Years, 1983–1990* as we follow Stevie Ray Vaughan, day by day, night after night.

Index

About the Author

© LORIE LEIGH LAWRENCE

Craig Hopkins is internationally recognized as a leading authority on the life and music of Stevie Ray Vaughan. This expertise has grown steadily through years of musicianship, rock and blues fanhood and devout Stevie Ray Vaughan appreciation. What began as casual research and a modest, quarterly newsletter, born from tried and true enthusiasm for the blues and curiosity about Vaughan, Hopkins' work has evolved into what could be considered the most detailed account of any musician yet. With meticulous research, a museum-quality music memorabilia collection, endless hours interacting with Vaughan's fan base, dozens of interviews with those who knew Vaughan best and sheer day-by-day dedication, Hopkins shares the magnificence of the world's most pivotal guitarist. *Stevie Ray Vaughan: Day by Day, Night After Night, His Early Years, 1954–1982* and the companion volume, *His Final Years, 1983–1990* encapsulate this enormous effort by Hopkins, providing a rich, intimate biographical account that is almost cinematic.

Hopkins has been recognized by the Blues Foundation as a vital contributor to the world of blues. His unprecedented books on Stevie Ray Vaughan have earned him the Blues Foundation Keeping the Blues Alive Award for Literature, an award that recognizes an individual's lifetime body of work and its significance to the genre. Hopkins shares the KBA honor with such blues greats as Robert Palmer, B. B. King, Dave Ritz, Honeyboy Edwards, Billy Wyman, Robert Gordon, Dick Waterman and Peter Guralnick, among others. Though the *Stevie Ray Vaughan: Day by Day, Night After Night* volumes are at the forefront of Hopkins' historical work, he continues to celebrate Vaughan's life through his website, www.StevieRay.com, and remains a committed collector and researcher.

In addition to his role as an author, Hopkins has been a trial lawyer (successfully arguing in the U.S. Supreme Court), judge, banker, racquetball pro, custom picture framer, guitar teacher and a director of a nonprofit assistance program for artists. He is based in Texas, where he continues to focus his energies on music-related endeavors, including the development of a museum to house his enormous memorabilia collection.

KEEPING THE
BLUES
·ALIVE·